KENNIKAT PRESS SCHOLARLY REPRINTS

Dr. Ralph Adams Brown, Senior Editor

Series on

LITERARY AMERICA IN THE NINETEENTH CENTURY

Under the General Editorial Supervision of

Dr. Walter Harding

University Professor, State University of New York

R. W. EMERSON

EDINBURGH, 1848.

Heliotyped from a painting by DAVID SCOTT.

THE

GENIUS AND CHARACTER

OF

EMERSON

*LECTURES AT THE CONCORD SCHOOL
OF PHILOSOPHY*

EDITED BY

F. B. SANBORN

KENNIKAT PRESS
Port Washington, N. Y./London

THE GENIUS AND CHARACTER OF EMERSON

First published in 1885
Reissued in 1971 by Kennikat Press
Library of Congress Catalog Card No: 72-122663
ISBN 0-8046-1312-5

Manufactured by Taylor Publishing Company   Dallas, Texas

TO

A. BRONSON ALCOTT,

THE FOUNDER

OF

THE CONCORD SCHOOL OF PHILOSOPHY,

𝕿𝖍𝖎𝖘 𝖁𝖔𝖑𝖚𝖒𝖊 𝖎𝖘 𝕴𝖓𝖘𝖈𝖗𝖎𝖇𝖊𝖉

BY ITS AUTHORS.

CONCORD, MASSACHUSETTS,
October 10, 1884.

PREFACE.

THE Faculty of the Concord School of Philosophy have preferred until now not to make any formal publication of the lectures read at their summer sessions, leaving each lecturer free to print his own if he chose. Many of the lectures have thus been printed, in volumes or in magazines; and the newspapers have each year published reports, more or less imperfect, of the lectures and conversations. In 1882 one of the journalists (Mr. BRIDGMAN), who had been most careful in his reports, was authorized to publish a volume of abstracts (in which were included a few complete addresses and poems) under the title of "Concord Lectures on Philosophy," which appeared early in 1883. The present volume, however, is the first which has been published by the School itself, — as an indication of its method of discussion as well as in tribute to the memory of its most illustrious teacher. It contains all the Essays and Poems read in the special course of 1884 on "The Genius and Character of Emerson" (except that of Mr. ALBEE on "Emerson as an Essayist," which the author has withheld for publication elsewhere), and also two Poems read at the session of 1882. The lectures on Immortality are not included, and will not be published by the School. Mr. FISKE's lecture has been printed in a volume by Houghton, Mifflin, & Co., and those by Dr. PEABODY, Dr. HARRIS, Dr. HOLLAND, and Mr. DAVIDSON will doubtless be printed by the authors.

In quoting from Emerson's poems in this volume, the various essayists have cited the lines in the form and manner they thought best, — one sometimes repeating in another guise or connection what his colleague had before cited. The editor has allowed these quotations to stand as they were read, — referring the reader to the different editions of Emerson's poems for the text as the poet printed it.

The heliotype of Emerson in this volume is from a photograph, by permission of the Concord Library, of David Scott's portrait, representing Emerson as he stood before his Scotch audiences in the winter of 1847–1848; painted at Edinburgh in 1848, and never before copied. The view of the Orchard House and Hillside Chapel was taken in 1881 by Mr. E. Chamberlain, of Medfield, through whose courtesy it is here printed as the best representation of the rural environment of our School which has yet been made.

CONTENTS.

PAGE

THE CONCORD SCHOOL OF PHILOSOPHY ix

I. EMERSON AND BOSTON. *Mrs. E. D. Cheney* . . . 1

II. EMERSON AND ALCOTT. — Passages from the Diary
and Correspondence of Mr. Alcott 36

III. EMERSON AS AN AMERICAN. *Julian Hawthorne* . 68

IV. A FRENCH VIEW OF EMERSON. *M. René de
Poyen Belleisle* 92

V. EMERSON'S RELIGION. *Dr. C. A. Bartol* . . . 109

VI. EMERSON AS PREACHER. *Miss E. P. Peabody* . 146

VII. EMERSON AMONG THE POETS. *F. B. Sanborn* . . 173

VIII. POEMS IN HONOR OF EMERSON:

1. Miss Emma Lazarus 215
2. Ellery Channing 216
3. F. B. Sanborn 224
4. Mrs. E. C. Kinney 231

IX. EMERSON'S ETHICS. *Edwin D. Mead* 233

X. EMERSON'S RELATION TO SOCIETY. *Mrs. Julia
Ward Howe* 286

PAGE

XI. EMERSON'S VIEW OF NATIONALITY. *George Willis Cooke* 310

XII. EMERSON'S PHILOSOPHY OF NATURE. *William T. Harris* 339

XIII. EMERSON AS SEEN FROM INDIA. *Protap Chunder Mozoomdar* 365

XIV. EMERSON'S ORIENTALISM. *William T. Harris* . 372

XV. EMERSON'S RELATION TO GOETHE AND CARLYLE. *William T. Harris* 386

XVI. ION : A MONODY. *A. Bronson Alcott* 420

INDEX 427

THE CONCORD SCHOOL OF PHILOSOPHY.

A BRIEF sketch of the origin and purpose of this institution may properly be given here, since it was the last enterprise of a general character in which Mr. EMERSON engaged, and derived a portion of its interest from his connection with it. This connection was not very close, however, since its opening was delayed until those later years of his life when he withdrew from an active part even in conversation; but he was fully cognizant of its aims, and in the most friendly relation to its founders, the chief of whom was Mr. ALCOTT. It had been the hope of Mr. ALCOTT for many years to establish in the town of his chosen residence a conversational school of philosophy and literature; and the collection of a library by him and his English friends in 1842 had reference to such an institution. But circumstances were unfavorable until, in 1878, the visit of Dr. JONES of Illinois, and the conversations in which he participated, suggested to Mr. ALCOTT and

his friends that the time had come for announcing
the enterprise. Accordingly, in the spring of 1879,
under the advice and with the co-operation of Mr.
EMERSON, the late Professor PEIRCE, of Harvard University, Mrs. CHENEY, Professor HARRIS, and other
friends of Mr. ALCOTT, the public, or such as chose to
come, were invited to the first session of the School,
which was opened in Mr. ALCOTT's study, at the Orchard House, now the residence of Professor HARRIS.
The attendance much exceeded the expectation of the
Faculty, although the session was longer than has
since been found expedient, — the term being six
weeks, and the chief lecturers five in number, occupy-
ing the five week-days before Saturday, which was
given up to single lectures on general topics. During the next three years the sessions were five weeks;
in 1882 and 1883, four weeks; and in 1884, two
weeks. The Programme in the successive years was
as follows: —

FIRST YEAR'S PROGRAMME. 1879.

Mr. A. BRONSON ALCOTT. — 1. Welcome, and plan of future
conversations. 2. The Powers of the Person in the descending scale. 3. The same in the ascending scale. 4. Incarnation. 5. The Powers of Personality in detail. 6.
The Origin of Evil. 7. The Lapse into Evil. 8. The
Return from the Lapse (the Atonement). 9. Life Eternal.
10. Valedictory.

Dr. WILLIAM T. HARRIS. — 1. How Philosophical Knowing
differs from all other forms of Knowing; the Five Intentions of the mind. 2. The Discovery of the First

HILLSIDE CHAPEL. AND ORCHARD HOUSE.

Principle, and its Relation to the Universe. 3. Fate and Freedom. 4. The conscious and unconscious First Principle in relation to human life. 5. The Personality of God. 6. The Immortality of the Soul. 7. Physiological Psychology. 8. The Method of study in Speculative Philosophy. 9. Art, Religion, and Philosophy in relation to each other and to man. 10. The Dialectic.

Mrs. EDNAH D. CHENEY. — 1. The general subject of Art. 2. Greek Art. 3. Early Italian Art. 4. Italian Art. 5. Michael Angelo. 6. Spanish Art. 7. German Art. 8. Albert Dürer. 9. French Art. 10. Contemporaneous Art.

Dr. H. K. JONES. — 1. General content of the Platonic Philosophy. 2. The Apology of Socrates. 3. The Platonic idea of Church and State. 4. The Immortality of the Soul. 5. Reminiscence as related to the Pre-existence of the Soul. 6. Pre-existence. 7. The Human Body. 8. The Republic. 9. The Material Body. 10. Education.

Mr. DAVID A. WASSON. — 1. Social Genesis and Texture. 2. The Nation. 3. Individualism as a Political Principle. 4. Public Obligation. 5. Sovereignty. 6. Absolutism crowned and uncrowned. 7. Representation. 8. Rights. 9. The Making of Freedom. 10. The Political Spirit of '76.

Professor BENJAMIN PEIRCE. — 1. Ideality in Science. 2. Cosmogony.

Mr. T. W. HIGGINSON. — 1. The Birth of American Literature. 2. Literature in a Republic.

Mr. THOMAS DAVIDSON. — 1. The History of Athens as revealed in its topography and monuments. 2. The Same, continued.

Mr. RALPH WALDO EMERSON. — Memory.

Mr. F. B. SANBORN. — 1. Social Science. 2. Philanthropy and Public Charities.

Rev. Dr. CYRUS A. BARTOL. — Education.

Mr. HARRISON G. O. BLAKE. — Selections from Thoreau's Manuscripts.

SECOND YEAR'S PROGRAMME. 1880.

Mr. A. BRONSON ALCOTT. — Five Lectures on Mysticism:
1. St. John the Evangelist. 2. Plotinus. 3. Tauler and
Eckhart. 4. Behmen. 5. Swedenborg. Mr. Alcott also
delivered the Salutatory and Valedictory.

Dr. H. K. JONES. — Five Lectures on The Platonic Philosophy,
and five on Platonism in its Relation to Modern Civiliza-
tion : 1. Platonic Philosophy; Cosmologic and Theologic
Outlines. 2. The Platonic Psychology ; The Dæmon of
Socrates. 3. The Two Worlds, and the Twofold Con-
sciousness ; The Sensible and the Intelligible. 4. The
State and Church ; Their Relations and Correlations.
5. The Eternity of the Soul, and its Pre-existence. 6.
The Immortality and the Mortality of the Soul ; Personal-
ity and Individuality ; Metempsychosis. 7. The Psychic
Body and the Material Body of Man. 8. Education and
Discipline of Man ; The Uses of the World we live
in. 9. The Philosophy of Law. 10. The Philosophy of
Prayer, and the " Prayer Gauge."

Dr. WILLIAM T. HARRIS. — Five Lectures on Speculative
Philosophy, namely : 1. Philosophic Knowing. 2. Philosophic First Principles. 3. Philosophy and Immortality.
4. Philosophy and Religion. 5. Philosophy and Art. — Five
Lectures on the History of Philosophy, namely : 1. Plato.
2. Aristotle. 3. Kant. 4. Fichte. 5. Hegel.

Rev. JOHN S. KEDNEY, D.D. — Four Lectures on the Philosophy of the Beautiful and Sublime.

Mr. DENTON J. SNIDER. — Five Lectures on Shakspeare :
1. Philosophy of Shakspearian Criticism. 2. The Shakspearian World. 3. Principles of Characterization in
Shakspeare. 4. Organism of the Individual Drama.
5. Organism of the Universal Drama.

Rev. WILLIAM H. CHANNING. — Four Lectures on Oriental and
Mystical Philosophy : 1. Historical Mysticism. 2. Man's
Fourfold Being. 3. True Buddhism. 4. Modern Pessimism.

Mrs. EDNAH D. CHENEY. — 1. Color. 2. Early American Art.

Mrs. JULIA WARD HOWE. — Modern Society.

Mr. JOHN ALBEE. — 1. Figurative Language. 2. The Literary Art.

Mr. F. B. SANBORN. — The Philosophy of Charity.

Dr. ELISHA MULFORD. — 1. The Personality of God. 2. Precedent Relations of Religion and Philosophy to Christianity.

Mr. HARRISON G. O. BLAKE. — Readings from Thoreau's Manuscripts.

Rev. Dr. CYRUS A. BARTOL. — God in Nature.

Rev. Dr. ANDREW P. PEABODY. — Conscience and Consciousness.

Mr. EMERSON. — Aristocracy.

Rev. Dr. FREDERIC H. HEDGE. — Ghosts and Ghost-seeing.

Mr. DAVID A. WASSON. — 1. Philosophy of History. 2. The Same.

(In place of an expected lecture of Professor PEIRCE, who was too ill to be present, there was a conversation on Hawthorne.)

THIRD YEAR'S PROGRAMME. 1881.

Mr. A. BRONSON ALCOTT. — Salutatory, Valedictory, and Five Lectures on the Philosophy of Life.

Dr. WILLIAM T. HARRIS. — *First Course: Philosophical Distinctions.* 1. Philosophy Distinguished from Opinion or Fragmentary Observation; The Miraculous *vs.* The Mechanical Explanation of Things. 2. Nominalism of Locke and Hume; Pantheistic Realism of Hobbes, Spinoza, Comte, and Spencer *vs.* the Realism of Christianity. 3. The Influence of Nature upon the Human Mind; the Emancipation of the Soul from the Body. 4. Sense-Impressions and Recollections *vs.* Memory and Reflection; Animal Cries and Gestures *vs.* Human Language. 5. The Metaphysical Categories used by Natural Science, —

Thing, Fact, Atom, Force, Law, Final Cause or Design, Correlation, Natural Selection, Reality, Potentiality, and Actuality.

Dr. HARRIS. — *Second Course: Hegel's Philosophy.* 1. Hegel's Doctrine of Psychology and Logic; his Dialectic Method and System. 2. Hegel's Doctrine of God and the World, — Creator and Created. 3. Relations of Kant and Hegel. 4. Hegel's Distinction of Man from Nature; Two Kinds of Immortality, that of the Species and that of the Individual. 5. Hegel's Doctrine of Providence in History; Asia *vs.* Europe as furnishing the contrast of Pantheism and Christianity. 6. Hegel's Theory of Fine Arts and Literature as reflecting the development of Man's Spiritual Consciousness.

Dr. HIRAM K. JONES. — *First Course: The Platonic Philosophy.* 1. The Platonic Cosmology, Cosmogony, Physics, and Metaphysics. 2. Myth ; The Gods of the Greek Mythology ; The Ideas and Principles of their Worship, Divine Providence, Free Will, and Fate. 3. Platonic Psychology. The Idea of Conscience ; The Dæmon of Socrates. 4. The Eternity of the Soul, and its Preexistence. 5. The Immortality of the Soul, and the Mortality of the Soul : Personality and Individuality ; Metempsychosis.

Dr. JONES. — *Second Course: Platonism in its Relation to Modern Civilization.* 1. The Social Genesis; The Church and the State. 2. The Education and Discipline of Man; The Uses of the World we live in. 3. The Psychic Body and the Material Body of Man; The Christian Resurrection. 4. The Philosophy of Law. 5. The Philosophy of Prayer, and the " Prayer Gauge."

Mr. DENTON J. SNIDER. — Five Lectures on Greek Life and Literature.

Mrs. JULIA WARD HOWE. — 1. Philosophy in Europe and America. 2. The Results of Kant.

Mrs. EDNAH D. CHENEY. — The Relation of Poetry to Science.

Rev. J. S. KEDNEY, D.D. — Three Lectures on the Philosophic Groundwork of Ethics.

Mrs. AMALIA J. HATHAWAY. — Schopenhauer.

President JOHN BASCOM. — Freedom of the Will.

Mr. EDWIN D. MEAD. — Philosophy of Fichte.

Mr. S. H. EMERY, Jr. — System in Philosophy.

Rev. F. H. HEDGE, D.D. — A Lecture on Kant.

Professor GEORGE S. MORRIS. — A Lecture on Kant.

Mr. F. B. SANBORN. — 1. Roman Literature. 2. English and German Literature. 3. American Literature and Life.

Mr. JOHN ALBEE. — Faded Metaphors.

Rev. Dr. C. A. BARTOL. — The Transcendent Faculty in Man.

Dr. ELISHA MULFORD. — The Philosophy of the State.

Dr. ROWLAND G. HAZARD. — Philosophical Character of Channing.

President NOAH PORTER. — A Lecture on Kant.

Professor JOHN W. MEARS. — A Lecture on Kant.

Professor JOHN WATSON. — The Critical Philosophy in its relation to Realism and Sensationalism.

Mr. H. G. O. BLAKE. — Readings from Thoreau's Manuscripts.

FOURTH YEAR'S PROGRAMME. 1882.

Mr. A. BRONSON ALCOTT. — Four Lectures on The Personal, Generic and Individual Mind. 1. Personality, Divine and Human. 2. The Descending Scale of Powers. 3. Individualism. 4. Immortality, Individual or Personal?

Dr. HARRIS. — Five Lectures on the History of Philosophy, three on Fichte's Philosophy, and two on Art. 1. Socrates and the Pre-Socratic Philosophy. 2. Aristotle's De Anima (his distinctions between Nutrition, Feeling, and Thinking). 3. Gnosticism and Neoplatonism. 4. Christian Mysticism : Bonaventura and Meister Eckhart. 5. The Philosophy of the Bhagavat Gita. 6. Fichte's " Destination of Man." 7. Fichte's Wissenschaftslehre — Theoretical. 8. Fichte's Wissenschaftslehre — Practical. 9. Historical Epochs of Art. 10. Landscape Painting — Turner.

Dr. JONES. — Eight Lectures on Christian Philosophy. *First Course: Chapters in the History of Philosophy.* 1. Premises, Predications, and Outlines of Christian Philosophy. 2. The Relation between Common-sense and Philosophy. 3. The Relation between Science and Philosophy. 4. The Relation between Experience and Philosophy.

Dr. JONES. — *Second Course: Truths that are always Old and always New in the History of Human Thought.* 1. The Genesis of the "Maya." 2. The Philosophy of Religion and the Law of the Supernatural. 3. The Community of the Faiths and the Worships of Mankind. 4. The Symposium.

Dr. KEDNEY. — Three Lectures on Hegel's Æsthetics. 1. Critique of Fundamentals. 2. Critique of Symbolic Art and of Classic Art. 3. Critique of Romantic Art. 4. The Philosophy of Professor Ferrier, with a Prelude on Berkeley.

Mr. F. B. SANBORN. — Three Lectures on Oracular Poetry. 1. Hebrew, Egyptian, and Greek Oracles. 2. Persian and Christian Oracles. 3. The Oracles of New England.

Rev. Dr. BARTOL. — The Nature of Knowledge.

Prof. JOHN WATSON, of Kingston. — Three Lectures on Schelling. 1. Schelling's Relations to Kant and Fichte. 2. Early Treatises, Transcendental Idealism, and Philosophy of Identity. 3. Later Philosophy, and Transition to Hegel.

Miss E. P. PEABODY. — Childhood.

Mr. JOHN ALBEE. — Poetry.

Mrs. E. D. CHENEY. — Nature.

Dr. GEORGE H. HOWISON. — Two Lectures on German Philosophy since Hegel.

President PORTER. — Kantian Ethics.

Mrs. J. W. HOWE. — Idols and Iconoclasts.

Rev. R. A. HOLLAND. — Atomism.

Dr. R. G. HAZARD. — 1. Man as Creative Power. 2. Utility of Metaphysical Pursuits.

Mr. G. P. Lathrop. — The Symbolism of Color.
Mr. Alexander Wilder. — Alexandrian Platonism.
Rev. Dr. McCosh. — The Scottish Philosophy.
Mr. F. B. Sanborn. — Readings from Thoreau's Manuscripts.

In addition to the regular lectures of 1882, the recent death of Mr. Emerson was commemorated by a Poem and address by Mr. Sanborn, and the following exercises on the commemoration day : —

Address, by Rev. Dr. Bartol ; Ion : a Monody, by Mr. Alcott ; Emerson as a Poet, by Joel Benton ; Reminiscences of Emerson, by Mrs. Howe ; Dialectic Unity in Emerson's Prose, by Dr. Harris ; A Visit to Emerson, by Mr. Albee ; Poem, — " Consolation," — by Mrs. Martha P. Lowe ; Emerson as a Philosopher, by Dr. Alexander Wilder ; Reminiscences of Emerson, by Mrs. E. D. Cheney.

Fifth Year's Programme. 1883.

Dr. William T. Harris. — *First Course ; Elementary Lessons in Philosophy.* 1. Space and Time Considered ; Basis of Kantian Philosophy. Ground of certainty deeper than Scepticism or Agnosticism. 2. Causality and Self-cause ; Force Transient and Persistent; Self-existent Energy underlying all change. 3. Fate and Freedom ; Individuality ; Distinction of Reality and Potentiality from True Actuality, of Phenomenon from Substance. 4. Laws of Thought, the Principles of Identity, Contradiction, and Excluded Middle ; Categories of Being, Essence, Cause, and Personality.

Dr. Harris. — *Second Course.* 1. The Absolute a personal Reason. Discussion of Plato's insight (Tenth Book of the Laws) and Aristotle's (the eighth book of his Physics and the eleventh of his Metaphysics). 2. Triune Nature of God. — St. Augustine, St. Thomas Aquinas, St. Anselm, - ·

Justice and Grace in the Divine Nature. **3.** The World as Revelation of the Divine First Cause, — Nature and Man : the doctrine of Evolution ; the Orders of Being as Progressive Revelation of the Divine. **4.** Immortality of the individual man in the light of Psychology, — in the light of the Christian Religion ; the Vocation of Man in the Future Life.

Dr. G. H. HOWISON. — 1. Hume's Aim and Method ; the Problem, as handed over to Kant. 2. Kant's Mode of Dealing with this Problem. 3. The Strength and Weakness of Kant's Methods and Results. 4. The Same Subject, concluded ; The Outlook from Kant.

Professor WILLIAM JAMES. — Three Lectures on Psychology.

Mr. DENTON J. SNIDER. — Four Lectures on Homer and the Greek Religion. 1. Literary Bibles, — Homer. 2. The Iliad. 3. The Odyssey. 4. The Gods.

Dr. KEDNEY. — Two Lectures on Art Appreciation and the Higher Criticism.

Mr. F. B. SANBORN. — 1. The Puritanic Philosophy, — Jonathan Edwards. 2. The Philanthropic Philosophy, — Benjamin Franklin. 3. The Negation of Philosophy. 4. The Ideal and Vital Philosophy, — R. W. Emerson.

Mr. JOHN ALBEE. — The Norman Influences in English Language and Literature.

Rev. Dr. BARTOL. — Optimism and Pessimism, — a Personal Equation.

Miss E. P. PEABODY. — Milton's Paradise Lost.

Mrs. E. D. CHENEY. — A Study of Nirvana.

Mr. EDWIN D. MEAD. — Carlyle and Emerson.

Mrs. J. W. HOWE. — A Conversation, — Margaret Fuller.

Mr. JULIAN HAWTHORNE. — A Lecture on Novels.

Mr. DAVID A. WASSON. — Herbert Spencer's Causal Law of Evolution.

Mr. LEWIS J. BLOCK. — Platonism and its Relation to Modern Thought.

Mr. H. G. O. BLAKE. — Readings from Thoreau's Manuscripts.

SIXTH YEAR'S PROGRAMME. 1884.

Readings from Mr. Alcott's Diary and Correspondence.
Fourteen Lectures on the Genius and Character of Emerson.
1. Emerson's View of Nature; by Dr. HARRIS, of Concord. 2. Emerson's Religion; by Dr. BARTOL. 3. Emerson's Ethics ; by Mr. EDWIN D. MEAD. 4. Emerson's Relation to Society; by Mrs. JULIA WARD HOWE. 5. Emerson as seen from India ; by PROTAP CHUNDER MOZOOMDAR, of Calcutta. 6. Emerson as an American ; by Mr. JULIAN HAWTHORNE, of New York. 7. Emerson as Preacher ; by Miss E. P. PEABODY. 8. A French View of Emerson ; by M. RENÉ DE POYEN BELLEISLE. 9. Emerson and Boston ; by Mrs. E. D. CHENEY. 10. Emerson as an Essayist; by Mr. JOHN ALBEE. 11. Emerson and Thoreau, — a Conversation. 12. Emerson's View of Nationality ; by Rev. G. W. COOKE. 13. Emerson among the Poets ; by Mr. F. B. SANBORN. 14. Emerson's Relation to Goethe and Carlyle ; by Dr. HARRIS.
Five Lectures on Immortality ; by Rev. A. P. PEABODY, D.D., of Cambridge, Mr. JOHN FISKE, of Cambridge, Rev. R. A. HOLLAND, D.D., of New Orleans, Mr. THOMAS DAVIDSON, of Cambridge, and Dr. HARRIS, of Concord.

SEVENTH YEAR'S PROGRAMME.

At the adjournment of the Concord School, Aug. 2, 1884, it was announced that the next session would open about July 20, 1885, and would continue for two weeks or more ; the general topic to be, " Goethe and Modern Science," considered under two main heads : I. Goethe's Genius and Work. II. Is Pantheism the Legitimate Outcome of Modern Science ?

The special subjects of each lecture are not yet definitely fixed, nor are the lecturers assigned, except in part; but the following may be taken as a provisional arrangement, — liable to be changed before the final announcements are made in June, 1885: —

I. *Goethe's Genius and Work.* 1. Goethe and Modern Science; by T. STERRY HUNT, of Montreal. 2. Goethe and Religion; by Rev. Dr. R. A. HOLLAND. 3. Goethe's Relation to Kant and Spinoza in Philosophy; by Mr. F. L. SOLDAN, of St. Louis. 4. Goethe, the French Revolution and its Results. 5. Goethe and Art. 6. Goethe and Modern Education. 7. Goethe's Faust; by Professor HARRIS and Mr. D. J. SNIDER. 8. Goethe's Relation to English Literature; by F. B. SANBORN. 9. Goethe's Classical and Oriental Studies. 10. The Novelettes in "Wilhelm Meister;" by Professor HARRIS. 11. "Wilhelm Meister" as a Whole; by Mr. D. J. SNIDER. 12. Goethe and Schiller; by Rev. Dr. BARTOL. 13. The Women of Goethe; by Mrs. JULIA WARD HOWE. 14. The Elective Affinities; by Mr. S. H. EMERY, Jr., of Concord. 15. Goethe's Titanism; by Mr. THOMAS DAVIDSON. 16. Goethe's Self-Culture; by Mr. JOHN ALBEE.

General lectures on Goethe, by Dr. H. K. JONES, Prof. G. H. HOWISON, Mrs. CHENEY, and others, are expected.

II. *A Symposium: Is Pantheism the Legitimate Outcome of Modern Science?* Papers by Rev. Dr. PEABODY, Mr. JOHN FISKE, Professor HARRIS, and others.

The management of the Concord School, from the beginning, has been in the hands of a Faculty, the officers of which have been Mr. A. BRONSON ALCOTT, *Dean,* Mr. S. H. EMERY, Jr., *Director,* and Mr. F. B. SANBORN, *Secretary.* These three, with Dr. WILLIAM T. HARRIS, Dr. H. K. JONES, Miss PEABODY, Mrs. CHENEY, Mr. SNIDER, Dr. KEDNEY, Dr. HOLLAND, or so many of these and the other lecturers as happen to be in Concord, constitute the Faculty for the time being; but the permanent and active members are Messrs. ALCOTT, HARRIS, EMERY, and SANBORN. In the second year of the School the Hillside Chapel was built, with the aid of a small fund given by Mrs. ELIZABETH THOMPSON, of New York; and all the sessions are now held there.

The variety of subjects considered during the six summers that the School has existed show that its scope is not a narrow one; and the wide diversity of opinion among those who have spoken from its platform may serve as a guarantee that no limitation of sect or philosophical shibboleth has been enforced. The aim of the Faculty has been to bring together a few of those persons who, in America, have pursued, or desire to pursue, the paths of speculative philosophy; to encourage these students and professors to communicate with each other what they have learned and meditated; and to illustrate, by a constant reference to poetry and the higher literature, those ideas which philosophy presents. The design was modest, and in no ambitious sense a public one; nor have the Faculty been persuaded, by the attention their experiment has aroused, to diverge from the natural and simple path first chosen. The first purpose of the School is conversation on serious topics, — the lectures serving mainly as a text for discussion, while dispute and polemical debate are avoided. In this we have sought to follow the example of him whom this volume of essays and poems portrays, and whose method in philosophy has proved so attractive to many who may never reach the same intellectual results. What is sought in the discussions at Concord is not an absolute unity of opinion, but a general agreement in the manner of viewing philosophic truth and applying it to the problems of life.

F. B. S.

CONCORD, Oct. 10, 1884.

THE GENIUS AND CHARACTER OF EMERSON.

I.

EMERSON AND BOSTON.

By MRS. EDNAH D. CHENEY.

ALTHOUGH his ancestors were of the old stock of
Concord ministers, our Emerson was born in Boston
in 1803.[1] Shall we rejoice at this? Ordinarily we
are glad that the child should draw his first breath
in the fresh air of the country, and " babble of green
fields " in his infancy, that they may give a touch of
Nature and Religion to his old age, even were it
spent, like Shakspeare's immortal profligate's, among
the foul vices and base pleasures of a city. But
Nature's own darling child, henceforth to be her
tenderest lover and wisest interpreter, was born

---

[1] Some of the old friends of Mr. Emerson are under the impression that he was born in Harvard, Mass., where his father lived
some time ; but the testimony of his family is explicit and decided
that he was born in Summer Street, Boston. One of his earliest
recollections was of sitting upon the wall and looking longingly at
the pears in a neighbor's garden.

1

within the limits of the town; for blessed Mother Nature knew that her child would never forsake her, but that, clinging too closely to her breast, he might not learn the sterner lessons of wisdom which only the life of humanity in association can teach. It was given to him, therefore, to blend the virtues both of the city and of the country in the practical wisdom, the ripe good sense, the broad humanity, the poetic beauty, and the unfailing serenity of his life. Coming from under his pines at Concord, he was no stranger in the streets of our eager and bustling city; it was the same old native town which he ever loved and believed in, and whose influence is clearly traceable in his life and writings. I count it a great felicity for him, and for us, that he thus partook of the life of the city from his very youth, and so became not merely the poet of outward Nature, but the seer of Humanity. How have the greatest men loved their city homes! Jesus was wont to retire to the Mount of Olives for lonely meditation and prayer; but he wept over Jerusalem as a mother weeps for her lost child. Dante might choose his home in all the wide, beautiful world; but to be out of the streets of Florence was exile to him. Socrates never cared to go beyond the bounds of Athens. The great universal heart welcomes the city as a natural growth of the eternal forces, and

> " Nature gladly gives it place,
> Adopting it into her race,
> And granting it an equal date
> With Andes and with Ararat."

Emerson has many a severe word for the city, as every sensitive soul shrinks at times from the rude contact of average, struggling humanity, and longs to say, in weary mood,

> " Good-by, proud world ! I 'm going home."

Indeed, at such times

> " The politics are base,
>   The letters do not cheer,
> And 't is far in the deeps of history
>   The voice that speaketh clear.
> Trade and the streets ensnare us,
>   Our bodies are weak and worn ;
> We plot and corrupt each other,
>   And we despoil the unborn."

Writing to Carlyle concerning New York, he says : " I always seem to suffer some loss of faith on entering cities ;" and yet he acknowledges that the poor fellows who live there " do get some compensation for the sale of their souls." But Emerson also recognizes that the town is under the care of Nature, who does not desert humanity even in the crisis of its struggle. How often does the weary toiler take comfort from his lines, —

> " The inevitable morning
>   Finds them who in cellars be ;
> And be sure the all-loving Nature
>   Will smile in a factory.
>   .   .   .   .   .
> " Still, still the secret presses,
>   The nearing clouds draw down ;
> The crimson morning flames into
>   The fopperies of the town.
>   .   .   .   .   .

" And what if Trade sow cities
        Like shells along the shore,
    And thatch with towns the prairie broad,
        With railways ironed o'er ?
    They are but sailing foam-bells
        Along Thought's causing stream,
    And take their shape and sun-color
        From him that sends the dream."

He says : —

" We can ill spare the commanding social benefits of cities ; they must be used, yet cautiously and haughtily, and will yield their best values to him who best can do without them."

" Keep the town for occasions ; but the habits should be formed to retirement."

" Cities give us collision. 'T is said London and New York take the nonsense out of a man."

Boston town as Emerson knew it in his childhood was in its happy youth, when Nature still lay all about it ; and was like a family association, where every man knew his neighbor, and there was a common bond of good-fellowship among all. The Common was still the training-ground and cow-pasture, and the boy's little feet roamed freely over it, with no caution to " keep off the grass." Yet it was already a place consecrated by historic memories. The British had built fortifications upon it during the war ; and when the Constitution was adopted a procession had carried an old long-boat, named the " Old Confederacy," to the Common, and there burned it amid the shouts of the rejoicing people. The Common was endeared to every one as the theatre of his sports and exercises in youth, or of the quiet walks for thought and contemplation or the sweet converse of lovers, in later years.

Emerson's childhood in Boston was during a period of commercial activity and pecuniary prosperity, when the career was open to talent, and every boy might look forward to success and fame in life. Yet economy was necessary in the household of the widowed mother; and thus the true-hearted boy learned the lessons of conscientious frugality for the sake of noble good, which are so conspicuous in his thought. But these were blended with a generous wisdom, which counselled to spend for one's genius, but not for show in the eyes of others. His chapter on "Wealth" is full of the wisdom of the saint and the practical sagacity of Poor Richard : —

"As long as your genius buys, the investment is safe, though you spend like a monarch."

"Spend for *your* expense, and retrench the expense which is not yours."

"But vanity costs money, labor, horses, men, women, health, and peace, and is still nothing at last, — a long way leading nowhere."

"A good pride is, as I reckon it, worth from five hundred to fifteen hundred a year."

Very early he found the help of the city in getting the novel he craved from the circulating library; but when his aunt reproached him for spending six cents on such a luxury while his mother's needs were so constant, he left the story unfinished, and did not take out the second volume. The wise mother did not keep her boy tied to her apron-strings, but at eight years old sent him to the grammar school, that his life might be rooted in the common ground with his fellow-citizens. This grammar school was probably one whose course of instruction was laid down in 1784 by a committee of which Samuel Adams was a member. Dilworth's spelling-book, containing a brief treatise on English grammar, was the only text-book required. Arithmetic included vulgar and decimal fractions; while the Bible and Psalter were the only reading-books. We do not know how much this programme had been extended in 1811. In 1814 he became a Latin School boy. The Latin School is a peculiarly "Boston institution," and was founded in the very earliest period of her history. Boston has always believed in beginning to grow at the top; and long before she had primary schools for her children she had her college and Latin School, to keep learning alive and furnish leaders in the great warfare against the enemy of souls. The aristocracy that founded the Latin School is not that of selfishness and greed, — "the best for me, and the worst for the rest of the world," — but it holds the doctrine of *noblesse oblige,* and teaches that the highest service must have the fullest preparation. The poorest boy may share its privileges; but he is expected to pay for them by superior work done in

the course of his life, — not by sinking into the
readiest means for gaining wealth or ignoble ease.
The honorable names among our Latin School boys
have justified this claim.

If Emerson often read the book of genius by
stealth, instead of conning the stupid lessons of routine, he still accomplished the work of preparation
for college ; and he got from his public-school training the best results of an acquaintance with the
future men of his age and country. These early
companionships, like family ties, have a special value
in binding us to acquaintance with those unlike us
in tastes and habits, whom we might not seek from
choice. They save us from living in a petty world of
our own choosing, as well as from the dreary experience of the aristocratic lady who said that " the longer
she lived the more she realized how little there is outside of one's own circle." Emerson's high courtesy
could always meet all on equal terms, and the poorest of servants or the highest of nobles alike felt of
kin to him when he gave them the benediction of
the morning.

The commercial prosperity which existed during
his childhood was followed by the hated embargo
and the war with England, which had such a disastrous influence on the business of Boston, changing it
from a purely commercial to a manufacturing town.
During the war the British cruisers could be daily
seen in the harbor, and volunteer companies were engaged in defending commerce and in building forts.

Politics furnished the theme of all intellectual conversation, and Emerson must have found his young mind broadened and enriched by the exciting discussions of the time. The master of the school once invited his boys to spend the next day in helping to throw up defences against the enemy at Noddle's Island, now East Boston.

Party spirit raged fiercely throughout the nation, and especially in Boston. The French Revolution had aroused the greatest activity of thought on political and social questions, and the party divisions of that day did not represent a mere scramble for office, but the opposite sides of the most important problems of social and political economy. While the Democrats held those generous views which captivate the young mind, on the other side was an array of personal character and historic reputation which could not but command the respect of a modest and reverent nature ; so that, as Emerson afterwards said, "One party had the best ideas and the other the best men." An orphan boy, much under the influence of wise and sweet women, Emerson was not bound to follow a father's party in politics, and may early have learned the great lesson of unpartisan patriotism which he so fully carried out. As a young man of eighteen or nineteen he may have heard the animated discussions in regard to the adoption of the city charter, and may have remembered Josiah Quincy's eloquent eulogiums on the town meetings when he wrote afterwards to Carlyle, —

" I will show you (as in this country we can anywhere) an America in miniature in the April or November town meeting. Therein should you conveniently study and master the whole of our hemispherical politics, reduced to a nutshell, and have a new version of Oxenstiern's little wit, and yet be consoled by seeing that here the farmers, patient as their bulls of head-boards (provided for them in relation to distant national objects by kind editors of newspapers), do yet their will, and a good will, in their own parish." [1]

Nothing of the spirit of the cockney ever came of his city birth and training. The city was a centring of forces which could accomplish great results, but the simple working life of the country supplied the life-blood which gave it strength and power of action. He recognized the function of great centres of population, but also their dangers. France has held herself compact and firm in her intellectual life, amid countless revolutions, greatly through the centralizing influence of her metropolis, to which the eye of every boy of talent and ambition turns as to his polar star. Emerson said of England : " The nation sits in the immense city they have builded, a London extended into every man's mind, though he live in Van Diemen's Land or Cape Town ; " and he recognized Carlyle as a " product of London." Germany must yet find or make a central city (perhaps the Berlin

[1] This passage was equally descriptive of Concord, however, where it was written, and where Emerson made his home constantly from 1834 to his death in April, 1882.

of Frederick the Great) before she can become a truly united nation. How wisely have Florence, Turin, Milan, and Naples yielded local prejudices and made Rome, with its far-reaching historic memories, the centre of the new Italian government and life!

More than any city on this continent Boston has been a real uniting centre for a large and intelligent population. All over New England, men have said as Emerson wrote to Carlyle, " I am spending the summer in the country, but my address is Boston;" and as the iron links have been more closely woven around the hills and through the valleys, the interchange has become so constant (as the citizen seeks health and refreshment in every quiet village by the mountain or seaside, and the dweller in the country comes to the city for lessons and lectures, opera and concert) that dress and manners are hardly distinguishable, and each part can " call the farthest brother."

How truly Emerson felt that the city did not shut men out from the sublimity of the universe is shown in that glorious passage on the stars with which he opens the great prose poem of " Nature," — " Seen in the streets of cities, how great they are!" We please ourselves with thinking that he had never lost the feeling with which he first looked up through the vista of the narrow streets of Boston, and caught the shining of the Eternal in the stars; and that ever after they had a glory for him there which he did not find on the mountain-top, or the broad ocean, or as they bent nearer and more lovingly to him on the plains of Concord.

When he entered Harvard College in 1817, the life at Cambridge, in College and Divinity School, did not break his relation to Boston; for the two were then closely united, and Commencement Day was a general holiday. The mild Kirkland was President; Channing, Everett, and Ticknor were among his professors; Josiah Quincy, son and grandson of Josiah, the most Bostonian of Bostonians, who might live at Quincy but prayed to be buried in Boston, was a classmate. More important than college and divinity lectures, however, was the influence of Everett's and Channing's eloquence. The indifference shown by Everett to the great moral conflict of the age destroyed so much of his personal influence in his later years, that it is difficult for us to realize that his eloquence aroused the enthusiasm of Emerson and Elizabeth Peabody and Margaret Fuller; but he had not then lost the faith and love of youth, and he may have helped the young man to that temperance of thought and sobriety of manner which never failed him, but blended happily with his never-ceasing earnestness and enthusiasm. Dr. Channing was then preaching in his Federal Street Church, and Edward Everett, leaving his pulpit in Boston, had become a professor at Cambridge, from which position he entered Congress in 1825, and in due time became Governor of Massachusetts. Emerson says of him in 1820: —

"There was an influence on the young people from the genius of Everett which was almost comparable to that of Pericles in Athens. He had an inspiration which did not go beyond his head, but which made him the master of elegance. If any of my readers were at that period in Boston or Cambridge, they will easily remember his radiant beauty of person, of a classic style; his heavy large eye, marble lids which gave the impression of mass that the slightness of his form needed; sculptured lips; a voice of such rich tones, such precise and perfect utterance, that, although slightly nasal, it was the most mellow and beautiful and correct of all the instruments of the time. The word that he spoke, in the manner in which he spoke it, became current and classical in New England. . . . He had nothing in common with vulgarity or infirmity; but, speaking, walking, sitting, was as much aloof and uncommon as a star. The smallest anecdote of his conversation or behavior was eagerly caught and repeated; and every young scholar could recite brilliant sentences from his sermons, with mimicry, good or bad, of his voice. Every youth was his defender, and boys filled their mouths with arguments to prove that the orator had a heart."

Although Emerson preached for a short time at New Bedford and other places, he accepted a call to settle in Boston as his rightful place, and was installed as colleague with Henry Ware in 1829 over the Second Church, in Hanover Street. Welcomed by the pastor and congregation, and " charming them by the beauty of his elocution and the direct and sincere manner in which he addressed them," all seemed to promise a long and happy relation.

Although in style his discourses were not unlike those of his predecessors and contemporaries, — Channing, Buckminster, etc., — yet the great spirit within them was felt by those in harmony with him; while it was clear that "God had let loose a thinker upon the planet,"[1] and that men must beware for their frail shells of conventionalism, which he would inevitably break down. When the expanding life made it necessary for him to give up some of the customary observances, especially the form of public prayer and the celebration of the Lord's Supper, a general discussion was aroused throughout the city. I remember as a school-girl listening to the comments of my dressmaker on "this minister who did not go into the pulpit in the spirit of prayer."

The impersonality of his action in thus leaving the established church of his ancestors is shown by the tender affection which he ever cherished for it. As he truly wrote, —

> " We love the venerable house
>   Our fathers built to God.
>   In heaven are kept their grateful vows,
>   Their dust endears the sod."

[1] Nothing could more fitly describe the coming of Emerson to the world of Boston and the influence of his transcendental thought than his own words : "Beware when the great God lets loose a thinker on this planet ; then all things are at risk. It is as when a conflagration has broken out in a great city, and no man knows what is safe or where it will end. There is not a piece of science that its flank may not be turned to-morrow; there is not a literary reputation but the so-called eternal names of fame that may not be revised and condemned."

He recognized

> " How anxious hearts have pondered here
>   The mystery of life,
> And prayed the Eternal Spirit clear
>   Their doubts, and end their strife."

To many, who

> " In this church a blessing found
>   Which filled their homes again,"

the loss of his weekly ministrations seemed irreparable. Many years after, I read manuscript notes taken of his sermons by a woman whose life was fashioned to peace and purity ; and her daughter used to cherish in memory one of his parochial visits, when he took her on his lap and showed her the barberry blossom, and how its stamens sprang up at the touch of a pin or an insect.[1]

The places in Boston associated with Emerson as a minister are chiefly at the North End. His church was in Hanover Street, not far from Father Taylor's Bethel, and his parsonage was in Chardon Street, near Bowdoin Square. In later times he for years frequented the old American House in Hanover Street, and would shut himself up there to finish a lecture which the music of his pines had not given him leisure for ; and I have pleased myself in thinking that the ancient memory of the church in which

---

[1] The public record of his work as a preacher is very meagre. It is highly desirable that those who recollect him at that period should give their reminiscences to the public, as Miss Peabody has done to-day.

he ministered sanctified to him this street, which to others might seem the very abode of mammon-worship and vulgarity.

After a year's absence spent in travelling for the benefit of his health, in 1833–1834, Emerson returned to Boston, but not to the work of the Unitarian ministry. He preached only once in his old church, — on the occasion of the death of a friend, — and he soon went to Concord, and made his home there ever afterward. But in thus leaving Boston he was not severed from it. He still found there his intellectual companionship and his spiritual parish. He was no longer the boy in her schools, or the preacher in her churches ; but on the lecture platform he found opportunity for the freest and fullest expression of his life and thought. Nor can we say that " he came unto his own, and his own received him not." From the time that he began his first course of lectures in Boston, in 1835, a circle of friends, admirers, and disciples gathered about him, who never faltered in their allegiance, and who found in his words their highest moral and spiritual inspiration and their richest intellectual enjoyment. He never drew a noisy crowd ; he rarely spoke in the largest halls of the city ; but a moderate-sized room was filled with an audience of the most intelligent, cultivated, and earnest men and women. The same faces might be seen there, week after week and year after year ; and when almost for the last time he repeated a lecture at the Old South Church in 1880 for the benefit of its funds, it was touching to see the gray heads bent eagerly forward to catch his words, — the hearing of the listener having grown dull, and the silvery voice of the speaker low, while the chord of sympathy and love was still unbroken between them. A generation grew up under the benediction of those great words in which ever the noblest principles and highest faith were appealed to; and among them were found the lofty men and "honorable women not a few," who have upheld the standard of education, morals, and pure philanthropy in Boston, and who have been the earnest workers in every good cause.

The portrait by David Scott[1] recalls his expression and action in the lecture-room during that early period. The rapt expression of intense thought was emphasized by the peculiar action of the hand, which Scott has given. His voice was modulated by every shade of feeling, but had always a peculiar resonance which gave spirit and life to its tones; and it answered to that glance of the eyes which recalled Mrs. Child's comparison of light shining out from a temple. But the charm of manner was intimately connected with the thought, and was not that superficial readiness which pleases everybody. Newspaper writers and School-ship boys thought it awkward and embarrassed.[2] He never wearied his audience; he was

[1] Heliotyped for this volume.

[2] Perhaps every anecdote is worth preserving. Mr. Emerson once addressed the boys on board the Reform School-ship. He disliked extemporaneous speaking, and he was embarrassed and confused by

a perfect artist in the correspondence between the value of the thought and the beauty of the expression, and his sentences were like jewels whose brilliancy drew your attention before you knew their worth. He was very scrupulous in regard to time, never keeping his audience more than an hour, but often tantalizing them by suddenly closing his lecture when seemingly much of his manuscript remained unread.

One of the richest treasures which Emerson found in Boston was the old sailor-preacher, Father Taylor. This son of the forecastle possessed a poetic insight and imagination only equalled by his warm heart and fervent devotion. Utterly undaunted by pretensions of any kind, he saw clearly through all shams, and recognized the true ring of the Divine wherever he heard the note. Mr. Emerson delighted in his wit and his wisdom, often went to hear him preach, and subscribed to his Bethel. His *bon mot* in regard to Emerson has often been repeated, but I will give it as I had it from the lips of Governor Andrew, to whom Father Taylor had said it : —

"Mr. Emerson," said Father Taylor, "is one of the sweetest creatures God ever made. But there is a screw

the novel audience. A few days after, the teacher of reading, wishing to impress upon the boys of the ship the importance of ease and freedom of utterance, mimicked the awkwardness and confusion of an inexperienced speaker, and asked, "Now, boys, what should you think if you heard a man speak so?" "Should think it was Mr. Emerson," shouted the irrepressibles of the forecastle.

loose somewhere in the machinery; yet I cannot tell where it is, for I never heard it jar. He must go to heaven when he dies, for if he went to hell the Devil would not know what to do with him. But still he knows no more of the religion of the New Testament than Balaam's ass did of the principles of the Hebrew grammar."

As the poor beast spoke the word of the Lord, in spite of his ignorance of grammar, so Father Taylor seemed to intimate that Emerson had entered into the life of heavenly grace, though he did not go through the portals of Christianity. The last time I saw Father Taylor, — possibly the last time he and Emerson met, — was at a meeting of the friends of the Fifty-fourth (colored) Regiment of Massachusetts Volunteers, at Chickering's Rooms, on Friday, March 20, 1863, to raise means for supplying them with an outfit like that of other regiments sent from this State in the war. Father Taylor was very old and infirm, and spoke little, but his presence on the platform was significant. Mr. Emerson came in from the anteroom with his face on fire with indignation, as I never saw it on any other occasion, and announced to the audience that he had just learned that South Carolina had given out the threat that colored soldiers, if captured, should not be treated as prisoners, but be put to death. " What answer does Massachusetts send back to South Carolina ? " he said. " Two for one!" shouted voices in the audience. " Is that the answer that Massachusetts sends?" he asked;

and the audience responded with applause. He retired from the platform, it seemed to me a little appalled at the spirit he had raised.

While there was never a time when Emerson was not recognized by the circle of wise and beautiful souls who formed his parish in Boston, his Divinity School Address and other utterances in regard to theological topics undoubtedly gave sincere pain to many who had been numbered among his thoughtful friends, and still greater offence to the superficial crowd that were unable to appreciate his thoughts. It was the fashion among a certain clique to sneer at his lectures as vague, whimsical, and incomprehensible. "Nothing but whipped syllabub," said a literary man now well-nigh forgotten, — "but I like syllabub." I once heard the late George S. Hillard say, "*I* don't understand Mr. Emerson," in a tone which plainly implied that he considered the loss to be on Emerson's side. To the same effect the tremendous dictum of the great lawyer, Jeremiah Mason, whose imposing stature overawed lesser men, has been often repeated : "*I* don't understand Emerson ; my gals do." It is said that Mr. Mason really enjoyed every lecture, although he could not quite accept the new light. After hearing the lecture on "Memory," a smart young lawyer approached a lady the next evening who was talking of it to a friend. "Oh, it was all very pretty and pleasant," he said, "but no real thought in it! I can't remember anything he said, can you ?" "Yes," replied the lady ;

" he said 'shallow brains have short memories.'"
The wife of a minister with whom he had exchanged
in 1830 said, " Waldo Emerson came last Sunday
and preached a sermon with his chin in the air, in
scorn of the whole human race."

During some seasons the enjoyment of Emerson's
lectures was prolonged by a social gathering at the
hospitable rooms of Mr. James Fisher or Miss E. P.
Peabody. Mr. Emerson would offer his escort to one
of his friends to walk to these rooms, and Theodore
Parker, Mr. Alcott, and other favored guests followed.
Here the timid girl, who had listened in rapt awe
and delight to the great speaker, was made happy by
a grasp of his hand and a kindly beam from his eye ;
and the tones of his voice filled the night air with
music, as if the winds of heaven were playing over
an Æolian harp.

The influences of these lectures, from 1835 to 1865,
on the growing mind of Boston in those days, is
simply inestimable. In the language of one of his
hearers, " His words not only fired the thoughts of
his hearers, quickened their consciences, and pierced
their hearts, but they modelled their lives." I always
recall the question of another earnest young woman,
which shows the estimation of a Bostonian : " Which
could you have least spared out of your life, — the
Common, or Ralph Waldo Emerson ? " Perhaps none
but a Boston child, to whom the Common had been
Nature's very self, would understand the force of the
comparison. Theodore Parker was wont to "thank

God for the sun, the moon, and Ralph Waldo
Emerson." It was hard to tell what were Nature's
teachings and what his, they were so fully one.
In later years, — from 1855 onward, — Emerson was
chosen to speak for Boston on many important occasions. He spoke very frequently to the great
congregation which Theodore Parker had gathered
together, and gave voice to the feelings of heroism
and patriotism called forth by the Civil War. He
took his stand by the hero of Harper's Ferry in
1859, in a lecture before the Parker Fraternity, and
at the meeting for sympathy with John Brown's
family held in Tremont Temple. In 1863, when a
grand festival was held in the Music Hall to celebrate Lincoln's Proclamation of Emancipation, he
read his " Boston Hymn." That he gave this name
to the poem embodying his lofty ideal of American
life, shows his feeling that the city of his birth
ought to stand as representative of the principles
and virtues which should lead the national life.
He also wrote the poem for the centennial celebration, in 1873, of the destruction of the tea in
Boston Harbor; and it seems as if the spirit of boyhood and fun, which belonged to the days of the
fights between North End and South End on the
Common, came back to him as he chronicled the half-
mad exploit of the Indians who threw the tea over-
board, under the direction of Sam Adams, in 1773.

A certain almost forgotten institution, the Town
and Country Club, where Concord and Boston were

expected to meet and exchange the wisdom of the world and of Nature, was established by Mr. Alcott about 1848, and Mr. Emerson and others heartily joined in the scheme. Great was the indignation among the faithful women who found that membership was confined to one sex. The word "club" had no feminine then. Some of the aggrieved sex perpetrated a poem to express their feelings, — of which I can only remember a comparison with Socrates, who did not scorn the wisdom of Diotima. To the "Parliaments of the Times" and other good meetings held there, however, women were cordially invited; and it was delightful to see the eager pleasure with which Mr. Emerson listened to every speaker. When the New England Women's Club was formed, in 1865, he was at once made an honorary member. He frequently came to its meetings, and read some of his most personal and charming papers there. Among these was the first draught of his reminiscences of his beloved Aunt Mary, since published in the "Atlantic." In his letters to Carlyle he alludes to his Boston Saturday Club, as if he had there found a congenial circle. He always delighted in meeting thoughtful men, whose pursuits differed from his own; and this was what the Saturday Club gave him, from 1856 till 1880.

Mr. Emerson was born in Boston, married a Bostonian in 1829, preached and lectured in Boston, and was a member of Boston society for many years, though his home was twenty miles away in Concord.

What Boston thought of him I have pointed out; but the tables are now turned, and what Emerson thought of Boston is more important than what a Boston clique once thought of him. In his correspondence with Carlyle we catch many hints of his feeling about the good city. That he looked upon it as having a pretty distinct individuality and character is very evident, and this trait of Boston was certainly dear to him. It is one way in which we recognize the influence of the city. He was the least egotistical of men; but he guarded the sacredness of individual personality most jealously, and was a true idealist in always insisting that it be kept in due relation to the universal.

He was not blind to the faults of his native town, and knew how he was regarded by many; but he was more interested in the recognition of Carlyle's merit, in 1836–1838, than of his own. Speaking to Carlyle about a friendly notice of his work by Alexander H. Everett, he says: "I am delighted, for this man represents a clique to which I am a stranger, and which I supposed might not love you. It must be you shall succeed when Saul prophesies." He seems proud and hopeful of the mental condition of Boston as tried by the Carlyle test. He "hopes to have a work on the First Philosophy in Boston," and does not doubt its reception. "Boston contains some genuine taste for literature, and a good deal of traditional reverence for it," he adds; and he evidently has satisfaction and pleasure in the reception of his lectures, which he "found much indulgence in reading." He fully recognized that he had found his place in the Lyceum at Boston, and that it depended upon the speaker to make of it what he could. "I see not why this is not the most flexible of all organs of opinion, from its popularity and its newness, permitting you to say what you think, without any shackles of prescription. . . . You may handle every member and relation of humanity. What could Homer, Socrates, or Saint Paul say, that cannot be said here?" He adds (this was in 1837), "I find myself so much more and freer on the platform of the lecture-room than in the pulpit, that I shall not much more use the last; and do now only in a little country chapel at the request of simple men, to whom I sustain no other relation than that of preacher. But I preach in the lecture-room, and then it tells, for there is no prescription. You may laugh, weep, reason, sing, sneer, or pray, according to your genius. It is the new pulpit, and very much in vogue with my northern countrymen. The audience is of all classes, and its character will be determined always by the name of the lecturer. Why may you not," he says to Carlyle, "give the reins to your wit, your pathos, your philosophy, and become that good despot which the virtuous orator is?"

He identifies himself with the city, and says, "We could easily get up for you a course of lectures in Boston;" but during the "storm in our wash-bowl," which followed the Address at the Divinity School, in 1838, he will not involve Carlyle in his supposed unpopularity. How soon any such feeling against him was dissipated, however, is shown by the full attendance at his next course of lectures. His "Boston Parish" did not secede from him. In this parish, as he says, were "all the bright boys and girls in New England, quite ignorant of each other, . . . who do not wish to go into trade, and do not like morning calls and evening parties. They are all religious, but hate the churches; they reject all the ways of living of other men, but have none to offer in their stead." He must have felt the fullest recognition of his thought by his audiences; and in his relation to them was the happy blending of fellow-citizenship with the fresh fragrance of his country home. Even "the solid men of Boston" will understand Carlyle; and he dares to suggest that "a prayer from Boston, Massachusetts, is as worthy of serious and prompt granting as one from Edinburgh or Oxford."

At the Boston Athenæum, which he loved to frequent, he had read Carlyle's "Diamond Necklace" and the "Mirabeau" three weeks before his presentation copy came; and as we read these lines, a vision of the rapt face and intent attitude with which he seized the new thoughts of his friend rises before us. Oh! happy city, where such men lived and read!

Yes, Emerson was ours. We claim him by birth, by blood, by mutual service rendered, by the indissoluble ties of gratitude, by steadfast, unfailing love. There is a Boston of degraded politics, of noisy bluster, of scramble for wealth, which was not his, and does not bear his seal upon it. But he was patient even with this rough, coarse element; and in spite of it, as he stood by the ballot-box, he believed that the majority of men tried to vote right, and he never despaired of the uplifting of the masses. There is another Boston whose blood, running blue in its veins, unstirred by sympathy with the groans of the slave, and intrenched in egotistic pride, despaired of the Republic, and sought to erect itself into an aristocracy of wealth or learning. This Boston strove to throw scorn upon the higher law, and to ridicule the prophet whose truth it could neither receive nor understand. But he knew well what a thin crust of selfishness overlay the real deep heart of humanity which was underneath it; and he rejoiced when the sons of the men who in 1850–1852 had driven the fugitive slave out of their harbor, and closed their doors upon Kossuth, gave, in the Civil War ten years after, their young lives for their country, in tardy reparation for the wrongs of the slave. Emerson's Boston held " men whom to name, the voice breaks and the eye is wet," — men " of noblest affections, whose name is a motive-power and regulator to our city, — refusing all office, but impossible to spare." During the Civil War, he says: " A multitude of young men are growing up here of high promise, and I compare gladly the social poverty of my youth with the power on which these draw. The Lowell race again in our war yielded three or four martyrs so able and tender and true that James Russell Lowell cannot allude to them in verse or prose but the public is melted anew." "All these," he says to Carlyle, "know you well, have read and will read you, — yes, and will prize and use your benefaction to the College [at Cambridge] ; and I believe it would add hope, health, and strength to you to come and see them." I cannot but regret that Carlyle's bequest of books did not go to the Boston Library, open to all, and furnishing help to students from Canada to California; but the Cambridge scholar rejoiced at the association of his dear friend with his *Alma Mater.*

Oh, blessed heart ! ever young, that rejoiced thus in the new life and the rich opportunity offered to others, never groaning that the former times were better than these, and incapable of despair of the race that God had begotten. But while he felt the kind reception and sympathetic response from his young and enthusiastic auditors, like every true artist of that day he saw the want of intelligent, thorough criticism ; and in his thought of going to England, the hope entered of meeting there critics who would rouse him to put forth his full strength. " At home, no man makes any proper demand on me, and the audience I address is a handful of men and women too widely scattered to dictate to me that which they are justly entitled to say."

In the dark days of the Antislavery contest, and during the war, he was not separated from his fellow-citizens. His word was sought and heeded in every crisis ; and if his quiet manner and scholarly habits kept him from the excitement of the political convention, he was always squarely on the side of right and freedom. " As if every sane man were not an Abolitionist ! " he said, in his speech on the outrage against Charles Sumner. This speech, made at a meeting in Concord, reported at the time in the daily newspapers, and then almost forgotten by its author till recalled to his memory at the death of Mr. Sumner, deserves to be placed beside the famous orations of antiquity for its condensed power of thought and feeling, and for its influence in changing the minds of men. It was the best voice of New England and of Boston that spoke through him, as he tenderly and reverently closed with these words : —

" I wish that he may know the shudder of terror that ran through all this community on the first tidings of this brutal attack. Let him hear that every man in New England loves his virtues ; that every mother thinks of him as the protector of families ; that every friend of freedom thinks him the friend of freedom. And if our arms at this distance cannot defend him from assassins, we confide the defence of a life so precious to all honorable men and true patriots, and to the Almighty Maker of men."

No one knew better than Emerson how all the surroundings and experiences of life go to make up

" The being that I am,
When I am most myself."

While his horizon was large, and many influences came into his life from inheritance and surroundings, there are marked traits in his character which we cannot but ascribe to the fact that Boston was his birthplace. " Boston *is* the hub of the solar system ; you could n't pry that out of a Boston man if you had the tire of all creation for a crowbar," says the witty Dr. Holmes ; and Emerson never needed any other spot from which to draw the great circle of infinity but that on which he stood. The relation of man to the universe was as confident as it was modest. That in him this sense of relation was per-fect in humility and courtesy, while in other men it was blatant and brazen, does not prove that the feeling sprang from no common source. The " wee modest crimson-tippèd " daisy has to own its cousin-ship with the flaunting white-weed and showy Rudbeckia. But with all her pride, Boston loves moderation and understatement and the fine re-serve of the gentleman. " I wish cities could teach their best lesson of quiet manners," says Emerson. She does not take on tricks of speech, but calls the dear old Common by its homely name. How thor-oughly Emersonian is this trait ! It is English, indeed, and he loved the English blood and speech, and I think had no special fondness for any other tongue. Yet, like Boston, whose nickname of the American Athens is well bestowed, he was rather a Greek than an Englishman, — Greek in the fineness of his perceptions, in his love for the subtler ele-ments of thought, his belief in the purity of beauty ; he was full of delight in new ideas, strong in his own individuality, but ready for all mental hospitality. Yet he was the Greek blended with the Puritan, — for as in Boston the old leaven of that strong Puritan race is still working, so in him was the stern Calvinism of his fathers, which believed in eternal decrees, and in the absoluteness and omnipotence of right. The same fidelity to belief which obliged the men of Boston and Salem to obey the letter of the word, and "not suffer a witch to live," led them on to the modern radicalism which is equally loyal and in its way sometimes equally narrow. Emerson was saved from the extremes of the past or the present by the sanity of his nature and the entire absence of personal regards. Yet without his line of Puritan descent he would not have been the man he was, — relinquishing office, friends, and public regard for the sake of truth. The Puritan spirit breathes through all his brave utterances : —

> " When duty whispers low, *Thou must,*
> The youth replies, *I can.*"

It was only in the city that he could have had the sympathy of such a group of scholars and thinkers as he found in Boston, and he well understood how much he owed to relation with other men. While he found the benefit of solitude, it was because he could carry into it such a precious freight of thought which he had garnered from life.

He says : " 'T is wonderful what sublime lessons I have once and again read on the bulletin-boards in the streets. Everybody has been wrong in his guess except good women, who never despair of an ideal right." He loved solitude, but he was closely linked with society, saying, " I follow, I find, the fortunes of my country in my privatest ways."

Mrs. Cheney here read, as illustrative of what she had said concerning Emerson's relation to the Boston of his youth, the following letter from Miss Sarah Clark, a pupil of Allston in art and of Emerson in thought : —

MARIETTA, Ohio, July 20, 1884.

DEAR MRS. CHENEY, — I would I were with you at Concord on the day to which you invite me to contribute. This invitation gratifies me immensely ; but I doubt if I can find anything to say on the proposed subject. I have never thought of Emerson as related to Boston. Yet it may not be an unfruitful theme. I remember when he announced six lectures to be read there, I wondered how one who seemed so wholly to belong to " thought's interior sphere " could find anything to say to a public assembly. But he already had his public which came at his call; and when those clear-cut sentences, those selected words, fell from his lips, it became evident that he had a power of throwing light into his abstractions that could easily admit many minds to that illumination. His voice, his manner of saying these wise words, you all remember. Was there not a note of authority, as well as of persuasive sweetness, that made all his hearers take his words to heart ? It was as if behind him some other power had spoken. It may be that Boston produced him ; but I think rather it was a singular good-fortune, or Heaven's grace, that gave him to us.

His little public grew year by year. Those who at first cried, " Is this man mad ? " came to respect the pure sanity of his utterances ; his influence was felt in circles wider and wider, till he became a power in the whole intellectual world. Whether he was or was not a product of Boston, he certainly loved his city and his country. Who has uttered better words of love than these to " Boston " ? —

> " The rocky nook, with hill-tops three,
>   Looked eastward from the farms,
> And twice each day the flowing sea
>   Took Boston in its arms."

Or who has said a better word for our earliest battle-ground than this immortal verse ? —

> " By the rude bridge that arched the flood,
>   Their flag to April's breeze unfurled,
> Here once the embattled farmers stood,
>   And fired the shot heard round the world."

Or the 4th of July Ode read at Concord in 1857, with its grandly poetic opening image ? —

> " Oh, tenderly the haughty day
>   Fills his blue urn with fire;
> One morn is in the mighty heaven,
>   And one in our desire."

These, with the " Emancipation Hymn," show the burning heart of a patriot unchilled by the philosophy that was sometimes accused of coldness ; but in his personal intellectual relation with many minds what seeds were sown, and what fructification ensued ! Immeasurable forces these, and of unmeasurable duration. They cannot be counted, they cannot be estimated. Emerson was patriot to the heart's core; but he was not only a patriot, he was an intellectual force that valued liberty wherever man is found. He was not merely an intellect, but he had the poet's grasp, which holds in one hand the seen and the unseen. He was not merely the poet, he was like the sun which searches out and stimulates life-seeds hidden in the dark earth, waiting for this warm energy to unfold them. Concord is right to talk of him; he is her best subject.

But I should weary you long before I should exhaust the countless streams into which my theme runs. Why should I speak longer, when he has spoken for himself? The poem of "Boston," read in Faneuil Hall, Dec. 16, 1873, on the Centennial Anniversary of the destruction of the Tea in Boston Harbor, is written with the freedom of a boyish muse, and the irregular stanzas seem to pour out like a gurgling brook from the overflow of his memory and heart. Who that saw and heard him as he read it will ever forget the youthful gleam in his face, and the loving tones of his voice? And how clearly did his own boyhood and youth in the old town rise up to his mind as he spoke these lines:—

BOSTON.

The rocky nook, with hill-tops three,
    Looked eastward from the farms,
And twice each day the flowing sea
    Took Boston in its arms;
The men of yore were stout and poor,
And sailed for bread to every shore.

And where they went, on trade intent,
   They did what freemen can ;
Their dauntless ways did all men praise, —
   The merchant was a man ;
The world was made for honest trade, —
To plant and eat be none afraid.
    .   .   .   .   .   .

Old Europe groans with palaces, —
   Has lords enough and more ;
We plant and build by foaming seas
   A city of the poor ;
For day by day could Boston Bay
Their honest labor overpay.

We grant no dukedoms to the few,
   We hold like rights and shall, —
Equal on Sunday in the pew,
   On Monday in the mall ;
For what avail the plough or sail,
Or land or life, if freedom fail ?

The noble craftsman we promote,
   Disown the knave and fool ;
Each honest man shall have his vote,
   Each child shall have his school ;
A union then of honest men,
Or union nevermore again.
    .   .   .   .   .   .

They laughed to know the world so wide ;
   The mountains said, " Good day ;
We greet you well, you Saxon men,
   Up with your towns and stay ! "
The world was made for honest trade, —
To plant and eat be none afraid.

" For you," they said, " no barriers be,
   For you no sluggard rest ;
Each street leads downward to the sea,
   Or landward to the West."

O happy town beside the sea,
  Whose roads lead everywhere to all ;
Than thine no deeper moat can be,
  No stouter fence, no steeper wall !

Kings shook with fear, old empires crave
  The secret force to find,
Which fired the little State to save
  The rights of all mankind.

But right is might through all the world,
  Province to province faithful clung,
Through good and ill the war-bolt hurled,
  Till Freedom cheered and the joy-bells rung.

The sea returning day by day
  Restores the world-wide mart ;
So let each dweller on the Bay
  Fold Boston in his heart,
Till these echoes be choked with snows,
Or over the town blue ocean flows.

Let the blood of her hundred thousands
  Throb in each manly vein,
And the wit of all her wisest
  Make sunshine in her brain ;
For you can teach the lightning speech,
And round the globe your voices reach.

And each shall care for other,
  And each to each shall bend, —
To the poor a noble brother,
  To the good an equal friend.

A blessing through the ages thus
  Shield all thy roofs and towers !
God with the fathers, so with us,
  Thou darling town of ours !

II.

EMERSON AND ALCOTT.

PASSAGES FROM THE DIARY AND CORRESPONDENCE OF MR. ALCOTT, — READ AT THE OPENING OF THE SCHOOL OF PHILOSOPHY, JULY 23, 1884.

MR. SANBORN said: Among the topics proposed for the discussion we are about to commence concerning the "Genius and Character of Emerson," was one on "Emerson's Friendships." But not the least of the misfortunes which the continued illness of Mr. Alcott brings to us, is this one, — that it deprives us of the voice and the thought of that friend of Emerson who stood beside him for nearly half a century, and who could best have spoken on this delightful theme. Among the qualities of our friend and master, none was more conspicuous or more charming than his loyalty in friendship. His Arab in the poem "Hermione," who in other passages utters the sentiment of Emerson, nowhere speaks more truly than in saying,

> "I am of a lineage
> That each for each doth fast engage;"

and that noble poem which precedes the essay on
"Friendship" describes no friend more faithfully than
Emerson himself : —

> " I fancied he was fled, —
>   But, after many a year,
>   Glowed unexhausted kindliness
>   Like daily sunrise there."

To no person was this high companionship per-
mitted for a longer and more intimate term than to
Mr. Alcott; and we have therefore asked him to
allow us the public reading from his Diaries and
Correspondence in the last fifty years, of a few
passages which illustrate the relation between the
two friends, and which also fix the date of certain
events in Emerson's career.

Mr. Alcott first met Emerson, and heard him
speak from Dr. Channing's pulpit, in 1829; but their
acquaintance did not begin until after our Connecticut Pestalozzi had returned from Philadelphia and
opened in Boston his celebrated school for children
at the Masonic Temple, in 1834–1835. Early in 1835,
and before knowing Emerson, Mr. Alcott had spent
an evening with Allston the painter, at his house in
Cambridgeport; and as these two men of genius—
Allston and Emerson — had many traits in common,
we may first hear what Mr. Alcott said in his Diary
of Jan. 13, 1835, concerning the artist : —

" I was particularly impressed with the uncommon
artlessness and modesty of this man of genius, — a man
of higher endowments and skill in the art of painting

than perhaps any other person in our country. I felt myself in the presence of a superior spirit, — an external shaping of the higher traits of the human soul; the power of genius was there. This is a man of genius; and how rarely does the spirit, while invested in flesh, behold such manifestation of its inner life! How rarely doth the soul come forth in shapes of beauty, of truth, and breathe into the dead forms of matter and of words the inspiring life of its own divinity! And yet this same man — this spirit of celestial energy — lives in an obscure mansion, away from the noise and stir of every-day life; seldom is his name pronounced; and who are those that behold his face? Verily, he knoweth his mission; he showeth himself only to the spiritually visaged, like himself."

How exactly is Emerson, the seer and poet, depicted in this sketch of the superior artist! A few weeks later, after several interviews with Dr. Channing, then at the height of his renown and influence as a preacher in Boston, Mr. Alcott goes to hear Emerson lecture (Feb. 5, 1835), and makes this inadequate record: —

"This evening I heard Rev. Mr. Emerson give a lecture, at the Temple, on the 'Character of Michael Angelo.' This is the *second* lecture of a course embracing Biographical Sketches of eminent men, before the Society for the Diffusion of Useful Knowledge. I did not hear the first lecture. Miss Peabody informs me that it was a beautiful one. The speaker took a general view of the Theory of Life, and of the means to be used in order to realize it. Few men among us take nobler views of the mission, powers, and destinies of man than Mr. Emerson. I hope the people of this city will go and learn of him the conditions of virtue and wisdom, — by what self-denial, what exertions, these are to be sought and won. The lives of the great and good are examples of this strife of the soul."

Again, Feb. 12, 1835, he says : —

" I heard Mr. Emerson's lecture on 'Martin Luther,' at the Temple. There was much in it bespeaking a high philosophy of life as conceived in the mind of the speaker ; and the application of the analysis of Luther's character was beautiful and profound. He deemed Luther not less a *poet* than a *practical man ;* and if not a philosopher in the common sense of the term, he was a prophet, speaking and acting from an imperative above reason."

The Diary contains no more notices of this course of lectures, in which was that remarkable one on " Milton," afterwards printed in the " North American Review ; " nor do we find records of interview and conversation between the two friends. But that they were already becoming intimate is seen by this entry of July 12, 1835 : —

" A few days since, Mrs. Morrison, of Philadelphia, came in town, bringing me letters from Mr. Russell. Last evening she saw several of our friends, — persons with whom we wished her to be made acquainted. Among these were the following : Mr. Waldo Emerson, Charles Emerson, Mr. and Mrs. D. L. Child, Mr. S. J. May, Miss

Elizabeth and Miss Mary Peabody [now Mrs. Horace Mann], Mrs. Bliss [now Mrs. George Bancroft], Miss Mary Emerson, Miss Elizabeth Hoar, and others."

Here we see the names of several persons of that Concord circle into which Mr. Alcott afterwards came ; but as yet he had never visited the town. Later in the summer, August 23, he writes : —

"I have been in attendance at the American Institute of Instruction, — at the State House in the daytime, at Chauncy Hall in the evening. On Thursday, at eleven o'clock, Rev. Mr. Furness, of Philadelphia, gave an introductory address on the 'Spirit of the True Teacher,' — an eloquent performance. At 4 P. M. Rev. Mr. Emerson, of Concord, gave a lecture on the 'Means of Inspiring a Taste for English Literature.'

"These two lectures were of a more spiritual character than have been presented to the Institute on former occasions. They inspire hope. They are proofs that sometimes more is felt in the community than the material. The members of the Institute — many of them teachers from the country, persons of narrow views and superficial attainments — were unprepared to follow the lecturers ; yet they seemed to listen with interest, and to feel, if they did not appreciate, the truths announced."

Through this year (1835) Mr. Alcott was deep in the study of Plato and the Bible, which he found in accord with each other and with his own thoughts; and he was also in close communication with those readers of Carlyle who were inviting him to New

England, and were proposing a new magazine, to be called " The Transcendentalist," of which mention is made in Emerson's letters to Carlyle of March 12, and April 30, 1835. Of this project Emerson wrote: —

" Dr. Channing lay awake all night, he told my friend last week, because he had learned in the evening that some young men proposed to issue a journal, to be called ' The Transcendentalist,' as the organ of a spiritual philosophy. . . . If Mr. Carlyle would undertake a journal of which we have talked much, but which we have never yet produced, he would do us great service, and we feel some confidence that it could be made to secure him a support. It is to be called ' The Transcendentalist,' or 'The Spiritual Inquirer,' or the like, and F. H. Hedge was to be the editor. Hedge is just leaving our neighborhood, to be settled as a minister two hundred and fifty miles off in Maine, and entreats that you will edit the journal. He will write, and I please myself with thinking I shall be able to write under such auspices."

To this invitation Carlyle listened and responded (May 13, 1835): —

" The Boston ' Transcendentalist,' whatever the fate or merit of it prove to be, is surely an interesting symptom. There must be things not dreamt of over in that Transoceanic Parish, and I shall cordially wish well to this thing, and hail it as the sure forerunner of things better. Innumerable tumults of Metaphysic must be struggled through, and at last Transcendentalism evolve itself as the *Euthanasia* of Metaphysic altogether. May it be sure ! may it be speedy ! "

Mr. Alcott's record of this premature movement, which found expression in "The Dial" five years later, is in a letter to his friend Russell at Philadelphia, of which we only find the heads given in his Diary of March, 1835. These are the following : —

"SPIRIT OF LIFE IN BOSTON. — *Persons :* Dr. Channing, Mr. Allston, Dr. Follen, Mr. [James] Walker, Mr. Hedge, Mr. Emerson, Mr. H. Ware, Jr., Mr. Waterston, [Father] Taylor, Mr. [C.] Francis, Mr. [G.] Ripley, Mr. May, Miss Peabody, Mrs. Follen, Mrs. Child.

" ' THE TRANSCENDENTALIST.' — Hedge, Emerson, Peabody, Clarke, Ripley [no doubt as contributors].

"Republication of Coleridge, Abbott's Works [Rev. Jacob Abbott], ' North American,' ' Examiner,' ' Observer.'

"READINGS. — Plato, Coleridge, Hesiod, Boëthius, Bockshirmer [a forgotten German writer on the Will], ' Sartor Resartus,' T. C. Upham."

What effect all this spiritual movement had on the thought of Mr. Alcott may be seen in his Diary. His mind was moving on the same lines with the mind of Emerson, and they read in part the same books. Mr. Alcott writes, from March to August, 1835 : —

" My own conceptions of life are confirmed in the happiest manner in the Platonic theory. In Plato, as in Jesus, do I find the Light of the World, even the *supersensual* light, that lighteth every one who cometh into the world of sense, and essayeth to regain that spirit it seemeth to have lost by the incarnation of itself. The true study of man is man. When this is felt as it ought to be, natural science will receive an impulse that we cannot at present conceive of. Then we shall begin at the beginning, and not, as now, at the end; we shall trace things in the order of their production, see them in the process of formation, growth, consummation, — the only true way of apprehending them, the method of philosophy. Without this method all our boasted acquisitions are fragments, unintelligible parts, broken members of a whole, whose outline we have not pictured in our ideal, and therefore want the standard by which to resolve these parts to their true place in the great Whole. The unity of truth is wanting; glimpses only are given of this Whole, and we content ourselves with the dim survey of parts, becoming parts ourselves. . . . As Man is my study, — universal as well as individual man, — man in his elements, embracing views of him in all stages of his career, — in his pre-existent life, his infancy, childhood, youth, manhood, decline, resumption in God, — so doth all Nature, in its manifold relations, present innumerable topics for consideration, as the framework and emblem of this same Being. Man, the Incarnate Spirit; God, the Absolute Spirit; Creation, the emblem of these two, — such are my topics of speculation and inquiry. As in the morning twilight the sun paints in the horizon the radiant glories of his own visage upon the clear and serene azure, announcing to the risen world the coming day; even so doth the Divinity, in this terrestrial life, shed forth on the dim forms of mind and matter some intimation of his own celestial visage; prophesying, in these visible and invisible things, the coming of his own Day, which is Eternity; of his own life, which is Immortality, and Light without obstruction."

This last passage is dated Aug. 4, 1835 ; and at the close of the month (August 30), after listening to a sermon by Mr. Hedge, Mr. Alcott wrote : —

" The spiritual philosophy appeared as the life of this sermon. Of the few men among us who are believers in this philosophy, the following are the most interesting ; indeed, they comprise all the thorough disciples of the transcendent and metaphysical life, as revealed in the theory of Jesus. The number is, however, daily increasing ; for a spiritual idea has gone forth in our community, and the religious instinct apprehends its glory. Let me arrange these prophets of the present time according to their apprehension of the spiritual ideal : Dr. Channing, Dr. Follen, Mr. R. W. Emerson, Mr. Hedge, Mr. R. H. Dana, Mr. Furness, Mr. Allston, Mr. Walker, Mr. J. F. Clarke, Mr. Peabody, Mr. Frothingham."

At a later date Mr. Alcott placed Emerson at the head of this list, where he properly belonged, and where he might also have placed his own name. The two brethren were drawing closer together ; and a few weeks later Mr. Alcott paid his first visit to Concord (Oct. 17, 1835). Under date of Oct. 20, 1835, the Diary says : —

" On Saturday afternoon I came to Concord with Mr. George P. Bradford. We reached the residence of Mr. Emerson after a ride of three hours. The evening was passed in very interesting conversation. On Sunday, various topics of an intellectual and spiritual character were resumed. On most subjects there was striking conformity of taste and opinion. We had much talk on the character and life of Christ. On this there was some disparity of idea, more the effect, I deem, of difference of association than of thought. Mr. Emerson's fine literary taste is sometimes in the way of a clear and hearty acceptance of the *spiritual.* Carlyle is his ideal; his portrait I saw for the first time. I have not found a man in whose whole mind I felt more sympathy than in his. These two persons [Mr. and Mrs. Emerson] have and represent a *new idea of life.* I have found a man who, with all his taste for Grecian literature and philosophy, can apprehend something spiritual in Christianity. To him it is not 'altogether foolishness;' for he has the sense of the Human, and the love and faith of the Pure and the Perfect in Universal Man. With his brother, Mr. Charles Emerson, I had some interesting conversation. He has much of his brother's spirit. They are both scholarlike in their views and tastes, and yet the man is not lost in the scholar. To have a few such friends is the joy and comfort of life. In communion with such the Spirit finds itself, and, for the brief time of their presence, forgets its independent life, — being lost in the common Being of Humanity."

The day on which Mr. Alcott returned to Boston from this Concord visit (Oct. 21, 1835) was that when Garrison was mobbed in the city by "gentlemen of property and standing;" and the first errand, after reaching Boston, was to visit, with Mrs. Alcott, the Antislavery leader in the Leverett Street Jail, where he was confined by the authorities. At an earlier date in the same year (August 1), the Diary records Mr. Alcott's presence at an emancipation meeting in Julien Hall, where George Thompson, the English

Abolitionist, spoke, and where several slaveholders from the South were present. Mr. Alcott writes:

" Mr. Thompson was eloquent and impassioned, as usual; but in a singular compound of imagery brought forth some very clear and true points to the eye of the audience. The slaveholders seemed somewhat astounded by this strange display of sense, principle, wit, satire, humor, pathos, practical and theoretic wisdom thus showered upon them. Before he had concluded his philippic (or by what name it shall be called), they deliberately rose and left the room. After the meeting they were found standing at the passage, to get a nearer glance at Mr. Thompson as he passed, — perhaps to intimidate him and others. I took my stand near the door to watch their movements. Meanwhile Mr. Thompson's carriage had come to another passage-way, and he was driven off, leaving these disaffected men to go home without causing disturbance. Before they left the door, however, one of them said to the bystanders : ' We will give five hundred dollars for him in any one of the slaveholding States.' I said, ' And what would you do with him ? ' ' Do with him ? ' said he, with a look of mingled malignity and scorn, uttering at the same time an oath, ' we would hang him ! ' ' Yes,' said another, ' if we had him at Vicksburg, we would bring Lynch's law to bear upon him at once.' And they departed."

The two Transcendentalists were then Emancipationists also, and they bore their testimony publicly in after years. What were the opinions of Mr. Alcott in 1835 on " the character and life of Christ," which he discussed with Mr. Emerson, may be seen in this autobiographical passage from the Diary, dated Sunday, Sept. 27, 1835 : —

" In 1833 I was a disciple of Experience, trying to bring my theories within the Baconian method of Induction, and took the philosophy of Aristotle as the exponent of humanity, while my heart was even then lingering around the theories of Plato, without being conscious of it. A follower of Aristotle was I in theory, yet a true Platonist in practice. Christianity had not found its philosophical interpretation at that time in my heart; its spirit was striving for forms agreeable to the understanding. The heart's problems were seeking solution from the skill of the head. I was looking outward for the origin of the human powers, making more of phenomena than I ought; studying the concrete, without a sense of the grounds on which this was dependent for its form and continuance. It was Coleridge that lifted me out of this difficulty. The perusal of the ' Aids to Reflection,' the ' Friend,' and the ' Biographia Literaria ' at this time gave my mind a turn toward the spiritual. I was led deeper to seek the grounds even of experience, and found the elements of human consciousness not in the impressions of external nature, but in the spontaneous life of Spirit itself, independent of experience in space and time. Thus was I relieved from the philosophy of sense. Since that time I have been steadily pursuing the light thus let in upon me, and striving to apprehend, represent, and embody it, not only in theory but in practice. The lights of Aristotle, Plato, Bacon, bright and glorious as they are, have all been lost in the transparent radiance of the gospel of Christ, who is the exponent of human nature, and whose theory of life and being is a sublime synthesis of Infinite and Absolute. The analysis of this sublime theory is a work to which I devote myself; Christ in act, word, spirit, I seek to know."

It was out of this frame of mind that Mr. Alcott's "Conversations on the Gospels" grew, — the book which was so brutally attacked by the Boston newspapers when it appeared two years later, and which Mr. Emerson so generously defended. Meantime the two friends were drawing still closer together, each giving up, perhaps, something of his own opinion in deference to the other. Thus in 1835 Mr. Alcott went to spend his thirty-sixth birthday with Emerson at Concord, returning Dec. 1, 1835. The Diary, under date of December 2, says : —

"Last evening I returned, having had a very pleasant time with him and his friends. I shall seek his face and favor as a precious delight in life. While at Concord I saw Rev. Mr. Hedge also; with him and Mr. Emerson I had some very interesting conversation. These men are the most earnest spiritualists of the time. I found much in their ideas and purposes of like character with my own. Time shall unfold what we may do for the good of humanity. I was pleased to find so ready and sincere apprehension of some of my favorite theories from persons whom I could respect, and who were without guile ; persons whose culture places them on the mount of clear vision, and who know what they see. Rev. Mr. Goodwin, of Concord, and Dr. Ripley spoke encouragingly to me also."

This was the spring-time of Transcendentalism, before it had aroused enemies, and united itself with social, political, and religious movements which excited the most violent hostility and scorn. The mild weather of spring soon turned to fierce storms and cold east-winds, under which the apostles of the Newness shivered and struggled for years. Poverty, neglect, contempt, misrepresentation, were their lot; but they had a good cause and good courage. Emerson in particular stood up among them like a champion, and received on his sunny shield the blows aimed at others as well as at himself. When the "Daily Advertiser," in March, 1837, attacked Mr. Alcott's book of "Conversations on the Gospels," and the school in which he was holding such talks with children, Mr. Emerson wrote in defence of his friend, and to Mr. Alcott wrote thus :—

"I hate to have all the little dogs barking at you, for you have something better to do than to attend to them; but every beast must do after its kind, and why not these? And you will hold by yourself, and presently forget them. Whatever you do at school, pray let not the pen halt, for that must be your last and longest lever to lift the world withal. But you will bide your time, and, with views so large and secular, can better afford to wait than other men. I never regretted more than in this case my own helplessness in all practical contingencies. For a knowing and efficient friend can do a man with a mob a better service than he himself. But I was created a seeing eye, and not a useful hand."

4

In copying this letter into his Diary, Mr. Alcott, in April, 1837, makes this comment : —

" It is much to have the vision of the seeing eye. Did most men possess this, the useful hand would be empowered with new dexterity also. Emerson sees me, knows me, and, more than all others, helps me, — not by noisy praise, not by low appeals to interest and passion, but by turning the eye of others to my stand in reason and the nature of things. Only men of like vision can apprehend and counsel each other. A man whose purpose and act demand but a day or an hour for their completion can do little by way of advising him whose purposes require years for their fulfilment. Only Emerson, of this age, knows me, of all that I have found. Well, every one does not find *one* man, one *very man, through and through.* Many are they who live and die alone, known only to their survivors of an after century."

So said Alcott in 1837 ; and four years after, Carlyle, on receiving from Emerson the first volume of " Essays," said almost the same thing, and with quite the same feeling : —

" The voice of one crying in the desert ! It is once more the voice of a *man.* Ah me ! I feel as if in the wide world there were still but this one voice that responded intelligently to my own ; as if the rest were all hearsays, melodious or unmelodious echoes ; as if this alone were true and alive."

This same Diary of 1837 contains a prophetic and critical passage concerning Emerson, which may be quoted as the first prediction of the exact place our poet-philosopher was to take among the leaders of thought. In January, forty-seven years ago, after "Nature" had been published, but when few had read it, Mr. Alcott thus delineated, with sure eye and hand, the genius and fame of its author : —

"Emerson the lecturer always kindles a sublime sentiment when, in those deep and oracular undertones which he knows well when and how to use, he speaks of the divine entities of all being. A solemn, supernatural awe creeps over one as the severe pathos of his manner and the unaffected earnestness of his bearing come upon the senses. At long intervals of remark — now bordering almost on coarseness, from the terms that he weaves into his diction, and the picture of vulgar life that he draws with a Shakspearian boldness of delineation respecting farmers, tradesmen, beasts, vermin, the rabid mob, the courtesan, the under as well as the upper vulgar, and now sliding into all that is beautiful, refined, elegant, in thought, speech, action, and vocation — he bursts upon the hearer in strains of thought and charms of diction that overpower the soul by their bewildering, lofty grandeur. The burlesque, in a twinkling, is transformed into the serious ; the bold and sketchy outline becomes a deep, sublime idea. His is the poet's, not the logician's power ; he states, pictures, sketches, but does not reason. His appeal is through the imagination and the senses to the mind. He leaves things in the place where Nature left them, never deranging that order for a special, logical analysis. Nature shines serenely through the calm depths of his soul, and leaves upon its unruffled surface the images of all her works. . . . The day shall come when this man's genius shall shine beyond the circle of his own city and nation. It shall flash across the wide water, and receive the homage of other peoples. Emerson is destined to be the high literary name of this age. Other men we have who ply small trade in the nooks and corners of this wide sea, and whose wares are peddled at this place and that; but this man's genius is cosmopolitan, and shall be in demand wherever man has risen above the mere mechanics and utilities of life."

Where shall we find, after all these years, a closer criticism of Emerson's eloquence than this, to which the *post-mortem* remarks of Arnold and Morley are like descriptions of the living soul drawn in the dissecting-room ? Emerson himself, however, in a letter to Mr. Alcott of May, 1837, opened the secret of his own success with the world as a writer, while at the same time giving high and wise advice to his friend. He wrote thus : —

"In the few moments' broken conversation I had with you a fortnight ago, it seems to me you did not acquiesce at all in what is always my golden view for you, as for all men to whom God has given 'the vision and the faculty divine ;' namely, that one day you would leave the impracticable world to wag its own way, and sit apart and write your oracles for its behoof ! Write ! let them hear or let them forbear ; the written word abides until, slowly and unexpectedly and in widely sundered places, it has created its own church. And my love and confidence in that silent Muse is such, that, in circumstances in which I can easily conceive myself placed, I should prefer some manual or quite mechanical labor as a means of living, that should leave me a few sacred hours in the twenty-four, to any attempt to realize my idea in any existing forms called intellectual or spiritual, where, by defying every settled usage in society, I should be sure to sour my own temper."

In commenting on this advice (which was sound), and after a visit to Emerson in Concord, Mr. Alcott makes some striking remarks, which show, however, that even he did not then fully appreciate the breadth and variety of his friend's powers. Mr. Alcott wrote thus : —

"Emerson, true to his genius, favors written works. He holds men and things at a distance ; pleases himself with using them for his own benefit, and as means of gathering material for his own work. He does not believe in the actual ; his sympathies are all intellectual. He persuades me to leave the actual, devote myself to the speculative, and embody my thought in written works. Emerson idealizes all things. This idealized picture is the true and real one to him, — all else is nought. Even persons are thus idealized, and his interest in them and their influence over him exist no longer than this conformity appears in his imagination. Beauty, beauty, — this it is that charms him. But beauty has pure and delicate tastes ; and hence all that mars or displeases this sense, with however much of truth or of goodness it may be associated, is of no interest to the mind. Emerson seeks the beauty of truth. With him all men and things have a beauty ; but this is the result of his point of vision, and often falls wide of the actual truth. To give pleasure, more than to impart truth, is his mission ; what is beautiful in man, nature, or art, this he apprehends, and with the poet's power sets forth. His genius is high and commanding ; he will do honor to his age. As a man, however, this visit has somewhat modified my former notions of him. He seems not to be fully in earnest. Fame stands before him as a dazzling award, and he holds himself somewhat too proudly, nor seeks the humble and sincere regard of his race. His life has been one of opportunity, and he has sought to realize in it more of the accomplished scholar than of the perfect man ; a great intellect refined by elegant study, rather than a divine life radiant with the beauty of truth and holiness."

In this criticism the insight is keen, but not always just. As Chaucer says, "there are more stars in the sky than a pair ;" and it is not by this balanced antithesis that great men are to be judged. There was what astronomers call a "nutation" in Emerson's genius ; he inclined now this way and now that, but the circle of his orbit brought him always round to his place. He bowed to beauty for what it claimed, but not at the expense of justice and the upright.

Not long after the visit to Concord which suggested this criticism on Emerson, Mr. Alcott heard his friend give a lecture in Boston on "Ethics," bringing out his view of conscience and the moral laws as illustrated by the example of just men. Upon this lecture, considering both its thought and its style, the Diary thus passes judgment (Feb. 15, 1837) : —

"Emerson is always impressive when he comes to the elucidation of great and eminent natures. In discoursing on these, the awful front of truth, the severe grandeur of beauty, the commanding presence of justice, look forth upon the hearer in their divine majesty of outline. These are realities, and have their root and life in the Spirit. They are great natures, above change, above harm. They know of no peril, but dwell serenely in the bosom of Spirit, of which man and nature are the visible types.

"But this man's genius has little in common with the spirit and temper of this age. It is the herald of a future time, when nature and life shall have other significance than that which they now wear; when all things shall be viewed through a nobler organ than the external sense, and subserve other purposes than mere corporeal use. The old enthusiasm for honest and simple bravery, the love of all that is noble and fair, — these elements reappear in our modern. Observe his style: it is full of genuine phrases from the Saxon. He loves the simple, the natural; the thing is sharply presented, yet graced by beauty and elegance, both of conception and diction. Our language is a fit organ as used by him. Its sensualism, the filth and dust that had bedaubed it as it was used by coarse natures during the last generations, until all its idioms and commonplaces tell the story of our declension from honor and purity, are all washed away, and we hear clean and classic English once more from Northern lips. Shakspeare, Sidney, Browne, speak again to us, and we recognize our affinity of speech with the fathers of English diction. Poesy and philosophy lisp once more their native accents, uniting beauty with grandeur, grace with force, and asserting the original sweetness and richness of our own tongue. Emerson is the only instance of original style among Americans. Who writes like him? Who can? None of his imitators, surely."

So much for the style, which is, at least, part of the man. In 1839, Mr. Alcott has a passage on his friend's characteristics which still better expresses them. He writes : —

"I propose spending a few days in Concord with Emerson. We have much, I fancy, to say on the present aspects and tendencies of the times. A day of controversy is coming over our heads. Renovating influences are at work in the very heart of society; old forms are soon to be cast off. The soul is shedding its slough, and renewing itself. The timid, the besotted, are looking on with fear. Views with which our names are associated are to be assailed as the prolific cause of this overturn of things. We are to be made the butt of sectarian scandal. Persecutions fierce and unrelenting are to be waged against us. Our tempers are to be tried. I shall like to learn the mood of this my brother as he looks out from the seclusion of his rural retreat.

"Brother! That is a kindling name. I feel the sentiment of kindred quicken within me as I write it. He *is* a brother of mine, and an only one. All other men seem strange to me when I think of him ; for no other knows me so well, and I value none so dearly. I may confide in him. Bravest among my contemporaries, he walks the earth magnanimously ; and I behold his front, and despair not of men. A spirit like his shall not be cowed. An insight like his shall gain its meed of honor. My brother, we

shall do and dare. God is on our side. We believe in the
Real, and shall come off victorious in our warfare against
the Seeming."

The passages drawn from the Diary of 1837 have
been chiefly taken from Mr. Alcott's comments, week
by week, on a course of twelve lectures which Emerson
gave in the winter of 1836–1837, in Boston, on what
he called "The Methods and Philosophy of History,"
but which Mr. Alcott, who heard them all, said related to "the omniscience of spirit." The Diary for
February, 1837, furnishes these remarks : —

"Mr. Emerson lectured this week on politics, — sound
doctrines, I thought, in fit phrase. His audience enlarges
from week to week. I am glad the people come to hear
these discourses, which serve to arouse the noble faculties and adapt the senses to something supersensual and
permanent. But they will not understand aright. Better attain but glimpses, however, than remain in sluggish
obscurity, sense-ridden and sense-beguiled. They seem to
listen to him as marvelling children to a riddle-telling
elder, anxious to fathom the puzzle that drops from his
lips and pleasing their dull wits with his mystic lore.
Need enough is there of some statement of the divine
order and beauty of things, and especially in this city.
All minds seem to be enveloped in the bewildering haze
of sensualism. Ideas are not ; spirit is not ; brains and
hands move all things. The world is a busy workshop,
exchange, or inn ; and whosoever plies most dexterously
the organs that he hath, whether of brain, hand, or belly,
doth manfully his duty, and is an accepted member of the

body social. Channing's ethics touch not these functions of the social order ; Brownson's reasonings stay not the rabid instincts of the populace ; nor Graham's invectives stop the career of intemperance and debauchery, in high places and low. Emerson can scarce do more than please ; for vain is the hope of undermining the foundations of men's belief in shows and shapes, while the philosophy of the speaker is itself deemed a beautiful show, and himself a skilful puzzler of men's brains. Not on those who hear these lectures will the principles which they announce take abiding effect. Another day, another age, are to espouse and live in harmony and love with them. The divine truths which these utter will be sown in the soil of young and fertile spirits ; and these shall gather the harvest in the old age of the seedsman and the sower. He shall reap in due time of the fruits of his toil, and the thankful laboriousness of self-chosen disciples shall minister to his decline."

The state of things here described, which will be recognized by those who remember the Presidency of Van Buren in New England, led Mr. Alcott, as well as Emerson, Garrison, and other reformers, to attempt measures and form plans to change what they found so wrong. In the prosecution of his plans for a simpler mode of social life, a better education, and a truer worship, Mr. Alcott, in the year 1842, felt strongly the importance of visiting England and entering into acquaintance with the men and women there who seemed to be cherishing the same purposes with himself. He had for years corresponded with some of these persons, particularly with Mr. Heraud, a literary man, and Mr. Greaves, a disciple and friend of Pestalozzi. Mr. Emerson entered cordially into Mr. Alcott's plans in this respect, and was the principal person who contributed to the fund which was raised for this Transcendental embassy. Writing to Mr. Alcott on the 12th of February, 1842, Mr. Emerson said : —

" I am far from thinking that the project should be dropped. If it shall continue to seem profitable and desirable to you, as it has appeared, it will seem so to me. I think you need the diversion and the stimulus which so total a change in your habits and company will afford, without considering what farther contingencies may accrue."

Accordingly, on the 8th of May, Mr. Alcott sailed for England, and there spent several months, returning Oct. 20, 1842, accompanied by two English Socialists, Charles Lane and Henry C. Wright, who afterwards joined in his experiment of an ideal community at Fruitlands, in the town of Harvard. Before his return, Emerson, who was then editing " The Dial," printed in that magazine (October, 1842) an excellent account of Mr. Alcott's mission to England and the companionship which he found there :

ENGLISH REFORMERS.

Whilst Mr. Sparks visits England to explore the manuscripts of the Colonial Office, and Dr. Waagen on a mission of art, Mr. Alcott, whose genius and efforts in the great art of education have been more appreciated in England than in America, has now been spending some months in that country, with the aim to confer with the most eminent educators and philanthropists, in the hope to exchange intelligence, and import into this country whatever hints have been struck out there on the subject of literature and the First Philosophy. The design was worthy, and its first results have already reached us. Mr. Alcott was received with great cordiality of joy and respect by his friends in London, and presently found himself domesticated at an institution managed after his own methods and called after his name, — the School of Mr. Wright, at Alcott House, Ham, Surrey. He was introduced to many men of literary and philanthropic distinction, and his arrival was made the occasion of meetings for public conversation on the great ethical questions of the day.

Mr. Alcott's mission, besides making us acquainted with the character and labors of some excellent persons, has loaded our table with a pile of English books, pamphlets, periodicals, flying prospectuses, and advertisements proceeding from a class very little known in this country and on many accounts important, — the party, namely, who represent Social Reform. Here are Educational Circulars and Communist Apostles, Alists, Plans for Syncretic Associations and Pestalozzian Societies, Self-supporting Institutions, Experimental Normal Schools, Hydropathic and Philosophical Associations, Health Unions and Phalansterian Gazettes, Paradises within the reach of all men, Appeals of Man to Woman, and Necessities of Internal Marriage, illustrated by Phrenological Diagrams. These papers have many sins to answer for. There is an abundance of superficialness, of pedantry, of inflation, and want of thought.

It seems as if these sanguine schemers rushed to the press with every notion that danced before their brain, and clothed it in the most clumsily compound and terminated words, for want of time to find the right one. But although these men use a swollen and vicious diction, yet they write to ends which raise them out of the jurisdiction of ordinary criticism. They speak to the conscience, and have that superiority over the crowd of their contemporaries which belongs to men who entertain a good hope. Moreover, these pamphlets may well engage the attention of the politician, as straws of no mean significance to show the tendencies of the time.

Mr. Alcott found little in the condition or the population of England in 1842 to encourage his labors there; but he did find a few enthusiastic persons who partook of his own philanthropic idealism, and were eager to join his private efforts at social reform in New England. Some of his observations on persons and events in the mother country may here be cited : —

"*July* 18, 1842. Returned to Alcott House. 19*th.* Had much conversation with Mr. Wright on our union in New England. He inclines to return with me. *Evening.* — We walked to Wandsworth (six miles), and had a lively conversation there on education, and engaged to resume our conversation there on Tuesday evening next.

"*July* 20. Dined with W. J. Fox, and met Harwood, Dr. Elliotson, Mr. Lalor, and others. The conversation was prolonged till late in the evening, and ran on various topics, — Pythagorean diet, taxes, government, magnetism,

poetry, 'The Dial,' Emerson, etc.   It gave me little satisfaction.   There was much argument, protestation, and but
little from the heart.   Our Club in its dotage, even, was
wiser far.   I seemed to have fallen on Dr. Channing and
the Unitarian Association.

"*July* 21. Called on J. M. Morgan, and saw his painting of a design for his 'Self-Supporting Institution,' at
his rooms in Holborn.   He discoursed long, and with
great good-will, on his plans for relieving the needy and
distressed; but relies on the Church for support, and seeks
to redeem his own name from disgrace by denying his
former intimacy with Mr. Owen.   He is another sad instance of apostasy from the principles so livingly affirmed
by Mr. Greaves.   I recognized but little of the wide
humanity that pervades his 'Hampden in the Nineteenth Century.'   Morgan, Biber, Heraud, Oldham, Smith,
Marston, — these are all fallen; and there remain but
Lane and Wright in whom the divine fire still burns.   I
saw George Thompson again, and heard O'Connell, Joseph
Hume, M. P., Joseph Sturge, and Sydney Smith, at the
Anti-Corn-Law Conference at the King's Arms, West-
minster.   The meeting reminded me of our Abolition and
Non-resistance conventions; and the speakers, of Garrison,
Wright, and Phillips.   Fierce denunciation, discontent,
sedition, desperation, rang throughout the hall; but neither
people, delegates, nor leaders seemed at all aware of the
remedy for the social evils under which they are now
writhing in sorrow, disappointment, hunger.   It is not
bread nor wages (and so I told Thompson), but property,
gain, and the lust of gain, — these are the parents of the
ills they suffer.   But Thompson is too busy to hear, and
the people too hungry to believe.

" Had a short interview with Robert Owen at his rooms in Pall Mall. He read me a letter which he had just written, addressed to Sir Robert Peel, proposing his remedy for the distress of the nation ; but he seemed but little wiser than the Premier, Parliament, and Reformers. Property, property still, and the people still left enslaved to their lusts and passions. He asked me to breakfast with him at my convenience, which I promised to do, but scarce know why. 'T is a base errand, this of eating and drinking with lions, and I am getting heartily ashamed of it. Surely, I am made for better things. *Evening.* — At Heraud's. Barham, Marston, Wright, and others, were there. We discussed printing a new journal, to be supported by contributions from the Old World and the New, and issued quarterly. A good deal was said. Heraud and Barham deem Carlyle's interest essential to its success with the public. I put the work on its own merits, quite independent of names, and Wright agrees with me. I gave them the theory of my new journal : the hopes it must meet, the audience it must create, the contributors it must secure. I proposed that it should answer to something like this : 'The Janus : An Ephemeris of the Permanent in Religion, Philosophy, Science, Art, and Letters.' My idea was obviously too broad and daring for them, and so we separated.

" Two letters from my wife at the close of this stormful day. I read them, and found peace in the gardens of Concordia."

Nearly twenty years later Mr. Alcott's project of an international magazine was carried out in some degree by the establishment of the " Atlantic

Monthly." With Carlyle, to whom Emerson sent him with warm commendatory letters, Mr. Alcott had no good fortune ; the two friends of Emerson proved antipathetic to each other. In a letter to Mrs. Alcott, her husband wrote : —

"June 25, 1842.

"I rode to Chelsea and passed an hour with Carlyle. Ah, me ! Saul amongst the prophets ! It must have been a dark hour with him. He seemed impatient of interruption ; faithless, quite, in all social reforms. His wit was sombre, severe, hopeless ; his very merriment had madness in it ; his humor was tragic even to tears. There lay smouldering in him a whole French Revolution, a Cromwellian rebellion ; nor could the rich mellowness of his voice, deepened as it was and made more musical by his broad Northern accent, hide from me the restless melancholy, the memory feeding on hope, the decease of all prophecy in the grave of history. I told him the dead only dealt with the dead ; that the living breathed only with the living. The man is sick ; he needs rest. I know his ailment ; I know its cure. Emerson will sadden when you tell him what I write ; but here is another of the thousand confirmations of that suicide by the pen in which literature abounds. I will not turn on my heel to see another man· ; and the women are tragic all (Mrs. Carlyle, Mrs. Fox, etc.), — these doleful daughters of Britain, they mourn even in their joys."

"August 2.

"I have seen Carlyle again ; but we quarrelled outright, and I shall see him not again. Greatness abides not here ; her home is in the clouds, save when she descends on the meadows or treads the groves of Concord."

Nevertheless, Mr. Alcott did call once more on Carlyle, but he was not at home. A few days after he wrote this letter to Mr. Alcott : —

CHELSEA, Sept. 22, 1842.

MY DEAR SIR, — I am very sorry to have been out the other day when you called again. I suppose it is my last chance of seeing you in England. You leave me, too, as an incorrigible heretic and infidel, which verily I am not, yet must be content to seem for the present! Well, I will wish you a right pleasant reunion with your native friends, with those whom you know better than you do me. To hear that your scheme of life prospers to the utmost possible extent will, you may depend upon it, be always happy news to me. Though not precisely my church, I do reckon it a branch of the true church, very worthy to spread and root itself according to its power in a world so overgrown with falsity and jungle as ours is. . . . I was absent in Suffolk when your invitation to the Conference reached me. I can add no more but that sad word, adieu! May all good Powers watch over you, guide you well, and ever better towards your true aim. I remain always,

Yours very sincerely,

T. CARLYLE.

Our last extract shall be taken from the brief Diary for 1846, when Mr. Alcott, after his experiences in England and at Fruitlands, was again established in Concord, at the Hillside Cottage, in which Hawthorne succeeded him, and which has since been known and described as The Wayside. Looking out from this "loophole of retreat" in January, 1846,

5

and having lately read Carlyle's book on Cromwell, which Mr. Alcott had found him toiling over in 1842, the Concord mystic thus writes, justly and prophetically : —

" Carlyle's new book comes opportunely. This nation seems lost to every sense of right ; the spark of freedom that inflamed the breasts of our fathers is extinct in their Republic. In the midst of a revolution we seem not to know it, nor that the principles for which Luther and Cromwell contended, and which constitute our inheritance, are trodden under foot in the counsels and acts of Congress. The Reformation is still in progress, and Providence invites us to carry it forward and give it permanency in worthy institutions. Freedom in Church, in State, in the Family, in our bosoms and estates, — these are the demands of Protestantism in 1846. The family is the cradle of the Commonwealth ; the private house is the council-chamber of the Republic. Every man has some faint sentiment of this, and human history is the record of struggles for his own freedom or subjection. The ascendency of a spiritual philosophy in the finer and better minds, and particularly in the youth of our day, is an omen of hope. A silent, gradual, and yet perceptible amendment is taking place, and the final settlement of the new is near and sure. The old order is crumbling away ; the new powers with which modern science has charged the civilized world have given fresh impulse to enterprise in our people, — opened new and wider fields for their extension. Our social and geographical position affords additional incentives and opportunity for a broader display of the national character. The Northern genius is successfully competing with Nature ; and, no less than the Southern ambition, is adding new territories to the already overgrown Republic. This great secular interest, thus called into vigorous existence and furnished with new facilities by its broader field of action, is coming in conflict with existing social and political institutions, and arraying the extreme sections of the country against each other. The struggle has begun. The base and wicked alliance between freedom and slavery — the source of national discord — must issue soon in the dissolution of the present political confederacy. . . .

" The change in the business of men is no less remarkable than in their thinking; the magnetic and steam couriers match the intuitive philosophy and religion. Man is constructing organs for the mind ; the dynamic forces of his being are forging facile engines, alike of ponderous metal and the subtilest fluid. Flame, Lightning, Intuition, Enthusiasm, are become his readiest porters and runners. ' Feed me,' cries Body, querulously, ' and I'll feed thee.' ' Nay,' quoth the Soul, ' thou canst give me no bread ; thou canst not even grow bread for thyself. 'T is of my good pleasure that thou art ; by me are formed all thine organs. I feed thy heart with Piety, thy mind with Science, thy hand with Art ; and sustain thee in comfort all thy life long, in this little mansion and world to which I am a party in making it for thee. But a worldling and hireling art thou, ever discontented with thy fodder and wages.'

" Noblest of benefactors is the thinking Soul ; all men, in some sort and time, are beggars, and receive its alms."

III.

EMERSON AS AN AMERICAN.

By JULIAN HAWTHORNE.

It might be said, both that the time has passed, and that it is not yet come, to assign Emerson his place among the thinkers of the world; but it can never be out of place to remark that his bent and genius were profoundly and typically American. So far as his thoughts and opinions had color, it was that of his native soil. He believed in our great experiment; he was not disheartened by our mistakes; he had faith that the goodness and wisdom of humanity would, in the long run, prove more than equal to the goodness and wisdom of any possible man; and that men would, at last, govern themselves more nobly and successfully than any individual monarch could govern them. He speaks, indeed, of Representative Men; but he was no hero-worshipper, like Carlyle. A hero was, to him, not so much a powerful and dominating personality, as a relatively impersonal instrument of God for the accomplishment of some great end. It would follow from this that humanity is the greatest hero of all; and

Emerson, perhaps, believed — in this sense if not otherwise — that God has put on human nature. In the American Republic he saw the most promising field for the unhampered working-out of this Divine inspiration within us.

But he was American not by determination only, but by the constitution of his mind. His catholic and unflinching acceptance of what truth soever came to him was in accordance with the American idea, though not, unfortunately, with the invariable American practice. As our land is open to the world to come and inhabit it, so was his mind open to all vigorous and progressive ideas, be their hue and parentage what they might. It were rash to predict how soon America will reach his standard of her ideal ; but it is encouraging to remember that nothing in her political construction renders its final attainment impossible.

It is not with us as with other peoples. Our position seems vague, because not primarily related to the senses. I know where England or Italy is, and recognize an Englishman or an Italian ; but Americans are not, to the same extent, limited by geographical boundaries. America did not originate as did European nations : they were born after the flesh, but we after the spirit. Their frontiers must be defended, and their race kept distinct ; but highly though I esteem our immeasurable East and West, North and South, our Pacific and our Atlantic and our Gulf of Mexico, I cannot help deeming these a secondary matter. If America be not more than these United States, then the United States are little better than a penal colony. It is convenient, no doubt, that a great idea shall find a suitable stage and incarnation; but it depends not upon these things. It was accidental, or I would rather say providential, that the Puritans came to New England, or that Columbus discovered the continent for them; but the body is instrumental merely: it enables the spirit to take hold of its mortal affairs, just as the hilt enables us to grasp the sword. Had the Puritans not come to New England, still their spirit would have lived, and somehow made its place. How many Puritans, indeed, for how many previous ages, had been trying, and failing, to get foothold in the world! They were known by many names; their voice was heard in many tongues: the hour for them to touch their earthly inheritance had not yet struck. But the latent impetus meanwhile accumulated, and the "Mayflower" was driven across the Atlantic by it at last!

And the "Mayflower" sails still between the Old World and the New. Day by day it brings new settlers, if not to Boston Bay, and Castle Garden, and the Golden Gate, at any rate to our mental ports and wharves. I cannot take up a European newspaper without finding an American idea in it. Many of us make the trip to Europe every summer; but we come back, and bring with us many more who come to stay. I do not specify the literal emigrants in the steerage ; they may or may not be Americans. But England and the Continent are full of Americans who were born and may die there, and who may be better Americans than the Bostonian or the New Yorker who votes the Republican, or the Democratic, or even the Independent ticket. Whatever their birthplace or residence, they belong to us, and are with us. Broadway and Washington Street, New Hampshire and Colorado, extend all over Europe. Russia tries to banish them to Siberia, but in vain. Are mountains and prairies solid facts ? — the geography of the mind is more stubborn ! I dare say there are oblique-eyed, pig-tailed New Englanders in the Celestial Empire. Though they may never have visited these shores, or heard of Kearney, they think our thought, have apprehended our idea, and by and by they or their heirs will cause it to prevail.

It is useless to hide our heads in the grass, and shun to rise to the height of our occasion. We stand as the fulfilment of prophecy ; we attest a new departure in moral and intellectual development, — or which of us does not, must suffer annihilation. If I deny my birthright as an American, I vanish and am not missed ; an American takes my place. The position is not altogether luxurious : you cannot sit and hold your hands. Hard and unpleasant things are expected of you, which you neglect at your peril. It is like the fable of the mermaid : she loved a mortal youth, and in order to win his affection prayed for the limbs and feet of a human maiden. Her prayer was answered, and she met her prince; but each step she took was as if she trod on razors. So it is fine to sit at ease and reflect on being American; but when we must arise and do an American's duty, how sharp the razors are!

We do not always stand the test; flesh and blood do not differ essentially on different sides of the planet. Possibly we are too numerous. It were strange if here and there among fifty millions, one were not quite a hero. Possibly, indeed, that little original band of "Mayflower" Pilgrims has not greatly multiplied since their disembarkation, so far as their spiritual progeny are concerned. We do not find a succession of Winthrops and Endicotts in the chair of the Governor and on the floor of the Senate. Bridget serves us in the kitchen; but Patrick, more helpful yet, enters the Legislature and serves the State. But turn and turn about is fair play; and we ought once in a while to take off our coat and do unto Patrick as he does unto us.

When we get in a tight place we are apt to slip out under a plea of European precedent; but was it not to avoid European precedents that we came here? America should take the highest ground in her political and commercial relations. Why must the President of the Western Union, for instance, or a late Governor of Massachusetts, be cited as typical Americans? The dominance of such men has effects out of proportion with their personal acts. What they may do is of small import: the mischief is in their inclining us to believe (as Emerson puts it) in two gods. They make the morality of Wall Street and the White House seem a different thing from that of the parlor and nursery. "He may be a little shady on 'Change," we say, " but a capital fellow when you know him." But if I am a capital fellow when you know me, I can afford to be shady in my business. I can endure public opprobrium so long as it remains public: it is the private cold looks that trouble me.

In short, we have two Americas, — the street-corner and newspaper America, and the ideal America. At present, the former makes the most noise; but the latter has made the former possible. A great crowd is drawn together for some noble purpose, — to declare a righteous war, or to pass a just decree. But there are persons on the outskirts unable to hear the orators, and with time hanging idle on their hands, who take to throwing bricks, smashing hats, or perhaps picking pockets. They may have assembled with virtuous and patriotic intentions; under favorable circumstances they might themselves have been the orators. Virtue and patriotism are not private property; at certain times any one may possess them. And, on the other hand, how often do we see persons of high respectability and trust turn out sorry scamps! We vary according to our company and the event: the outlook may be sordid to-day, but during the Civil War the air was full of heroism. So the real and the ideal America, though far apart in one sense, are, in another, as near as our right hand to our left. They exist side by side in each one of us. But civil war comes not every day; nor do we desire it, even to show us once more that we are worthy of our destiny. Some less expensive and quieter method must remind us of that. And of such methods none, perhaps, is better than to review the lives of Americans who were truly great: to ask what their country meant to them; what they asked of her; what virtues and vices they detected in her. Passion may be generous, but cannot last, and coldness and indifference follow; but in calm moods reason and example reach us, and their lesson abides.

Although many a true American is born and dies abroad, Emerson was born and died here. In the outward accidents of generation and descent, he could not have been more American than he was. Of course, one prefers that it should be so. A rare gem should be fitly set. It helps us to believe in ourselves to know that Emerson's ancestry was not only Puritan but clerical; that through his heart ran the vital thread of the idea that created us. We have many traits not found in him; but nothing in him is not a sublimation and concentration of something in us; and such is the selection and grouping of the elements that he is a typical figure. Indeed, he is all type; which is the same as to say there is nobody like him. And, mentally, he is all force; his mind acts without natural impediment or friction, — a machine that runs unhindered by the contact of its parts. As he was physically lean and slender of figure, and his face but a welding together of features, so there was no adipose tissue in his thought. It is pure, clear, and accurate, and has the fault of dryness, but often moves with exquisite beauty. It is not adhesive; it sticks to nothing except to the memory, nor anything to it. After ranging through the philosophies of the world, it emerges clean and characteristic as ever. It has many affinities, but no adhesion; it is not always self-adherent. There are in any of his essays separate statements presenting no logical continuity; but though this may cause anxiety to disciples of Emerson, it never troubled him. Wandering at will in the garden of moral and religious philosophy, it was his part to pluck such blossoms as he saw were good and beautiful, — not to discover their botanical relationship. He might, for art or harmony's sake, arrange them according to their hue or fragrance; but it was not his affair to go further in their classification.

This intuitional method, how little soever it satisfies those who want their thinking done for them, — who want not only all the cities of the earth, but straight roads to connect them, — carries its own justification. " There is but one Reason," is Emerson's saying; and we confess again and again that the truth he asserts is true indeed. Even his divergences from the truth, when he is betrayed into them, confirm the rule; for these are seldom intuitions at first hand, but intuitions from previous intuitions, — deductions. They are from Emerson, instead of from the Absolute; tinted, instead of colorless. They show a mental bias, redeeming him back to humanity. We love him the more for them, because they imply that for him, too, was a choice of ways, and that he struggled and watched to choose the right.

We are so wedded to systems, and so prone to connect a system with a man, that Emerson's absence of system strikes us as a defect. But truth has no system, nor has the human mind. We cannot bear to be illogical, and enlist, some under this philosopher's banner, some under that; and so sacrifice to consistency at least half the truth. We cross-examine our intuitions, and ask them, not whether they are true in themselves, but what are their tendencies. If they would lead us to stultify some past conclusion to which we stand committed, we drop them like hot coals. This, to Emerson, was the nakedest personal vanity. Recognizing his finiteness, he did not covet consistency. One thing was true to-day: to-morrow, its opposite. Was it for him to elect which should have the preference? To reject either was to reject all: it belonged to God to reconcile such contradictions. Between Infinite and finite can exist no ratio; and the Creator's consistency implies the inconsistency of the creature.

Emerson's Americanism, therefore, was Americanism in its last and purest analysis, — which is giving him praise, and to America hope. But let me not pay him, who was so full of modesty and humility, the ungrateful compliment of holding him up as our permanent ideal. It is his tendency, his quality, that are valuable, and only in a minor degree his actual results. All human results are limited, and according to the epoch. Emerson does not solve for all time the problem of the universe. He solves nothing; but, what is more useful, he gives impetus and direction to lofty endeavor. He does not anticipate the lessons of the ages; but he teaches us so to deal with circumstance as to secure the good instead of the evil issue. New horizons opening before us will carry us beyond the scope of Emerson's surmise; but we shall not easily improve upon his aim and attitude. In spaces beyond the stars are marvels such as it has not entered into the mind of man to conceive; but there, as here, the right aspiration will still be upward, and the right conduct still be humble and charitable.

I spoke of Emerson's absence of system; yet his writings have coherence by virtue of their single-hearted motive. Those with whom, in this tribute to our beloved poet and sage, I have the honor to be associated, will doubtless notice, as I do, how the whole of Emerson illustrates every aspect of him. Whether your subject be his religion, his ethics, his social aspects, or what not, your picture gains color and form from each page that he has written. All that he is permeates all that he has done. His books cannot be indexed, and he can treat no topic without incorporating in his statement the germs at least of all his thought and belief. In this respect he illustrates the definition of light, — the presence of the general at the particular. And, to say truth, I am somewhat loath to diffract this pure ray to the arbitrary end of my special theme. Why speak of him as an American? He was American because he was himself. But America gives less limitation than other nationalities to a generous and serene personality.

Emerson's " English Traits " perhaps reveal his American traits more than most that he has written. We are described by our criticisms of others: the exceptions we take are the mould of our own figures. So this volume affords valuable glimpses of Emerson's contours. And it is almost as remarkable a work for him to write, as a volume of his essays would be for any one else ; it is to his other books as flesh and blood to spirit. Emersonian flesh and blood, it is true, and semi-translucent; but it completes the man for us : without it, he would have been too problematical. Those who never personally knew him may here finish and solidify their impressions of him. His sympathy with England and the English is beyond our expectation of the mind that evolved " Nature " and " The Over-Soul." The grasp of his hand, I remember, was firm and stout, and we perceive those qualities in the cordiality of " English Traits." And it is an objective book ; it affords a unique basis for comparing his general human faculty with that of other men. He relents from the airy heights he treads so easily, and descends to measure himself

against all comers. He means only to report their
stature, leaving himself out of the story; but their
answers reveal the questioner. We suspect (though
he did not) that his English friends were put to it
to keep the pace of their clear-faced, penetrating,
attentive visitor.

He has seldom said of his own countrymen such
comfortable things as he vouchsafes to the English:
as a father who is severe with his own children will
freely admire others, for whom he is not responsible.
Emerson is stern towards what we are, and arduous
indeed in his estimate of what we ought to be. He
intimates that we are not quite worthy yet of our
continent, — have not yet lived up to our blue
china. In America the geography is sublime, but
the men are not. Even our more presentable public
acts are due to the money-making spirit. The benefaction derived in the great West from railroads
vastly exceeds any intentional philanthropy on record.
He will not celebrate the Forty-niners, though ad-
mitting that California gets civilized in this immoral
way; and is fain to suppose that, just as there is
a use in the world for poisons, so the world cannot
move without rogues. Huge animals (like America)
nourish huge parasites, and the rancor of the disease
attests the strength of the constitution. He ridicules
our unsuspecting provincialism. " Have you seen
the dozen great men of New York and Boston?
Then you may as well die!" He does not spare our
tendency to declamation; quotes a shrewd foreigner's

remark that whatever we say has a little the air of a speech, and proceeds to ask whether the American forest has refreshed some weeds of old Pictish barbarism just ready to die out. He finds the especial foible of American youth to be — pretension; and remarks, suggestively, that we talk about the "key of the age," but the key of all ages is imbecility ! He will not be reconciled to the mania for travel : there is a restlessness in our people that argues want of character ; can we never extract this tape-worm of Europe from our brains ? Yet he concedes that we go to Europe to be Americanized, and has faith that one day we shall cast out the passion for Europe by the passion for America. As for our political doings, — politics is an after-word, a poor patching : we shall learn to supersede politics by education. He sympathizes with Lovelace, and holds that freedom and slavery are inward, not outward, conditions. Slavery is not in fetters, but in feeling; you cannot by external restrictions eradicate the irons ; and the way to emancipate the slave is to make him comprehend his inviolable dignity and freedom as a human being. Amelioration of outward circumstances will be the effect, but can never be the means, of mental and moral improvement. Nothing, he affirms, is more disgusting than the crowing about liberty by slaves, as most men are, and the flippant mistaking for freedom of some paper preamble, like a Declaration of Independence, or the statute right to vote. Our America has a bad name for superficialness. Great men and great nations have not been boasters and buffoons, but perceivers of the terrors of life, and have nerved themselves to face it. Nor will he be deceived by the clamor of blatant reformers. "If an angry bigot assumes the bountiful cause of Abolition, and comes to me with his last news from Barbadoes, why should I not say to him, 'Go, love thy infant; love thy woodchopper; be good-natured and modest; have *that* grace, and never varnish your hard, uncharitable ambition with this incredible tenderness for black folk a thousand miles off!'"

He does not shrink from questioning the validity of some of our pet institutions, — universal suffrage, for instance. In old Egypt the vote of a prophet was reckoned equal to one hundred hands, and was much underestimated. Shall we, then, he asks, judge a country by the majority, or by the minority? By the minority, surely! 'T is pedantry to estimate nations by the census, or by square miles of territory, or other than by their importance to the mind of the time. The majority are unripe, and know not yet their own opinion. Yet he would not counsel organic alteration in this respect, believing that with the progress of enlightenment such coarse constructions of human rights will adjust themselves. He concedes the sagacity of the Fultons and Watts of politics, who, noticing that the opinion of the million was the terror of the world, grouped it on a level, instead of piling it into a mountain, and so contrived to make of this terror the most harmless and energetic

6

form of a State. But, again, he would not have us regard the State as a finality, or as relieving any man of his individual responsibility for his actions and purposes. Confide in God, and not in your money, nor in the State because it is the guard of it. The Union itself has no basis but the good pleasure of the majority to be united. The wise and just men impart strength to the State, not receive it; and if all went down, they and their like would soon combine in a new and better constitution. Yet let us not forget that only by the supernatural is man strong, — nothing so weak as an egotist. We are mighty only as vehicles of a truth before which State and individual are alike ephemeral. In this sense we, like other nations, shall have our kings and nobles, — the leading and inspiration of the best; and he who would become a member of that nobility must obey his heart.

Government, which has been a fossil, must, he says, become a plant: statute law should express, not impede, the mind of mankind. Feudalism succeeds monarchy, and this, again, is followed by trade; the good and evil of which is, that it would put everything in the market, — talent, beauty, virtue, and man himself. Trade has done its work; it has faults, and will end, as the others. We need not fear its aristocracy, because, not being entailed, it can have no permanence. In the time to come we shall, he hopes, be less anxious to be governed: government without governors will, for the first time, be adamantine; each man shall govern himself in the interests of all. These are radical views, but Emerson asks whether every man is not sometimes a radical in politics? Men are conservative when they are least vigorous or most luxurious; for Conservatism stands on man's limitations, Reform on his infinitude.

But the age of the quadruped is going out; the age of brain and heart is coming in. We are still too pettifogging and imitative in our legislative conceptions; our Legislature should become more catholic and cosmopolitan than any other. Strong natures are inevitable patriots; let us be strong enough to trust in humanity. The time, the age,— what is that but a few prominent persons and a few active persons who epitomize the times? There is a bribe possible for any finite will; but the pure sympathy with universal ends is an infinite force, and cannot be bribed or bent. The world wants saviors and religions: society is servile from want of will; but there is a destiny by which the human race is guided, — the race never dying, the individual never spared; its law is, you shall have everything as a member, nothing to yourself. Referring to the various communities so much in vogue some years ago, he holds them valuable, not for what they have done, but for the indication they give of the revolution that is on the way. Communities place faith in mutual support; but only as a man puts off from himself external support is he strong, and will he prevail. He is weaker by every recruit to his banner. A man ought to compare

advantageously with a river, an oak, or a mountain.
He must not shun whatever comes to him in the way
of duty : the only path of escape is — performance!
He must rely on Providence, but not in a timid or
ecclesiastical spirit; no use to dress up that terrific
benefactor in the clean shirt and white neck-cloth
of a student of divinity. We shall come out well,
despite whatever personal or political disasters; for
here, in America, is the home of man. After de-
ducting our pitiful politics, — shall John or Jonathan
sit in the chair and hold the purse ? — and making
due allowance for our frivolities and insanities, there
still remains an organic simplicity and liberty, which,
when it loses its balance, redresses itself presently,
and which offers to the human mind opportunities
not known elsewhere.

Whenever Emerson touches upon the fundamental
elements of social and rational life, it is always to
enlarge and illuminate our conceptions of them. We
are not wont, for example, to question the propriety
of the sentiment of patriotism. We are to swear by
our own *Lares* and *Penates*, and stand by the American eagle, right or wrong. But Emerson instantly
goes beneath this interpretation, and exposes its
crudity. The true sense of patriotism is almost the
reverse of the popular sense. He has no sympathy
with that boyish egotism, hoarse with cheering for
our side, for our State, for our town: the right patriotism consists in the delight which springs from

contributing our peculiar and legitimate advantages
to the benefit of humanity. Every foot of soil has its
proper quality; the grape on two sides of the fence
has new flavors; and so every acre on the globe,
every family of men, every point of climate, has its distinguishing virtues. This admitted, Emerson yields
in patriotism to no one; he is only concerned that
the advantages we contribute shall be as many instead of as few as possible. This country, he says,
does not lie here in the sun causeless; and, though
it may not be easy to define its influence, men feel
already its emancipating quality in the careless self-
reliance of the manners, in the freedom of thought,
in the direct roads by which grievances are reached
and redressed, and even in the reckless and sinister
politics, — not less than in purer expressions. Bad
as it is, this freedom leads onward and upward to a
Columbia of thought and art, which is the last and
endless end of Columbus' adventure. Nor is this
poet of virtue and philosophy ever more truly patriotic, from his spiritual stand-point, than when he
casts scorn and indignation upon his country's sins
and frailties: —

" But who is he that prates of the culture of mankind?
Go, blindworm, go, — behold the famous States harrying Mexico
With rifle and with knife!

" Or who, with accent bolder, dare praise the freedom-loving
mountaineer?
I found by thee, O rushing Contoocook, and in thy valleys,
Agiochook,
The jackals of the negro-holder!
. . . .

" What boots thy zeal, O glowing friend, who wouldst indignant rend
     The northland from the south ?
     Wherefore ? to what good end ? Boston Bay and Bunker Hill
        would serve things still ; — things are of the snake !

          .   .   .   .

     'T is the day of the chattel, — web to weave, and corn to grind;
     Things are in the saddle, and ride mankind ! "

It is worth noting that he, whose verse is uniformly so abstractly and intellectually beautiful, kindles to passion whenever his theme is America. The loftiest patriotism never found more ardent and eloquent expression than in the hymn sung at the completion of Concord Monument, on the 19th of April, 1836.   There is no rancor in it, no taunt of triumph, —

          " The foe long since in silence slept," —

but throughout there resounds a note of pure and deep rejoicing at the victory of justice over oppression, which Concord Fight so aptly symbolized.   In " Hamatreya " and " The Earth-Song " another chord is struck, of calm, laconic irony.   Shall we too, he asks, — we Yankee farmers, descendants of the men who gave up all for freedom, — go back to the creed outworn of feudalism and aristocracy, and affirm of the land that yields us produce,

          " 'T is mine, my children's, and my name's " ?

Earth laughs in flowers at our boastfulness, and asks, —

               " How am I theirs,
               If they cannot hold me,
               But I hold them ? "

Or read "Monadnoc," and mark the insight and power wherewith the significance of the great facts of Nature is stated : —

" Complement of human kind, having us at vantage still,
   Our sumptuous indigence, O barren mound, thy plenties fill !
   We fool and prate ; thou art silent.and sedate.
   To myriad kinds and times one sense the constant mountain doth
      dispense ;
   Shedding on all its snows and leaves ; one joy it joys, one grief it
      grieves.
   Thou seest, O watchman tall, our towns and races grow and fall,
   And imagest the stable good for which we all our lifetime grope,
   And though the substance us elude, we in thee the shadow find.
      .   .   .   .

   Thou dost supply the shortness of our days,
   And promise, on thy Founder's truth, long morrow to this mor-
      tal youth ! "

No other poet with whom I am acquainted has caused the very spirit of the land — the mother of men — to express itself so adequately as Emerson has done.

Emerson is continually urging us to give heed to this grand voice of hills and streams, and to mould ourselves upon its suggestions. The difficulty and anomaly consist in the fact that we are not native ; that England, quite as much as Monadnoc, is our mother ; that we are heirs of memories and traditions reaching far beyond the times and boundaries of the Republic. We cannot assume the splendid child-likeness of the great primitive races, and exhibit the hairy strength and unconscious genius that the poet longs to find in us. He remarks somewhere that the culminating period of good in Nature and the world is at just that moment of transition, when the hairy juices still flow plentifully from Nature, but their astringency and acidity is got out by ethics and humanity.

It was at such a period that Greece attained her apogee; but our experience, I think, must needs be different. Our story is not of birth, but of regeneration, — a far more subtile and less obvious transaction. The Homeric California, of which Bret Harte is the reporter, is not, in the closest sense, American. "A sturdy lad from New Hampshire or Vermont," says Emerson, "who in turn tries all the professions, — who teams it, farms it, peddles, keeps a school, preaches, edits a newspaper, goes to Congress, buys a township, and so forth, in successive years, and always, like a cat, falls on his feet, — is worth a hundred of these city dolls. He walks abreast with his days, and feels no shame in not studying a 'profession,' for he does not postpone his life, but lives it already."

That is poignantly said; and yet few of the Americans whom we recognize as great have had such a history; nor, had they had it, would they on that account be any the more American. On the other hand, the careers of men like Jim Fiske and Jay Gould might serve well as illustrations of the above sketch. If we must wait for our national character until our geographical advantages and the absence of social distinctions manufacture it for us, we are likely to remain a long time in suspense. When our foreign visitors begin to evince a keener interest in Beacon Hill and Fifth Avenue than in the Mississippi and the Yellowstone, we may infer that we are assuming our proper stature relative to our physical environment. " The Land," says Emerson, " is a sanative and Americanizing influence, which promises to disclose new virtues for ages to come." Well, when we are virtuous we may, perhaps, spare our own blushes by allowing our topography symbolically to celebrate us, and when our admirers would worship the purity of our intuitions, refer them to Walden Pond; or to Mount Shasta, when they would expatiate upon our lofty idealism. Meanwhile, it is perhaps true that the chances of leading a decent life are greater in a palace than in a pigsty.

But this is holding the poet too strictly to the letter of his message; and at any rate the Americanism of Emerson is better than anything that he has said in its vindication. He is the champion of the Republic; he is our future living in our present, and showing the world, by anticipation, what sort of excellence we are capable of. A nation that has produced Emerson, and can recognize in him flesh of her flesh and bone of her bone, — and, still more, spirit of her spirit, — that nation may look forward with security. But he has done more than to prophesy of his country: he is electric, and stimulates us to fulfil our destiny. To use a phrase of his own, we cannot hear of personal vigor of any kind — great power of performance — without fresh resolution. Emerson helps us most in provoking us to help ourselves. After Concord Fight, it is Emerson who has made Concord's reputation, — or, rather, its reputation has been he. More victorious even than the embattled farmers of a century ago, he attracted invaders instead of repelling them. No one can take his place, now that he is gone; but the memory of him, and the purity and vitality of the thoughts and of the example with which he has enriched the world, will abide longer than many lifetimes, and will renew again and again, before an ever-widening audience, the summons to virtue and the faith in immortality which were the burden and the glory of his song.

The pleasantest kind of revenge is that which we can sometimes take upon great men in quoting of themselves what they have said of others. It is easy to be so revenged upon Emerson, because he has been so broadly generous and cordial in his appreciation of human worth. "If there should appear in the company," he observes, "some gentle soul who knows little of persons and parties, of Carolina or Cuba, but who announces a law that disposes these particulars, and so certifies me of the equity which checkmates every false player, bankrupts every self-seeker, and apprises me of my independence on any conditions of country, or time, or human body, — that man liberates me. I am made immortal by apprehending my possession of incorruptible goods." Who can state the mission and effect of Emerson more tersely and aptly than in those words ?

But he does not need eulogiums, and it seems half ungenerous to force them upon him now that he can no longer defend himself. So I will conclude by repeating a passage, characteristic of him both as a man and as an American, which perhaps conveys a sounder and healthier criticism, both for us and for him, than any mere nerveless admiration. For great men are great only in so far as they liberate us; and in courting their tyranny we undo their work. The passage runs thus : —

"Let me remind you that I am only an experimenter. Do not set the least value on what I do, or the least discredit on what I do not, — as if I pretended to settle anything as true or false. I unsettle all things : no facts to me are sacred, none profane. I simply experiment, — an endless Seeker, with no Past at my back ! "

IV.

A FRENCH VIEW OF EMERSON.

BY M. RENÉ DE POYEN BELLEISLE.

> " Le poète inspiré, lorsque la terre ignore,
>   Ressemble à ces grands monts que la nouvelle aurore
>   Dore avant tous à son réveil ;
>   Et qui, longtemps vainqueurs de l'ombre,
>   Conservent jusque dans la nuit sombre
>   Les derniers rayons du soleil."

MESDAMES, MESSIEURS : Si je débute par ces vers de Victor Hugo, c'est que je trouve qu'il y a admirablement exprimé l'idée que je me fais du poëte ; et, que si un mot, un seul, pouvait exprimer mon opinion sur Emerson ; je dirai : c'est un poëte. Mais il ne s'agit pas de le comparer ici avec d'autres poëtes ni d'examiner ce qu'il n'a pas fait ou ce qu'il aurait pu faire. La méthode critique la plus simple et la plus sûre quand on se trouve en présence d'un poëte à étudier, c'est de rechercher d'abord quelle était sa conception générale de son art et en second lieu comment il s'y est conformé.

En ce qui concerne Emerson, la première partie de cette étude est facile, car dans ses Essais il a plus d'une fois et longuement exposé ses vues sur la poésie. Ce qu'il y a de mieux à faire c'est donc de le laisser parler pour lui-même, ou du moins tenter de vous faire entendre un écho de sa voix puissante.

L'homme, placé dans l'Univers au milieu des phénomènes de la Nature et des manifestations sans cesse renaissantes de l'activité de ses semblables, a d'abord un sentiment de diversité infinie. Le poëte est l'homme qui, doué d'une vue plus puissante que le commun des hommes, pénètre au-delà de ces apparences, de cette variété, et découvre derrière cette diversité de la surface une unité qui est au fond. Plus il s'approchera de ce point central où tout s'unit et plus grand sera le Poëte. Dans son expression la plus élevée, la Poésie se confond avec la Religion; les plus grand poëtes sont les instructeurs religieux, et les Bibles des nations seront écrites. Si l'œuvre du Poëte est un miroir dans lequel toute la Nature vient se refléter fidèlement; si en lisant ses vers nous entendons le bruissement des feuilles des arbres; si la tempête y hurle, si les passions y grondent et si l'Amour y soupire ce qu'il a de plus tendre et de plus délicat, — ce poëte là, son nom est sur toutes les lèvres; c'est Shakespeare! Si s'absorbant dans sa contemplation de la Nature, il s'efforce de traduire l'esprit qui s'en dégage, de découvrir sous l'effet la cause qui est encore plus belle, ce poëte c'est Wordsworth! Si, au contraire, tournant sa vue plus particulièrement vers l'homme, il observe ses ridicules, ses travers, ses passions, ses vices, et s'il saisit le Protée malgré ses innombrables transformations, ce poëte c'est Molière! Cette intuition puissante, voilà ce qui fait le Poëte et voilà ce

qui fait qu'Emerson est un poëte. " Poetry," a dit
Lord Bacon, " accommodates the shows of the world
to the desires of the mind." C'est bien là la définition
qu'il conviendrait d'appliquer à sa poésie, c'est du
reste celle qu'il donne lui-même sous une autre
forme, lorsqu'il dit : " C'est l'expression de l'esprit
parlant d'après ce qui est idéal et non d'après ce qui
est apparent."

Mais parmi les poëtes quelle sera la place d'Emerson ? Parmi les premiers et les plus grands. Sa
poésie est de celle qui se confond avec la religion
elle-même. Seulement, il faut s'entendre sur la
valeur des mots. Lorsqu'on parle d'Emerson, il est
important de définir ceux qu'on emploie avec la plus
grande exactitude, car il ne tient pas compte en s'en
servant du sens que l'habitude a faussement pu leur
attribuer. La religion est le sentiment de l'Infini,
c'est l'âme s'élevant vers les choses qui sont invisibles
et éternelles, c'est le sentiment qui s'empare de l'âme
en présence du double problème de notre origine et
de notre destinée. L'homme religieux est celui qui
croit qu'il n'est rien dans la création, pas même
l'atome le plus petit, qui ne soit destiné à servir une
fin générale et universelle. La religion nous révèle
le lien subtil qui unit toutes choses. Rien n'est
isolé dans la Nature, tout se rattache à une cause, et
la cause suprême trouve son expression dans l'ordre
moral de l'Univers. Si l'on vient m'objecter que ces
vues sont tant soit peu imprégnées de mysticisme, je
dois humblement confesser que je suis incapable de

discerner jusqu'à quel point j'en suis coupable. Je
ne suis pas assez profondément versé dans les sys-
tèmes philosophiques pour savoir où commence et où
finit le mysticisme. Pour moi c'est le paroxysme du
sentiment religieux, c'est l'extase à laquelle l'âme
arrive par la contemplation de la vérité morale;
mais, s'il y a du danger à s'abandonner à l'exaltation
de ce sentiment, Emerson n'y tombe pas; l'importance qu'il attache à l'individualité de l'homme l'en
préserve. Si comme on l'a dit sa tête est quelquefois
entourée de nuages, ses pieds sont toujours fortement
plantés sur le sol et ne quittent pas la terre.

Il fait de sa raison l'emploi le plus intrépide et le
plus actif, et, l'applique sur tous les objets qui en sont
dignes, car, non seulement son esprit est religieux,
mais aussi profondément philosophique. Ce mot de
philosophe, nous ne le comprenons pas cependant de
la même façon que Mr. Matthew Arnold; et, nous
n'avons pas de peine à lui accorder qu'Emerson n'a
pas été un philosophe ainsi qu'il l'entend. Non, il
n'a pas le génie constructif des Platon, des Kant, des
Spinosa, mais, est-ce bien le génie constructif de ces
grands hommes qui leur a gagné notre admiration?
Pour ma part, je croirai plutôt que la place qu'ils ont
su conquérir parmi les maîtres de la pensée humaine,
ils la doivent non pas à leurs constructions, plus ou
moins en ruines aujourd'hui; mais à la beauté de
leurs idées, à leur profondeur, à l'impulsion féconde
qu'ils ont donné à l'esprit humain. Si le génie constructif est la condition *sine quâ non* du philosophe,

il nous faut abandonner ce titre pour Emerson ; mais
que nous l'appellions le Penseur, le Sage, le Prophète
il n'en demeure pas moins toujours le même pour
nous.   Mais pourquoi, après tout, renoncer à ce mot
de philosophe ? il est trop beau pour ne pas le con-
server.   Emerson est " an endless seeker without any
past at his back," mais il est encore quelque chose de
plus pour nous, et nous pouvons, certes, lui appliquer
la définition du philosophe que Thoreau a faite ;
" To be a philosopher is not merely to have subtle thoughts, or even to found a school, but so to
love wisdom as to live according to its dictates a
life of independence, simplicity, magnanimity, and
trust."

Mais après avoir dit qu'Emerson était un poëte,
il semble, pour ainsi dire, oiseux de tant insister sur
ses tendances religieuses et philosophiques.   Ce mot
poëte dit tout ; car, dans ma pensée, un poëte doit être
nécessairement un homme religieux et un philosophe.
La philosophie est le sol fertile, où la plante poétique
prendra fortement racine.   Il n'y a pas d'incompati-
bilité, l'une n'exclut pas l'autre.   Le soleil, qui va
chercher jusque dans les entrailles de la terre les
semences pour les féconder, est aussi le peintre admirable qui donne aux fleurs leur splendide éclat.

Si après avoir essayé de définir le Poëte, nous essay-
ons de pénétrer plus profondément dans son œuvre, si
nous fixons notre attention sur ses idées, nous pouvons
jeter sur elles un rapide coup d'œil en les groupant
autour des trois points principaux qui contiennent

tout ce qu'il est important pour l'homme de connaître. Dieu, la Nature et l'homme, voilà le fonds éternel de toute spéculation humaine.

Et d'abord pour commencer par Dieu, il me semble que toute l'œuvre d'Emerson peut se concentrer, se résumer dans ce seul mot ; c'est là ce point central vers lequel tout converge, duquel tout rayonne. Quelque soit le sujet qu'Emerson traite, quelque soit la position qu'il occupe sur la circonférence, nous sommes sûrs qu'il suivra toujours le rayon qui le ramènera infailliblement au Centre. Dieu est tout, il est dans tout et partout. Emerson n'est pas un métaphysicien et par conséquent nous n'avons pas à approfondir ses vues sur la nature de Dieu. Croit-il à la personalité de Dieu ? Ses affirmations sont assez larges pour qu'on puisse leur donner la signification qu'on est porté à accepter : "Self-existence is the attribute of the Supreme Being." Ainsi que l'a fait remarquer Mr. G. W. Cooke, il serait très injuste de limiter l'idée qu'Emerson a de la divinité à ce qu'il a dit sur Dieu. L'idée qu'il a de l'âme repose sur celle qu'il a de Dieu, et il ne sépare pas un seul instant ces deux idées. Sa conception de l'âme nécessite la croyance dans l'existence de Dieu comme une Intelligence suprême. Une âme qui pense ne peut avoir rien de commun avec une Essence qui ne pense pas ; une âme qui a confiance en elle-même ne peut pas s'absorber dans un Océan de vie, mais le secret de sa force est dans sa parfaite harmonie avec un principe libre et intelligent comme elle-même.

7

La Nature est le symbole de l'Esprit Universel, c'est l'œuvre de Dieu, et ses apparences n'ont de réalité qu'en lui.   Ici nous nous trouvons en présence des critiques que l'on prodigue à l'idéalisme. L'homme sensuel qui retient avec force les choses dont il tire ses jouissances, traitera de fou celui qui voudra· lui faire croire que ces choses ne sont qu' apparentes.   Néanmoins, tout ce que nous voyons, tout ce que nous sentons, tout ce qui, en un mot, nous tombe sous les sens, ne sont que des accidents. Ce qui n'est pas accidental, mais absolu et nécessaire, c'est l'Esprit qui a créé tout cela.   Nous n'entendons pas cependant par là transformer le monde extérieur en une vaste fantasmagorie, ni changer la vie en une hallucination, mais nous affirmons que notre certitude de la réalité de l'existence des phénomènes extérieurs est basée sur un témoignage plus sérieux que celui des sens : "The Universe," dit Emerson, "is the externization of the soul. . . . The world is mind precipitated, the volatile essence is forever escaping again into the state of free thought.   Hence the pungency and virtue of every natural object on the mind.   Man imprisoned, man crystallized speaks to man impersonated."   Non certes nous ne voulons pas jeter des pierres à cette mère si belle, nous ne voulons salir et souiller le doux nid qui nous abrite. L'amour de la Nature est un des traits les plus caractéristiques d'Emerson, il se révèle avec force dans toutes ses œuvres ; mais dans aucun de ses écrits, ce sentiment n'est aussi vif que dans " Nature."   En

lisant ce livre, il me semble que j'assiste au spectacle
de l'aurore. Je sens mon front caressé par la brise
matinale, je vois le soleil commencer à darder ses
premiers rayons et les légers nuages qui flottent à
l'horizon s'empourprer dans l'immensité claire. Je
me laisse entraîner par l'enthousiasme du poëte, car
c'est un vrai chant qui résonne à mes oreilles ; et,
parfois même je crois saisir de vrais accents de
passion.

Si la Nature est la contre-partie de l'âme, son but
est évidemment de servir à l'éducation et aux besoins
de l'homme. Emerson renferme les différents services
qu'elle peut nous rendre dans les différentes catégories
de Commodité, de Beauté, de Langage et de Discipline. Ce qu'il dit du Langage m'intéresse particulièrement, d'autant plus que j'y trouve la définition
de sa poésie elle-même, — définition qui peut se for-
muler ainsi : " La Poésie est l'expression d'un fait
spirituel par un symbole naturel." Le Poëte prend
possession de la Nature toute entière et s'en sert pour
exprimer ses pensées. Il donne une voix à toute
créature et fait de l'univers une immense trope :
"L'imagination," dit Emerson, "peut être définie l'usage
que la raison fait du monde extérieur," et, comme
exemple, il cite Shakespeare ; il parle de ses merveil-
leux Sonnets avec un enthousiasme entraînant ; mais
ce qu'il dit de Shakespeare peut s'appliquer aussi à
lui-même. La poésie d'Emerson c'est vraiment la
Nature traduite en pensée ; il a fait entrer dans sa
trame le brin de paille que l'hirondelle avait dans

son bec, son livre est parfumé de l'odeur des pins, sa voix est aussi douce que le frémissement des gerbes d'épis, et que le murmure des ruisseaux qui coulent sous l'herbe.

À l'œil perçant du poëte une loi de progrès se manifeste dans cette belle Nature qu'il contemple et il suit le mouvement ascensionnel dans l'échelle des êtres :

> " A subtle chain of countless rings
>   The next unto the farthest brings ;
>   The eye reads omens where it goes,
>   And speaks all languages the rose ;
>   And striving to be man the worm
>   Mounts through all spires of form."

L'homme ! voila donc le dernier anneau de la chaine, le couronnement de l'œuvre, le roi de la création. L'homme, c'est la matière arrivée au point où elle a conscience de son existence. L'homme a un âme ; et cette âme est l'étincelle divine qui vient du foyer central. L'âme c'est Dieu dans l'homme ; et Dieu est l'être où s'unissent toutes les individualités. Il n'y a pas de mouvements lyriques comparables à ceux d'Emerson lorsqu'il parle de cette unité et de cette identité de l'âme humaine : " This central fire which, beaming out of the lips of Etna, lightens the capes of Sicily ; and flaming now out of the throat of Vesuvius, illuminates the towers and vineyards of Naples. It is one light which beams out of a thousand stars ; it is one soul which animates all men." De cette haute conception de ce qui constitue notre individualité, Emerson fait découler la première règle sur laquelle il édifiera sa morale. Sonore et perçante comme la note du clairon, il lance cette phrase, " Trust thyself, every heart vibrates to that iron string."

Mais cette confiance en nous-mêmes, pour en jouir il faut que nous fassions le sacrifice de tout ce que nous avons de personnel et d'égoïste en nous. Pour que nous puissions compter sur nous-mêmes, il est nécessaire que nous ayons d'abord pleine et entière confiance dans les éternelles lois de l'Univers.

> " Les éternelles lois, comme un fleuve puissant,
> Poursuivent lentement leur cours irrésistible ;
> Rien ne peut résister à ce flot qui descend
> Dont l'œil ne saisit pas le flux imperceptible.
>
> " Notre barque, flottant sur cette onde paisible,
> Profite de leur force en y obéissant,
> Rase le sein des eaux et glisse en s'y berçant,
> Se laissant entraîner par un guide invisible.
>
> " Nous n'avons pas besoin d'un incessant travail ;
> La voile peut tomber et la rame être oisive,
> S'il est bien dirigé, l'esquif au port arrive.
>
> " Mais il faut fermement tenir le gouvernail,
> Et surtout se garder d'aller en sens inverse ;
> Car alors en passant la vague nous renverse."

C'est notre obéissance à ces lois qui seule peut nous rendre forts. " Lorsqu'un homme," dit Emerson, " travaille dans la direction du Bien ; il est aidé par toutes les forces de l'Univers. Ce sont ces lois immuables, c'est cet ordre éternel des choses que les hommes accusent dans leur folie. C'est ce même Pouvoir bienfaisant qu'ils appellent Fatalité, lorsqu'ils se sentent blessés pour avoir tenté de le violer." " 'Tis weak and vicious people who cast the blame on Fate ; the right use of Fate is to bring up our actions to the loftiness of Nature. Rude and invincible, except by themselves, are the elements ; so let man be, let him empty his breast of his windy conceits and show his lordship by manners and deeds on the scale of Nature. A man should compare advantageously with an oak, a river, or a mountain."

> " Autour de toi, le rocher, l'arbre,
> Le granit et le bloc de marbre,
> Obéissent tous à la loi ;
> Et tout te répète sans cesse
> Que tu dois faire avec sagesse
> Ce qu'ils font sans savoir pourquoi.

> " Ces vastes mers et ces montagnes,
> Ces larges fleuves et ces campagnes,
> Tout cela n'appartient qu'à toi ;
> Et tu fais croître ta puissance
> Par ta sublime obéissance
> Au grand Pouvoir qui t'a fait roi ! "

Cette confiance que nous devons avoir en nous-mêmes, c'est la vertu mère de toutes les autres, c'est le principe fécond qui nous fera nous retrouver nous-mêmes. Il changera la face de notre religion, de notre politique, de notre littérature. Nous ne serons plus des imitateurs, mais nous oserons être nous-

mêmes. Nous ne nous contenterons pas d'une admiration stérile pour les œuvres du passé ; mais nous
essaierons nous aussi de les égaler et de les surpasser.
Le sens d'indépendance spirituelle, d'après Emerson,
est comme cet admirable vernis de la rosée ; grâce
auquel cette vieille terre et toutes ses productions
sont rendues chaque matin nouvelles et brillantes
sous la dernière touche de l'artiste. Non, nous ne
nous laisserons pas décourager par les gloires du
passé. Les grands hommes qui nous ont précédé
nous les considérerons comme des plongeurs heureux
dans cet Océan, dont le fond est encore pavé de perles
dont nous pouvons nous emparer.

> " Oui, d'autres ont plongé dans cette mer profonde,
> Ils sont allés chercher la perle au fond de l'onde ;
> Quand ils sont revenus, ils l'avaient à la main ;
> Mais, l'océan toujours en trésors abonde,
> C'est à nous de chercher à dépouiller son sein,
> Ceux qui le tenteront, n'essaieront pas en vain."

Comment Emerson se sert-il de ses idées ; ou, en
d'autres termes ; quelle est sa méthode ? Je pro-
nonce là un mot qui sonne étrangement quand on
parle d'Emerson ; il est généralement pris dans une
acception si pédantesque qu'il est vraiment dange-
reux de l'employer. La méthode d'Emerson est
toute poétique. Il y a une phrase de Montaigne,
que du reste Emerson s'est appropriée, et qui
exprime admirablement ce que j'ai dans la pensée.
"Les abeilles," dit Montaigne, "qui pillotent de ci,
de là, font le miel qui est tout leur ; ce n'est plus ni

thym ni marjolaine." Le poëte est cette abeille;
tout dans l'homme et dans la Nature l'attire, et le miel
qu'il en distille est sa pensée. Peu importe le sujet
qu'il prend, il en fera toujours sortir la grande leçon.
Comme Wordsworth il pourrait dire aussi : —

> " To me the meanest flower that blows can give
> Thoughts that do often lie too deep for tears."

Qui ne connaît ces vers charmants au Rhodora ?

> En Mai lorsque des vents les soufles sont moins rudes,
> Je vis le Rhodora parer nos solitudes ;
> Il étalait ses fleurs tremblantes sur les eaux
> Pour charmer le désert, l'onde entre les roseaux
> Ses pétales flottaient éclatantes et belles
> Sur le sombre ruisseau qu'égayait sa beauté ;
> Le cardinal eût pu, tout pâle à son coté,
> Pour courtiser la fleur venir baigner ses ailes.
> Rhodora ! les sages demanderont pourquoi
> Ce charme sur la terre est gaspillé par toi ?
> Réponds : que si pour voir, l'œil s'ouvre à la lumière,
> D'être aussi, la beauté, s'excuse à sa manière.
> Si de te voir ici mon âme s'étonna
> Je n'ai rien demandé rivale de la rose ;
> Car dans mon ignorance humblement je suppose
> Que le même Pouvoir qui t'y mit, m'y mena.

Rien n'est trop petit, rien n'est indigne de fixer la
pensée du poëte, car tout aboutit au même but ; tout
aussi émane de la même cause ; c'est toujours la même
essence qui recoit les différents noms d'Amour, de
Justice, de Tempérance, de même que cet immense
océan qui change de noms sur les différents rivages
qu'il baigne.

Cette considération de la méthode d'Emerson
m'amène naturellement à parler de son style. Mr.
John Burroughs dans un article inséré dans le Century d'Avril dernier, dit que les grands écrivains ont
deux façons d'exhiber leur style, dans la conception
et le dessein, aussi par le fini et le traitement. Il
reconnait qu'Emerson possède la seconde qualité
dans toute son étendue et que rien n'est comparable à la perfection de sa phrase, mais il semble con-
clure que la première qualité lui fait défaut. Ce
n'est pas mon avis ; si je ne vais pas jusqu'à trouver
chez Emerson une conception et un dessein comme
dans l'œuvre d'un peintre ou d'un compositeur, j'y
découvre une unité réelle qui est plus profonde encore,
et qui vient de la tendance uniforme et constante de ses
pensées, une unité de but, si je puis m'exprimer ainsi.

Mr. Burroughs a été plus heureux lorsqu'il applique
à Emerson la fameuse phrase de Ste. Beuve, qui parle
du grande poëte, non pas comme de celui qui a le
mieux fait au point de vue de la perfection acadé-
mique ; mais de celui qui suggère le plus, qui excite,
féconde, vous laisse beaucoup à deviner et à compléter.
C'est ce que fait Emerson. À ceux qui disent ne pas
le comprendre, il a lui-même répondu d'avance : —

> " O mortal ! thy ears are stones,
> These echoes are laden with tones
> Which only the pure can hear.
> Thou canst not catch what they recite
> Of Will and Fate, of Want and Right,
> Of man to come, of human life,
> Of death and fortune, growth and strife."

Emerson est un Réformateur ; le colonel Higginson à ce propos l'a fait remarquer. Nul n'a une physionomie aussi marquée que lui à cet égard. Il est arrivé en effet que des hommes ont fait des révolutions dans la littérature ou dans la vie, sans d'abord se rendre bien compte du résultat qu'ils allaient atteindre. Emerson dès ses premiers pas avait au contraire pris l'attitude qu'il devait toujours garder et dont il n'a jamais dévié. Qu'on relise les premières lignes de " Nature ; " il est impossible d'affirmer plus nettement ses intentions réformatrices.

La sanction des enseignements d'Emerson est dans sa vie, qui présente un rare exemple d'unité et de consistence. Jamais une vie n'a servi de commentaire aussi éclatant aux écrits d'un homme. Que l'on compare le ton de l'Adresse devant le Divinity College en 1838, avec celle qui est intitulée " Progress of Culture." Quelle hardiesse dans la première ! quelle sérénité dans la seconde ! C'est que dans le long espace de temps qui s'était écoulé entre elles, bien des évènements étaient survenus, et, que leurs résultats avaient plus que jamais augmenté sa foi dans l'humanité. Il avait assisté à la grande crise que son pays avait traversé. Il était fier de l'héroïsme d'une nation qui s'était soulevée toute entière contre la honte de l'esclavage. C'est avec une confiance paisible qu'il voyait le soleil se coucher dans un ciel sans nuages ; et que dans la joie de son cœur il s'écriait : " I read the promise of happier times and of better men ! "

Emerson est un Américain ; il l'est par le caractère déterminé et hardi de sa pensée, par les grâces particulières de sa forme. Il fallait sans doute une terre vierge pour nourir cette vigoureuse plante ; une individualité aussi puissante que la sienne ne pouvait se produire qu'au milieu d'une société qui permet à l'homme de se développer en pleine liberté et de tirer de ses facultés tous les secours qu'il peut en attendre. Ce sera, Mesdames et Messieurs, l'éternel honneur de votre pays, d'avoir mérité ce grand homme. Puisse-t-il en produire d'autres semblables à lui ! Puissent leurs voix puissantes nous arrêter sur les pentes glissantes où nous roulons. Puissent-ils nous aider à nous retrouver nous-mêmes, en augmentant notre foi dans la liberté de la volonté, notre respect pour la personalité humaine.

J'ai parlé d'un poëte, et, j'ai conscience, hélas ! d'être resté bien au-dessous du sujet que j'avais à traiter ; mais j'aurais, en passant du moins, laissé tomber ma modeste couronne aux pieds de sa blanche statue.

> Penseur ! en te lisant j'apprends à me connaître,
> Et je deviens moi-même, en écoutant ta voix ;
> Tu parles comme un homme et non pas comme un maître,
> Car tu veux simplement montrer ce que tu vois.
>
> L'Univers est régi par d'éternelles lois,
> Il faut que l'homme accepte et sache se soumettre ;
> Mais il augmente ainsi la force de son être,
> Il grandit, s'il s'incline en se disant : "Je dois !"

On t'appelle écrivain, philosophe ou poëte,
Mais de l'homme pour moi tu fus le vrai prophète,
Et je te nommerai mon guide et mon sauveur.

Car tu m'as éclairé d'une vive lumière.
Grâce à toi, je suis fort pour fournir ma carrière ;
Mon cœur s'est enflammé de ta noble ferveur.

V.

EMERSON'S RELIGION.

By REV. C. A. BARTOL, D.D.

ARTISTS sometimes paint their own portraits. In describing Emerson's religion I shall make him, as far as possible, sit, not to me, but to himself. The soul is shy in its devotions. It enters the closet and shuts the door. What I worship is my secret, says Rubinstein. To know a man's religion, we must surprise him on his knees; and that is an intrusion and offence. George Washington, whose nature had but a tropical calm, being interrupted at his prayers by an importunate knocking at his chamber, arose, and, putting at once wrath for humility, thrust his sword through the panel of the door.

That Emerson, though no such volcano, — rather a cool observer and unimpassioned saint, — was a pious man, and that religion was a feeling raised in him to the highest power, was proved to me by the rapture in his look after a service in his house nearly half a century ago.

> " His eyes let out more light than they took in ;
> They told not when, but did the day begin."

Such light, as Wordsworth says, "never was on sea or land." Yet Emerson broke with the organized religion of the Church, not on a point of faith, but of form. A born idealist, carrying or carried by his idealism sometimes to excess, offended by the deacons' creaking boots as they bore around the consecrated elements in their hands, he forswore his clerical part in that particular ceremony as unsuited to the Occidental mind, and proposed a change in the administration of the Lord's Supper; which his parish not accepting, he resigned his place, parting with grief from his flock. Many years after, when, on a different issue, of removing between church and congregation the sacramental line, I was ready to leave my post, he advised me to remain, and reform from the inside; and he spoke then to me of his own pain in the rupture of the pastoral tie. At one time he queried if Christianity were a blessing. By triangulating the points of his early experience we may measure his position. The business of the pulpit, function of the preacher, he never decried. When Dr. Bellows congratulated him on his independence as a free lance, he replied, "If there be a load to draw, a harness is a good thing." He had but slipped from an unfit tackle : —

> " Why should the vest on him allure,
>   Which I could not on me endure ? "

Yet not with the investiture did he confound the thing. " Let us converse aside," he said to me, when

I differed from him about the person of Christ. Doubtless he swung from and then back to Christianity, but never quite away ; as the magnetic meridian cannot forsake, but leaves and returns to the pole, — is now returning, astronomers say.

> " One accent of the Holy Ghost
>   The heedless world hath never lost."

What treatise on Scripture inspiration or apostolic succession are not these lines more than worth ? The critic of Emerson has a hard time, finding that Emerson is always beforehand in his trade, and always criticises and answers himself. We can read but one face of the coin at a time, and he never forgets to turn it over. Father Taylor wanted to navigate, he said, on the edge of the pit. Emerson's ship tacks close to the reef, and zigzags into port. He flouts the ritual, and gives it its revenge : "A whole popedom of forms one pulsation of virtue can uplift and vivify." There are two oxen always in his team, and the farther they strain apart the surer and stronger they pull. He is an optimist, extravagant to declare the brothel or gallows a step upwards.

> " Yet spake yon purple mountain,
>   Yet said yon ancient wood,
>   That night or day, that love or crime,
>   Sends all men to the good."

But shall slavery escape his lash ? Does he not see every drop of Mr. Webster's blood point down ? Is he charged with inconsistency, he pleads sincerity.

As an expert marksman hits and flattens in the target his first bullet with a second, so he makes his sentences each other's butt, the spirit of truth always the aim. He claims a first hand with Deity, and says, " Off, ye lendings ! " to traditions.

> " By God, I will not be an owl,
> But sun me in the capitol."

Yet he bows to the majestic and venerable institution that hands down revelations from age to age. Still, he asks, " Why not have an original relation to Nature, our own works and words, and worship ? "

He is an immigrant from some other land, like David; a pilgrim and stranger on the earth, like Paul, coming from and seeking a city foreign to this world, where he is not quite naturalized and at home. As a vessel touches at Bermuda or the Azores, he is a visitor who must weigh anchor and cannot stay; and this posture or aspect is the expression of that sense of the Infinite in which, more than in any feeling of dependence, or owning of obligation, or reading of Nature's volume between the lines, or effort at personal perfection, or otherwise defined mood of mind or condition of life, religion consists. He interrogates all observances and creeds, bids them report at head-quarters of the intellect; will see and judge for himself, and not look through others' spectacles. The divine personality he doubts, but leaves his speculation, like Joseph's coat, in the hands of the harlot when he prays. To Mr. Arnold's " Power not

ourselves that makes for righteousness," he would say,
" Is it not our *self ?* "

" Himself from God he could not free."

The boundary line or stone betwixt man and his
Maker, he thinks, was never found. He can scarce
say *Thou* to Him of whom he is part. Seven generations in him of ministerial blood have so lifted and
refined his thought, that he cannot rush rashly into the
Great Presence, or pray to order at a set time in a set
place. His installation in New Bedford was stopped
by his request to the committee that the public
prayers should be optional. He offered prayer in
the Divinity School Chapel before his Address. But
it was impersonal, — to Infinite Wisdom and Goodness to grant light to our lowliness, — as I still
remember the terms which I heard, and which a rev-
erend brother at the time, loving him, yet pronounced
to be no prayer. But it was an articulation, for a
moment, of the prayer without ceasing in a loyal
heart, a continuation of what had begun or been
eternal,

" Or ever the wild Time coined itself
Into calendar months and days."

Every man of ideas, identified with principles which
are everlasting, seems to us and to himself to have
pre-existed, as Plato says, and been loved, like Jesus,
before the foundation of the world. Emerson says
he knows not whether these thoughts, which so animate and exercise him, will house again in just such

8

a frame, only that they cannot be sick with any sickness, or die any death. He is not an accredited representative of, nor a seceder from, the Church which first suckled and at last sucked him back; but he insisted to the last his name should be on her books. He said, as the Master bids, *Yea, yea*, as well as *Nay. nay;* but his *Yes* was more than his *No*. *Aliquando Ecclesia in exiguis.* "Sometimes the Church is composed of the smallest number of persons," says an ancient father. It may be, as avers the Apostle, in a house, or, let us add, in one breast full of saintly company, like Channing's, standing for the dignity of human nature; or Garrison's answering, when reproached with not going to meeting, that he sometimes preached to himself. Emerson, when he felt and celebrated the world-warming spark,

> " The axis of the star,
> The sparkle of the spar,"

proclaimed the universal divinity; though he tells us when we are with God we count not the congregation, The Muse teaches a living God.

> " Into the fifth himself he flings,
> And conscious Law is King of kings."

His doctrine of the access of the Spirit to the private soul is not new, but very old. The Montanists maintained that the Holy Ghost had not spent itself on the formulas of belief and worship understood and agreed upon in the society of the faithful, but had left some things still to be said. American Emerson, like the French Montaigne, was the Roman Montanus over again. Despite Councils of Nice and Chalcedon, and theological triumphs of Saint Augustine, modern history demonstrates the indispensable additions to the Hebrew Bible, without which all nations would still be subject to kings, slaves would cringe under their masters' whip, women would neither bare their heads nor cut their hair, nor open their mouths save to husbands at home; records would be put for truth, the killing letter for the enlivening spirit, and God be a child that cannot find his tongue. Discarding Trinitarian absurdities, Emerson also scores the pale negations of Unitarianism. Whatever part of the so-called Liberal, Radical, Free Religious host switches off into materialism and immorality, leaving the main track of the Transcendental movement, as a curve on the railway at length reaches the opposite point of the compass, has none of his sympathy. He reverts to his ancestry. The old Puritan in him revives. He greets a new Orthodoxy rather than any liberty of sin. He says, " A little Calvinism does not hurt the flavor of the bread."

Labor is respectable; and this man is a working bee in the hive, not a self-indulging, sensual, honey-eating drone. When one praised to him the privilege of vacation, the delicious summer-rest, he said, "That poppy grows among the corn." " The miller, like the poet, is a lazy man, setting his wheel in the stream;" but his watching is work. The poet culti-

vates and reaps, not with plough and hoe, scythe or
sickle.

> " One harvest from thy field
>   Homeward brought the oxen strong ;
> A second crop thine acres yield,
>   Which I gather in a song."

When I invited him once as a guest, he said, " I
must not forsake my tasks."   All the sects may well
waive claim of property in a man so human and
humane.   He belongs to no denomination, but to the
humanity in all.   When the German poet Schiller
was asked why he subscribed to no form of religious
belief, he answered, " Because I am so religious."
When our own Olmsted, of the Sanitary Commis-
sion, was asked why he absented himself from
church, he replied, " Because going to meeting hurts
my religious feelings."   Church and Saviour were
not finalities with Emerson ; and the Bible was to
the entire revelation no more than are the wheat-
grains among mummies in the Pyramids to all the
harvests of the world.

Emerson came to illustrate and verify again one
of the great texts of Holy Writ from the voice of
God to John in Patmos : " He that hath an ear, let
him hear what the Spirit saith unto the churches ; "
and if not one of the seven in Asia escaped then, why
should any of the thousand in America be excused
now ?   The prophet must not cease to call the priest
to account.   He does not break the idols, but puts
them out of the way or exposes their deformity ; and,

though he loves Nature, he makes not, with some of the scientists, a huge idol of her. Rather with Plato he sees but a child's picture-book in all the astronomy; says the screen is too thin to hide the cause, — the outward universe but a shining, peaceful apparition to be interrogated; and that the transport of life comes when this vast creation reverently withdraws before its Author. None more than Emerson has lived next-door neighbor to truth. "Who is this that turns aside into the thicket from the throng?" asks Goethe in his poem. It was Moses at Mount Sinai, Paul in Arabia, Jesus in the wilderness, and Emerson a worshipper in the woods.

> "And when I am stretched beneath the pines,
> Where the evening star so holy shines,
> I laugh at the lore and the pride of man,
> At the sophist schools and the learnèd clan;
> For what are they all, in their high conceit,
> When man in the bush with God may meet?"

Organ though he be of the religious sentiment, which is vocal in his least syllable and with his last tone, Emerson will be popular only with a class, — the finest spirits, a sifted audience of select men and women, — because he lacks rush and passion, does not flame or flow. Rather he climbs where but few can find footing and breath, to dilate and conspire with the morning wind. But to whoso keeps pace with him he gives confidence and peace, a feeling that the world is not base metal, but its Maker, as the Persian Omar Khayam says, a good fellow. Prayer,

Emerson calls the soliloquy of a beholding and jubi-
lant soul ; meaning not his own or any separate,
but that one all are part of, which, as Moses said,
takes satisfaction in its own responsive work. This
participation is not David's prayer, " Cleanse me
with hyssop," or Luther's, " Thou must hear me ; "
but Wordsworth's, — " his mind a thanksgiving to the
Power that made him." Emerson is Adam before the
Fall. The ground is not cursed for his sake or in his
view. He sees no warning angel with flaming sword
turning every way on the wall. Thorns and briers
fulfil for him no threat. A weed is but a plant
whose uses have not been discovered. All the two
hundred thousand conceal virtue. He would say,
with the Stoics, pain of child-birth or other sort is
no evil. He scouts the notion of doom. The poetry
of his late incompetent critic, Matthew Arnold, perfect in finish and classic in form, is devoid of cheer ;
suggests monumental sculpture, or the adorning of a
tomb, — as the Rubayat is the dogma of death and
splendid mausoleum of human hope. Emerson's lines
are an emancipation proclamation set to music, a
resurrection to that immortality and identity he told
his friend Sanborn he held to. He has not written
a verse that does not refresh and exhilarate. He
never for an instant panders to despondency and
despair. If, in Henry Vaughan's figure, such a bird
sing not now in some other grove out of mortal sight,
what a loss in Nature ! What is the use ? Says
Victor Hugo, " It were unfair if the great expectations

of a child be not met;" and, if God be not bankrupt, his promissory note will not go to protest. Louis Agassiz accounted for the scientists' neglect of the supernatural by their being tired, and too much absorbed in the natural even to consider the miraculous; and Emerson, in the early flush of his genius, was so conscious of the life that is, that he considered as a sort of peeping, all curiosity about that to come. But he was just to the subject in his later years; the key-hole became a window; he reverted to the ancient faith; God and heaven were bound in one volume to his mind. He saw how evolution, like phrenology, deals with structure. It is the book of Exodus, not Genesis. Mind from matter were an effect greater than the cause. Mind from mind has a warrant against dissolution and beyond fate. Revering the law of duty, he did not resolve religion into morality, but spoke of it as *the sentiment.* An intelligence like his, the most uncommitted and impartial of our time, deserves for its judgment great respect. What, indeed, but failure can wait on such a fight with the instinct of mankind in all ages and every land, as the attempt to reduce religion to ethics, and cut the blossom from the root? Whoever has such a purpose, it will spew out of its mouth. We cannot force religion on another, as we may compel him to do his civil duty. We may have no image in us of God which were a mental idolatry. But the race will always feel and hear from what it cannot comprehend. In vain will any objector brand it as unknowable or unknown.   He and his cargo of definitions will be swamped in the sea of glory we are full of and float in, by the united, inseparable constitution of things with the soul.   Emerson's place in the choir of this hosanna and hallelujah will be his crown.

"But why not *do* something?" screams Carlyle, with a voice to be heard across the Atlantic, to his friend; who might reply, quoting himself, "Is not a thought the ancestor of every act?"   But his answer is, that music, not discord, is the core of the world, and anthems better and truer than growls.   A sad woman spoke to her legal counsellor of the hollowness of this life, trusting he would give her some courage.   How her heart was damped as with a wet sheet, as he observed, "Well, Madam, all the same let us keep up the sham."   So much talk of shams from the Chelsea philosopher not only dejects, but is further from the fact than the Concord sage's lesson from the bee's

"Merry breezy bass."
.   .   .   .   .
"Leave the chaff, and take the wheat."

The American's note is a chant, the Englishman's is prolonged into cant: we stumble on his page.

Emerson practised on the outcome of his own definition of religion, — to do and suffer all for others' sake.   Goethe says it is man's business to enact hell on the earth.   But in a drama of heaven Emerson performed, to prove that what is morose is false.   He is not the whole manhood, or its only scribe.   He is not fond of the night-side. He is dainty, and lifts his robe, as a lady does treading through the mire. In his " English Traits" he shuns the shame, unlike those Hebrew scouts of old charged with spying out the nakedness of the land. The world-wide poem of " Faust" is to him a disagreeable composition. He would walk backward to throw a cover on indecency, like Noah's sons. His admiration for Walt Whitman's firm stroke and unborrowed strain halts at the bald spots on his page. " Not that we would be unclothed, but clothed upon," he cries with Paul. But, discriminating what is unfit for literature, his perception has no drawback. That an observer so quick, a surveyor so wide, whose imagination was an eye and his passions asleep, his brain at least as full as his heart was warm, should advise the reading of all the bibles on bent knees, is a great evidence and vote on behalf of religion. His faith was faithfulness.

> " Nor knowest thou what argument
> Thy life to thy neighbor's creed hath lent."

Emerson, supposed irreligious, was pre-eminently religious, because, not bewildered or diverted like a butterfly by the multitude of gay phenomena, he clung to the noumena, the real and invisible, and his conduct corresponded to his belief. Dogma is thought to be the parent of creed ; but behavior returns the compliment, and fashions the faith. Through all the spectacle and panorama of sensible impressions, coat of many colors, protean forms, he, as Plato bids, exer-

cised his intellect.   His mind and heart sought the
object of worship.   The atheist leaps like a grass-
hopper from appearance to appearance; the pan-
theist fails to distinguish appearance from reality.
He fixed on the unity in the universe.   He marked
the spiritual motives, perpetual forces, beautiful laws;
he saw them at work in trifles as manifest as in the
vast domain, life a game played with a mill or a million, and from all aberration he noted recovery sure
as the planet's or the comet's curve.

> " And while the lamp holds out to burn,
>   The vilest sinner may return."

He translates the old into a new couplet: —

> " And the joy that is sweetest
>   Lurks in stings of remorse."

To him, as to Wordsworth, all is full of blessings.
There is Boston and Concord, Bunker Hill and the
"dear old Devil not far off," — a shadowy personage to
be made a jest of.   Life is a normal school, in which
he instructs his class, the highest in rank, but not
the most numerous; and he is, unawares, the clear
pattern of his own bright lesson.   He embodied —
and was incarnate in every feature and gesture —
what he taught, affording " the luxury of a religion
that does not degrade."   Nothing can alienate, dis-
locate, set him at odds with God.   He is reconciled;
he falls " soft on a thought."

Shall we then indorse his criticism on this wheel
or fandango of articles and rites which we call the

Church, the same complaint in substance he makes on the common spawn of the species we belong to,—

> " Add their nine lives to this cat,
> Stuff their nine brains in his hat " ?

Does his description hold of the poor preacher as spectral, while the snow-storm is real ? Is the sacred truth "but behooted and behowled" ? Let his picture pass for humor. Plato would shut such poetry, with that of Hesiod and Homer and with the enervating music, out of his republic. Let me plead for the poor preacher, to whom a certain " fellow-feeling makes me wondrous kind." He does not in his plain homily grasp the naked thunderbolts of Jove, which slip from all fleshly hands. He does not receive, but transmits, link after link, through long circles and wide ranges, the first full shock. It must be weakened, for the feeble children of men to bear. The efficacy of certain medicines depends on their dilution, and the high potency of moral principle on its nice adaptation to the patient's strength. Meat for men, milk for babes. When Dr. Walker was told the sermon had been very dull one Sunday morning, he said he doubted not it was very good, — no ambitious sensational undertaking to capture and astonish by an ambitious official with his chin in the air, but a modest rehearsal of familiar and yet forgotten or neglected duties. Commonly it is well to serve not high-spiced brands, but brown bread, which Fields told me he furnished. Water is more wholesome than wine. Andrews Norton being in the assembly, Ephraim

Peabody said unquestionably the great professor had despised the logic, and been mortified by the law of the discourse. The strings which the violinist screws too tight before he begins, crack before he gets through, and all for the time is over with the piece he would play. Transcendental catgut will not always bear the strain put upon it, while the hurdy-gurdy in the street pleases the crowd and fears no casualty. " Hear the good artists, hear the bad, and compare," said Rubinstein to his pupil. Ordinary human nature, trudging like Shakspeare's boy " unwillingly to school," must not be reproved too harshly in the slow entertainment and moderate stint.

But Emerson, in his own poems about the " Day's Ration " and the Days like hypocritic dervishes, with artless cunning of self-reproof and owning of however lamented limits, sufficiently refutes his own argument or rules his case of exorbitant demand out of court. He goes ahead ; but a good locomotive knows how to back and couple with the train. It must not be forward too far. Loose on the track, flying to and fro, it is called a wild engine, hauling neither passengers nor freight. Such, perhaps, are some of Emerson's excursions. He is one of his own forerunners. Far off his trumpet sounds and stirs. Genius is always sublime in its call. Rubinstein liked not our most famous American preacher's telling his audience they could not be expected to go beyond their strength. " No," he affirmed, " they must do the impossible. I tell my pupils they must try to surpass Beethoven, or not study at all." But we accuse God when we are hard on congenitally weak and slenderly endowed men. I sympathize with the under-dog. I think Emerson, the genial and gentle, sometimes punishes his opponent too sorely, badgers conservatives, and with blockheads and laggards is too severe. But he spares the person, while he assails the class. Only against a few persons did I hear him speak. He is aware of and ever ready to return from his over-statement and excess. He says, — perhaps the passage I heard is not in print, — " We censure the rich, the fashionable, and luxurious folk ; but we go to their houses to find they are lovers, and our hasty judgment is reversed." His weapon has a trenchant edge and tremendous swing. Admirable is Milton's line of the Son of God routing the hosts of Satan : —

> " Half his strength he put not forth."

He would disperse but not destroy ; and enjoining, we must not exact or insist on, angelic virtue save in ourselves ; with the two-edged sword of conscience smiting in more than out. Plato sees the ideal ; the incarnation he does not expect. But superior gift or character is impatient with low attainment. We bolt in vain if the bolters be no better than the rest. Not from any vulgar soul, but from Homer, Dante, Milton, even John and Jesus, come the awful pictures of that underworld where sinners are like flies we poison and burn, only that worm dieth not and the fire is not quenched. The infernal upholstery is chalked large, the figures made colossal, because so far off the eye will fetch them down to a small and fitting size. A large dose is brought, when only a little can be got down. It would, one said, have totally depraved Jonathan Edwards to realize the menaces he flung. Emerson atones for his repudiation of the old theology by painting the earthly scene as taunted with churls and little men. But he recants, retracts his satire, prophesies good out of all that is bad and low, graciously descends to the folk, not only from the proud hill in Cheshire, but from the Monadnoc of his mind. He scorns the mass as refuse, the majority of voices as base; yet how quick our acrobat turns, recovers, and falls on his feet!

> " The pariah hind
> Admits thee to the perfect mind."

He cannot be an ecclesiastic when the Church is so corrupt that financial gamblers are communicants in regular standing, to " be sharp as a Baptist deacon " is a motto for the market, and memorial windows are put in cathedrals for persons who have no title to the sacred honor beyond their sect or wealth. Yet Emerson has no conceit of doing without the Church, — the institution which does the thinking for Balzac's Breton gentleman and cavalier, who fancies it is enough for him to draw his sword and act.

On the fact that religion is not an interest of the individual or of all individuals alone, but a social

principle, it was not in the line of Emerson's thought
— more deep and lofty than wise and broad — to lay
adequate stress. He is not to be blamed that he stuck
to his mission. We must not expect a seer to be
an organizer, any more than a microscopist to be a
helmsman, or an astronomer an engineer. We must
supplement his calling, extend his vision, and perhaps correct his view. In the irony of his " Sartor
Resartus," — an essay hinted in Swift's " World in a
Suit of Clothes," — Carlyle walks over a track of
philosophy quite beyond Emerson's beat. Browning,
in his satirical poem, makes Bishop Blougram the
unbelieving objector's match. Society, civil or religious, must have its symbols and symbolical books.
To discard ordinances and forms were to abolish its
vocabulary and cut out its tongue. To confine its
communication to improvised spontaneous speech in
its worship, were both to abolish literature and to
remand the community from arbitrary characters to
picture-language and natural signs. Altar, temple,
synagogue, mosque, meeting-house, and conventicle,
with their architecture and various inward and outward order, are the style and alphabet of a common
prayer and praise, in token that men are not to go
away each to his own selfish solitude with so much
of the bread of life as he can get hold of, as a dog
runs off with a bone to gnaw ; but in their instruc-
tions and devotions to have some sort of Lord's Supper to sit down together to, as in a house we have a
table as well as a sideboard ; and, though on occasion

we may carry a lunch in our pocket, we come back habitually to a joint and punctual feast.

So, but from poverty of imagination, and a horse-jockey kind of wit, did Theodore Parker call the elements nothing but baker's bread and grocer's wine, and say "the Lord ate veal with Abraham;" and that it is whining through an attorney to pray in the name of Christ. Emerson was kept from such grossness by his sagacity and charity no less than his good taste. Delivering his blow, he dreamed not the nail he hit was the only one in the common weal's fabric to drive. Abstractions and generalizations will not, without particular prescriptions, heal and save the sick and lost. All space is a temple, but we need some visible shrine. All days are holy; suppose we begin with one ? God is everywhere; but, lest ignorant creatures think him nowhere, trample his universal sanctuary with violence and noise, and find no ground reverently to put off the shoes from their profane and hasty feet, let Protestant service and Romish mass remind them he is at least somewhere ! Better the superstition that besots than the Sadducee-ism that desolates and disenchants. It is a mechanical age. We have political and theological machines, and must withstand their brute tyrannic force, and get the best resultant we can. But if all contract, compromise, and concerted action fall under the head of machinery, it were as prudent to wipe out mills and railroads, hunt around everybody for his own fig-leaf, and go only afoot, as to disintegrate nations by dissolving civil government or ecclesiastical rule. " In company or on the street," says Bismarck, " I am not an individual, but an event." He means Germany. Of the units, society is the source, not the sum. Will you destroy with dynamite and petroleum the religious emblems? Blow up, then, judicial benches with like explosion, and put flag and shield into the same fire! The world is a cipher. Only for what it signifies do we care. The soul is the numeral. Time and space are but the floor and curtain-slides of an illusory and transitory stage. Certainly there may be minutiæ and mummeries in the Church of but artificial import, which justification of reason cannot reach; but no passwords of an army, no signals at sea, no travellers' beckonings or business telegrams, have consequences greater than decent religious observances for the human heart. Rufus Choate humorously said of a certain witness, that he had overworked the participle. We overwork all the parts of speech, and expect to do everything with words.

> " No mountain can
> Measure with a perfect man."

Yet no man, says Emerson, can feed us ever. Man, measure of all things, has his measure in every human sample yet. Even in our present favorite we must note what is limitary and left out as well as catholic and large. Perhaps from his imperfect comprehension comes his atomic style. Cardinal Newman has a running hand because borne on amid the social or ecclesiastical stream. How can the conscious and unconscious in speech and character be combined? In certain pieces of orchestral music the general movement of the wind and string instruments is broken in upon from the unseen outside by some herald's, horseman's, huntsman's messenger-horn, on which the strain pauses for a moment and then relapses into the even tenor of its way. With whatever jars in the execution, it is a grand symphony whose score is set in the human generations. The discord is not in the composition, but in the censorious critic's ear. But room is provided for the clarion of the prophet to interrupt the uniform sleepy notes in their course. Emerson arrived, after many a Hebrew and Pagan oracle, to blow the old trumpet again. To him how many owe it that they are now awake, while all the performers within hailing distance of the oracular summons and recall bend with new zeal to their several parts.

Mr. Arnold, who has forgot the dreams and got so bravely over the supposed illusions of his youth, putting for them the depressing doubts and hopeless speculations of his age, while he prizes Emerson's spiritual substance, eschews, as not good tissue, his literary style. Moses, David, Jesus as reported by his amanuenses, Paul too, and James, under this self-confident critic's cleaver must lose their heads, as writers and authors, on the same block. They too are no weavers of words, whose work is figured by the loom; but brief, sententious, pictorial, ejaculatory, a quiver

full of arrows being rather their type. Is there not
a good prophetic and oracular as well as a didactic
or dialectic style? Emerson's is not the only, and
may not be the best. It is not consecutive, a logical demonstration, or a spontaneous combustion. It
is neither a conflagration nor a flood. It is good
form, nevertheless. Its growth is not that of a flower,
but a gem. He makes of green wood a fire, sometimes hot, anon going out. He is an intermittent
geyser, a fountain that does not always play. But
he draws from the heart of Nature and the river of
God. Rationalizing writers spin from their brains:
he waits patient as a bivalve for the tide. It is not
passion, but peace, in this racket of the world of
mental uneasiness hushed and drowned so poorly by
travel in a million trains. When his tripod speaks,
it articulates the everlasting word. It is an even
motion, no spurt. Goodness, in Emerson, appears at
its high-water mark, — like the successive lines the
coast-tide leaves, as if it were ruled on the ocean-
cliffs. It was absolute, punctual worth. All the watches
oscillate and go a little wrong: he was like the Cambridge Observatory, and gave us sidereal time, but for
which to refer to there would be variations incorrigible and without end. His was no piecemeal probity.
Reverent, not abject; high, not haughty; pride and
humility one and the same. In the conflict between
the world-spirit and the Holy Spirit, in which the
former is so apt to get the upper hand, he was a
pentecostal man, planting himself on his instincts

till the huge world came round to him. He was not
content with average virtue, or with the available,
because unprincipled, nominee. The bawling dema-
gogue in yonder court-house, he told me, blew him,
as he walked, across the road with the breath of his
mouth. He refused his hand to the philanthropist
on the trickster's side. When Theodore Parker's Harvard College friends wanted to adjourn and lobby to
get for him a literary honor, the truthful, impolitic
Emerson voted not to postpone. In his tenderness
was pluck. Seeing what stuff his virtue was made
of, the article seems cheap which is hawked about
the streets. We thank him for another example of
what God cannot afford to throw away.

In the Italian engraving of Raphael's "Marriage of
the Virgin" is the imprint, that if the yet beardless
artist could produce such a work, never did finer
dawning announce a splendid day. I am reminded
of this inscription by Emerson's first sermons (passages of these from the manuscripts having been
read to me), which, though somewhat florid, prefigure
the style of his poems and essays. His language
from the first was like a reminting of old coins from
which edge and figure have been worn off. He knew
and could reveal the power that lurks in a word.
All words in their origin are potencies, dynamites,
few of which, as most writers place them, go off.
Emerson explodes his in a better fashion than elocu-
tionists teach; and they are not from his hands any
Nihilist's infernal machines. Never was war more

holy than he waged against injustice and untruth. Great as was his genius, it is surpassed by his moral worth. Reformers have their angles, philanthropists their bitter and uncharitable side. He gave to none gall and vinegar to drink. Should I be suffered to select the three great characters of American history, I should name Washington, Lincoln, — the lily out of Illinois mud, — and Emerson. In the religious sphere, Unitarianism has given us Channing; Methodism, Taylor; Quakerism, Whittier; Transcendentalism, Emerson, — a soul religious because reverent for what deserves to be revered. Plato says the child must be so revered by the parents that they will do nought they would not have him repeat. What gold or gems deserve to spell such a line! Goethe would teach reverence threefold, — for what is beneath as well as above and within. Emerson's posture was expectance to be surprised and pleased with divine revealings, which he watched for as astronomers for new heavenly bodies or for the aurora, never wanting himself to shine, but to be eclipsed. He longed for the Deity to come out of hiding in every person and at every point. It is a small testimony, but I have not known anybody who won more my own respect; and on such religiousness, as in certain quarters of fancied intelligence it goes out of fashion, let us lay stress. Emerson's thoughts and moods change. We must make an average or personal equation of them at diverse earlier or later times. But there is no need of a varying judgment or discount of what he

was, his last days his best.   His memory failed ; and
how much we can afford to forget !   His spiritual
growth did not cease or slow.   No American or contemporary in any land has had a finer brain ; but it
did not rob his heart of blood.   He was not of those
who think the universe a great Saturn devouring men,
and profess with equanimity to bury forever their
dead.   In his view, the agnostics and materialists

> "With science poorly mask their hurt."

He would not have written, at the end of life, of

> "The grief whose balsam never grew."

Emerson was a minister who had taken off the
gown.   As overseer of Harvard University, he thought
prayer the highest act of the human mind.   His was
a virile, not sentimental, vote.   To some his gracious
form and manner suggested a feminine mind ; and
his friend Henry James said one might feel a love
for him as for a woman.   But he was rugged in his
opinion as Bismarck or Carlyle.   I asked him if he
approved of war.   "Yes," he said, " in one born to
fight ; " as Theodore Parker predicted the sword to
cut our Gordian knot of human bonds.   He delighted
in the heat and onset of Phillips's oratory, preferring
Phillips in his difference with Garrison ; but afterwards changing his mind.   His own tenderness was
but the glove or gauntlet of force.   He said John
Brown had made the gallows glorious like the cross.
But the glory of the Kansas raids and of Harper's
Ferry, great as it may have been, was not the same

as that of Gethsemane and Calvary. One star differ-
eth from another star in glory; though, when the hero
of Osawatomie became a martyr, the halo round his
head was a complementary color, at least, to that in
which Jesus died, and the sun of righteousness set to
rise again. Emerson admired will and power; wanted
the leader and "self of the nation" to appear, and the
giants of a new race to leap over the Western hills.
It was the rough original vigor, not the coarseness,
that pleased him in Walt Whitman's lines. Not
executive himself, he rejoiced in personal prowess
and accomplishment, and repeated with glee Horatio
Greenough's story of General Jackson, that when a
bank deputation of business men waited on him to
protest against the financial policy of the administration, having listened courteously like a polite host,
the President made but this reply: "Gentlemen, have
you done? Then it only remains for me to send for
Mrs. Eaton to come with her broom and sweep you
all out of the Capitol." "That," added Greenough, "not
Mr. Webster's logic, is what I call ability." Emerson relished strength, a touch of the mailed hand in
speech and literature. Of an English lecturer, Professor Owen, very soft-spoken in his style but bold
in his views, he said, "He has a surgical smile." He
expected revolutions in our theories of the world, and
greeted that herald of evolutionary doctrine, "Ves-
tiges of Creation," which Agassiz called a second-rate
book. But all was from and for the worship which
made the span betwixt his Essays and his songs.

The last half-century of his life overcame the prejudice that began at his break with the Church ; and never by personal traits was won victory more complete.   His charm on whoever met him never failed.   Father Taylor said, if Emerson went to hell it would change the climate, and the emigration would be that way.   He himself said of a winsome preacher, " He need not speak while he looks thus ; " as he said of a certain political agitator, " His eyes are but holes in his head."   He has celebrated in verse how all the powers of the soul ride on the eye ; and there was a soft penetration in his own which expressed the perfect blending of wisdom and love, — the keenest curiosity and loftiest rapture of the human mind.

No man's faith is determined by his own wit alone.   Tradition, heredity, and human consent cannot be shut off, as from the smallest vessel the air cannot be quite pumped out.   Paul declares, " After the way called heresy, so worshipped I the God of my fathers."   Webster said his was the belief that came down.   Emerson advised accepting the venerable and majestic form of piety transmitted, without criticism too minute, seeing the critical faculty has metes and should keep within bounds.   In his Historical Discourse, in Concord, 1835, the period of his supposed treason to the Church, he speaks of those who since the planting of the town had served God and never let go the hope of immortality.   The acknowledgment of the Supreme Being, he adds, brought the fathers hither.   In his last word, at

Cambridge, on this theme, he tells the students that to lose this confidence is to take the sun out of the sky. The extreme Independent fancies religion a private conceit, every man to spin his own. An atheistic lecturer whom, though on my friendly invitation, Emerson did not want to see, seems to some to imagine he can untwist its whole cord from the heart of mankind. But the thread is wrought into our fibre, not by our fingers, but by many a million hands, like spindles driven by a head of power. It is threefold, — deity, duty, destiny.

I linger, and am loath to leave contemplating this fine nature, fair creature, beautiful soul, served by an intelligence like a powerful glass well adjusted in every joint and lens, through which when he looked, as Goethe said of himself, he saw all there was; whatever and whoever he turned his instrument toward being disclosed, — the quality, not quantity, being what he would find. In the blackberry pasture, a thicket of ripeness, he said to me, " Let us eat one berry," wishing not to please his palate, but distinguish the taste. He was prophetic, not historic ; gazing for daybreak, not sunset. Like Thoreau, — who, when he had made a perfect pencil, dropped that business to try something else, — for improvement everywhere Emerson longed and toiled with good cheer. Even the half-pound he weighed more than he thought, he took as an omen of better things. The crescent of the Saracen's banner should be engraved on his shield or carved on his tomb. He was

a beholder, not one of the players in any game of
blind-man's-buff. He was no abbot of unreason, but
organ of reason, holding nought a calamity leaving
him his eyes. How speak of his delight at these
first pictures in God's great gallery, which Nurse
Nature shows ? He did not believe he should, after
this hour of mortal life, be turned out. We commend him to the Christian conviction he with the
great Apostle shared : —

> " Then shall we see as we are seen,
>   And know as we are known."

Some men, great or potent and influential as rulers,
actors, orators, preachers, reformers in their time, live
only as traditions, and leave in language little record
of their career. Emerson's works remain, — nothing
in American or modern English literature destined to
have a longer date, notable I know not whether more
for the weight they carry or the height they reach.
As the condor outsoars the sparrow and wren, as the
frigate outsails the birch canoe, so what is strong in
thought is lasting and swift. Rare and delightful as
was his public or private speech, no man's words depend less on the manner and voice. They walk well
without their author ; or, like birds pushed over the
edge of the parent-nest, fly at once. Yet within recollection no decease from our midst has withdrawn an
element like his, — atmosphere to breathe, climate to
heal. Some in their day imposing figures we do not
miss. Their mission ends, their funeral is in order ;

it seems proper they should die; the coffin-lid closes fitly over their remains. But though Emerson had reached a great age, we were not ready to part with him. We felt him in the air. He was an important friend, companion, kinsman, fellow-citizen, to the last; a wayfarer everybody was glad to greet; one whose enemy none could continue to be; a charmer, whose spell was not to be escaped. In our fine silk or broadcloth we look out with shrinking terror on the tramp. Who are the tramps, but such as, in robes or rags, on foot or in phaeton, pervade this earthly region and consume the corn they do not produce, men and women without worth or use? I have spoken of one no tramp, but a worker and traveller in the kingdom of God.

"Standing in the blithe air, my head uplifted into infinite space," says Emerson, "all mean egotism vanishes." He was the air and the sun he stood in, and needed not to speak of them apart from himself. He was a social, yet insulated, man. Jesus had his wilderness, Paul his Arabia, Mahomet the desert, and the Persian poet

"Wise Saadi dwells alone."

Emerson addresses his own person, —

"Go, lonely man ;"

and he complains that no man goes alone. "Consider," said a disagreeable man, "you only have to see me occasionally, — once in a while. I never get away from myself." Few people can bear themselves long, — hardly any one all the time. Emerson likes the tumultuous privacy of the storm, dear hermitage of Nature. See the trains and ships! Whither go the travellers by land or sea? Not to Europe, to Asia, to the Yosemite, White Hills, or North Pole; but away from themselves, away from home, away from God, — from the mountains, the unexplored regions, the Holy Land in their own souls. Emerson abode in his breast.

> " Who bides at home, nor looks abroad,
>   Carries the eagle and masters the sword."

He could endure and enjoy his own company, which was the divine angelic company, and when guests came he missed his mighty gods. But he was less solitary in his closet than among the stars. He muses, like the psalmist, till the fire burns, of thought and love and worship. But Nature, dear as she was, did not eclipse his spiritual visions, nor worldly noise drown the inward voice so dreadful to Adam and to every sinner, but such a solace to the upright. The soul in him had hushed her secret strife and become a pure and free personality, — author, as he says so few are, of its own actions; an original force, not the property of any party or sect. He preaches independence. Man, to him, is the Fourth of July of zoölogy. He laments the confounding of individuals in the mass, as soldiers wear uniform, hacks are ticketed, and a prisoner takes the number of his cell.

But, says Edmund Burke, when bad men combine, the good should associate. Religiously and politically so they must and will. Emerson's word is the grain of salt to keep the association from corruption, sound and sweet.

In one of his papers Mr. Emerson speaks of the vast loss when the brain of a great scholar gives way. The treasure of his own knowledge of things or words seemed at the close hid from him or locked up, and he could not find the key. In this oblivion, with cessation of the power of productive work, there was a pathos and beauty of stillness. "We are very ancient," he would answer to my inquiry after his health. Sometimes he would gently whistle, as if at the vanity of all that passes, — as the forgetful wind sweeps off the dust mortal beauty crumbles into, singing by the way in some casement or Æolian harp. But his love and worship did not decay; what Jean Paul Richter calls the night-flower of faith still continued blooming. Kindly feeling remained, kindred affection occupied the space left vacant by dates and names. As in a building a number of small rooms are turned for some solemn or festal purpose into a large hall, the partitions were taken down in his soul to make a temple of friendship and praise. Memory was always less to him than hope. Complete remembrance clogs the wings of the spirit ready to soar. Heaven is no rehearsal of the earth. He thought men overweighed with their past. "And he died, and he died," he said to me with wet eyes, of the brother who departed, for us, too soon.

> "Ask on, thou clothed eternity,
> Time is the false reply."

He is learning the meaning of his own words.

There are those who consider it impious to compare living worth with any old character sanctioned in the canon and the calendar. No person present in the world or lately deceased must be likened to Abraham, to Moses, to Jesus or Paul. Alas, we cannot detect a saint in the man round the corner or behind the door! There is no woman to rank as musician with Miriam, or is just such a seamstress as Dorcas! It were to mix sacred and profane. But,

> "Seigniors, are the old Niles dry?"

Has God failed? Are the prophets no more? Is there no vision now? We should almost be sorry the seers ever lived on earth, if they are dead and no member of their class survives. Every such example as I have been called to hold up is a protest against making ancient merit discredit that of to-day. Truth is as bright, love is as warm, adoration as lofty and uplifting now as thousands of years ago. A pianist said to me, there is a stamp of fine gold on Beethoven no later composer should expect to match; as if an old coin discovered in a pyramid, or a bit of the candlestick Titus robbed from the Temple at Jerusalem, had metal in it all the mines of Australia and California put together could not equal or repay ! The earth still yields. Heaven's breast is not shrunk. It nurses the soul still: else itself were empty and at fault.

Our error or superstition is to mistake a man for a principle, and identify a name with a type. No name can be the whole thing ! Character is always current. God does not fall below himself. The human race is not running out. The light of the sun in the sky is as good as ever, and that of right-eousness in Asia or America cannot fail. Emerson was a pattern of integrity. As Goethe said of one, *this is a nature,* of peculiar property and singular impression, not to be confounded with any other, — remarkable for quality, not quantity. "God loveth not size." Not the mass of his head, but the lines in his face, expressed him. To be moderate and to omit was his gift. "Always understate," he said to Mr. Alcott.

> " I hung my verses in the wind ;
>   Time and tide their faults may find.
>   Have you eyes to find the five
>   Which five hundred did survive ? "

He said the chief excellence of style is suppres-sion, — an expedient so cheap, it is strange it is so seldom used. Reading a paper, he asked one by his side, in the midst of his recital, with wonderful modesty, if he had not better stop; as Rubinstein whispered to me of his piano recital, when all ears hung on his touch, "It is too long." They who move the world in art or government or war — Homer,

Shakspeare, Michael Angelo, Cæsar, Bonaparte — must have for part of their genius abundance, long flight, a certain precise aim and avoirdupois weight. Emerson, unsurpassed in height, lacked the spread and the motion or impulse of ambition to achieve. He was content to be clean and godly and deliver his soul. He leaves no single extensive performance. He was not caught, impressed, or enlisted by any one idea, object, or aspect of things. He makes no epic or drama. His songs are swallow-flights on eagle's wings. He coolly surveyed and reported, but did not conceive he had any special mission or part to enact, so he could be, as he was, faithful and true. Like Swedenborg, he united the keenest perception to a mystic sense. We may amend or complete, we cannot annihilate, his report. He did deliver his soul. He was essentially religious. The world to him was a haunted house : he never got over his surprise at being in it as one of the ghosts. "Wrangle who will, I will wonder." If he finds himself now in heaven, it is no astonishment to him, as he has had his surprise already on the earth. To exist is all. A genuine man, he was weakened by no contradiction in his own mind. From his influence there is no subtraction of a deviation or fault. He was whole, a sum total of wisdom and will. What he meant and was meant for was the same. Others might not agree with him ; he agreed with himself. He had below the "manners of the sky."

Only to hint a subject, not to explain a man, am I willing to speak. Into no pound of metaphysic can we drive the soul. Emerson thought Plato with his dialectic had but bit this apple of the world on one side. Rubinstein said all were ruined, were all found out. Our mind is the numeral for this cipher of the sphere; but it cannot fathom itself. We at once get beyond soundings when we launch on the intellectual sea. The North Pole seems to resent our search after its mysteries; but when ships sail across where the meridians meet, there will be a cover of Nature still remaining which no explorer will penetrate or break up. God and Heaven submit not to be analyzed. Our faith in the one, our hope of the other, is an instinct whose root is in both. But as abstractions they furnish no soil for any growth. We must contemplate them with our affections in the living creation, and in the concrete, before we can realize them in our thought or express them in our life. Sought as the net result of our logic, they vanish into thin air. With his imagination for an eye, Emerson was a perceiver; and he respected perception in himself and others, being as quick and glad to quote their perceptions as to announce his own. He notes, cites, and lauds every scrap of insight, or ripple of tidings over the ocean that heaves from the unknown shore toward which he sails.

10

VI.

EMERSON AS PREACHER.

By MISS E. P. PEABODY.

WHEN Mr. Sanborn wrote to me that I was appointed to this lecture, he told me that the subject assigned to me was " Mr. Emerson as Preacher," — not " Mr. Emerson in the Pulpit," as it stands in the printed programme. But I hold on to what I had immediately agreed to do, for I think Mr. Emerson was always pre-eminently the preacher to his own generation and future ones, but as much — if not more — out of the pulpit as in it; faithful unto the end to his early chosen profession and the vows of his youth. Whether he spoke in the pulpit or lyceum chair, or to friends in his hospitable parlor, or *tête-à-tête* in his study, or in his favorite walks in the woods with chosen companions, or at the festive gatherings of scholars, or in the conventions of philanthropists, or in the popular assemblies of patriots in times and on occasions that try men's souls, — always and everywhere it was his conscious purpose to utter a " Thus saith the Lord." It was, we may say, a fact of his pre-existence. Looking back through eight generations of Mr. Emerson's paternal ancestry, we find there were preachers in every one of them; the first being one of those Independents whom Archbishop Laud made an attempt to constrain to uniformity by dictating to him how he should regard the Sabbath, and on other ritualistic points, which the spirit of Luther's Reformation had reserved for the private judgment of redeemed souls. It marks the intrinsic conscience of Peter Bulkeley, that he would neither conform with his English pulpit, nor relinquish his profession; for he was a man of fortune, living on his hereditary property, and rich enough to live a layman's life amid the luxury of a scholar's leisure, which he was educated to value. But there was that spirit of consecration to his calling which seems a divine predestination, that compelled him to leave house and lands and turn his steps towards the Western wilderness, and dare all the dangers and hardships of breaking his way in it, to found a colony which was to be an independent church among the Indians. With them he made *concord* — which named the town — by a just purchase of land, and a Christian benevolence to them that was indeed not without parallel among the Independents. These Independents are never to be confounded with the later Puritans, who organized the pharisaical community that proudly denied the right of citizenship to Indians and all others not church-members, and also initiated a military policy towards the former that they attempted to justify to themselves from the Bible narrative of the conquest of Canaan by the children of Israel, — not discriminating the originally friendly, hospitable, trustful, and moral Indian from the heathen of ancient Syria, who were themselves recent invaders of that country, where they had established the cruellest and most licentious customs known in all antiquity; "passing their children through the fire to Moloch," and making the most vicious practices their rites of worship.

There is extant, in the public library of Concord, a volume of the writings of Peter Bulkeley, which, though in the form of the repulsive theology of the day, will prove, on careful analysis, to any thoughtful reader, that Mr. Emerson's remote ancestor had a spirit like his own, not to be paralyzed by ecclesiasticism or by the letter of sacred Scripture, but intrinsically moral, — worshipping God, not for his power, but for his righteousness. It is interesting to know — and it explains Mr. Emerson's affectionate relations with Concord — that many of the old families of Concord, besides the Emersons, of various names, are descendants of this grand old Independent. Mr. Emerson's grandfather, who died a chaplain of the Revolutionary army, consecrated the first fight of our war for civil independence with a prayer on the battle-field ; and his grandmother watched the fight from the study window of the Old Manse. Mr. Emerson's father, too, became minister of the First Church of Boston, in the meridian of his life, and was one of the earliest leaders of the liberal movement in that

city which ended in the Unitarian protest. This
second Mr. William Emerson left a family of sons
to the care of a mother who belonged to the excep-
tionally pious race of Haskins, strongly inclined to
mysticism in religion; and by this temperament the
desirable contrast was made with the more intellectual Emerson temperament; so that the union of
clear, cold intellect and warm, religious heart in the
subject of our discourse seems a divine providence.
Considering these antecedents, it is not surprising
that these brothers all naturally gravitated to the profession of preacher. The outlook at the time, however,
was not alluring to scions of the old Independent.
Although William Emerson, the eldest brother, went
to Germany to study for the Christian ministry, he
had not the nerve of his great ancestor; and, on
his return, shrank from the battle that he had dis-
cernment enough to see was impending, and took up
what he deemed the kindred profession of law. Edward and Charles also entered the latter profession,
with the most serious conceptions of its ideal, and
neither for fame nor fortune, — both being strong
Christians of the heroic old type. Our Mr. Emerson
always spoke of these brothers as his spiritual and
intellectual superiors; but I was told, by one who
knew them all intimately, that both of them regarded
him as the high-priest of their Holy of holies, rever-
encing his every intuition as a sacred oracle. Mr.
Emerson's poem, entitled " The Dirge," is the memorial of this rare fraternal relation.

My own acquaintance with Mr. Emerson dated from 1822, when I took a few private lessons from him in Greek, — a study that he was at the time immersed in, having just graduated from Harvard University, and being an assistant in the young ladies' school kept in his mother's house in Federal Street by his brother William. Mr. Conway mentions this circumstance in his very beautiful apotheosis of Mr. Emerson; and, as usual, entirely transforms, by his imaginative memory, something I probably did tell him, which I will take leave to repeat here, as I have often told it myself. It is true that both of us were very shy (Mr. Emerson then nineteen and I eighteen years old), and we did not get into a chatting acquaintance, but sat opposite each other at the study table, not lifting our eyes from our books, — I reciting the poems of the " Græca Majora," and he commenting and elucidating in the most instructive manner; and we were quite too much afraid of each other to venture any other conversation. When about to leave the city for what proved a two years' sojourn on the Kennebec, I sent for his bill, through his cousin George B. Emerson, who had introduced him to me. He came with that gentleman to say that he had no bill to render, for he found he could teach me nothing. It was then that, protected by his cousin's presence, he ventured to speak freely; and he poured out quite a stream of eloquence in praise of Mr. Edward Everett's oratory, of which I happened to express my admiration, and was delighted to find him as great an admirer of it as I was. Mr. Everett had just returned from Europe, and was lecturing in Boston on the panorama of Athens, which Mr. Theodore Lyman had presented to Harvard College. After this our acquaintance lapsed for ten years, comprehending all the time Mr. Emerson was studying divinity and preaching at the Second Church in Boston. Then he resumed it (in 1833) on occasion of reading a little paper of mine which his aunt, Miss Mary Emerson, — who was my great friend, and bent on bringing us into intimate acquaintance, — had found among some loose papers of a journal of thoughts I fitfully kept, on the same principle that Mr. Emerson kept a journal all his life. This paper was a very free paraphrase of the first chapter of the Gospel of Saint John, from the first verse to the fourteenth inclusive, in which I translated the word Logos into " moral truth-speaking," first by the things of Nature, then by the processes of conscious life and reason, etc.

He was on the eve of his first voyage to Europe, soon after the death of his first wife and the relinquishment of his Boston pulpit. He was at the time too feeble in health to make visits, and sent to me to come to his house in Chardon Street, where I found him quite absorbed in Goethe and Carlyle ; but he immediately turned his attention to Saint John's grand peroration, and we discussed every phrase of it. It was one of those conversations which " make the soul," to use a favorite expression of his aunt Mary's. It was, therefore, on the highest plane of human thought that we first met, our theme being the Eternal Relations of God, Nature, and Man; beginning an intercourse that continued there with more or less interval during his lifetime.

I had never heard Mr. Emerson preach while he was settled in Boston, for I was then always attending Dr. Channing's church, and so I did not learn the exceptional character of his preaching. My attention was first drawn to it by hearing that he had preached the sermon on the Lord's Supper that led to the loss of his pulpit. I heard of this from Dr. Channing, who at the same time expressed immense interest in so striking a proof of the moral independence as well as profound sincerity of the act. I remember he said he expected great things of him in future. He then told me that Mr. Emerson had, as was the custom of that day, put his name with him as a student when he began his study of divinity; but he had not become intimate with him, because he found, on talking with him, that he was quite competent to be his own guide, so far as human teaching could go. Dr. Channing himself had no desire to be Rabbi to any individual, nor a leader in the Church. He thought, as Mr. Emerson did, that one's own intellect and conscience, *used reverently*, were the best leaders of the spirit of a man into communion with the God of Truth.

Immediately after Mr. Emerson's return from

Europe, hearing he was to preach a sermon in his old pulpit, on occasion of the death of his friend Mr. Sampson (the most intimate friend he had had in his parish), I went to hear him. The sermon was a word-portrait of Mr. Sampson, which estimated him as the ideal Christian merchant. It was a wonderful discourse, as it seemed to me, who was familiar with, and had grown up on, the liveliest preaching of the time,—that of the leading Unitarians in the first vital vigor of their honest protest against the current Tritheism (for the doctrine of the Trinity had sunk to that in all the churches, whether old Congregational, Baptist, or Episcopal).

He began with saying that we might well doubt whether, if we had been contemporaries with Plato, we had found him out, if we did not find out in our own time some individuals who, like Plato, were in manifest living relation with the Infinite Mind in thought, or heart, or practical life. In the darkest times there were "seven thousand men in Israel who had not bowed the knee to Baal." There was even now some open vision. Mr. Sampson had this open vision ; and he invited his audience to contemplate with him his "conversation in the world," more especially in his business relations ; for in business, he said, as well as on the tower of contemplation, men could live with God face to face.[1]

---

[1] When, soon after its delivery, I begged Mr. Emerson to publish this sermon, which, it seemed to me, would immediately transform and elevate the practices of the business world in Boston, he

From this time forth I never omitted an opportunity of hearing Mr. Emerson preach. I went out from Boston to East Lexington to do so when I learned he was preaching there; and subsequently, when visiting at his house, as I frequently did in the first six years of his married life, I sought and obtained leave to read the sermons he had in manuscript. And I am free to affirm that they were all as truly transcendental as any of his later lectures and writings in prose or verse; if a volume of them could be printed to-day in their own form, it would interpret his later revelations, of which they are but a varied expression, and be of great advantage to a certain class of minds. I remember one upon the text, "We shall all appear before the judgment-seat of Christ," which, if it could be read in this place to-day, would, better than all my poor words, convey the view I would fain give of Mr. Emerson as always the preacher of the eternal life, entirely emancipated from the "letter which killeth," and minister of the Spirit which maketh alive. It showed his audience, and would show any reader of it, that we all are always before the judgment-seat of Christ, — always God is judging the world and passing sentence on every man, and he may hear it if he be sincere. There is no valid excuse for want of self-knowledge. The judgment-seat of Christ is

told me he had given it to Mrs. Sampson. I trust that Mr. Cabot will look it up and give it to the public even now; for, like everything else of Mr. Emerson's, it is of perennial interest.

within each of us, where we shall find it if we look for it earnestly, instead of the *ipse dixit* of the hour.

I wish I had time to speak of many other discourses that are fresh in my memory after more than forty years. In reading and comparing Mr. Emerson's two discourses, preached at forty years' interval, — the one the Divinity Hall Address, given in 1838 ; the other bearing the title of " The Preacher," in 1880, — it may be plainly seen that he was always a preacher of the Christ whose " glory was with the Father before the world was," " the same yesterday, to-day, and forever." But, from first to last, he never shut in his vision of the living God to the limitations of his own or any other individual conception ; for he dwelt and spoke in that temple of the moral sentiment in which all men commune with all other men as children of a common, impartial Father of the human race, and which, in the language of the old school-men, is " the Son," to whom " the Father giveth to have life in himself," in order that He may " behold His own glory in his face." Mr. Emerson understood and believed with Froebel — the cosmopolite prophet of the nineteenth century — what Jesus meant when he said that " whoever receiveth a little child in my name receiveth me, and whoever receiveth me receiveth Him that sent me."[1] Jesus of Nazareth realized to

[1] He says, in one of his Essays, " Infancy is a perpetual Messiah, which comes into the arms of fallen men, and pleads with them to return to Paradise."

him "the divinity that is in all men," — the divinity that first appears in the moral sentiment. He declares, in the Divinity Hall Address, that "the moral sentiment is the essence of all religion ; for," as he goes on to explain, "if a man is at heart just, then in so far is he God ; the immortality of God, the majesty of God, do enter into that man with justice."

I would I had space to copy out the whole of that pæan of praise to God living in the moral law, which makes the introduction to that wonderful discourse, whose eloquence is characteristic of him, — not like the whirlwind, the earthquake, or the fire, but the still, small voice, on hearing which Elijah veiled his face and worshipped. Who reads it with understanding will agree that Professor Thayer has well said : "There is in Emerson an inflaming religious quality which searches the soul of his readers with singular power. His morals are not merely morals ; they are morals on fire."

But to go back a little. In 1835 or 1836, when he was still supplying the pulpit at East Lexington, it was my privilege to make frequent visits to his house in Concord, and he would always invite me to go down with him in his chaise on Sundays. In one of these precious seasons for conversation, as we were returning to Concord, I repeated to him the reply of an unconsciously wise and pious woman of the congregation, with whom I had walked to the afternoon meeting, and had asked her why the society did not call to settle over them an eminent preacher that Mr. Emerson had sent in his stead on a previous Sunday, secretly hoping that they would do so, for he craved him as a near neighbor. "Oh, Miss Peabody," her words were, "we are a very simple people here; we cannot understand anybody but Mr. Emerson." "There is a 'tell' for a Transcendentalist," said I to him playfully, thinking he would laugh in contrasting it with the current cant in Boston among the Philistines, who said they "could not understand Mr. Emerson." But he did not laugh. On the contrary, with an accent that was almost pathetic, he replied, "If I had not been cut off untimely in the pulpit, perhaps I might have made something of the sermon." "It is evident from this attentive Lexington audience," I said, "that you have already made something of the sermon." "Did you observe," he replied, "that row of venerable, earnest faces of old men who sit just in front of the platform? It would be rather difficult to be frivolous when speaking to them. But in the back part of the hall there were some young men turning over the leaves of a hymn-book. No preacher can be satisfied with himself when he leaves any of his audience at leisure to turn over the leaves of a book." "That is a high standard," I replied. And soon he added, in a livelier tone, "Henceforth the lyceum chair must be my pulpit. The word of moral truth makes one of any place." And we both fell into silence for the remainder of our drive, as I went back in thought to that old conversation in Chardon Street, on the proem of Saint John's Gospel.

I think I have shown you reason to agree with me that it was Mr. Emerson's conscious life-purpose to minister the Living Spirit, whom he sought alike in the material universe and in human history, in literature and in ethics, in art, and, above all, in his own heart and imagination. In every form of his utterance he touched the profound depth of poetry, whether he sung in verse or spoke in prose. Much of his prose is as melodious as his verse, — witness his first publication on "Nature," his lecture on the "Method of Nature," and the opening, and indeed the whole, of his Address at Divinity Hall, already alluded to, which was not to me alone the apocalypse of our Transcendental era in Boston. For, if the life-less understanding of the day mistook it for a denial of Christ, we now see that upon those whose hearts "the forms of young imagination had kept pure," and whom the pulpit entirely ignored or seldom addressed, it flashed the first light of the revelation of "the friend of man," whom he then affirmed that an effete ecclesiasticism had made "the enemy of man."

And here I take leave to introduce another personal reminiscence. I had the happiness of listening to this truly prophetic discourse; and when, soon after, he was correcting the proof-sheets of it for the press, I was visiting at his house. One day he came from his study into the room where his wife and myself were sitting at our needle-work, and said, "How does this strike your Hebrew souls?" proceeding to read the paragraph containing the above expression, which begins with the words, "This Eastern monarchy of a Christianity," etc. I said, "You will put a capital 'F' to the word 'friend'?" He seemed to reflect a few moments, and then deliberately replied, "No; directly I put that capital 'F' my readers go to sleep!"

He then went on to read another paragraph, which he remarked he had omitted to deliver because he thought he "was getting too long." It came immediately after the paragraph in which he accused the "historical Christianity" of corrupting all attempts to communicate living religion, "making Christianity a mythus, and founding the Church not on Jesus' principles, but on his tropes," and subordinating all individual natures to that of Jesus, "according to the portrait the vulgar drew of him."

I can recall only one word of this omitted paragraph, but remember perfectly the sense. It was a *caveat* anticipating the development of a new party, only half understanding him, which would fall into what he called the "puppyism" of a criticism irreverent of the person of Jesus. And this party did soon appear, and has not entirely passed away yet; some of our free religionists being guilty of this lack of just conception of "the one man who, alone in all history," as Mr. Emerson says, "estimated the greatness of man! One man was true to what is in

you and me. He saw that God incarnated himself
in man; and in the ecstasy of a sublime emotion
affirmed, 'through me God acts, through me God
speaks; would you see God, see me.'" I said, inter-
rogatively, "You will certainly print that passage,
for it will convict Mr. Ware of misunderstanding
and so misrepresenting you in his sermon." (Mr.
Henry Ware had just published a sermon contro-
verting, as he thought, the doctrine of Mr. Emerson's Address.) This was an unlucky suggestion of
mine; for, after a moment's silence, he replied: "No,
it would be shabby to spring upon Mr. Ware this
passage now. I must abide by what I delivered, whatever was its lack of full expression." I was struck
silent at the moment by this exhibition of an exquisite gentlemanly loyalty, the very poetry of self-
respect and politeness. But some months later, irri-
tated by many exhibitions of the "puppyism" he
had predicted, and which stupidly professed itself to
be Emersonian, I said to him, "Are you quite sure
you did not sacrifice a greater duty to a less, when
you decided not to publish that paragraph which
defined your exact meaning, lest it should put Mr.
Ware in the awkward predicament of having fought
a shadow?" He replied, deliberately but emphatically, "No." I wish I could remember to repeat in its
exact words the conversation that followed. I know
he expressed that gentlemanly courtesy was simply
social justice, and that anxiety to be personally understood, rather than to have the truth understood, was

the special weakness of the hour. Apology, and even explanation, were the blunders of egotism. Words were often more deceptive than silence, because of the meanings attached to them by a public which had ceased to think. He ended the conversation by saying, in illustration of his meaning, " Whoever would preach Christ in these times must say nothing about him !" These words, uttered in that low tone of the moral imperative, which all who heard his first lectures must remember, let me completely into the secret of his method, giving me the key to unlock the meaning alike of what he said and what he did not say. As I pondered on it that day, I called to mind the words of Jesus as reported by Saint John from his discourse at the last supper : " It is expedient for you that I go away from you ; unless I go away, the Spirit of truth, which is the Comforter, will not come unto you."

Whether Mr. Emerson is to be followed by others in this severe method of preaching the Christ by devout silence, may perhaps be a question. The late Mr. Maurice, who suffered from the ecclesiastical verbosity and ritual trifling of his time a lifelong martyrdom, as the recently published memoirs of him reveal, answered a similar question by dropping from his vocabulary the word Christianity, seeing it to be a human abstraction merely, confusing those seeking the secret of life with as many significations as there are denominations in the Church, and individual thinkers; therefore leading away from that divine

11

life manifested in Jesus Christ *par eminence.* Both Maurice and his most effective apostle, George Macdonald, always say Christ, instead of Christianity, when they would set forth the true goal of human living, as the deliverer from the vicious subjectivity of the mere thinker which dries up the fountains of life. With the same intent Mr. Emerson said that it was the duty of the individual to affirm all that his experience had proved to be true, and never to be satisfied short of a generalization covering a principle. He had the faith that our growing experience would contain the solution of all questions, the consummation of all hopes, the satisfaction of all unselfish desires, inasmuch as the social law was intercommunication of experiences forevermore. His humility was a quickening hope, not a weak agnosticism, — the humility of a son of God who feels that all that his Father has will duly become his. He never presumes to call the Unknown unknowable.

But I do not mean to say that the "golden silence" which heightened the effect of Mr. Emerson's "silvern speech," when he preached those truths that he felt were hidden from his times by the prevalent technics of the pulpit, was a prudential expedient that he contrived to meet a practical difficulty: it came from something deeper and higher, that characterized his individuality; it was the unforgotten instinct of the child, who often cannot utter the name of God, precisely because he sees Him with the spiritual eye of pre-existence. I heard Mr. Emerson once say to Mr. Orestes A. Brownson, who was pressing on him the duty of explanation, "I feel myself to be in the midst of a truth I do not comprehend, but which comprehends me." It was this truth before which he bowed with the devoutness which hushes the Hindoo worshipper to the utterance of the mystic Om; which makes the Hebrew, when in the books of the Law and Prophets he comes to the word Jehovah (which means *was and is and is to come*, translated in the Pentateuch "the Lord God," and in the Septuagint "the Eternal"), to stop and bow in silence; which impels a worshipper to fall on his face and shut out the light (that is defined by Hegel as "the presence of the Universal at the particular," whether we mean material light, or Reason with its relative poles); which made the army of the angels in Milton's magnificent fable "veil their faces with their wings" when the chariot of Christ rolled in a bloodless victory over the battle-field of heaven, and found no contending armies, for the enemy had vanished as soon as "far-off his coming shone." In Mr. Emerson, the Infinite of Being was an intuition "beyond the reach of thought," which is the act of the growing understanding, likened by himself to a man going out in a dark night with a farthing candle to find something. What he discovered with his farthing candle he declared, in words that shine and words that burn, putting his readers at a stand-point open on all sides to the sky of the Universal Truth, which comprehends the seer and the seen too ; and then, with the delicate reserve of a spiritual modesty which never says " I," he pauses, to let his hearer or reader supply the ellipses, not attempting to utter the unutterable, which we nevertheless know as we know the fixed stars, wondering what they are. Such silence is eloquent.

> " The silent organ loudest chants
> The master's requiem."

But the individual's right of reserve Mr. Emerson severely limited to boundaries of his experience. He recognized the duty of every individual, who is a fraction of his generation, on which is doubtless laid the obligation to transmit what it has received from foregone generations, augmented by what he has gained from his own experience in its characteristic individuality ; but this truth could only be expressed in words illuminated by action strictly according to the nature of things, — a phrase he generally used for action according to the will of God ; for he avoided using words whose meaning he agreed with and even reverenced, when their original lustre had been lost by long lying in the dusty ruts of the highways of custom.

And no more than Jesus, who "without a parable opened not his mouth," did Mr. Emerson preach merely in the pulpit form of sermons. He preached still more in song, when his intellect, as well as morals, is seen to be on fire, in worship. Witness

the "Ode to Beauty." Beauty is to him no abstraction made by his own mind from lovely concrete
forms, but the " Infinite One " —

> "gliding through the sea of form,
> Like the lightning through the storm,
> Somewhat not to be possessed,
> Somewhat not to be caressed ; "

to whom, in a transport of devout ecstasy, he prays,

> "Dread Power, but dear
> If God thou be,
> Unmake me quite,
> Or give thyself to me !"

And again, in "The Problem," where he sings of the
genesis, not of Nature's "beauteous forms" alone, but
of the mind's creations, — the great sculptures of
antiquity, the architectures of Egypt, Greece, Rome,
and the Middle Ages, — "the litanies of nations," "the
canticles of love and woe," and all the wonders that
"rise in upper air"

> "Out of thought's interior sphere."

For the Infinite Goodness and the Infinite Beauty live
also as the Infinite Truth, whose coming "full circle"
he celebrates in the "Uriel," — another anthem of
praise to Him who is to be worshipped with all the
mind as well as heart and might; and all three are
summed in the "Ode to Bacchus" (the Greek Bacchus,
not the Roman), in which he so importunately prays

to be "given to drink" of the "wine that never grew
in the belly of the grape:" —

> " Wine of wine,
>   Blood of the world,
>   Form of forms, and mould of statures,
>   That I, intoxicated,
>   And by the draught assimilated,
>   May float at pleasure through all natures,
>   The bird-language rightly spell,
>   And that which roses say so well.
>
>   .   .   .   .   .   .
>
> " Pour, Bacchus ! the remembering wine ;
>   Retrieve the loss of me and mine !
>   Vine for vine be antidote,
>   And the grape requite the lote !
>   Haste to cure the old despair, —
>   Reason in Nature's lotus drenched,
>   The memory of ages quenched ;
>   Give them again to shine ;
>   Let wine repair what this undid ;
>   And where the infection slid,
>   A dazzling memory revive ;
>   Refresh the faded tints,
>   Recut the aged prints,
>   And write my old adventures with the pen
>   Which on the first day drew,
>   Upon the tablets blue,
>   The dancing Pleiads and eternal men."

And again in the " Woodnotes," when he hears the
pine-tree declare : —

> " Ever fresh the broad creation,
>   A divine improvisation,
>   From the heart of God proceeds,
>   A single will, a million deeds.

Once slept the world an egg of stone,
And pulse and sound and light had none ;
And God said, ' Throb !' and there was motion,
And the vast mass became vast ocean,

.   .   .   .   .   .

Pouring of his power the wine
To every age, to every race ;
Unto every race and age
He emptieth the beverage ;
Unto each and unto all,
Maker and original.
The world is the ring of his spells,
And the play of his miracles.
As he giveth all to drink,
Thus or thus they are and think.
He giveth little, he giveth much,
To make them several or such.
With one drop sheds form and feature,
With the second special nature ;
The third adds heat's indulgent spark ;
The fourth gives light which eats the dark ;
In the fifth drop himself he flings,
And conscious Law is King of kings."

Time would fail me to give specimens of all the utterances of this tongue of fire, which retrieves the disastrous confusion of the old Babel, that has corrupted by dividing the religion of nations, and eclipsed the Eternal Christ almost totally ; while Mr. Emerson in his use of the words Brahm, Pan, Apollo, the Greek Bacchus, Uriel, and other burning personifications of the Persian Muse, revivifies the Pentecostal Muse and brings home to the imagination of this duller modern time the various attributes of the Eternal Spirit ; making a language of his own, that creates unity of understanding in all who speak the differing and therefore imperfect languages of man in their partial creeds. Do we not hear this in the great lyric utterances I have already recited? To which I must add, from "The Sphinx," the answer of the poet to her conundrum: —

> "Deep love lieth under
>   These pictures of time;
> They fade in the light of
>   Their meaning sublime!
>
> "The fiend that man harries
>   Is love of the Best;
> Yawns the pit of the Dragon
>   Lit by rays from the Blest;
> The Lethe of Nature
>   Can't trance him again,
> Whose soul sees the Perfect,
>   Which his eyes seek in vain.
>
> "Profounder, profounder,
>   Man's spirit must dive;
> To his aye-rolling orbit
>   No goal will arrive;
> The heavens that now draw him
>   With sweetness untold,
> Once found, — for new heavens
>   He spurneth the old.
>
> "Pride ruined the angels,
>   Their shame them restores;
> And the joy that is sweetest
>   Lurks in stings of remorse."

Do not these last two lines contain the deepest secret of the Christ that Jesus revealed, — God's forgiveness of sin, which justifies the supreme gift of the freedom to will, through which man may be lifted into the divine sonship, eternal in the bosom of the Father, — a vast overpayment even for the experience of sin, which being overcome, qualifies us to seek and save others?

> " Draw if thou canst the mystic line
> Severing rightly his from thine,
> Which is human, which divine."

I will not attempt to read the whole of what is to me the most profoundly touching of all Emerson's divine songs, the " deep Heart's " reply in the " Threnody," when he himself came up from the most transforming personal experience of his life, expressed in that wild wail over the child lost to him for " the forever of this world," that for a long time plunged him into a deep of sorrow of which the first part of the poem is the all but unequalled expression. But at length he found what fully developed the human tenderness, that gave the last divine touch to the decline of his life. I have said that this rich strain of poetry was of all his utterances the most touching to me. For several years before this season of his personal experience he was struggling to bear the loss of his brother Charles with the dignity of a man. To the question I had put to him, " Is there not something in God corresponding to and justifying this human sensibility?" he had replied, " No!" And at that period of his life he seemed to measure spiritual strength by a man's stoical denial of the fact of pain. His intellectual fire could not smelt the ore of human suffering. A gentleman who stood with him at his brother Charles's grave, said he turned away from it with the words, " Death is an absurdity ! "

It required nothing short of a father's love to open his ear to the tender voice of the Divine Father, who sung in his bereaved heart this healing song : —

> " I came to thee, as to a friend,
>   Dearest! to thee I did not send
>   Tutors, but a joyful eye,
>   Innocence that matched the sky,
>   Lovely locks, a form of wonder,
>   Laughter rich as woodland thunder,
>   That thou might'st entertain apart
>   The richest flowering of all art:
>   And, as the great all-seeing Day
>   Through smallest chambers takes its way,
>   That thou might'st break thy daily bread
>   With prophet, Saviour, and Head ;
>   That thou might'st cherish for thine own
>   The riches of sweet Mary's Son,
>   Boy-Rabbi, Israel's paragon!
>   And thoughtest thou such guest
>   Would in thy hall take up his rest?
>
>   .   .   .   .   .   .
>
>   High omens ask diviner guess !
>
>   .   .   .   .   .   .
>
>   To-morrow, when the masks shall fall
>   That dizen Nature's carnival,
>   The Pure shall see by their own will,
>   Which overflowing Love shall fill.

> 'T is not within the power of fate,
> The fate-conjoined to separate.
>
> . . . . .
>
> . . . what is excellent,
> As God lives, is permanent.
> Hearts are dust ; heart's loves remain ;
> Heart's love will meet thee again ! "

Not only do all his great apocalyptic chants, but nearly all his smaller pieces, — such as, " Rhea," "Each and All," " The Rhodora," " Hamatreya," " Lines to J. W." (I might copy out the whole table of contents from his two volumes of poetry), — seem a true preaching, even " The Mountain and the Squirrel," in this instance keenly practical, sometimes catching up our spirits into the vision of principles, sometimes kindling private virtue and patriotic heroism, and sometimes plunging the soul into the unfound infinite. In one of his lectures he defined prayer as, "a plunge into the unfound infinite." It seems to me, therefore, that I am not irreverent, but reverent, when, as my last word, I say of him, more and more " the multitude hears him gladly," for, like Jesus, he preaches " with authority," and not as the Scribes.

POSTSCRIPT.

There was no time for a conversation after I closed my reading, as Mrs. Cheney's lecture and mine had taken up the usual time of the session; but to a question that was asked just as we broke up, " What was Mr. Emerson's attitude towards religious institutions ? " I will here take leave to reply. It was an essentially temporary one, like that he held to the technics of the pulpit of his day. His attitude towards the Lord's Supper naturally brought him into sympathy with the Quakers on the point of stated times for public prayer; and he actually ceased to go to meeting on Sundays because church-going also had at that time become merely perfunctory. But I heard him say, at that very date, that to meet together to consider all our duties in the light of the Divine Omnipresence was by far the most legitimate of human assemblies; and he considered it a great misfortune to society that it had become such a routine that "a devout person" (he meant his own ardently Christian wife) said, "It seems wicked to go to church."

At the time he ceased to go to church he was making a pulpit of the study-table where he composed his lectures. He never abandoned his office of preacher. I heard him say, in the last half of his life, "My special parish is young men inquiring their way of life." He always favored their free access to him, and it would not be easy to count those to whom a *tête-à-tête* with him gave the clew of Life eternal.

In the last of his life, when the infirmities of old age tied his tongue, and he could no longer minister the word of moral truth to others, he resumed his early habit of going to church himself on Sundays; and his wife told me he thanked her for bringing up his children to do so.

VII.

EMERSON AMONG THE POETS.

By F. B. SANBORN.

I WISH to speak of Emerson, and not merely of a poet; for to me he was a poet and much more. And therefore my theme is, " Emerson among the Poets," — the man whom we saw and heard, and read and loved, amidst those men with whom his gifts gave him rank; who, like him, were poets and something more. It was among his gifts that he could feel the poetic impulse not only in himself but in others; that he knew and tested high poesy, not so much by a critical faculty and by study, as by native inspiration and appreciation. The great poets addressed him as one of themselves; he was not of their audience, but of their choir. Homer says : —

> " The gods are to each other not unknown,
> Though far apart they dwell," —

and those earthly gods, the poets, can recognize one another in all disguises, because in them the godhead is more than the apparent disguise, — " the man is paramount to the poet," as Emerson said of

Milton. Had the Concord seer never written a line
of verse, he would still have been a poet by virtue of
that insight, that clairvoyance of the imagination,
which is the one indispensable token of poetic power.
The " accomplishment of verse," as Wordsworth terms
it, is another thing ; not usually divorced entirely
from the poetic insight, but only in a few rare instances (as in Shakspeare, Milton, Dante, and Homer) completely united and fused with it.   Even
then a third rarity is wont to be absent, — a mascu-
line soul capable of controlling these gifts of genius,
and constituting their possessor a true man as well
as a true poet.   Toward this threefold unity of insight, expression, and will, — this union of what Emerson calls " the Knower, the Sayer, and the Doer,"
— Dante approached nearer than Shakspeare, and
Milton nearer than Dante ; though in the strictly
poetic gifts Shakspeare surpassed them both.   If
we were to look in recent times for the highest example of this union, we should find it in Emerson
rather than in Wordsworth, in Victor Hugo, or even
in Goethe, who has passed for fifty years as the most
perfect type of these blended powers.   In poetic expression Goethe generally, and Wordsworth often,
surpass Emerson ; in poetic insight neither of them
is so lofty nor so well sustained.   In the acts of
life, as Victor Hugo has played a grander part than
Wordsworth or Goethe, so Emerson, in his own
sphere and for all time, must be deemed to have excelled the great Frenchman.   That force and purity

of will which gives Milton his pre-eminence among
English poets was a quality no less marked in Emerson, whose fortune it was, also, to be thrown on a
time when this austere greatness of soul, like Milton's, could give to genius its best sanction, and
stamp its impression most durably on succeeding
times. For the delight and instruction of England
and America Shakspeare has been wondrously effective, far beyond Milton; but for the spiritual gov-
ernance and advancement of the two nations, he can
bear no comparison with that blind poet, —

> " In whom is plainest taught and easiest learned
> What makes a nation happy and keeps it so."

This parallel between the Puritan and the Transcendental poet, between Milton and Emerson, is
not only obvious in itself, but is thrust upon us by
the description which Emerson gave of Milton half
a century ago, and in which he unconsciously and
prophetically described himself. This essay, which
was first a lecture in Boston, and afterwards (in
1838) an article in the "North American Review,"
has not been included by Dr. Emerson in the recent
edition of his father's writings, and I may therefore
cite from it the more freely, as not being accessible
to all. Says Emerson : —

" Milton is rightly dear to mankind, because in him,
among so many perverse and partial men of genius, —
in him humanity rights itself, the old eternal goodness finds
a home in his breast, and for once shows itself beau-

tiful. Among so many contrivances as the world has
seen to make holiness ugly, in Milton, at least, it was so
pure a flame that the foremost impression his character
makes is that of elegance. His gifts are subordinated to
his moral sentiments; yet his virtues are so graceful that
they seem rather talents than labors. The victories of the
conscience in him are gained by the commanding charm
which all the severe and restrictive virtues have for him.
Yet in his severity is no grimace or effort; he serves from
love, not from fear. He is innocent and exact, because
his taste was so pure and delicate. He acknowledges to
his friend Diodati, at the age of twenty-one, that he is
enamoured, if ever any was, of moral perfection. 'For,
whatever the Deity may have bestowed upon me in other
respects, he has certainly inspired me, if ever any were
inspired, with a passion for the good and fair.' The in-
differency of a wise mind to what is called high and low,
and the fact that true greatness is a perfect humility, are
revelations of Christianity which Milton well understood.
They give an inexhaustible truth to all his compositions.
Milton — gentle, learned, delicately bred in all the elegancy of art and learning — was set down in the stern,
almost fanatic society of the Puritans. Susceptible as
Burke to the attractions of historical prescription, of roy-
alty, of chivalry, of an ancient church illustrated by old
martyrdoms, and installed in cathedrals, he threw himself, the flower of elegancy, on the side of the reeking
conventicle, the side of humanity, but unlearned and un-
adorned. He advises that in country places, rather than
trudge many miles to a church, public worship be maintained nearer home, as in a house or barn, saying : 'We
may be well assured that He who disdained not to be

born in a manger, disdains not to be preached in a barn.'
Though drawn into the great controversies of the times,
he is never lost in a party. His private opinions and
private conscience always distinguish him. That which
drew him to the party was his love of liberty, ideal liberty ; this, therefore, he could not sacrifice to any party.
The most devout man of his time, he frequented no
church ; probably from a disgust at the fierce spirit of
the pulpits. And so, throughout all his actions and opinions, he is a consistent spiritualist, or believer in the omnipotence of spiritual laws. He wished that his writings
should be communicated only to those who desired to see
them. He thought nothing honest was low. The tone of
his thought and passion is as healthful, as even, and as
vigorous as befits the new and perfect model of a race of
gods. It was plainly needful that his poetry should be a
version of his own life, in order to give weight and solem-
nity to his thoughts, by which they might penetrate and
possess the imagination and will of mankind. His fancy
is never transcendent, extravagant ; his imagination ministers to character. Milton's sublimest song is the voice
of Milton still. Indeed, throughout his poems one may
see, under a thin veil, the opinions, the feelings, even the
incidents of the poet's life still reappearing."

I have here been giving the very words of Emerson, now and then changed in their connection ; and
do you not see how closely they apply to the author
himself ? Neither is this because of any marked
similarity in the fortunes of the two men, but by
reason of that superiority of the man to his circumstances, and even to his endowments, in each case.

These endowments, indeed, were widely different. That perfect command of verse for every form of expression, in which Milton excels every English poet, even Shakspeare, was denied to Emerson, who in turn excelled Milton in the sustained force and beauty of his prose. Like Milton's, however, it is the prose of a poet ; and, as he says of Milton's, "not the style alone but the argument also is poetic, and we read one sense in his prose and in his metrical compositions."

Let us then pause to consider what poetry is, and what it has in common with prose. For these two styles of writing are not distinct from each other, as air and water are, — one ethereal, the other terrestrial, one visible, the other invisible and seen only in its effects ; but they are contrasted manifestations, rather, of the single human intelligence, and blend in their source, however distinct may be their course in literature. The basis of poetry is Imagination and the higher Reason ; the basis of prose is the Understanding or Common-Sense. Yet neither prose nor poetry rejects Fancy, Wit, and Memory, — those three graces of literature ; nor does prose exclude Imagination and the supreme Reason ; nor yet does Poetry abhor Common-Sense, while often flying high above it. Thus Coleridge — himself a good poet, and a follower of his own rule — said : " Poetry must first be good sense; a palace may well be magnificent, but first it must be a house." On the other hand, prose must have something more than good sense in order to be eloquence, which is the highest form of prose. There is eloquence in poetry too; and in this noble quality we see the union of prose and poetry. For example, we take no offence at a good prose translation of the great poets who wrote Sanscrit, Greek, Latin, Persian, or Italian; but the translation must be eloquent, or we never call it good. What we admire in the poetical books of the Bible, as they appear in our common version, is their eloquence, through which, as through a clear glass, we see their essential poetry and truth, though not a shred be left of what in Hebrew was metrical. Can the plainest prose translation deprive the Bhagavat Gita of its poetic eloquence, or quench the magnificence of Hafiz, of Saadi, of Firdûsî, or of the antique, half-fabulous Zoroaster? It is this Zoroaster, indeed, to whom is ascribed what is still the best description of the poet and his genius; for in his oracular manner he was understood to say: "Poets are standing transporters; their employment consists in speaking to the Father and to Matter; in producing apparent copies of unapparent natures, and thus inscribing things unapparent in the apparent fabric of the world." This is more imaginative, and therefore better, than the famous definition of Bacon, — "Poetry accommodates the shows of things to the desires of the mind."

But can anything be better than the sayings of Emerson himself on this subject, of which he was the only modern master? Thus, he said: —

" Poetry is the perpetual endeavor to express the spirit of the thing."

" Poetry is the only verity, — the expression of a sound mind speaking after the ideal, and not after the apparent."

" Its essential work is that it betrays in every word instant activity of mind, shown in new uses of every fact and image ; all its words are poems."

" God himself does not speak prose, but communicates with us by hints, omens, inference, and dark resemblances in objects lying all around us."

" Poetry teaches the enormous force of a few words, and, in proportion to the inspiration, checks loquacity. It requires that splendor of expression which carries with it the proof of great thoughts. The great poets are judged by the frame of mind they induce ; and to them, of all men, the severest criticism is due."

It was upon the profound truth here expressed — that "great poets are judged by the frame of mind they induce " — that Matthew Arnold should have based any criticism he might have to make on Emerson as a poet. Tried by that standard, how different would have been the verdict ! especially if it be true, as Ben Jonson said, that " the principal end of poetry is to inform men in the just reason of living." Mr. Arnold began by making those impossible comparisons of our poet with Cicero, Voltaire, Swift, and Addison, — a collocation which inevitably reminded us of the Irish statuary in the Groves of Blarney, —

> " Bold Neptune, Plutarch, and Nicodemus,
> All standing naked in the open air."

The Irish poet who thus revels in the incongruous does it for the sake of compliment, and not, like our English censor, by way of anticipating the awful doom of posterity. Yet, after yielding to Time, as he condescendingly says, " all that Time can take away," — imagine the dispenser of " sweetness and light " in the rôle of Fame,

> " While panting Time toils after him in vain," —

after this severity of award he also falls into the eulogistic strain of the Hibernian bard : —

> " So now to finish this brave narration
> Which all my genius could not entwine,
> But were I Homer or Nebuchadnezzar,
> 'T is in every feature I would make it shine."

Assuming this laudatory part, and in some degree regaining the right use of his reason, Mr. Arnold proceeds to compare Emerson with Marcus Aurelius, as " the friend and aider of those who would live in the spirit." He certainly was that, and more ; and he did resemble Marcus Aurelius more than he resembled Nebuchadnezzar or Swift or Voltaire. And yet the likeness of Emerson to the imperial stoic was not a very close or confusing one. For Marcus Aurelius was in no sense a poet, and hardly an appreciator of the poets ; while Emerson was both a poet of high rank, as I shall hope to show you, and also the best appreciator of poets that the modern world has seen. If Mr. Arnold, in the great heap of his wisdom, had chosen to compare Emerson with Plutarch, the precursor of Marcus Aurelius, and much more than that emperor " the friend and aider of those who would live in the spirit," we should have said that the comparison was more just; for Plutarch, in his genius and his influence, — nay, even in his style of writing, — was the prototype of Emerson; not in all respects, but under the limitations and with the individual peculiarities that distinguish all men of one era from all men of every other. Plutarch was no poet, to be sure, but a dear lover and quoter of the best poetry; and to him we owe the currency, and often the preservation, of noble passages in the Greek poets, just as we owe to Emerson the quotation and currency of some of the noblest passages in English and Persian poetry. Plutarch was garrulous too, as Emerson never was, well knowing, as he said, that " poetry teaches the enormous force of a few words, and, in proportion to the inspiration, *checks loquacity.*" Yet the loquacious Plutarch, like the reserved and concentrating Emerson, knew life at its source and in its thousand saliencies, as Shakspeare did; and had he been a poet, might have been that impossible being — the Shakspeare of antiquity — whom we must now piece together out of Pindar, Æschylus, Plato, and Aristophanes, and still come short of the wonderful genius we name Shakspeare.

Mr. Symonds, a learned and sometimes a felicitous English critic, when seeking to explain the short brilliancy of dramatic poetry in England during the

time of Elizabeth and James, finds occasion to apply
the term "clairvoyance" to the dramatic genius of
the English poets. He says : —

"The ancient Greeks and the Italians of the Renaissance possessed clairvoyance in the plastic arts. The
present age is clairvoyant in science, and the application
of science to purposes of utility. At each great epoch of
the world's history the mind of man has penetrated more
deeply than at others into some particular subject; has
interrogated Nature in its own way, solving for one period
of time intuitively and with ease problems which before
and after it has been unable with pains to apprehend in
the same manner. In the days of our dramatic supremacy
the apocalypse of man was more complete than at any
other moment of the world's history. Shakspeare and his
contemporaries reveal human passions, thoughts, aspirations, sentiments, and motives of action, with evidence
so absolute that the creations even of Sophocles, of Calderon, of Corneille, when compared with these, seem to
represent abstract conceptions or animated forms rather
than the inner truth of life. This clairvoyance gave them
insight into things beyond their own experience. Shakspeare painted much that he had never seen ; and it was
true to Nature. This power, in a greater or less degree, was
shared by his contemporaries ; they owed it to that intuition
into human character which was the virtue of their age."

It was also, if not the virtue of Emerson's period
and environment, at least the endowment of himself,
of Margaret Fuller and Hawthorne, and others of his
fellowship.

Mr. Arnold once defined genius as "mainly an affair of energy," and contrasted the English literary "genius" with the French "openness of mind and flexibility of intelligence." The Elizabethan age, he said, produced "a literature of genius;" and then with characteristic carping he complained of the poverty of its results, and lauded the power and fecundity of the French "literature of intelligence" in the great century of Louis XIV. Against this judgment Mr. Symonds protests, rightly, and says that "the memory of the Elizabethan poets, like the memory of youth and spring, is now an element of beauty in the mental life of a people too much given to worldly interests. The blossoms, too, of that spring-time of poetry, unlike the pleasures of youth or the flowers of May, are imperishable." What the Elizabethan age was to English literature, the Transcendental period was to the literature of New England; and our spring-time of poetry, though late and brief in comparison with that which saw the blossoming of Sidney's, Spenser's, Raleigh's, Marlowe's, and Shakspeare's genius, will be as imperishable as theirs. The climate and the soil of Massachusetts were not favorable to the flowers that bloom around the Muses' fountain; yet the mayflower and the violet could open there, and another plant there was which the shepherd of our meadows found: —

> "Amongst the rest a small unsightly root,
>   But of divine effect, he culled me out;
>   The leaf was darkish, and had prickles on it,
>   But in another country, as he said,

> Bore a bright golden flower, but not in this soil ;
> Unknown, and like esteemed, and the dull swain
> Treads on it daily with his clouted shoon ;
> And yet more med'cinal is it than that moly
> Which Hermes once to wise Ulysses gave."

We have seen the lofty scholar from Cambridge or Oxford tread as heavily on our unnoticed and divine flower as Milton's ploughman did ; but the virtue and beauty of the plant were there all the same. To trample or browse on flowers is the botany of the ox ; and to neglect or note with scorn a new form of poetry is habitual with all but the best critics. Emerson said, — and Arnold may well heed this, — "The reason that we set so high a value on any poetry — as often on a line or a phrase as on a poem — is that it is a new work of Nature, as a man is. It must be as new as foam and as old as the rock. But a new verse comes once in a hundred years ; therefore Pindar, Hafiz, Dante, speak so proudly of what seems to the clown a jingle." Emerson would never say for himself what we must say for his best verses, in the words that Shakspeare wrote of his own sonnets : —

> "Nor marble, nor the gilded monuments
> Of princes, shall outlive this powerful rhyme."

What, then, are some of the best poems of Emerson, and why will they be permanent ? We say that "The Sphinx," "Uriel," some passages in "Woodnotes," the "Ode to Beauty," "The Forerunners," "Hermione," "Merlin," "The Three Loves," and the

"Threnody" will survive; that those short poems which he chose out from his "Discontented Poet's" portfolio, as mottoes for the essays, will be as permanent as they are oracular; and that many of his epigrams will go down to posterity with those in the Greek Anthology. Of more personal poems, "The Dirge," "Saadi," "Rhea," "The Titmouse," "The Days," "Terminus," and some portions of those new poems that appear in the last edition, may be cited as giving in the best manner the poet's portrait of himself. But there is not a poem which he gave to the world in his lifetime — hardly a verse — that does not contain something worth preserving when the more ambitious poems of other men are allowed to perish. This will seem extravagant to some of you; but time will bear out what is here said, as it has already brought forward into the light these verses that were once so obscure and unknown.

And why are these verses — too often fantastic, rude, or harsh — to outlive the more polished and melodious poetry of other men? First, because of their superior tone. They speak as having authority, and not as the Scribes. They are oracular, not with ostentation or for effect, but with weight. He is the one modern poet that " uses Nature as his hieroglyphic," and has "an adequate message to convey thereby." Observe how naturally these symbols fall to his use. He is describing the common experience of a lonely youth who through the magic of

love comes into communion with the wide world, —
and thus he writes in "Hermione" : —

> "In old Bassora's schools, I seemed
> Hermit vowed to books and gloom, —
> Ill-bestead for gay bridegroom ;
> I was by thy touch redeemed ;
> When thy meteor glances came,
> We talked at large of worldly fate,
> And drew truly every trait.

> "Once I dwelt apart,
> Now I live with all ;
> As shepherd's lamp on far hillside
> Seems, by the traveller espied,
> A door into the mountain heart, —
> So didst thou quarry and unlock
> Highways for me through the rock."

In the same poem (which seems to be but little read)
we find that superb homage which genius pays to the
object of its love, and which makes the poet the darling of the sex that loves to be worshipped : —

> " If it be, as they said, she was not fair,
> Beauty 's not beautiful to me,
> But sceptred genius, aye inorbed,
> Culminating in her sphere.
> This Hermione absorbed
> The lustre of the land and ocean,
> Hills and islands, cloud and tree,
> In her form and motion.

> " I ask no bauble miniature,
> Nor ringlets dead
> Shorn from her comely head,
> Now that morning not disdains,
> Mountains and the misty plains,
> Her colossal portraiture ;

They her heralds be,
Steeped in her quality,
And singers of her fame
Who is their muse and dame.

.   .   .   .   .   .

South-wind is my next of blood ;
He is come through fragrant wood,
Drugged with spice from climates warm,
And in every twinkling glade,
And twilight nook,
Unveils thy form.
Out of the forest way
Forth paced it yesterday,
And when I sat by the watercourse,
Watching the daylight fade,
It throbbed up from the brook."

As none has written so well the lore of noble love,
so none has more sententiously set forth the gospel
of friendship, in this brief poem : —

FRIENDSHIP.

A ruddy drop of manly blood
The surging sea outweighs ;
The world, uncertain, comes and goes,
The lover rooted stays.
I fancied he was fled, —
And, after many a year,
Glowed unexpected kindliness,
Like daily sunrise there.
My careful heart was free again,
"O friend," my bosom said,
"Through thee alone the sky is arched,
Through thee the rose is red ;
All things through thee take nobler form,
And look beyond the earth ;

> The mill-round of our fate appears
> A sun-path in thy worth.
> Me too thy nobleness hath taught
> To master my despair ;
> The fountains of my hidden life
> Are through thy friendship fair."

The permanence of Friendship, in contrast with the flitting, fugitive nature of Love, is well marked in this poem ; for Friendship, as the French say, " is Love without his wings." Emerson understood this, like every other part of the lore which Love imparts, and which is fully known only to women and to poets ; and he perceived that magnanimity was the shibboleth in Love's camp. Observe the advice he gives to lovers, which not only in purity but in profound art and wisdom goes far beyond Ovid's or Petrarca's or even Shakspeare's doctrine and discipline of love : —

> " Give all to Love ; obey thy heart :
>   Friends, kindred, days, estate, good-fame,
>   Plans, credit, and the Muse, —
>   Nothing refuse.
>   'T is a brave master, — let it have scope :
>   Follow it utterly, — hope beyond hope :
>   High and more high it dives into noon,
>   With wing unspent,
>   Untold intent ;
>   But 't is a god ; knows its own path
>   And the outlets of the sky.

> " It was never for the mean ;
>   It requireth courage stout,
>   Souls above doubt,
>   Valor unbending ;

Such 't will reward, — they shall return
More than they were, and ever ascending.

   .   .   .   .   .   .

Cling with life to the maid ;
But when the surprise,
First vague shadow of surmise,
Flits across her bosom young,
Of a joy apart from thee, —
Free be she, fancy-free :
Nor thou detain her vesture's hem,
Nor the palest rose she flung
From her summer diadem.

"Though thou loved her as thyself,
As a self of purer clay, —
Though her parting dims the day,
Stealing grace from all alive ;
Heartily know
When half-gods go
The gods arrive."

In another tone, but to the same effect, he sings in
" Rhea " : —

" When a god is once beguiled
By beauty of a mortal child,
And by her radiant youth delighted,
He is not fooled, but warily knoweth
His love shall never be requited.
And thus the wise Immortal doeth, —
'T is his study and delight
To bless that creature day and night ;
From all evils to defend her ;
In her lap to pour all splendor ;
To ransack earth for riches rare,
And fetch her stars to deck her hair :
He mixes music with her thoughts,
And saddens her with heavenly doubts :

> All grace, all good his great heart knows,
> Profuse in love, the king bestows :
> Saying, ' Hearken, Earth, Sea, Air !
> This monument of my despair
> Build I to the All-Good, All-Fair.
>
> .   .   .   .   .   .
>
> These presents be the hostages
> Which I pawn for my release.
> See to thyself, O universe !
> Thou art better, and not worse,' —
> And the god, having given all,
> Is freed forever from his thrall."

It is in the longer poem, however, — " Initial, Dæmonic, and Celestial Love," — that Emerson treats
most fully of the universal passion ; yet not here
like a boy with his spelling-lesson, nor a school-
master with his protasis and apodosis, his thus and
therefore, but in the free manner of the great artist,
whose sketch contains more of feeling and picture
than the mosaic of lapidaries. In this wonderful
chart of love he begins with the first voyage of
Cupid, and arrives, by magic isle and wild ship-
wreck, at the harbor of the celestials, where the freed
spirits,

> " Borne o'er the bosom of the untrammelled deep,
> Ride in the heavenly boat and touch new stars."

In the first part of this poem, " The Initial Love,"
Emerson is sportive as Mercutio, a gay bachelor who
is in the first freshness of his adventure, and pub-
lishes his hue-and-cry for the son of Venus as a
Greek poet might : —

" Venus, when her son was lost,
   Cried him up and down the coast.

   .   .   .   .   .   .

He came late along the waste,
Shod like a traveller for haste ;
With malice dared me to proclaim him,
That the maids and boys might name him."

So the young poet accepts the challenge, and goes on like Mercutio painting the portrait of Queen Mab : —

" Boy no more, he wears all coats,
   Frocks, and blouses, capes, capotes ;
He bears no bow or quiver or wand,
   Nor chaplet on his head or hand.
Leave his weeds and heed his eyes, —
   All the rest he can disguise.
In the pit of his eye 's a spark
Would bring back day if it were dark.

   .   .   .   .   .   .

Fleeter they than any creature, —
   They are his steeds, and not his feature ;
Inquisitive and fierce and fasting,
Restless, predatory, hasting ;
And they pounce on other eyes
   As lions on their prey.

   .   .   .   .   .

Heralds high before him run ;
He has ushers many a one ;
He spreads his welcome where he goes,
And touches all things with his rose.
All things wait for and divine him, —
How shall I dare to malign him,
Or accuse the god of sport ?
I must end my true report, —

   .   .   .   .   .   .

"He is wilful, mutable,
  Shy, untamed, inscrutable,
  Swifter-fashioned than the fairies,
  Substance mixed of pure contraries ;
  His vice some elder virtue's token,
  And his good is evil-spoken.

    .   .   .   .   .   .

  Shun him, nymphs, on the fleet horses !
  He has a total world of wit ;
  Oh how wise are his discourses !
  But he is the arch-hypocrite.

    .   .   .   .   .

  He is a Pundit of the East,
  He is an augur and a priest,
  And his soul will melt in prayer,
  But word and wisdom is a snare ;
  Corrupted by the present toy,
  He follows joy, and only joy.
  There is no mask but he will wear ;
  He invented oaths to swear.

    .   .   .   .   .   .

  Boundless is his memory ;
  Plans immense his term prolong ;
  He is not of counted age,
  Meaning always to be young.
  And his wish is intimacy, —
  Intimater intimacy,
  And a stricter privacy ;
  The impossible shall yet be done,
  And, being two, shall still be one."

Here ends the Mercutio phase of the poet, and when he next speaks, in " The Dæmonic Love," it is in a more serious tone, and with an air of solemn warning, something like that of Lucretius, but with a higher meaning. Now appears that docrine of magic influences of which we catch glimpses here and there all through Emerson's imaginative writing.   His theory of Dæmons is plainly yet fancifully stated : —

> " Close, close to men,
>   Like undulating layer of air,
>   Right above their heads,
>   The potent plane of Dæmons spreads ;
>   Stands to each human soul its own,
>   For watch and ward and furtherance,
>   In the snares of Nature's dance ;
>   And the lustre and the grace
>   To fascinate each youthful heart,
>   Beaming from its counterpart,
>   Translucent through the mortal covers,
>   Is the Dæmon's form and face.
>   To and fro the Genius hies, —
>   A gleam which plays and hovers
>   Over the maiden's head,
>   And dips sometimes as low as to her eyes.
>
>   .   .   .   .   .   .
>
>   Sometimes the airy synod bends
>   And the mighty choir descends,
>   And the brains of men thenceforth,
>   In crowded and in still resorts,
>   Teem with unwonted thoughts :
>   As when a shower of meteors
>   Cross the orbit of the earth,
>   And, lit by fringent air,
>   Blaze near and far, —
>   Mortals deem the planets bright
>   Have slipped their sacred bars,
>   And the lone seaman, all the night,
>   Sails, astonished, amid stars."

These Dæmons are both good and bad, black and white, like the genii that attended on the ancients ;

and when Love comes under the power of " Dæmons less divine," the issue is disastrous : —

> " The Dæmon ever builds a wall,
>   Himself encloses and includes,
>   Solitude in solitudes :
> In like sort his love doth fall.
>
>   .   .   .   .   .   .
>
>   He doth elect
>   The beautiful and fortunate,
>   And the sons of intellect,
>   And the souls of ample fate,
>   Who the Future's gates unbar, —
>   Minions of the Morning Star.
>   In his prowess he exults,
>   And the multitude insults.
>   His impatient looks devour
>   Oft the humble and the poor ;
>   And, seeing his eye glare,
>   They drop their few pale flowers,
>   Gathered, with hope to please,
>   Along the mountain towers, —
>   Lose courage, and despair.
>   He will never be gainsaid, —
>   Pitiless, will not be stayed ;
>   His hot tyranny
>   Burns up every other tie.
>   Therefore comes an hour from Jove
>   Which his ruthless will defies,
>   And the dogs of Fate unties.
>   Shiver the palaces of glass ;
>   Shrivel the rainbow-colored walls,
>   Where in bright Art each god and sibyl dwelt
>   Secure as in the zodiac's belt ;
>   And the galleries and halls,
>   Wherein every siren sung,
>   Like a meteor pass.

> For this fortune wanted root
> In the core of God's abysm, —
> Was a weed of self and schism ;
> And ever the Dæmonic Love
> Is the ancestor of wars
> And the parent of remorse."

And now we come to the culmination of this three-fold poem, — " The Celestial Love," which restores and completes this broken vision of the grand passion. It is no longer Cupid, the boy-god, nor the tyrannical and exclusive Dæmon of whom these dithyrambic verses, imaginative and inconsequent as the strophes of a Greek chorus, chant to us ; we hear the Divine voice itself : —

> " But God said, —
> ' I will have a purer gift ;
> There is smoke in the flame ;
> New flowerets bring, new prayers uplift,
> And love without a name !
>
> . . . . . .
>
> " ' Deep, deep are loving eyes,
> Flowed with naphtha fiery sweet :
> And the point is paradise,
> Where their glances meet ;
> Their reach shall yet be more profound, .
> And a vision without bound.'
>
> . . . . . .
>
> " Higher far,
> Upward into the pure realm,
> Over sun and star,
> Over the flickering Dæmon film,
> Thou must mount for love ;
> Into vision where all form

In one only form dissolves,
In a region where the wheel
On which all beings ride
Visibly revolves ;
Where the starred, eternal worm
Girds the world with bound and term ;
Where unlike things are like,
Where good and ill,
And joy and moan,
Melt into one.
There Past, Present, Future, shoot
Triple blossoms from one root ;
Substances at base divided
In their summits are united ;
There the holy Essence rolls
One through separated souls ;
And the sunny Æon sleeps,
Folding Nature in its deeps ;
And every fair and every good,
Known in part or known impure
To men below,
In their archetypes endure.
The race of gods,
Or those we erring own,
Are shadows flitting up and down
In the still abodes.
The circles of that sea are laws
Which publish and which hide their cause."

This is mysticism, and the very romance of mysticism, — intelligible to some, musical to all, — and breathing deeply of Plato and the Orientals, who, more than all others, were the torch-bearers to Emerson in his philosophy. Of that I do not speak, but of his poetry, which in this instance rises to its highest flight, and far beyond those meaningless

melodies of Edgar Poe which caught the ear of
the world in Emerson's time. But now follows the
ethical lesson delivered from this height of the
imagination : —

> " Pray for a beam
>   Out of that sphere,
>   Thee to guide and to redeem.
>
> .   .   .   .   .   .
>
>   Counsel which the ages kept
>   Shall the well-born soul accept.
>   As garment draws the garment's hem,
>   Men their fortunes bring with them.
>
> .   .   .   .   .
>
> " Not less do the eternal poles
>   Of tendency distribute souls.
>   There need no vows to bind
>   Whom not each other seek, but find.
>   They give and take no pledge or oath, —
>   Nature is the bond of both :
>   No prayer persuades, no flattery fawns, —
>   Their noble meanings are their pawns.
>   Plain and cold is their address,
>   Power have they for tenderness ;
>   And, so thoroughly is known
>   Each other's counsel by his own,
>   They can parley without meeting ;
>   Need is none of forms of greeting ;
>   They can well communicate
>   In their innermost estate ;
>   When each the other shall avoid,
>   Shall each by each be most enjoyed.
>
>
> " Not with scarfs or perfumed gloves
>   Do these celebrate their loves ;
>   Not by jewels, feasts, and savors,
>   Not by ribbons or by favors,

But by the sun-spark on the sea,
And the cloud-shadow on the lea,
The soothing lapse of morn to mirk,
And the cheerful round of work.
Their cords of love so public are,
They intertwine the farthest star :
The throbbing sea, the quaking earth,
Yield sympathy and signs of mirth.

. . . . . .

Even the fell Furies are appeased,
The good applaud, the lost are eased.

" Love's hearts are faithful, but not fond,
Bound for the just, but not beyond ;
Not glad, as the low-loving herd,
Of self in other still preferred, —
But these have heartily designed
The benefit of broad mankind ;
And they serve men austerely,
After their own genius, clearly,
Without a false humility ;
For this is Love's nobility, —
Not to scatter bread and gold,
Goods and raiment bought and sold ;
But to hold fast his simple sense,
And speak the speech of innocence,
And with hand and body and blood
To make his bosom-counsel good.
He that feeds men serveth few ;
He serves all who dares be true."

" What extraordinary language for a vestry-meet-
ing!" shuddered the English bishop, when his American brother related the unsanctified confession of
his quarrelsome church-warden. What an uncommon ending is this for a love-poem, you will say, —
this noble maxim, which does not in the least remind

us of Romeo and Juliet. Our Mercutio has been
transformed into Romeo, and the amorous Montague
again into the Platonic poet, — and now this soaring
Muse alights and reappears as one

> " Of those budge doctors of the Stoic fur,
>   Praising the lean and sallow abstinence."

The changes are bewildering, I confess, — but the
doctrine of this stoic is admirable, and he has drawn
it direct from the book of Love, in which not even
Shakspeare was better read. Nor do we find in
Emerson those low and jesting commentaries on the
heavenly text which Shakspeare could not avoid
writing in; while, on the other hand, Emerson avoids
those marginal references to Aristotle and the scho-
lastic theology which chill and weary the reader of
Dante's love-poems. Of the four great scholars in
the philosophy of Love, — Plato, Dante, Shakspeare,
and Emerson, — our countryman pierced nearer to
the heart of the matter than the Greek, the Tuscan,
or the Englishman, — not excepting Shakspeare's
" sugared Sonnets," nor that mysterious poem ascribed to him, " The Phœnix and Turtle," which
Emerson thought so " quaint and charming in diction, tone, and allusions, and in its perfect metre and
harmony," as to be poetry for poets alone. Emerson
added, what will apply well to much of his own
verse : " This poem, if published for the first time,
and without a known author's name, would find no
general reception ; only the poets would save it."

I have dwelt at this length on Emerson's love-poems, because it is by their treatment of this universal subject that poets are judged and tested. I do not know from what page of Milton Mr. Arnold took the dictum that poetry ought always to be " simple, sensuous, or impassioned," but it is chiefly to love-poetry, narration, and description that this test would apply ; and Milton himself, in his highest flights, disregarded it completely, as the Greek dramatists, and Pindar, Lucretius, Dante, and Shakspeare had done before him, — and as Mr. Arnold (to compare great things with small) has since done. Montaigne or Aristotle, to say nothing of Plato, could have supplied us with a better test. Says Montaigne, speaking of style : " The precepts of the masters, and still more their example, tell us that we must have a little insanity, if we would not have still more stupidity. A thousand poets drawl and languish in prose ; but the best of the ancient prose (and the same with verse) glows throughout with the vigor and daring of poesy, and assumes an air of inspiration. The poet, says Plato," — I am still quoting Montaigne, who gives his own quaint form to the passage in Plato's Laws, — "the poet, sitting on the Muses' tripod, pours out, like mad, all that comes into his mouth, as if it were the spout of a fountain, without digesting or weighing it ; and so things escape him of various colors, of opposite natures, and with intermittent flow. Plato himself is wholly poetic ; the old theology is all poetry, say the scholars ; and the First

Philosophy is the original language of the gods." To this wild rule Emerson conforms; and still more to that saying of Aristotle in his Poetics, — "Poetry is more philosophical and more earnest than history," — φιλοσοφώτερον καὶ σπουδαιότερον ἱστορίας ποίησις ἐστίν. By history, as Professor Davidson has shown, Aristotle here meant all account of and research into fact, — while poetry is the artistic spirit. Or, as Professor Davidson says, "History is in its highest form a matter of the understanding; poetry is based upon the reason." And this reason is not only more philosophical and more earnest than the understanding of man, but it moves by swifter and less connected steps, — is winged where the understanding is footed or crawling. Its wings are insight and imagination, and its logic is a flight and not a stairway, — or at the slowest, a "flight of stairs," in which surprise awaits every ascending step.

> " ' Pass in, pass in,' the angels say,
>   ' In to the upper doors, —
>   Nor count compartments of the floors,
>   But mount to Paradise
>   By the stairway of surprise.' "

Montaigne, who read all the poets, if he did not discriminate very wisely between them, said also: "Strange to say, we have many more poets than we have good judges and interpreters of poetry; it is easier to write it than to appreciate it." I have already said that Emerson was first of all an appreciator of poetry; and Mr. Arnold, little as we should

guess it from his criticism on Emerson, was formerly
capable of recognizing poetry when he saw it. In his
Introduction to that valuable collection, "Ward's
English Poets," Mr. Arnold wrote, as commentary on
Aristotle's just quoted maxim, —

"The substance and matter of the best poetry acquire
their special character from possessing, in an eminent
degree, truth and seriousness. The superior character of
truth and seriousness [by which he means Aristotle's
"philosophy" and "earnestness"], in the matter and substance of the best poetry, is inseparable from the superiority of diction and movement, marking its style and
manner. So far as high poetic truth and seriousness are
wanting to a poet's matter and substance, so far also will
a high poetic stamp of diction and movement be wanting
to his style and manner."

Then taking up that wondrous poet, Chaucer, of
whom Emerson said, "I think he has lines of more
force than any English writer except Shakspeare,"—
Mr. Arnold says : "Something is wanting to the
poetry of Chaucer which poetry must have before it
can be placed in the glorious class of the best ; and
there is no doubt what that something is. It is the
earnestness, the high and excellent seriousness, which
Aristotle assigns as one of the grand virtues of poetry. Chaucer's view of things and his criticism of
life has largeness, freedom, benignity ; but it has not
this high seriousness. Homer's criticism of life has
it, Dante's has it, Shakspeare's has it ; " and he might
have added, for it is eminently true, "Emerson's has

it." He does say, however, and the remark is more just in its application to Emerson than to any except these three, " The greatness of the great poets, the power of their criticism of life, is that their virtue is sustained," — not fitful like that of poor Villon the French scamp-poet, or the English dramatists of Shakspeare's time. And then, in this essay of four years ago, Mr. Arnold makes these just observations concerning Pope and Gray, whom, in his Emerson lecture, he had the whim of setting above our poet in point of style : —

"Do you ask me whether Pope's verse, take it almost where you will, is not good ? —

'To Hounslow Heath I point, and Banstead Down ;
Thence comes your mutton, and these chicks my own.'

I answer, Admirable for the purposes of a high-priest of an age of prose and reason. But do you ask me whether such verse proceeds from men with an adequate poetic criticism of life ; from men whose criticism of life has a high seriousness, or even has poetic largeness, freedom, insight, benignity ? I answer, It has not and cannot have them ; it is the poetry of the builders of an age of prose and reason. Though they may write in verse, though they may be in a certain sense masters of the art of versification, Dryden and Pope are not classics of our poetry ; they are classics of our prose. Gray is our poetical classic of that literature and age. He has not the volume or the power of poets who, coming in times more favorable, have attained to an independent criticism of life. But he lived with the great poets ; he lived, above all, with the

Greeks, and he caught their poetic point of view for re-
garding life.   The point of view and the poetic manner
are not self-sprung in him, — he caught them of others ;
and he had not the free and abundant use of them.   But
whereas Addison and Pope never had the use of them,
Gray had the use of them at times.   He is the scantiest
and frailest of classics in our poetry, but he is a classic."

This is unjust to Gray ; but it was far more unjust
to Emerson to place Gray above him, as Mr. Arnold
did last winter.   In one point only did Gray excel
Emerson, — in the art of versification ; which is a
lower gift than either poetic insight or poetic expression, in both which Emerson greatly excelled Gray.
But in " high seriousness," in " poetic largeness, freedom, benignity," in his whole criticism of life, our Concord poet-philosopher stood far above the poet-pedant
and virtuoso of English Cambridge, sweet and stirring
as were the strains of Gray.   Compare the " Elegy in
a Country Churchyard " with the " Threnody," the
" Dirge " and " In Memoriam," — contrast these two
verses only, and tell me which is the greater poet : —

> " Can storied urn, or animated bust,
>   Back to its mansion call the fleeting breath ?
> Can honor's voice provoke the silent dust,
>   Or flatt'ry soothe the dull, cold ear of death ?

> " Turn the key and bolt the door, —
>   Sweet is death for evermore.
> Nor haughty hope, nor swart chagrin,
> Nor murdering hate can enter in.
> All is now secure and fast ;
> Not the gods can shake the Past."

Here is the same number of syllables in the two competing stanzas, the same theme, the same tone of mind; but how much higher is the insight of Emerson! Or compare, if your love for Gray does not too much mortify you to do so, his Epitaph on Sir William Williams, with Emerson's Ode on the death of Colonel Shaw. The English hero was killed at the siege of Belleisle, the French town from which our friend M. de Poyen derives his local name.

THE EPITAPH.

Here, foremost in the dangerous paths of fame,
　Young Williams fought for England's fair renown ;
His mind each Muse, each Grace adorned his frame,
　Nor envy dared to view him with a frown.

At Aix his voluntary sword he drew,
　There first in blood his infant honor sealed ;
From fortune, pleasure, science, love he flew,
　And scorned repose when Britain took the field.

With eyes of flame and cool undaunted breast,
　Victor he stood on Belleisle's rocky steeps ;
Ah, gallant youth ! this marble tells the rest,
　Where melancholy friendship bends and weeps.

This is Gray, not at his best, we must own, — but it is Gray and his age. Now listen to Emerson, who " was not of an age, but for all time."

THE ODE.

So nigh is grandeur to our dust,
So near is God to man,
When Duty whispers low, *Thou must,*
The youth replies, *I can.*

Oh, well for the fortunate soul
Which music's wings infold,
Stealing away the memory
Of sorrows new and old !
Yet happier he whose inward sight,
Stayed on his subtile thought,
Shuts his sense on toys of time
To vacant bosoms brought.
But best befriended of the God
He who in evil times,
Warned by an inward voice,
Heeds not the darkness and the dread ;
Biding by his rule and choice,
Feeling only the fiery thread
Leading over heroic ground,
Walled with mortal terror round,
To the aim which him allures ;
And the sweet Heaven his deed secures.
Peril around, all else appalling,
Cannon in front and leaden rain,
Him Duty through the clarion calling
To the van, called not in vain.

Stainless soldier on the walls,
Knowing this, — and knows no more, —
Whoever fights, whoever falls,
Justice, after as before,
Justice conquers evermore ;
And he who battles on her side,
God, though he were ten times slain,
Crowns him victor glorified,
Victor over death and pain.

Here ends the memorial ode ; but then the poet, having paid his tribute to courage and friendship, resumes the perpetual chant which celebrates the

might of the Unseen Powers, and which distinguishes
Emerson's verse among all the oracles of the modern
world : —

THE EPODE.

> Blooms the laurel which belongs
>   To the valiant chief who fights ;
> I see the wreath, I hear the songs
>   Lauding the Eternal Rights,
> Victors over daily wrongs ;
>   Awful victors, they misguide
>   Whom they will destroy,
>   And their coming triumph hide
>   In our downfall, or our joy :
> They reach no term — they never sleep —
>   In equal strength through space abide ;
> Though, feigning dwarfs, they crouch and creep,
>   The strong they slay, the swift outstride ;
>   Fate's grass grows rank in valley clods,
>   And rankly on the castled steep, —
>   Speak it firmly ! these are gods,
>   All are ghosts beside.

If we would restore Gray to anything like his fair
place among poets after this mortifying comparison,
we must turn to his best ode, " The Bard," which in
expression, not in theme nor insight, is on a level
with Emerson's best verse : —

> " On a rock whose haughty brow
>   Frowns o'er old Conway's foaming flood,
>   Robed in the sable garb of woe,
>   With haggard eyes the poet stood ;
>   (Loose his beard, and hoary hair
>   Streamed, like a meteor, to the troubled air) ;
>   And, with a master's hand, a prophet's fire,
>   Struck the deep sorrows of his lyre : —

'Hark ! how each giant-oak, and desert cave,
Sighs to the torrent's awful voice beneath !
O'er thee, O King, their hundred arms they wave,
Revenge on thee in hoarser murmurs breathe ;
Vocal no more, since Cambria's fatal day,
To high-born Hoel's harp, or soft Llewellyn's lay.
   Cold is Cadwallo's tongue
   That hushed the stormy main ;
Brave Urien sleeps upon his craggy bed ;
   Mountains, ye mourn in vain
   Modred, whose magic song
Made huge Plinlimmon bow his cloud-topped head.
   On dreary Arvon's shore they lie
Smeared with gore, and ghastly pale :
Far, far aloof the affrighted ravens sail ;
   The famished eagle screams, and passes by.
Dear lost companions of my tuneful art !
   Dear as the light that visits these sad eyes,
Dear as the ruddy drops that warm my heart, —
   Ye died amidst your dying country's cries.
No more I weep. They do not sleep.
   On yonder cliffs, a grisly band,
I see them sit, — they linger yet,
   Avengers of their native land.
    .   .   .   .   .   .

Fond impious man ! think'st thou yon sanguine cloud,
   Raised by thy breath, has quenched the orb of day ?
To-morrow he repairs the golden flood
   And warms the nations with redoubled ray.
Enough for me ; with joy I see
   The different doom our fates assign,
Be thine despair, and sceptred care, —
   To triumph, and to die, are mine.'
He spoke, and headlong from the mountain's height
Deep in the roaring tide he plunged to endless night."

It must be admitted that Gray wrote verse with more
skill and harmony than Emerson : so far Mr. Arnold

was correct in his criticism.   But then how little had Gray to utter in verse, compared with the oracles and canticles of Emerson !   " Byron had nothing to say, but he said it magnificently !" was the pithy verdict of Emerson on his youthful favorite, whom he sometimes quoted in his Essays.   We measure poets first by what they tell us, next by the words they use, and lastly by the skill with which they weave these words into verse.   "Homer's words," says Aristotle, in the Poetics, "are the only words that have energy, movement, and action ; they are words of substance."   Emerson, also, used words of this sort; and in one of his unpublished pieces, " The Discontented Poet," he thus described in fanciful terms the poet's dictionary : —

> " The gallant child, where'er he came,
>   Threw to each fact a tuneful name.
>   The things whereon he cast his eyes
>   Could not the nations rebaptize,
>   Nor Time's snows hide the names he set,
>   Nor last posterity forget.
>   Yet every scroll whereon he wrote
>   In latent fire his secret thought,
>   Fell unregarded to the ground,
>   Unseen by such as stood around.
>   The pious wind took it away,
>   The reverent darkness hid the lay.
>   Methought like water-haunting birds,
>   Divers or dippers, were his words ;
>   And idle clowns beside the mere
>   At the new vision gape and jeer ;
>   But when the noisy scorn was past,
>   Emerge the wingèd words in haste.
>   New-bathed, new-trimmed, on healthy wing,
>   Right to the heaven they steer and sing."

This is the history of every poet's dialect, so far as he makes it anew; and such has been the fortune of Emerson's. His vocabulary is rich and novel, and he has brought it well into acceptance. But in marshalling these words he felt his inadequacy, and in this was the " discontented poet " of whom he wrote. He lamented his imperfect use of the metrical faculty, which he felt all the more keenly in contrast with the melodious thoughts he had to utter, and the fitting words in which he could clothe these thoughts. He would have written much more in verse if he had been content with his own metrical expression as constantly as he was delighted with it sometimes. But it is also true that he purposely roughened his verse, and threw in superfluous lines and ill-matched rhymes, as a kind of protest against the smoothness and jingle of what he called "poetry to put round frosted cake." The passage from his " Merlin," which Mr. Albee has quoted to us, is preceded by this introduction to that great but unequal poem : —

" Thy trivial harp will never please
    Or fill my craving ear ;
Its chords should ring as blows the breeze,
    Free, peremptory, clear.
No jingling serenader's art,
    Nor tinkle of piano strings,
Can make the wild blood start
    In its mystic springs.
The kingly bard
Must smite the chords rudely and hard,
As with hammer or with mace ;

> That they may render back
> Artful thunder, which conveys
> Secrets of the solar track,
> Sparks of the supersolar blaze.
> Merlin's blows are strokes of fate.
>
> .   .   .   .   .
>
> " By Sybarites beguiled,
> He shall no task decline ;
> Merlin's mighty line
> Extremes of nature reconciled, —
> Bereaved a tyrant of his will,
> And made the lion mild."

Pursuing this thought of the magical power which the poet can wield, and which he strove to attain, Emerson closes " Merlin " with these lines : —

> " Subtle rhymes with ruin rife,
> Murmur in the house of life,
> Sung by the Sisters as they spin ;
> In perfect time and measure they
> Build and unbuild our echoing clay,
> As the two twilights of the day
> Fold us music-drunken in."

In the " Bacchus," which stands next to " Merlin " in the volumes, the same theme is carried forward, with a change of imagery ; and I may properly close with its mystical aspiration, which leaves our poet in the timeless, immortal existence, out of which he came and to which he has returned,—a pilgrim of the eternal and melodious spheres.   It has been read in part by Miss Peabody, but you will easily pardon the repetition.

BACCHUS.

. . . . .

We buy diluted wine ;
Give me of the true, —
Whose ample leaves and tendrils curled
Among the silver hills of heaven,
Draw everlasting dew ;
Wine of wine, blood of the world,
Form of forms, and mould of statures,
That I, intoxicated,
And by the draught assimilated,
May float at pleasure through all natures ;
The bird-language rightly spell,
And that which roses say so well.

. . . . .

Wine which Music is, —
Music and wine are one, —
That I, drinking this,
Shall hear far Chaos talk with me ;
Kings unborn shall walk with me ;
And the poor grass shall plot and plan
What it will do when it is man.
Quickened so, will I unlock
Every crypt of every rock.

I thank the joyful juice
For all I know ; —
Winds of remembering
Of the ancient being blow,
And seeming-solid walls of use
Open and flow.

Pour, Bacchus ! the remembering wine ;
Retrieve the loss of me and mine !
Vine for vine be antidote,
And the grape requite the lote !

Haste to cure the old despair, —
Reason in Nature's lotus drenched,
The memory of ages quenched, —
Give them again to shine ;
Let wine repair what this undid ;
And where the infection slid,
A dazzling memory revive ;
Refresh the faded tints,
Recut the aged prints,
And write my old adventures with the pen
Which on the first day drew,
Upon the tablets blue,
The dancing Pleiads and eternal men.

VIII.

POEMS IN HONOR OF EMERSON.

I.

SONNET OF 1884. — Miss Emma Lazarus.

TO R. W. E.

As, when a father dies, his children draw
About the empty hearth, their loss to cheat
With uttered praise and love, and oft repeat
His all-familiar words with whispered awe, —
The honored habit of his daily law;
Not for his sake, but theirs, whose feebler feet
Need still that guiding lamp, whose faith less sweet
Misses that tempered patience without flaw; —
So do we gather round thy vacant chair,
In thine own elm-roofed, amber-rivered town,
Master and father!   For the love we bear,
Not for thy fame's sake, do we weave this crown,
And feel thy presence in the sacred air,
Forbidding us to weep that thou art gone.

New York, May, 1884.

II.

ODE OF 1845. — Ellery Channing.

If we should rake the bottom of the sea
　　For its best treasures,
　　And heap our measures, —
If we should ride upon the winds, and be
　　Partakers of their flight
　　By day and through the night,
Intent upon this business, — to find gold, —
Yet were thy story perfectly untold.

Such waves of wealth are rolled up in thy soul, —
　　Such swelling argosies
　　Laden with Time's supplies, —
Such pure, delicious wine shines in the bowl,
　　We could drink evermore
　　Upon the glittering shore, —
Drink of the pearl-dissolvèd, brilliant cup,
Be madly drunk, and drown our thirsting up.

This vessel richly chased about the rim
　　With golden emblems is, —
　　The utmost art of bliss;
With figures of the azure gods who swim
　　In the enchanted sea
　　Contrived for deity,
Floating in rounded shells of purple hue;
The sculptor died in carving this so true.

Some dry uprooted saplings we have seen,
      Pretend to even
      This grove of Heaven, —
This sacred forest where the foliage green
      Breathes music like mild lutes,
      Or silver-coated flutes,
Or the concealing winds that can convey
Never their tone to the rude ear of Day.

Some weary-footed mortals we have found
      Adventuring after thee;
      They, rooted, — as a tree
Pursues a swift breeze o'er a rocky ground, —
      Thy grand imperial flight
      Sweeping thee far from sight, —
As sweeps the movement of a southern blast
Across the heated Gulf, and bends the mast.

The circles of thy thought shine vast as stars;
      No glass shall round them,
      No plummet sound them,
They hem the observer like bright steel-wrought bars;
      Yet limpid as the sun,
      Or as bright waters run
From the cold fountain of an Alpine spring,
Or diamonds richly set in the King's ring.

The piercing of thy soul scorches the thought,
      As great fires burning,
      Or sunlight turning
Into a focus; in its meshes caught,

Our palpitating minds
    Show stupid, like coarse hinds;
So strong and composite through all thy powers
The Intellect divine serenely towers.

This heavy castle's gates no man can ope,
    Unless the lord doth will,
    To prove his skill
And read the fates hid in his horoscope;
    No man may enter there
    But first shall kneel in prayer,
And to superior gods orisons say, —
Powers of old time, unveiled in busy Day.

Thou need'st not search for men in Sidney's times,
    Or Raleigh fashion,
    And Herbert's passion, —
For us these are but dry preservèd limes;
    There is ripe fruit to-day
    Hangs yellow in display
Upon the waving garment of the bough;
The graceful Gentleman lives for us now.

Neither must thou turn back to Angelo,
    Who Rome commanded,
    And, single-handed,
Was architect, poet, and bold sculptor too:
    Behold a better thing
    When the pure Mind can sing;
When true philosophy is linked with verse,
When moral laws in rhyme themselves rehearse.

The smart and pathos of our suffering race
      Bear thee no harm;
      Thy muscular arm
The daily ills of living doth efface.
      The sources of the spring
      From whence thy instincts wing
Unsounded are by lines of sordid day;
Enclosed with inlaid walls thy virtue's way.

In city's street how often shall we hear
      It is a period
      Deprived of every god,
A time of indecision, and doom's near;
      What foolish altercation
      Threatens to break the nation!
All men turned talkers, and much good forgot, —
With score of curious troubles we know not.

By this account their learning you shall read,
      Who tell the story
      So sad and gory, —
People that you can never seek in need;
      The pygmies of the race,
      Who crowd the airy space
With counterfeit presentments of the Man
Who has done all things — all things surely can.

We never heard thee babble in this wise,
      Thou age-creator,
      And clear debater
Of that which this good Present underlies;

Thy course was better kept,
Than where the dreamers slept;
Thy sure meridian taken by the sun,
Thy compass pointing true as waters run.

In vain for us to say what thou hast been
To our occasion, —
This flickering nation,
This stock of people from an English kin, —
And he who led the van,
The frozen Puritan,
We thank thee for thy patience with his faith,
That chill delusive poison mixed for death.

So moderate in thy lessons, and so wise,
To foes so courteous,
To friends so duteous,
And hospitable to the neighbors' eyes;
Thy thoughts have fed the lamp
In Learning's polished camp;
But who suspects thee of this well-earned fame,
Or meditates on thy renownèd name?

The pins of custom have not pierced through thee
(Thy shining armor
A perfect charmer), —
Even the hornets of divinity
Allow thee a brief space;
And thy thought has a place
Upon the well-bound library's chaste shelves,
Where man of various wisdom rarely delves.

Within thy books the world is plainly set
    Before our vision,
    Thou keen physician!
We find there, wisely writ, what we have met
    Along the dusty path,
    And o'er the aftermath,
Where natures once world-daring held the scythe,
Nor paid to superstition a mean tithe.

Great persons are the epochs of the race;
    Then royal Nature
    Takes form and feature,
And careless handles the surrounding space;
    The age is vain and thin,
    A pageant of gay sin,
Without heroic response from that soul
Through which the tides diviner amply roll.

When thou dost pass below the forest shade,
    The branches drooping
    Enfold thee, stooping
Above thy figure, and form thus a glade;
    The flowers admire thee pass,
    In much content the grass
Awaits the pressure of thy firmest feet;
The bird for thee sends out his greeting sweet.

And welcomes thee, designed, the angry storm,
    When deep-toned thunder
    Steals up from under
The heavy-folded clouds; and on thy form

The lightning glances gay,
With its perplexing ray,
And sweep across thy path the speeding showers;
This pageantry doth fill thy outward hours.

Upon the rivers thou dost float at peace,
Or on the ocean
Feelest the motion;
Of every natural form thou hast the lease, —
Because thy way lies there
Where it is good and fair.
Thou hast perception, learning, and much art,
Propped by the columns of a stately heart.

From the deep mysteries thy goblet fills;
The wines do murmur
That Nature warmed her,
When she was pressing out from must the hills,
The plains that near us lie,
The foldings of the sky;
Whate'er within the horizon's bound there is,
From Hades' caldron to the blue God's bliss.

We may no more; so might we sing fore'er,
Thy thought recalling;
Thus waters falling
Over great cataracts from their lakes do bear
The power that is divine,
And bends their stately line:
All but thy beauty the cold verses have,
All but thy music, organ-mellowed nave.

NOTE. — In connection with this Ode of Mr. Channing which was read at the School of Philosophy from his second volume of "Poems" (Boston, 1847), there was also read an ode by the same poet to a son of Mr. Emerson when three years old, from which, at the desire of many who heard it, the following lines are here printed. The whole poem may be found in a little volume called "The Woodman and other Poems" (Boston, 1849), which has long been out of print, but exists in libraries here and there : —

"Child of the Good Divinity,
    Child of one
  Who shines on me
    Like a most friendly sun;
  Child of the azure sky
  (Who has outdone it in that eye,
  That trellised window in unfathomed blue), —
  Child of the midworld, sweet and true !
  Child of the combing crystal spheres
  Throned above this salt pool of tears, —
    Child of immortality,
  Why hast thou come to cheat the Destiny ?

"By the sweet mouth half-parted in a smile,
    By all thou art, —
  By the pat beating of thy criss-cross heart, —
  How couldst thou light on this plain homespun shore ?
  And — not upon thy own aerial riding —
  Fall down on earth, where turbid sadly pour
  The old perpetual rivers of backsliding ?

"Since thou *art* fast
  On our autumnal ball,
  Of thistle and specked grass weave thee a nest;
  Renounce (if possible) the mighty air-spanned hall,
    Cups of imperial nectar,
  Vases of transparent porphyry,
  Amethystine rings of splendor,
  Bright footstools of chalcedony, —

The alabaster bed,
Where in the plume of seraph sunk thy head,
To the full-sounding organ of the sphere,
   So amorously played
By the smooth, hyaline finger of thy peer !
  Be those blue eyes
    Thy only atmosphere !
  For in them lies
    What is than earth, than heaven more dear."

III.

ODE OF 1882. — F. B. Sanborn.

I.

Across these meadows, o'er the hills,
Beside our sleeping waters, hurrying rills,
Through many a woodland dark and many a bright
    arcade,
Where out and in the shifting sunbeams braid
An Indian mat of checkered light and shade, —
The sister seasons in their maze,
Since last we wakened here
From hot siesta the still drowsy year,
Have led the fourfold dance along our ways ; —
Autumn apparelled sadly gay,
Winter's white furs and shortened day,
Spring's loitering footstep, quickened at the last,
And half the affluent Summer went and came,
As for uncounted years the same, —
Ah me ! another unreturning spring hath passed.

II.

"When the young die," the Grecian mourner said,
"The spring-time from the year hath vanishèd,"
The gray-haired poet, in unfading youth,
Sits by the shrine of Truth,
Her oracles to spell,
And their deep meaning tell ;
Or else he chants a bird-like note
From that thick-bearded throat
Which warbled forth the songs of smooth-cheeked
      May
Beside Youth's sunny fountain all the day ;
Sweetly the echoes ring
As in the flush of spring ;
At last the poet dies,
The sunny fountain dries, —
The oracles are dumb, no more the wood-birds sing.

III.

Homer forsakes the billowy round
Of sailors circling o'er the island-sea ;
Pindar, from Theban fountains and the mound
Builded in love and woe by doomed Antigone,
Must pass beneath the ground ;
Stout Æschylus that slew the deep-haired Mede
At Marathon, at Salamis, and freed
Athens from Persian thrall,
Then sung the battle-call, —
Must yield to that one foe he could not quell ;
In Gela's flowery plain he slumbers well.

15

Sicilian roses bloom
Above his nameless tomb,
And there the nightingale doth mourn in vain
For Bion, too, who sang the Dorian strain :
By Arethusa's tide
His brother swains might flute in Dorian mood,
The bird of love in thickets of the wood
Sing for a thousand years his grave beside, —
Yet Bion still was mute, — the Dorian lay had died.

IV.

The Attic poet at approach of age
Laid by his garland, took the staff and scrip,
For singing-robes the mantle of the sage,
And taught gray wisdom with the same grave lip
That once had carolled gay,
Where silver flutes breathed soft, and festal harps
          did play ;
Young Plato sang of love and beauty's charm,
While he that from Stagira came to hear,
In lyric measures bade his princely pupil arm
And strike the Persian tyrant mute with fear.
High thought doth well accord with melody,
Brave deed with Poesy,
And song is prelude fair to sweet Philosophy.
But wiser still was Shakspeare's noble choice,
Poet and sage at once, whose varied voice
Taught beyond Plato's ken while charming every
          ear, —
A kindred choice was his, our poet, sage, and seer !

V.

Now Avon glides through Severn to the sea,
And murmurs that her Shakspeare sings no more ;
Thames bears the freight of many a tribute shore,
But on those banks her poet bold and free,
That stooped in blindness at his lowly door,
Yet never bowed to priest or prince the knee,
Wanders no more by those sad sisters led ;
Herbert and Spenser dead
Have left their names alone to him whose scheme
Stiffly endeavors to supplant the dream
Of seer and poet, with mechanic rule
Learned from the chemist's closet, from the surgeon's
    tool.
With us Philosophy still spreads her wing,
And soars to seek Heaven's King, —
Nor creeps through charnels, prying with the glass
That makes the little big, — while gods unseen may
    pass.

VI.

Along the marge of these slow-gliding streams,
Our winding Concord and the wider flow
Of Charles by Cambridge, walks and dreams
A throng of poets, — tearfully they go,
For each bright river misses from its band
The keenest eye, the truest heart, the surest minstrel-
    hand, —
They sleep each on his wooded hill above the sorrow-
    ing land.

Sadly their mound with garlands we adorn
Of violet, lily, laurel, and the flowering thorn, —
Sadly above them wave
The wailing pine-trees of their native strand ;
Sadly the distant billows smite the shore,
Plash in the sunlight, or at midnight roar :
All sounds of melody, all things sweet and fair,
On earth, in sea or air,
Droop and grow silent by the poet's grave.

VII.

Yet wherefore weep ?   Old age is but a tomb,
A living hearse, slow creeping to the gloom
And utter silence.   He from age is freed
Who meets the stroke of death, and rises thence
Victor o'er every woe ; his sure defence
Is swift defeat, — by that he doth succeed :
Death is the poet's friend, — I speak it sooth ;
Death shall restore him to his golden youth,
Unlock for him the portal of renown,
And on Fame's tablet write his verses down
For every age in endless time to read.
With us Death's quarrel is ; he takes away
Joy from our eyes, — from this dark world the day,
When other skies he opens to the poet's ray.

VIII.

Lonely these meadows green,
Silent these warbling woodlands must appear
To us, by whom our Poet-sage was seen
Wandering among their beauties, year by year, —

Listening with delicate ear
To each fine note that fell from tree or sky,
Or rose from earth on high, —
Glancing his falcon eye,
In kindly radiance, as of some young star,
At all the shows of Nature near and far,
Or on the tame procession plodding by
Of daily toil and care, — and all Life's pageantry;
Then darting forth warm beams of wit and love,
Wide as the sun's great orbit, and as high above
These paths wherein our lowly tasks we ply.

IX.

His was the task and his the lordly gift
Our eyes, our hearts, bent earthward, to uplift;
He found us chained in Plato's fabled cave,
Our faces long averted from the blaze
Of Heaven's broad light, and idly turned to gaze
On shadows, flitting ceaseless as the wave
That dashes ever idly on some isle enchanted;
By shadows haunted
We sat, — amused in youth, in manhood daunted,
In vacant age forlorn, — then slipped within the grave,
The same dull chain still clasped around our shroud.
These captives, bound and bowed,
He from their dungeon like that angel led,
Who softly to imprisoned Peter said,
"Arise up quickly! gird thyself and flee!"
We wist not whose the thrilling voice, we knew our
     souls were free.

X.

Ah ! blest those years of youthful hope,
When every breeze was zephyr, every morning
    May !
Then, as we bravely climbed the slope
Of life's steep mount, we gained a wider scope
At every stair, — and could with joy survey
The track beneath us, and the upward way ;
Both lay in light, — round both the breath of love
Fragrant and warm from Heaven's own tropic blew ;
Beside us what glad comrades smiled and strove !
Beyond us what dim visions rose to view !
With thee, dear Master, through that morning land
We journeyed happy ; thine the guiding hand,
Thine the far-looking eye, the dauntless smile ;
Thy lofty song of hope did the long march beguile.

XI.

Now scattered wide and lost to loving sight
The gallant train
That heard thy strain !
'T is May no longer, — shadows of the night
Beset the downward path, thy light withdrawn, —
And with thee vanished that perpetual dawn
Of which thou wert the harbinger and seer.
Yet courage ! comrades, — though no more we hear
Each other's voices, lost within this cloud
That Time and Chance about our way have cast, —
Still his brave music haunts the hearkening ear,

As 'mid bold cliffs and dewy passes of the Past.
Be that our countersign! for chanting loud,
His magic song, though far apart we go,
Best shall we thus discern both friend and foe.

CONCORD, May, 1882.

IV.

TWO SONNETS. — MRS. E. C. KINNEY.

EMERSON.

I.

LIKE some old Titan of majestic height,
His march has been with grand and solemn tread,
The brain profoundly working, while the head,
Circled by mists, was often hid from sight;
Yet from its cloud, when great thought flashed to
    light,
That mighty brain by the elect was read;
The many saw not, turned away instead,
His brightness, veiled, to them was only night.
But, as he walked, anon at either side
Fell pregnant seeds of thought, which, taking root
In minds long barren, showed the tender shoot
That later blossomed: clouds might genius hide,
Yet everywhere the great man planted foot,
His mark remains, and shall through time abide.

NEW YORK, April, 1882.

II.

DEAR Nature's Child, he nestled close to Her!
She to his heart had whispered deeper things
Than Science from the wells of learning brings:
His still small voice the human soul could stir,
For Nature made him her interpreter,
And gave her favorite son far-reaching wings, —
He soared and sang (as Heaven's lark only sings)
Devout in praise, Truth's truest worshipper.
With eyes anointed in his upward flight,
He quick discerned what was divine in men, —
Reading the humblest spirit's tongue aright:
Oh, Prophet, Poet, Leader! in thy light
How many saw beyond their natural ken,
Who follow now the star which led them then!

NEW CASTLE, N. H., Sept. 5, 1884.

IX.

EMERSON'S ETHICS.

By EDWIN D. MEAD.

I THINK the only thing which will secure to this Concord School of Philosophy a long remembrance will be the mention of it in Emerson's biography. When we are dead, men will read there, that in the evening of his life he was interested in these meetings and read lectures in them; and this mention will secure that men shall ask of them, to a day when else all questions had long ceased. It is proper, then, and worthy that we should give his thought that large measure of attention and of prominence which we do give it here and now. It is well that we American students of philosophy should seek to learn and to teach the doctrine of this greatest master of ours, and greatest — perhaps the only great — American philosopher. For, much more than philosopher, — so much more that the philosopher is but one simple element in the harmonious man, in nowise monopolizing or tyrannizing over temperament and powers, — yet is Emerson truly one of the greatest philosophers of all time, and has given the deepest answers in his time to the soul's Whence? and What? and Whither? So harmonious and synthetic is he, so interfused is his philosophy with life and poetry and beauty and counsel, that it is not a wholly grateful task to discuss him in that analytic and departmental manner which our programme imposes. Yet if by such discussion, by any stimulation of curiosity through the showing of Emerson's relation to those problems which everlastingly vex most men's minds, a more careful study of his own life-giving page is provoked in any, the price is surely not too high.

So much being said, it is with exceptional pleasure that I invite the attention of this serious company to the subject which has been given me, of Emerson's ethics. For I have been thinking long that in this time, when philosophic men are working more ingeniously and energetically to properly ground a system of morals than to do anything else in philosophy, the hint — and much more than the hint, the clear indication — of the direction which the next real and great advance in ethical theory must take is given us by Emerson. I believe that, just as Emerson has best given the insight which harmonizes idealism and the modern doctrine of evolution, — which shows indeed that the doctrine of evolution gets its adequate and rational ground only in a spiritual philosophy, — so he has made an ethical statement possible, large enough to take in both Kant and Spencer; and this in no mere eclectic fashion, but in the genuinely synthetic way of enriching and illuminating and explaining both, in a truth which is deeper and larger than theirs.

It has been impossible for me, in the brief time which is all that I have been able to give to the preparation of this essay, to do much more than present in some sort of systematic way such words of Emerson's own as best indicate and illustrate his great truth. Yet perhaps, after all, no one could do better than this; and I hope at least to make the conception clear and influential.

This truth is, that morality is the law of the universe as it is operative and consciously adopted in the soul of man, just as gravitation and the chemic forces are the same law of the universe operating otherwise.

I might repeat a score of passages in which this truth finds notable expression, to set as a sort of text before what I would say. I will here set two such passages, — passages which will be the better remembered because of the significant occasions of their utterance. The first is the closing words of the famous Harvard Address of 1838, an address which, as a whole, it is perhaps not unfair to pronounce the first free and full utterance of rational religion in America : —

" I look for the new teacher that shall follow so far those shining laws that he shall see them come full circle ; shall see their rounding, complete grace ; shall see the world to be the mirror of the soul ; shall see the identity of the law of gravitation with purity of heart; and shall show that the Ought, that Duty, is one thing with Science, with Beauty, and with Joy."

The other passage is from the address before the Free Religious Association, in 1869 : —

"I am ready to give, as often before, the first simple foundation of my belief : that the Author of Nature has not left himself without a witness in any sane mind; that the moral sentiment speaks to every man the law after which the universe was made ; that we find parity, identity of design, through Nature, and benefit to be the uniform aim ; that there is a force always at work to make the best better and the worst good."

" The identity of the law of gravitation·with purity of heart." " The moral sentiment speaks to every man the law after which the universe was made." Those are especially the texts which I would have remembered. It is one idea which speaks through both. Indeed, the most notable thing about this whole brief address of 1869, as still more about the address of 1880, upon "The Preacher," — Emerson's last great religious utterance, — is the way in which it revives and reiterates in some form almost every leading thought of the Address of 1838. But this rare consistency and persistency is the ever notable thing in Emerson. It is the superficial man that finds and talks of inconsistencies in Emerson. Never was so deep a thinker so mature at thirty ; and " Nature," his earliest essay, might still pass for the best, and a sufficient, summary of his philosophy.

I have chosen these two texts for a study of Emerson's ethics, not more because they were spoken on memorable occasions, than because those memorable occasions were religious occasions. The ethics of Emerson can never be dissociated from the religion of Emerson. The study of the one involves reference to the other. " How can we speak of the action of the mind under any divisions," he asks once himself, " as of its knowledge, of its ethics, of its works, and so forth, since it melts will into perception, knowledge into act ? Each becomes the other." Truest of all in Emerson's case is this melting of ethics and religion. Ethics ever becomes religion with him, and religion becomes ethics, in ways which we shall consider.

A few words concerning Emerson's religious thought are convenient and necessary at the very outset of this study of his ethics. And perhaps much ground can be cleared in no other way so quickly as by a brief statement of his attitude toward the popular religion, the creed of the Church. Of all the great religious thinkers of America, and almost of our time altogether, Emerson has been perhaps the most impatient of the Church and its doctrinal statements. Of this, this audience does not need to be reminded. But the matter of interest to us is the manner and purpose of his expressions of impatience, and the doctrine which inspires his criticism. He said : —

" We are all very sensible, it is forced on us every day, that churches are outgrown ; that the creeds are outgrown.

. . . The Church is not large enough for the man; it cannot inspire the enthusiasm which is the parent of everything good in history. . . . For that enthusiasm you must have something greater than yourselves, and not less. . . . But in churches every healthful and thoughtful mind finds itself in something less; it is checked, cribbed, confined."

" The Jewish *cultus* is declining; the Divine, or, as some will say, the truly Human, hovers, now seen, now unseen, before us."

" Swedenborg and Behmen both failed by attaching themselves to the Christian symbol instead of to the moral sentiment, which carries innumerable Christianities, humanities, divinities, in its bosom. What have I to do with arks and passovers, ephahs and ephods; what with heave-offerings and unleavened bread, chariots of fire, dragons crowned and horned, behemoth and unicorn? Good for Orientals, these are nothing to me. The more learning you bring to explain them, the more glaring the impertinence. Of all absurdities, this of some foreigner proposing to take away my rhetoric and substitute his own, and amuse me with pelican and stork instead of thrush and robin, palm-trees and shittim-wood instead of sassafras and hickory, seems the most useless."

" If a man claims to know and speak of God, and carries you backward to the phraseology of some old mouldered nation in another country, in another world, believe him not."

The animating feeling here is that no time or place was ever sacreder than ours, that God is in all history alike, and that we too sustain original relations with God. It is the same spirit as that of the opening lines of " Nature : " —

" The foregoing generations beheld God and Nature face to face; we through their eyes. Why should not we also enjoy an original relation to the universe? Why should not we have a poetry and philosophy of insight, and not of tradition; and a religion by revelation to us, and not the history of theirs? . . . The sun shines to-day also. There is more wool and flax in the fields."

" An original relation to the universe," — that word describes the spirit; and it is in the enforcement of this that he comes into collision with the Church upon its three doctrines of Miracle, the Bible, and Christ. His demand throughout is for an original relation and a uniform and universal law.

" The word Miracle, as pronounced by Christian churches, gives a false impression; it is Monster. It is not one with the blowing clover and the falling rain."

" I object, of course, to the claim of miraculous dispensation, — certainly not to the *doctrine* of Christianity. This claim impairs, to my mind, the soundness of him who makes it, and indisposes us to his communion. . . . It is contrary to that law of Nature which all wise men recognize; namely, never to require a larger cause than is necessary to the effect."

" The word miracle, as it is used, only indicates the ignorance of the devotee, staring with wonder to see water turned into wine, and heedless of the stupendous fact of his own personality. Here he stands, a lonely thought harmoniously organized into correspondence with the universe of mind and matter. What narrative of wonders coming down from a thousand years ought to charm his attention like this? . . . It seems as if, when the spirit of God speaks so plainly to each soul, it were an impiety to be listening to one or another saint. Jesus was better than others, because he refused to listen to others and listened at home."

" It is so wonderful to our neurologists that a man can see without his eyes, that it does not occur to them that it is just as wonderful that he should see with them; and that is ever the difference between the wise and the unwise : the latter wonders at what is unusual, the wise man wonders at the usual."

" Far be from me the impatience which cannot brook the supernatural, the vast ; far be from me the lust of explaining away all which appeals to the imagination, and the great presentiments which haunt us. Willingly I too say, Hail! to the unknown awful powers which transcend the ken of the understanding."

" It is not the incredibility of the fact," he says of various alleged marvels, " but a certain want of harmony between the action and the agent. We are used to vaster wonders. One moment of a man's life is a fact so stupendous as to take the lustre out of all fiction. But Nature never works like a conjurer. . . . The soul penetrated with the beatitude which pours into it on all sides, asks no interpositions, no new laws, — the old are good enough for it, — finds in every cart-path of labor ways to heaven, and the humblest lot exalted."

" We want all the aids to our moral training. We cannot spare the vision nor the virtue of the saints ; but let it be by pure sympathy, not with any personal or official claim. If you are childish, and exhibit your saint as a worker of wonders, a thaumaturgist, I am repelled. That claim takes his teachings out of logic and out of Nature, and permits official and arbitrary senses to be grafted on the teachings. It is the praise of our New Testament that its teachings go to the honor and benefit of humanity, — that no better lesson has been taught or incarnated. Let it stand, beautiful and wholesome, with whatever is most like it in the teaching and practice of men ; but do not attempt to elevate it out of humanity by saying, 'This was not a man,' for then you confound it with the fables of every popular religion, and my distrust of the story makes me distrust the doctrine as soon as it differs from my own belief."

He sees how much the New Testament loses in the charm of suggestion, of poetry and truth, by its connection with a church, and by the official place in which it is put : —

" Mankind cannot long suffer this loss, and the office of this age is to put all these writings on the eternal footing of equality of origin in the instincts of the human mind. It is certain that each inspired master will gain instantly by the separation from the idolatry of ages."

" Men have come to speak of the revelation as somewhat long ago given and done, as if God were dead."

" It is the office of a true teacher to show us that God is, not was ; that he speaketh, not spake."

" With each new mind, a new secret of Nature transpires ; nor can the Bible be closed until the last great man is born."

16

" The world is young : the former great men call to us affectionately. We too must write bibles, to unite again the heavens and the earthly world."

There is, you perceive, no trouble with the doctrine of inspiration, but rather a larger assertion of inspiration, — trouble only with the doctrine which limits inspiration. He cannot allow that the Holy Ghost was exhausted by one effort or a dozen ; it still and forever hovers over elect men with informations as surprising and commanding as those which came through Moses or Elias or Paul. There is no trouble with the supernatural, — trouble only with the provincial-supernatural, with the doctrine of the limitation or insulation of the divine energy. He asserts the natural-supernatural ; " in the universal miracle petty and particular miracles disappear." " The cure for false theology," he said, " is mother-wit. The scepticism which men say devastates the community cannot be cured or stayed by any modification of theologic creeds, much less by theologic discipline." " Forget your books and traditions, and obey your moral perceptions at this hour."

More strikingly than in his discussion of the Church's general doctrine of miracle and its doctrine of inspiration, does this conception of Emerson appear in his opposition to the Church's doctrine of Christ. I think that no man in late times, unless perhaps Fichte in Germany, has paid such notable, discriminating, and illuminating tribute to the mind of Christ as Emerson. " Until I read Emerson," said one of our ablest Congregational ministers to me, " I did not know the mind of Christ." But this tribute is always to Christ's pre-eminent possession of those qualities which constitute the glory of the human mind as such, and draws back at each suggestion of peculiarity and miracle : —

" The excellence of Jesus, and of every true teacher, is, that he affirms the Divinity in him and in us, — not thrusts himself between it and us. It would instantly indispose us to any person claiming to speak for the Author of Nature, the setting forth any fact or law which we did not find in our consciousness."

" Jesus has immense claims on the gratitude of mankind, and knew how to guard the integrity of his brother's soul from himself also ; but, in his disciples, admiration of him runs away with their reverence for the human soul, and they hamper us with limitations of person and text. Every exaggeration of these is a violation of the soul's right, and inclines the manly reader to lay down the New Testament, to take up the Pagan philosophers."

" The language that describes Christ to Europe and America is not the style of friendship and enthusiasm to a great and noble heart, but is appropriated and formal, — paints a demigod, as the Orientals or the Greeks would describe Osiris or Apollo."

" The Christian Church has dwelt — it dwells — with noxious exaggeration about the *person* of Jesus. The soul knows no persons. It invites every man to expand to the full circle of the universe."

" 'T is presumed there is but one Shakspeare, one Homer, one Jesus, — not that all are or shall be inspired. But we must begin by affirming. Truth and goodness subsist forevermore. . . . No historical person begins to content us."

" Jesus astonishes and overpowers sensual people. They cannot unite him to history, or reconcile him with themselves. As they come to revere their intuitions and aspire to live holily, their own piety explains every fact, every word."

" There are humble souls who think it the highest worship to expect of Heaven the most and the best; who do not wonder that there was a Christ, but that there were not a thousand; who have conceived an infinite hope for mankind; who believe that the history of Jesus is the history of every man, written large."

" Let a man believe in God, and not in names and places and persons. . . . Dare to love God without mediator or veil. Thank God for these good men, but say, I also am a man."

And particularly, in this connection, will be remembered the famous passage in the Divinity School Address : —

" Jesus Christ belonged to the true race of prophets. He saw with open eye the mystery of the soul. Drawn by its severe harmony, ravished with its beauty, he lived in it, and had his being there. Alone in all history he estimated the greatness of man. One man was true to what is in you and me. He saw that God incarnates himself in man, and evermore goes forth anew to take possession of his World. He said, in this jubilee of sublime emotion, ' I am divine. Through me, God acts; through me, speaks. Would you see God, see me ; or see thee, when thou also thinkest as I now think.'"

Having thus considered Emerson's assertion of the universal-supernatural, the perennial inspiration, and the common divine sonship, through his negation of the Church's doctrines of historical miracle, of a Bible with covers, and of an "only-begotten" son, we are prepared to understand better the aim and scope and spirit of his positive expositions of religion, and to see how his religious conception is the very foundation of, or rather almost one with, his moral conviction and philosophy.

Two well-known passages upon the Church and the worship of the future will serve us as a good starting-point for this part of our study. The first, as will be recognized, is from that inspired last page of the essay on "Worship," published in 1860 : —

"There will be a new church founded on moral science ; at first cold and naked, a babe in a manger again, the algebra and mathematics of ethical law, the church of men to come, without shawms, or psaltery, or sackbut ; but it will have heaven and earth for its beams and rafters ; science for symbol and illustration ; it will fast enough gather beauty, music, picture, poetry."

The other passage is from "The Preacher," published in 1880 : —

"We are in transition, from the worship of the fathers, which enshrined the law in a private and personal history, to a worship which recognizes the true eternity of the law, its presence to you and me, its equal energy in what is called brute nature as in what is called sacred history. The next age will behold God in the ethical laws, — as mankind begins to see them in this age, — self-equal, self-executing, instantaneous, and self-affirmed ; needing no voucher, no prophet, and no miracle besides their own irresistibility, — and will regard natural history, private fortunes, and politics, not for themselves, as we have done, but as illustrations of those laws, of that beatitude and love."

The new church will be "founded on moral science." "The next age will behold God in the ethical laws." It is, you perceive, one thought which speaks in both places. " In transition from a worship which enshrined the law in a private and personal history, to a worship which recognizes the true eternity of the law, its presence to you and to me." The law which the old worships have thus enshrined in a private and personal history is the moral law. To Emerson, as to Kant and to Carlyle, the purpose and the essence of religion is *the moral life,* and the significance and value of all saints and cults is in their illustration and enforcement of this.[1] " Hast

[1] This principle, thus generally stated, would not of course be denied by the really thoughtful and philosophic minds among those who attach a greater significance and value to the " personal history" and the cult than Emerson does. The principle, indeed, could scarcely be better asserted than in these words of Bishop Huntington : "The end of Christianity, the object of Revelation, the ideal of the Church, is personal character. Systems, theologies, creeds, sacraments, liturgies, missions, — all are for this ; unless this is produced somewhere, they fail. This making of character is our first concern."

thou reflected, O serious reader, Advanced-Liberal or other," asks Carlyle, in " Past and Present," " that the one end, essence, use, of all religion, past, present, and to come, was this only : To keep that same Moral Conscience or Inner Light of ours alive and shining ; — which certainly the ' Phantasms' and the ' turbid media' were not essential for ? All religion was here to remind us, better or worse, of the quite *infinite* difference there is between a Good man and a Bad; to bid us love infinitely the one, abhor and avoid infinitely the other, — strive infinitely to be the one, and not to be the other."

Emerson is full of passages urging this view. " The essence of Christianity," he said, in his eulogy of Parker, " is its practical morals. It is there for use, or it is nothing." " I consider theology," he says, — using theology, of course, in the popular, not in the philosophical, sense, — " to be the rhetoric of morals. The mind of this age has fallen away from theology to morals. I conceive it an advance."

" I think that all the dogmas rest on morals, and that it is only a question of youth or maturity, of more or less fancy in the recipient ; that the stern determination to do justly, to speak the truth, to be chaste and humble, was substantially the same, whether under a self-respect, or under a vow made on the knees at the shrine of Madonna."

" The creed, the legend, forms of worship, swiftly decay. Morals is the incorruptible essence, very heedless in its richness of any past teacher or witness, — heedless of their lives and fortunes. It does not ask whether you are wrong or right in your anecdotes of them ; but it is all in all how you stand to your own tribunal."

" The infant soul must learn to walk alone. At first he is forlorn, homeless ; but this rude stripping him of all support drives him inward, and he finds himself unhurt ; he finds himself face to face with the majestic Presence, reads the original of the Ten Commandments, the original of Gospels and Epistles ; nay, his narrow chapel expands to the blue cathedral of the sky."

" The popular religion echoes an original conscience in men. The commanding fact which I never do not see, is the sufficiency of the moral sentiment. We buttress it up, in shallow hours or ages, with legends, traditions, and forms, each good for the one moment in which it was a happy type or symbol of the Power ; but the Power sends in the next moment a new lesson, which we lose while our eyes are reverted and striving to perpetuate the old."

" The decline of the influence of Calvin, or Fénelon, or Wesley, or Channing, need give us no uneasiness. The builder of heaven has not so ill constructed his creature as that the religion — that is, the public nature — should fall out. The public and the private element, like north and south, like inside and outside, like centrifugal and centripetal, adhere to every soul, and cannot be subdued except the soul is dissipated. God builds his temple in the heart, on the ruins of churches and religions."

" The life of those once omnipotent traditions was really not in the legend, but in the moral sentiment and the metaphysical fact which the legends enclosed ; and these survive. A new Socrates, or Zeno, or Swedenborg, or Pascal, or a new crop of geniuses like those of the Elizabethan age, may be born in this age, and, with happy heart and a bias for theism, bring asceticism, duty, and magnanimity into vogue again."

" Men will learn to put back the emphasis peremptorily on pure morals, always the same, not subject to doubtful interpretation ; . . . to make morals the absolute test, and so uncover and drive out the false religions."

" We are thrown back on rectitude forever and ever, only rectitude,— to mend one ; that is all we can do. But *that* the zealot stigmatizes as a sterile chimney-corner philosophy. Now, the first position I make is, that natural religion supplies still all the facts which are disguised under the dogma of popular creeds. The progress of religion is steadily to its identity with morals."

" It accuses us that pure ethics is not now formulated and concreted into a *cultus*, — a fraternity with assemblings and holy-days, with song and book, with brick and stone."

" Ethics are thought not to satisfy affection. But all the religion we have is the ethics of one or another holy person. As soon as character appears, be sure love will, and veneration, and anecdotes, and fables about him, and delight of good men and women in him."

" Whenever the sublimities of character shall be incarnated in a man, we may rely that awe and love and insatiable curiosity will follow his steps."

" Is it quite impossible to believe that men should be drawn to each other by the simple respect which each man feels for another in whom he discovers absolute honesty ; the respect he feels for one who thinks life is quite too coarse and frivolous, and that he should like to lift it a little, should like to be the friend of some man's virtue ? for another who, underneath his compliances with artificial society, would dearly like to serve somebody, to test his own reality by making himself useful and indispensable ? "

"America shall introduce a new religion," he exclaimed ; and the new religion which he thus foresaw and prophesied was this religion of ethics. Already it seemed to him the religious feeling was preparing to rise out of its old forms " to an absolute justice and healthy perception," infusing " a new feeling of humanity into public actions."

It will not fail to occur to some here, that this whole view of ethical religion is strikingly approximated by the programme of the Societies for Ethical Culture, whose rise in various of our cities, starting with the work of Professor Adler in New York, is certainly one of the signs of the times, and a matter which seems to me deserving of the serious attention of religious men. And it is especially notable that Mr. Salter, the most speculative mind, perhaps, that is actively interested in this movement, remarked, in a recent address upon the philosophical basis of the movement, " I know not what true thought of mine you may not find, stripped of its imperfections of statement, in Emerson." In truth, I do believe that this movement, and all such, are notable approximations to the view of Emerson, and mark the effort of humanity to fulfil his prophecy. Wherein Mr. Salter's own expressed philosophy falls short of Emerson, and, as it seems to me, of truth, appears as well by testing it by our two passages in

"Worship" and "The Preacher" as otherwise. "A new church will be founded on ethical law," said Emerson in "Worship;" but he added, "The Laws are alive; they *know* if we have obeyed." "The next age will behold God in the ethical laws," he said in "The Preacher;" but mark deeply, — not simply behold the ethical laws, but behold God in the ethical laws. The points here involved are essentially the same as those involved in the ethical and religious thought of Fichte during his Jena period, with which most of those here are doubtless familiar. The evolution of Fichte's own thought from the conception of God as the moral law of the universe, to the conception of God as real ground, is worthy every student's careful study.

"God in the ethical laws." "The good laws are *alive.*" "The notion of virtue," Emerson says in the essay on Plato, "is not to be arrived at except through direct contemplation of the divine essence." "I am far from accepting the sentiment," he says elsewhere, "that the revelations of the moral sentiment are insufficient, as if it furnished a rule only, and not the spirit by which the rule is animated. . . . The sentiment itself teaches unity of source." "Men talk of 'mere morality,' which is much as if one should say, 'Poor God, with nobody to help him!' I find the omnipresence and the almightiness in the reaction of every atom in Nature. . . . Let us replace sentimentalism by realism, and dare to uncover those simple and terrible laws."

We are thus brought to the particular consideration of what morality is, in the philosophy of Emerson.   I defined his view, at the beginning, as this:
that morality is the law of the universe as it is
operative and consciously adopted in the soul of man,
just as gravitation and the chemic forces are the
same law of the universe operating otherwise.   And
we will here recall our two texts: "the identity of
the law of gravitation with purity of heart;" "the
moral sentiment speaks to every man the law after
which the universe was made."

"All power," says Emerson, "is of one kind, — a
sharing of the nature of the world."

"It is a short sight to limit our faith in laws to those
of gravity, of chemistry, of botany, and so forth.   These
laws do not stop when our eyes lose them, but push the
same geometry and chemistry up into the invisible plane
of social and rational life."

"It is the same fact existing as sentiment and as will
in mind, which works in nature as irresistible law, ex-
erting influence over nations, intelligent beings, or down
in the kingdoms of brute or of chemical atoms."

"I look on those sentiments which make the glory of
the human being, — love, humanity, faith, — as being also
the intimacy of Divinity in the atoms; and that man
is made of the same atoms as the world is, he shares the
same impressions, predispositions, and destiny.   When his
mind is illuminated, when his heart is kind, he throws
himself joyfully into the sublime order, and does with
knowledge what the stones do by structure."

It would perhaps be imposssible to find any single phrase which better defines Emerson's view of morality than this last, — *doing with knowledge what the stones do by structure.* We exist to an absolutely defined end ; and toward the fulfilment of that definition the absolute law of our being commands, as truly as the law of structure commands the inert and passive stone. "The weight of the universe," says Emerson, "is pressed down on the shoulders of each moral agent to hold him to his task. The only path of escape known in all the worlds of God is performance." But this performance, which is necessary, must, to make morality, be also voluntary. Man is free. He must do with knowledge, and by choice, what the stones do by structure, to fulfil his greater definition. "The last lesson of life," says Emerson, "the choral song which rises from all elements and all angels, is a voluntary obedience, a necessitated freedom."

Morality, then, is simply the health, the obedience, the perfection of our nature. It is the fulfilment of our definition, the triumph over the negative elements of the soul, the law of the universe reflected in the highest sphere. The moral law is the law of the universe. Says Emerson : —

"The universe is alive. All things are moral. The soul which within us is a sentiment, outside of us is a law. In us it is inspiration ; out there in Nature we see its fatal strength."

"A breath of will blows eternally through the universe of souls in the direction of the Right and Necessary. It is the air which all intellects inhale and exhale, and it is the wind which blows the worlds into order and orbit."

" If in sidereal ages gravity and projection keep their craft, and the ball never loses its way in its wild path through space, — a secreter gravitation, a secreter projection, rule not less tyrannically in human history, and keep the balance of power from age to age unbroken. For though the new element of freedom and an individual has been admitted, yet the primordial atoms are prefigured and predetermined to moral issues, are in search of justice, and ultimate right is done."

" The dice are loaded ; the colors are fast, because they are the native colors of the fleece ; the globe is a battery, because every atom is a magnet ; and the police and sincerity of the universe are secured by God's delegating his divinity to every particle."

" Morals are generated as the atmosphere is. 'T is a secret, the genesis of either ; but the springs of justice and courage do not fail any more than salt or sulphur springs."

" The constitution of the universe is on the side of the man who wills to do right. It is of no use to vote down gravitation or morals."

" Character," he says, " is nature in the highest form." Over and over, in the essays of Emerson, do we come upon sharp and striking definitions of character. I know of nothing which he defines so often by a phrase, as character. And you will observe that the definition is always a mere variation of the phrase I have quoted, " character is nature in the highest form," —

" Character is the moral order of the universe seen through the medium of an individual nature."

" Virtue is the adopting of the dictate of the universal mind by the individual mind. Character is the .habit of this obedience, and religion is the accompanying emotion, — the emotion of reverence, which the presence of the universal ever excites in the individual." [1]

" Character is the habit of action from the permanent vision of truth."

" Character is a will built on the reason of things."

" Character is a natural power, like light and heat, and all nature co-operates with it."

" The reason why we feel one man's presence, and do not feel another's," says Emerson, "is as simple as gravity. Truth is the summit of being; justice is the application of it to affairs. All individual natures stand in a scale, according to the purity of this element in them. . . . This natural force is no more to be withstood than any other natural force. We can drive a stone upward for a moment into the air, but it is yet true that all stones will forever fall; and whatever instances can be quoted of unpunished theft, or of a lie which somebody credited, justice must prevail, and it is the privilege of truth to make itself believed."

This fundamental idea in Emerson's ethics, that morality is simply the law of the universe, recurs so

---

[1] In accord with this definition of religion is the following : " The perception of this law of laws awakens in the mind a sentiment which we call the religious sentiment, and which makes our highest happiness."

constantly, and in such forcible and striking form, that it is difficult to set a limit to quotation. The following passage from " Nature " is important before we leave this portion of our subject, for the sake, especially, of the philosophical principle suggested at its close : —

" All things are moral ; and in their boundless changes have an unceasing reference to the spiritual nature. Therefore is Nature glorious with form, color, and motion, that every globe in the remotest heaven, every chemical change from the rudest crystal up to the laws of life, every change of vegetation from the first principle of growth in the eye of a leaf to the tropical forest and antediluvian coal-mine, every animal function from the sponge up to Hercules, shall hint or thunder to man the laws of right and wrong, and echo the Ten Commandments. Therefore is Nature ever the ally of Religion. . . . This ethical character so penetrates the bone and marrow of Nature, as to seem the end for which it was made."

This last thought is considered in detail, as will be remembered, in the chapter on " Discipline ; " and at the beginning of the chapter on " Idealism " occurs the notable remark: " A noble doubt perpetually suggests itself, whether this end of discipline be not the Final Cause of the universe, and whether Nature outwardly exists. . . . It is a sufficient account of that appearance we call the world, that God will teach a human mind, and so makes it the receiver of a certain number of congruent sensations, which we call sun and moon, man and woman, house and trade."

The grounds on which he proceeds to reject the extreme theory of Subjective Idealism will be remembered; and that theory is not necessary for the freest use of this thought of the ethical and disciplinary character of the universe. But it is interesting and significant that Emerson is here occupied with the same conception which Fichte declared so unreservedly in his essay on the "Ground of our Faith in a Divine Government." The world, said Fichte, is "nothing else than the rationally objectified perception of our own inner activity," "the objectified material of our duty." Not objectified, of course, in the sense of being made real, but rendered sensible, illustrating, — *versinnlichte* is the German word. "Die Welt is ja nichts weiter, als die nach Vernunftgesetzen versinnlichte Ansicht unseres eigenen inneren Handelns," "das versinnlichte Materiale unserer Pflicht." Emerson says : —

"Every natural process is a version of a moral sentence. The moral law lies at the centre of Nature and radiates to the circumference. . . . All things with which we deal preach to us. . . . The moral sentiment, which thus scents the air, grows in the grain, and impregnates the waters of the world, is caught by man and sinks into his soul. The moral influence of Nature upon every individual is that amount of truth which it illustrates to him. Who can estimate this? who can guess how much firmness the sea-beaten rock has taught the fisherman? how much tranquillity has been reflected to man from the azure sky, over whose unspotted deeps the winds forevermore drive flocks of stormy clouds, and leave no wrinkle or stain?

17

how much industry and providence and affection we have caught from the pantomime of brutes ? "

He says elsewhere : —

" A virtuous man is in unison with the works of Nature, and makes the central figure of the visible sphere. Homer, Pindar, Socrates, Phocian, associate themselves fitly in our memory with the geography and climate of Greece. The visible heavens and earth sympathize with Jesus."

The words in which Kant, in his " Kritik of Practical Reason," formulated the moral law are famous : " So act, that the maxim of thy will may always be the valid principle of a universal legislation." That is, morality is the conformity of our will to absolute or universal law. Precisely this is the thought of Emerson ; and it is noteworthy that he expressly remembers Kant in more than one statement of it.

"What is *moral ?*" he asks. " It is the respecting in action catholic or universal ends. Hear the definition which Kant gives of moral conduct : ' Act always so that the immediate motive of thy will may become a universal rule for all intelligent beings.' "

Again : —

"Morals is the direction of the will on universal ends. He is immoral who is acting to any private end. He is moral — we say it with Marcus Aurelius and with Kant — whose aim or motive may become a universal rule, binding on all intelligent beings."

" On the perpetual conflict between the dictate of this universal mind and the wishes and interests of the individual," he says, " the moral discipline of life is built. The one craves a private benefit, which the other requires him to renounce out of respect to the absolute good. . . . He that speaks the truth executes no private function of an individual will, but the world utters a sound by his lips."

" A man is a little thing whilst he works by and for himself ;" but " when his will leans on a principle, when he is the vehicle of ideas, he borrows their omnipotence."

" The first condition of success is secured in putting ourselves right. We have recovered ourselves from our false position, and planted ourselves on a law of Nature."

" Men who make themselves felt in the world avail themselves of a certain fate in their constitution which they know how to use."

" Gibraltar may be strong, but ideas are impregnable, and bestow on the hero their invincibility. ' It was a great instruction,' said a saint in Cromwell's war, ' that the best courages are but beams of the Almighty.' "

" Hitch your wagon to a star," is the homely, pithy word in which Emerson puts his doctrine into injunction. And perhaps his most adequate statement of the doctrine is the following : —

" The open secret of the world is the art of subliming a private soul with inspirations from the great and public and divine Soul from which we live."

Herein, it seems to me, is the superiority of Emerson to Kant. With Kant, the moral life appears almost as a chronic crucifixion, and we are forever suspicious whether an act be moral at all in so far as it is a pleasure. With Emerson, the moral life becomes by and by, to the healthy and obedient soul, a joy and an inspiration from the great God. "The law was given by Moses," says the old Bible writer, "but grace and truth came by Jesus Christ." And so it is here. There is no disparagement of the Kantian Sinai, but only added glory; yet severity itself appears as loveliness, and law is but another word for grace, obedience for joy.

I suppose we may say that three ethical theories essentially cover what occupies the attention of philosophical students to-day, — the three theories sufficiently indicated by the names of Kant and Mill and Spencer. But the essay of Mill is not concerned with what is really the urgent question with the purely philosophical student; namely, What is the genesis and meaning of the idea of right? For, somehow or other, as Emerson himself remarks, the idea of right *exists* in the human mind. It is a fixed quantity, — *a*, not *x*. It is here. It must be taken for granted at the outset of ethical inquiry, as truly as the perceptions of sense. The ethical question is not about the fact, but about its explanation and implication. I say that Mill's essay is not much concerned with this. The general counsel that men should act unselfishly for public ends is estimable; and it is certainly true that if they do not, society will ultimately fall, and individuals will suffer by it. But seventy years has little to do with what will ultimately happen to society by reason of anything; and I say that Utilitarianism has no imperative or adequate word for the selfish man who elects to take his chances with his selfishness. " If morality has no better foundation than a tendency to promote happiness," well observes Mr. Froude, " its sanction is but a feeble uncertainty. If it be recognized as part of the constitution of the world, it carries with it its right to command." Emerson says somewhere, " No matter how you seem to fatten on a crime, that can never be good for the bee which is bad for the hive ; " and whether true of bees or not, it is certainly true of men and the human hive, which are really what are here spoken of. But it is absolutely and universally true of humanity only because humanity is immortal, and because society is its redeemed form.[1]

With the real truth of Utilitarianism, Emerson was of course in heartiest accord. He was in most

[1] An important chapter in any complete study of Emerson's ethics would be upon his conception of the moral character of society as such. " Civilization depends on morality," he says. "The evolution of a highly destined society must be moral, it must run in the grooves of the celestial wheels ; " and he would have said as freely that morality depends on civilization or social institutions. Man creates moral institutions, which become themselves a moral power and conservator and canon and rebuke. There is a social ideal always extant, a higher always being born, which uplifts individuals above themselves. Emerson notes how the moral tone is immediately elevated and ennobled when men address large bodies or the nation.

natural accord with it; for, sovereign of idealists, Poor Richard himself was not more shrewd and practical than he. "The highest proof of civility," he said, "is that the whole public action of the State is directed on securing the greatest good of the greatest number." But he well knew that the greatest good is spiritual good, and that the greatest number is the whole. He well knew that the greatest good might lie in some act of justice that should decimate the material resources of a whole community. With a single word he exposed the spirit for which "Utilitarianism" too often stands: "Instead of enthusiasm, a low prudence seeks to hold society stanch; but its arms are too short: cordage and machinery never supply the place of life." And he touched the ultimate truth in the couplet, —

> " He that feeds men serveth few ;
> He serves all who dares be true."

And now what is Emerson's relation to the so-called ethics of evolution? Not in the least an antagonistic relation, but a vivifying and rationalizing one. His philosophy has abundant room for all the facts of evolution. His remarkable general anticipations of Darwinism have been frequently pointed out, and were dwelt upon by Dr. Harris in his lecture on "Nature." [1] But he would view a work

---

[1] I may refer to an article of my own in the "Princeton Review" for November, 1884, on "Emerson and the Philosophy of Evolution," as supplementing this portion of the discussion.

like Mr. Spencer's "Data of Ethics" as merely an account of processes, still without explanation. That explanation is the teleological principle, the truth that the eternally creative and informing Force is itself moral and ideal. Moral life is not something into which we drift. It is that thing whereto we are sent. The moral life is the centre, the genesis, and the commanding fact. "You must have a source higher than your tap." "We are made of the moral sentiment," says Emerson ; "the world is built by it, things endure as they share it ; all beauty, all intelligence, all health, exist by it. . . . An Eastern poet said that God had made Justice so dear to the heart of Nature that, if any injustice lurked anywhere under the sky, the blue vault would shrivel to a snake-skin and cast it out by spasms. But the spasms of Nature are years and centuries, and it will tax the faith of man to wait so long."

Belief in "a force always at work to make the best better and the worst good," — that, it will be remembered, was one of the four articles of Emerson's creed, which was read at the beginning. Keeping that in mind, viewing evolution simply as the method of the Moral Mind of the universe, then we shall find that there is no process described by Spencer which might not find proper place in the pages of Emerson. So notable indeed is the element of evolution in his own ethical discussions, that we may justly speak of the Spencerism that was in Emerson before Spencer, in the same way that we speak of the Darwinism there. Perhaps no single passage better combines Emerson's optimistic teleology and his doctrine of evolution than this : —

" Fate involves the melioration. No statement of the universe can have any soundness which does not admit its ascending effort. The direction of the whole and of the parts is toward benefit, and in proportion to the health. Behind every individual closes organization; before him opens liberty."

He also says : —

" The history of Nature, from first to last, is incessant advance from less to more, from rude to finer organization, the globe of matter thus conspiring with the principle of undying hope in man. . . . The best civilization yet is only valuable as a ground of hope."

To these two passages I add two others, in which the doctrine of evolution is treated in detail, with special reference to its ethical bearings : —

" Nature is a tropical swamp in sunshine, on whose purlieus we hear the song of summer birds, and see prismatic dew-drops, — but her interiors are terrific, full of hydras and crocodiles. In the pre-adamite, Nature bred valor only ; by and by she gets on to man, and adds tenderness, and thus raises virtue piecemeal. When we trace from the beginning, that ferocity has uses ; only so are the conditions of the then world met, and these monsters are the scavengers, executioners, diggers, pioneers, and fertilizers, destroying what is more destructive than they, and making better life possible. We see the steady aim of benefit in view from the first. Melioration is the law. The cruellest foe is a masked benefactor. The wars which make history so dreary have served the cause of truth and virtue. There is always an instinctive sense of right, an obscure idea which animates either party, and which in long periods vindicates itself at last. Thus a sublime confidence is fed at the bottom of the heart that, in spite of appearances, in spite of malignity and blind self-interest living for the moment, an eternal, beneficent necessity is always bringing things right; and though we should fold our arms, — which we cannot do, for our duty requires us to be the very hands of this guiding sentiment, and work in the present moment, — the evils we suffer will at last end themselves through the incessant opposition of Nature to everything hurtful."

The other passage is yet more striking : —

" Very few of our race can be said to be yet finished men. We still carry sticking to us some remains of the preceding inferior quadruped organization. We call these millions men; but they are not yet men. Half engaged in the soil, pawing to get free, man needs all the music that can be brought to disengage him. If Love, red Love, with tears and joy, if Want with his scourge, if War with his cannonade, if Christianity with its charity, if Trade with its money, if Art with its portfolios, if Science with her telegraphs through the deeps of space and time, can set his dull nerves throbbing, and by loud taps on his rough chrysalis can break its walls and let the new creature emerge erect and free, — make way and sing pæan ! The age of the quadruped is to go out, the age of the brain and of the heart is to come in. The time will come when the evil forms we have known can no more be organized. Man's culture can spare nothing, wants all the material. He is to convert all impediments into instruments, all enemies into power. The formidable mischief will only make the more useful slave. And if one shall read the future of the race hinted in the organic effort of Nature to mount and meliorate, and the corresponding impulse to the better in the human being, we shall dare affirm that there is nothing he will not overcome and convert, until at last culture shall absorb the chaos and gehenna. He will convert the Furies into Muses, and the hells into benefit."

" Behind every individual closes organization; before him opens liberty." No man ever laid greater stress upon organization and environment than Emerson. He says : —

" Men are what their mothers made them. You may as well ask a loom which weaves huckabuck why it does not make cashmere, as expect poetry from this engineer, or a chemical discovery from that jobber. Ask the digger in the ditch to explain Newton's laws ; the fine organs of his brain have been pinched by overwork and squalid poverty from father to son for a hundred years."

" I knew a witty physician who found the creed in the biliary duct, and used to affirm that if there was disease in the liver, the man became a Calvinist, and if that organ was sound, he became a Unitarian."

Many pages of the essay on " Fate " — on the whole, the greatest of the strictly ethical essays — are occupied by this strong showing of the tyranny

of circumstance. Some of his friends complained
that he ran the risk of making the argument for
circumstance and fate so strong that he could not
answer it. But he replied: "I dip my pen in the
blackest ink, because I am not afraid of falling into
my ink-pot. I have no sympathy with a poor man
I knew, who, when suicides abounded, told me he
dared not look at his razor. A just thinker will
allow full swing to his scepticism. I do not fear
scepticism for any good soul." "If you please to
plant yourself on the side of Fate," he said, "and
say, Fate is all; then we say, a part of Fate is the
freedom of man." "To hazard the contradiction, —
freedom is necessary." "Shall I preclude my future,"
he asks, in his Yankee manner, "by taking a high
seat and kindly adapting my conversation to the
shape of my head? When I come to that, the doc-
tors shall buy me for a cent."

"Behind every individual closes organization;
before him opens liberty." The latter is as necessary and as evident to Emerson as the former.
Freedom working through organization to freedom,
— that is the process which he sees; and the soul
of man is one of the rivulets of freedom. He
says : —

"We are sure that, though we know not how, necessity
does comport with liberty, the individual with the world,
my polarity with the spirit of the times. . . . Morals implies freedom and will. The will constitutes the man.
He has his life in Nature, like a beast : but choice is born

in him; here is he that chooses; here is the Declaration of Independence, the July Fourth of zoölogy and astronomy. He chooses, — as the rest of creation does not."

"Morals implies freedom." This principle has been declared by almost every great thinker from Plato and Aristotle to Kant. To me it seems self-evident. I think it must be regarded as an axiom in ethics. The tree obeys the law, but the tree is not moral. Morals implies freedom; but freedom is moral only when it obeys the righteous necessity. "Obedience alone," says Emerson, "gives the right to command."

"We throw ourselves by obedience into the circuit of the heavenly wisdom and share the secret of God."

"We arrive at virtue by taking its direction instead of imposing ours."

"If you wish to avail yourself of the might of the infinite forces, and in like manner if you wish the force of the intellect, the force of the will, you must take their divine direction, not they yours. Things work to their ends, not to yours, and will certainly defeat any adventurer who fights against this ordination."

"The education of the will is the object of our existence."

"All our power, all our happiness, consists in our reception of the hints of the soul, which ever become clearer and grander as they are obeyed."

"We need only obey. There is guidance for each of us, and by lowly listening we shall hear the right word."

" A point of education that I can never too much insist
upon is this tenet, that every individual man has a bias
which he must obey, and that it is only as he feels and
obeys this that he rightly develops and attains his legitimate power in the world. . . . In morals, this privatest
oracle is conscience ; in intellect, genius."

Morality, then, is the conscious adoption of the
universal, it is the controlling presence of the universal in the individual. Again and again we come
back to that great and simple thought. " Our first
experiences in moral as in intellectual nature," says
Emerson, " force us to discriminate a universal mind,
identical in all men. Certain biases, talents, executive skills, are special to each individual; but the
high, contemplative, all-commanding vision, the sense
of Right and Wrong, is alike in all. Its attributes
are self-existence, eternity, intuition, and command.
It is the mind of the mind. We belong to it, not
it to us. It is in all men, and constitutes them
men." Theodore Parker spoke no more absolutely,
and scarcely oftener, than Emerson of conscience as
" the voice of God."

" The moral sentiment comes from the highest place.
It is that which, being in all sound natures, and strongest
in the best and most gifted men, we know to be implanted
by the Creator of men. It is a commandment at every
moment and in every condition of life to do the duty of
that moment and to abstain from doing the wrong. And
it is so near and inward and constitutional to each, that

no commandment can compare with it in authority. All wise men regard it as the voice of the Creator himself."

" The inviolate soul is in perpetual telegraphic communication with the source of events. . . . If we should ask ourselves what is this self-respect, it would carry us to the highest problems. It is our practical perception of the Deity in man. It has its deep foundations in religion."

" Let man learn the revelation of all Nature and all thought to his heart ; this, namely, that the Highest dwells with him ; that the sources of Nature are in his own mind, if the sentiment of duty is there."

" It is impossible that the creative power should exclude itself. Into every intelligence there is a door which is never closed, through which the Creator passes."

" The soul of God is poured into the world through the thoughts of men. The world stands on ideas, and not on iron or cotton ; and the iron of iron, the fire of fire, the ether and source of all the elements, is moral force."

In one of the poems are these striking lines : —

> " But love me then and only, when you know
> Me for the channel of the rivers of God,
> From deep ideal fontal heavens that flow."

The following lines from " Saadi " will be well remembered : —

> " Open innumerable doors,
> The heaven where unveiled Allah pours
> The flood of truth, the flood of good,
> The Seraph's and the Cherub's food :
> Those doors are men : the Pariah hind
> Admits thee to the perfect Mind."

" In morals," I have quoted, " this privatest oracle is conscience; in intellect, genius." Emerson continually speaks of genius in almost the identical terms which he uses of morality, and always as the presence of the Divine and the yielding of ourselves to its control. Genius in men is " the Godhead in distribution." " Genius is an emanation of that it tells of." " Genius is religious."

> " The hand that rounded Peter's dome,
> And groined the aisles of Christian Rome,
> Wrought in a sad sincerity ;
> Himself from God he could not free ;
> He builded better than he knew.
> .   .   .   .   .   .
> The passive Master lent his hand
> To the vast soul that o'er him planned."

" We cannot look at works of art but they teach us how near man is to creating. Michael Angelo is largely filled with the Creator that made and makes men. How much of the original craft remains in him, and he a mortal man ! In him and the like perfecter brains the instinct is resistless, knows the right way, is melodious, and at all points divine. The reason we set so high a value on any poetry, — as often on a line or a phrase as on a poem, — is that it is a new work of Nature, as a man is."

" The delight which a work of art affords seems to arise from our recognizing in it the mind that formed Nature, again in active operation. It differs from the works of Nature in this, that they are organically reproductive. This is not, but spiritually it is prolific by its powerful action on the intellects of men. Hence it follows that a study of admirable works of art sharpens our perceptions of the beauty of Nature ; that a certain analogy reigns throughout the wonders of both ; that the contemplation of a work of great art draws us into a state of mind which may be called religious."

"There does not seem to be any limit to these new informations of the same Spirit that made the elements at first, and now, through man, works them."

A worker together with God,—that is the definition of the genius and of the moral man alike. A thinker of God's thoughts after him,—that is the true man of science. And an omnipresent and ultimately irresistible force is impelling humanity to this love and realization of the true, the beautiful, and the good.

> "The fiend that man harries
>   Is love of the Best ;
> Yawns the pit of the Dragon,
>   Lit by rays from the Blest.
> The Lethe of Nature
>   Can't trance him again,
> Whose soul sees the perfect,
>   Which his eyes seek in vain."

I have dwelt upon this similar treatment of genius and virtue by Emerson, because the point which I would next emphasize, as of great significance in his ethics, is that of the harmony and unity of the powers of the mind. I have already spoken at length of Emerson's general conception of the community of forces and the identity of law. "The identity of gravitation with purity of heart," as we will not forget, is our text. "All departments of life," he said, "feel and labor to express the identity of their law. They are rays of one sun; they translate each into a new language the sense of the other."

"Every fact is related on one side to sensation, and on the other to morals."

"Intellect and morals appear only the material forces on a higher plane."

"We are as much strangers in Nature as we are aliens from God. We do not understand the notes of birds."

"I delight in tracing those wonderful powers, the electricity and gravity of the human world."

"In proportion as a man's life comes into union with truth, his thoughts approach to a parallelism with the currents of natural laws, so that he easily expresses his meaning by natural symbols."

"There is but one Reason," he says in this connection. "The mind that made the world is not one mind, but *the* mind."

But nowhere does Emerson emphasize this conception of unity so strikingly as in its reference to the powers of the mind, and especially to genius and virtue. "There is genius," he says, "as well in virtue as in intellect."

"Men are ennobled by morals and by intellect; but those two elements know each other, and always beckon to each other, until at last they meet in the man, if he is to be truly great."

18

"So intimate is this alliance of mind and heart, that talent uniformly sinks with character."

"The moment of your loss of faith and acceptance of the lucrative standard will be marked in the pause or solstice of genius, the sequent retrogression, and the inevitable loss of attraction to other minds. The vulgar are sensible of the change in you, and of your descent, though they clap you on the back and congratulate you on your increased common-sense."

"The high intellect is absolutely at one with moral nature. A thought is imbosomed in a sentiment, and the attempt to detach and blazon the thought is like a show of cut flowers."

"I see that when souls reach a certain clearness of perception they accept a knowledge and motive above selfishness."

"Of two men, each obeying his own thought, he whose thought is deepest will be the strongest character."

"As much love, so much perception."

"All the great ages have been ages of belief."

"It was the conviction of Plato, of Van Helmont, of Pascal, of Swedenborg, that piety is an essential condition of science; that great thoughts come from the heart."[1]

"In the voice of Genius I hear invariably the moral tone, even when it is disowned in words."

"All high beauty has a moral element in it, and I find the antique sculpture as ethical as Marcus Antoninus, and the beauty ever in proportion to the depth of thought."

"The highest platform of eloquence is the moral sentiment. . . . I have observed that in all public speaking

[1] We remember here that word of Anselm's, — "I believe, in order that I may know."

the rule of the orator begins, not in the array of his facts, but when his deep conviction, and the right and necessity he feels to convey that conviction to his audience, — when these shine and burn in his address. . . . There is a certain transfiguration; all great orators have it, and men who wish to be orators simulate it."

"The finer the sense of justice, the better poet." The habit of injustice "takes away the presentiments."

"There was never poet who had not the heart in the right place. The old trouveur, Pons Capdueil, wrote: —

> ' Oft have I heard, and deem the witness true,
>   Whom man delights in, God delights in too.'

All beauty warms the heart, is a sign of health, prosperity, and the favor of God."

"Show me, said Sarona in the novel, one wicked man who has written poetry, and I will show you where his poetry is not poetry."

"In poetry, said Goethe, only the really great and pure advances us, and this exists as a second nature, either elevating us to itself, or rejecting us."

Does any intellectual man need to have this truth painfully enforced? Do we not all learn rapidly, as writers, as speakers, as public workers in any way, that there is no secret to success and power but that of simple sincerity; that every fond admixture of pretension or of pedantry instantly betrays itself and vitiates the effect; that there is no weakness but deception and diplomacy, and no power but truth? There is no power but truth. There is no success

but morality. "Civilization depends upon morality," says Emerson. All high private fortune depends
upon it no less.

"The soul at the centre of Nature has so infused its
strong enchantment into Nature, that we prosper when we
accept its advice, and when we struggle to wound its
creatures our hands are glued to our sides, or they beat
our own breasts."

"If I will stand upright, the creation cannot bend me.
But if I violate myself, if I commit a crime, the lightning
loiters by the speed of retribution, and every act is not
hereafter but instantaneously rewarded according to its
quality."

"There is a blessed necessity by which the interest of
men is always driving them to the right; and, again,
making all crime mean and ugly."

"Crime and punishment grow out of one stem. Character is always known. Thefts never enrich; alms never
impoverish; murder will speak out of stone walls. The
league between virtue and nature engages all things to
assume a hostile front to vice. All our political disasters
grow as logically out of our attempts in the past to do
without justice, as the sinking of some part of your house
comes of defect in the foundation."

"The laws of the soul execute themselves. There is
in the soul a justice whose retributions are instant and
entire. He who does a good deed is instantly ennobled.
He who does a mean deed is by the action itself con-
tracted. . . . If a man is at heart just, then in so far is
he God; the safety of God, the immortality of God, the
majesty of God, do enter into that man with justice."

The inevitable disaster of wrong is the guarantee of morality. The moral alone is strong. The moral alone can succeed. The moral is the measure of power. It is also the measure of health. This is a point upon which Emerson dwells with great force and frequency, — the interdependence of morals and mental and even bodily health. "Genius is health," he says, "and Beauty is health, and Virtue is health."

"No talent gives the impression of sanity if wanting the moral sentiment."

"The moral sentiment has the property of invigorating."

"Strength enters just as much as the moral element prevails."

Character is "that sublime health which values one moment as another, and makes us great in all conditions."

"The moral must be the measure of health."

"I have heard that whoever loves is in no condition old."

"It is certain that worship stands in some commanding relation to the health of man and to his highest powers, so as to be in some measure the source of intellect."

"A healthy soul stands united with the Just and the True, as the magnet arranges itself with the pole." [1]

"If your eye is on the eternal, your intellect will grow."

"Broader and deeper we must write our annals, — from an ethical reformation, from an influx of the ever new, ever sanative conscience."

[1] "He that has a soul unasphyxied will never want a religion ; he that has a soul asphyxied, reduced to a succedaneum for salt, will never find any religion, though you rose from the dead to preach him one." — CARLYLE.

Conversely, he says of health, "Health is the condition of wisdom." He lays down as the first obvious rule of life, — Get health. "Health is the condition of wisdom. . . . Sickness is a cannibal which eats up all the life and youth it can lay hold of, and absorbs its own sons and daughters. I figure it as a pale, wailing, distracted phantom, absolutely selfish, heedless of what is good and great, attentive to its sensations, losing its soul, and afflicting other souls with meanness and mopings, and with ministration to its voracity of trifles." He quotes with approval the word of Dr. Johnson, — "Every man is a rascal as soon as he is sick." He finds somewhat moral in all health and all beauty, and he preaches the duty of cheerfulness.

> " Set not thy foot on graves :
>   Hear what wine and roses say ;
>   The mountain chase, the summer waves,
>   The crowded town, thy feet may well delay.
>   .   .   .   .   .   .
> " Life is too short to waste
>   In critic peep or cynic bark,
>   Quarrel or reprimand :
>   'T will soon be dark ;
>   Up ! mind thine own aim, and
>   God speed the mark ! "

The progress of humanity is to completer health, a greater purity, a nobler knowledge, and a deeper joy.

"It is true there is evil and good, night and day ; but these are not equal. The day is great and final. The night is for the day, but the day is not for the night."

"Man helps himself by larger generalizations. The lesson of life is practically to generalize ; to believe what the years and the centuries say, against the hours ; to resist the usurpation of particulars ; to penetrate to their catholic sense."

With the most practical eye and hand to deal with evils and with sin, his philosophical optimism is absolute. "A hopeless spirit," he says, "puts out the eyes." Moreover, the deepest insight, like the deepest experience, worketh hope.

"Ever as you ascend your proper and native path, you rise on the same steps to science and to joy."

"Men are all secret believers in the Law alive and beautiful, else the word justice would have no meaning : they believe that the best is the true ; that right is done at last, or chaos is come."

It is the belief in Providence, in the Divine Nature, "which carries on its administration by good men."

"I find the survey of these cosmical powers a doctrine of consolation in the dark hours of private or public fortune. It shows us the world alive, guided, incorruptible ; that its cannon cannot be stolen nor its virtues misapplied. It shows us the long Providence, the safeguards of rectitude."

"I hope we have reached the end of our unbelief, have come to a belief that there is a divine Providence in the world, which will not save us but through our own co-operation."

"Nature works through her appointed elements ; and

ideas must work through the brains and the arms of good and brave men or they are no better than dreams."

" Will not man one day open his eyes and see how dear he is to the soul of Nature, — how near it is to him ? "

" The ancients believed in a serene and beautiful Genius which ruled in the affairs of nations ; which with a slow but stern justice carried forward the fortunes of certain chosen houses, weeding out single offenders or offending families, and securing at last the firm prosperity of the favorites of Heaven. It was too narrow a view of the Eternal Nemesis. There is a serene Providence which rules the fate of nations, which makes little account of time, little of one generation or race, makes no account of disasters, conquers alike by what is called defeat or by what is called victory, thrusts aside enemy and obstruction, crushes everything immoral as inhuman, and obtains the ultimate triumph of the best race by the sacrifice of everything which resists the moral laws of the world. It makes its own instruments, creates the man for the time, trains him in poverty, inspires his genius, and arms him for his task." If he fail, another shall rise. " Though ministers of justice and power fail, Justice and Power fail never."

It is in the contemplation of this " sublime and friendly Destiny by which the human race is guided," that Emerson rises to his highest inspirations. The thought of a mechanical, unconscious, automatic world is to him impossible. Neither morals nor intellect has so an explanation or a voucher.

" There is a persuasion in the soul of man that he is here for cause ; that he was put down in this place by the Creator to do the work for which he inspires him."

" Nature is too thin a screen; the glory of the One breaks in everywhere."

" Men do not see that *He*, that *It*, is there, next and within ; the thought of the thought ; the affair of affairs ; that he is existence, and take him from them and they would not be."

" O my brothers, God exists ; there is a soul at the centre of Nature and over the will of every man. . . . The whole course of things goes to teach us faith."

" Unlovely, nay frightful, is the solitude of the soul which is without God in the world."

" A man of thought must feel the thought that is parent of the universe. . . . The world is saturated with deity."

" The man who shall be born shall rely on the Law alive and beautiful, which works over our heads and under our feet."

The Law is alive; it *knows:* — this is ever his thought; and perhaps it is in a line of poetry that he has put the truth most adequately : —

> " And conscious Law is King of kings."

In this God's universe, he says,

> " What is excellent,
> As God lives, is permanent."

" I have heard," he says, — this is ever the form of his, Thus saith the Lord, —

" I have heard that whenever the name of man is spoken, the doctrine of immortality is announced ; it cleaves to his constitution. . . . All our intellectual action, not promises but bestows a feeling of absolute existence."

" A man speaking from insight affirms of himself what is true of the mind : seeing its immortality, he says, I am immortal ; seeing its invincibility, he says, I am strong."

But " the teachings of the high spirit are abstemious, and, in regard to particulars, negative." Emerson, too, is abstemious ; and any who are giving up their lives, in a spirit of uneasy curiosity, to fond discussions of a future life and other worlds are not living in the spirit of Emerson, and to my thinking are not laying the stress in a good place. It was, on the whole, a wise word of Thoreau, and an Emersonian word, — " One world at a time." " When I talked with an ardent missionary," said Emerson, " and pointed out to him that his creed found no support in my experience, he replied, ' It is not so in your experience, but is so in the other world.' I answer : ' Other world ! there is no other world. God is one and omnipresent ; here or nowhere is the whole fact.' " It is no question of the soul's eternal nature and immortal life, — no man's faith in that so entire. It is a rebuke of the irreligious blindness that does not see that the soul *is* immortal, not *will be,* and that eternity is one.

" In past oracles of the soul the understanding seeks to find answers to sensual questions, and undertakes to tell from God how long men shall exist, what their hands shall do, and who shall be their company, adding names and dates and places. . . . But we must pick no locks. We must check this low curiosity. An answer in words is delusive ; it is really no answer to the questions you ask. Men ask concerning the immortality of the soul, the employments of heaven, the estate of the sinner, and so forth. They even dream that Jesus has left replies to precisely these interrogatories. Never a moment did that sublime spirit speak in their *patois.* . . . It was left to his disciples to sever duration from the moral elements, and to teach the immortality of the soul as a doctrine, and maintain it by evidences. The moment the doctrine of the immortality is separately taught, man is already fallen. . . . These questions which we lust to ask about the future are a confession of sin. God has no answer for them. . . . It is not in an arbitrary ' decree of God,' but in the nature of man, that a veil shuts down on the facts of to-morrow ; for the soul will not have us read any other cipher than that of cause and effect. By this veil which curtains events it instructs the children of men to live in to-day. The only mode of obtaining an answer to these questions of the senses is to forego all low curiosity, and, accepting the tide of being which floats us into the secret of Nature, work and live, work and live ; and all unawares the advancing soul has built and forged for itself a new condition, and the question and the answer are one."

" Why should I hasten to solve every riddle which life offers me ? I am well assured that the Questioner who brings me so many problems will bring the answers also in due time. Very rich, very potent, very cheerful Giver that he is, he shall have it all his own way, for me."

" Of immortality, the soul when well employed is incurious. It is so well, that it is sure it will be well. It asks no questions of the Supreme Power."

Such, slightly and inadequately sketched, is Emerson's view of the moral life of man. My friends, it is my religion, — a truth sufficient to enable me, when I am faithful to it, to live strongly and joyfully; a-truth, I believe, by which any soul may enter any future with confidence and peace.

Wickedness may fill the earth and manifold corruptions taint society, but they that see that the law of the universe is the moral law, that morality is the soul's lawfulness and health and order, will be paralyzed by no thought of " moral interregnums." The immoral year is but the world's diastole. Tiberius is Christianity's gymnasium, and papal Borgias and Medicis manure the Reformation. Morality is sure, because it is of the nature of things ; but immorality is depravity. Crowd the cork to the bottom, but every atom is crowded up forever by the picture it carries of the sky. Morality has far deeper foundations than our passing purposes. Reality does not humor our imaginings. This one laments this other's atheism, as though his atheism cancelled God. And this one writes, " I was, but am not" on his tombstone, heedless of the smiles of the stars at the fatuity that fails to see that only an *I am* has any message. So fatuous is the thought that the universe leaves its morality to accident. " The conscience of man," says Emerson, " is regenerated as is the atmosphere, so that society cannot be debauched. The health which we call virtue is an equipoise which easily redresses itself, and resembles those rocking-stones which a child's finger can move, and a weight of many hundred tons cannot overthrow." Churches many and creeds many pass away, and " in the rapid decay of what was called religion timid and unthinking people fancy a decay of the hope of man;" but they that see the law " believe that man need not fear the want of religion, because they know his religious constitution,— that he must rest on the moral and religious sentiments, as the motion of bodies rests on geometry." " As soon as every man is apprised of the Divine Presence within his own mind, — is apprised that the perfect law of duty corresponds with the laws of chemistry, of vegetation, of astronomy, as face to face in a glass; that the basis of duty, the order of society, the power of character, the wealth of culture, the perfection of taste, all draw their essence from this moral sentiment, then we have a religion that exalts, that commands all the social and all the private action."

X.

EMERSON'S RELATION TO SOCIETY.

By MRS. JULIA WARD HOWE.

WHAT is society? or, if it comes to that, what *was* society? In the first place, an assemblage of human creatures whose humanity consisted largely in their power of discrimination and comparison between the various objects and advantages of life. Animals have habits, passions, affections, preferences, reasonings. Man must have always been able to compare the objects of these with a standard existing in his own mind, and then to compare them with each other. In this comparison, poor and rudimentary as it must once have been, the greater good constantly gained upon the lesser. The advantage of alliance was found to be greater than that of discord. Law was recognized as better than violence, temperance prevailed over excess, industry was seen to be more productive than rapine. The power of thought asserted its right to a nobler employment than the devising of fables for the superstitious, or of artifices for the covetous and ambitious. And so by slow steps we come from prehistoric man to the nineteenth century, and to that part of it in which the heaven of New England was bright with particular stars. We who were accustomed to the presence of these stars in the social firmament took very insufficient note of them. Which of us stops to rave about the sunlight, glorious and wonderful fact though it be? Take it away, and we recognize its constant and supreme office. While we have it, our life and it are so at one that we cannot much notice it.

Mr. Emerson's years surpassed by nine man's threescore and ten. His intellectual activity covers the whole period intervening between his early manhood and his seventy-first year. Yet I cannot find in what I have known of this time any evidence that the community at large felt itself either richer or safer for his presence. If this was true of the business world, it was equally true of the world of fashion. If I remember rightly, there were many years of his life in which his words and works were valued by a very small number of people. Has he not himself said, turning his face from his own Boston,

> " Good-by, proud world ! I 'm going home ;
> Thou art not my friend, and I 'm not thine " ?

The next strophe may tell us what he had seen there:

> " Good-by to Flattery's fawning face ;
> To Grandeur with his wise grimace ;
> To upstart Wealth's averted eye ;
> To supple Office, low and high ;
> To crowded halls, to court and street,
> To frozen hearts and hasting feet."

And a little further on he says : —

> " When I am stretched beneath the pines,
> Where the evening star so holy shines,
> I laugh at the lore and the pride of man,
> At the sophist schools, and the learnèd clan."

Even the recognized literary men of the time paid him little attention. The elder Dana, in those days at least, would have classed him with those whom he esteemed as eccentric disturbers of peace and religion. C. C. Felton, while professor of Greek at Harvard, wrote a notice of one of his books, which he compared to the orange-peel and water mentioned by Dickens's Little Marchioness, with the explanation that, " If you make believe very much, it is very good."

I remember having been sharply called to account some forty-five years ago for advising an acquaintance to attend the first course of lectures which he gave in New York; and I remember thinking that from an orthodox point of view I had been a little imprudent in so doing. In those days, and long after, Cambridge held him in doubtful and supercilious consideration. The world of fashion only in rare instances knew enough of him to laugh at him. Of course, there were exceptions to this. I think it must have been in 1843 that I heard of his having been invited after one of his lectures in Boston to the hcuse of Mr. Nathan Appleton; and the friend who mentioned this to me appeared much edified at the countenance thereby given to Mr. Emerson.

It would be instructive for us to compare Mr.

Emerson's attitude toward society with that of Margaret Fuller in the days in which each had a position of strangeness and novelty. I should say that Mr. Emerson's patient and cautious nature made his position a less aggressive one than that of his brilliant contemporary. Margaret's eloquence, which gave expression to the quick and vehement action of her mind, was less favorable to the formation of reserved judgment than was Mr. Emerson's more deliberate speech. Eloquent on foot Mr. Emerson was rarely or never. The glimpses of his genius showed him heights to be built up to, and this process was a slow one. I remember him as rather averse to extempore addresses, and as greatly preferring to read from a manuscript. On the other hand, we must remember that Margaret's encounter with the society of her youth was more of a hand-to-hand fight than Mr. Emerson was called upon to maintain. The fact of her sex aggravated in her case the displeasure which the worshippers of custom always visit upon innovators. In addition to this, a certain quality in her, difficult to define, often provoked hostility in those who knew her slightly, or not at all. Her critical attitude, her authoritative manner, and her somewhat novel method of imparting what she knew, brought upon her a wrath and ridicule which Mr. Emerson was not likely to encounter. For his *prime abord*, on the contrary, had in it nothing of challenge or defiance. A solemn suavity, saved by an overspreading cheerfulness, an eye in which severity of observation

19

and kindliness of judgment were strangely blended, — these traits of person and of character made Mr. Emerson's relations with those around him smooth at the start; and the severe sentences which he sometimes fulminated took by surprise those who looked into his genial countenance, and who heard those uncompromising rebukes through the silver medium of his voice.

I cannot follow here the steps by which he came to stand where we all remember him, in conceded eminence, as first in rank among our men of letters. We all know that each of these steps was brave, true, and independent. Clad in his wonderful temperament as in a seraph's golden armor, Mr. Emerson reviewed the forces of his time, showing neither fear nor favor to what he found amiss. Nothing did he set down in malice, nor aught extenuate. A single figure was he in his lone crusade; for though the field was full of brave fighters, no one of them followed his device. What could give one man the courage to expose so many shams, ignore so many false pretensions, assert so many unflattering convictions ? His knowledge of the value of what he had to give, and his determination to give it.

I remember as if it were a thing of yesterday the noble ring and scope of Mr. Emerson's Phi Beta Kappa Oration, delivered in the year 1837. What inspiration must his words have carried with them to those who stood in his serene presence, and who saw in his face the full beaming of his thought !

To me, at that time a youthful scorner of much that I did not understand, it sounded a new bugle-call, opened a new way. And I cannot but admire as a dispensation of Providence the gift of art and imagination through which the speaker's ingrained purity of soul was carried into the consciousness of all who heard him, and gave its tone to the hour, single and never to be forgotten.

The tardiness of Mr. Emerson's attainment of the recognition to which he was entitled is easily explained by the fact that he, like some of his peers, had to teach a new valuation to the community which assumed to judge him. Certain forms of belief, of reasoning, of expression, had in the minds of men become so hardened out of second nature into second death, that the fossilized community had become incapable of entertaining a novelty in either kind. To it religion meant a catechism and a creed, morality a bulwark of uncharities, art a catalogue of technical terms.

Now, Mr. Emerson was not the only person sent to blow up these coral reefs; but he wrought at them alone, because his manner of work was, above all, individual. He held to it, moreover, never borrowing Parker's hammer, nor Phillips's flashing artillery. His was the secret of a subtle solvent which changed enmity into friendship, and the titter of ridicule into the pæan of manly praise. Not the secret of base compliance this, but the finding of that deepest truth within whose domain all must agree.

The perfect politeness of Mr. Emerson's attitude in regard to society appears as much in what is remembered of his life as in his works. A great element of caution, a great sensitiveness to the rights and claims of others, sometimes made him a waiter where others dashed headlong into the fight. When he distinctly saw what to aim at, a single shaft from his bow flew far and hit the mark. He was, I should think, instinctively averse to all strife, delighting above all in the philosophic *coup-d'œil* which takes account of individual shortcomings only to lose sight of them in the final harmony. Keeping in view this determining characteristic of his mind, we must the more admire the unsparing frankness of his satire.

There are some rude truths which it is polite to utter, just as it would be polite to shake one's grandfather if he were sleeping to his hurt. The utterance of these truths was never shirked by Mr. Emerson; but his manner of imparting them rather encouraged those who were in error to come out of it, than condemned them to abide in their sins and await their punishment.

Forces, indeed, were not powers, in his view; and while he made due account of them, he did not unduly revere them. "The powers that be" he did not find in the rich merchants and haughty dames who represented wealth and social pretension, but in men and women of commanding mind and merit.

I do not remember him in the pulpit, but I think that, once out of it, he eyed it askance. Not the pulpit of Channing and Parker, but that from which a learned ignorance sought to impose its limits, — from which a surface morality forbade the digging of a deeper well. I once heard him say, in a Sunday discourse, that he entered the pulpit somewhat unwillingly, because it contained traditions which he neither wished to accept nor to reject. Many of these have melted away since that time. They were the prescriptions of an authority which then admitted neither question nor examination, but which has since learned to thrive upon both.

Mr. Emerson's power of critical appreciation is nowhere more fully shown than in his "English Traits." From the studious and laborious seclusion of his Concord home he went, in 1847, to the world's metropolis, — to London and its kindred cities. Recognition he surely found there, and of the best. The voyage was undertaken by the invitation of a number of associations much like our own lecture lyceums. The book tells us nothing of the success of the lectures which Mr. Emerson delivered in various towns of Great Britain, but we do not need to learn from it that his reputation and position at once introduced him to all that is best and most substantial in English society. The book startles us by its trenchant statements, which cut "deep down the middle" of English character. It is no less remarkable for the grasp and comprehension with which it presents the strong and redeeming points of the race. The first feature is illustrated in passages like the following,

which is not over-gratifying to those who claim that
their families came over with the Conqueror : —

"Twenty thousand thieves landed at Hastings. These
founders of the House of Lords were greedy and ferocious
dragoons, sons of greedy and ferocious pirates. They were
all alike. They took everything they could carry, they
burned, harried, violated, tortured, and killed. Such, however, is the illusion of antiquity and wealth, that decent
and dignified men, now existing, boast their descent from
those filthy thieves."

Mr. Emerson finds the English "led by a coarse
logic to worship wealth as the absolute test and cri-
terion of merit." He finds them much given also
to the service of the god Brag, whom he charitably
recognizes as an ancient Norse deity. He considers
them as preserved from over-quickness of judgment
by the mask of "a certain saving stupidity." On
the other hand, he says: "There is an English hero
superior to the French, the German, the Italian, or
the Greek. When he is brought to the strife with
fate, he sacrifices a richer material possession, and
on more purely metaphysical grounds. On deliberate
choice, and from grounds of character, he has elected
his part to live and die for, and dies with grandeur.
This race has added new elements to humanity, and
has a deeper root in the world." Well does he remark that the English have great range of scale, from
ferocity to exquisite refinement.

Since the days in which this book was written, the

attitude of Great Britain to the rest of the world has changed, not altogether for the better. She then appeared as the uncompromising foe of slavery : she has since become its apologist. A republican monarchy then, she has since appeared as an imperial autocracy.

We need not, for all this, suppose the values of the race to be lost. They still exist, and will assert themselves. But in the struggle and change of society the least worthy elements have attained a prominence which for the time gives to the very name " English " a significance very different from that which Mr. Emerson so cordially recognizes in the passage last quoted. The complex elements of the nationality make themselves felt, despite the long effort at assimilation. The fatality of its history perseveres, and every unrighteous conquest is called in question, though the wrongs inflicted have seemed to sleep the sleep of death for centuries. Is not Justice, after all, the enchanted princess who lies spellbound in her bower until the true knight finds his way to her and bears her forth in his strong arms, conquering and to conquer ?

Power is changing hands in the Island Empire, and the cherished immunities from change and disturbance are enjoyed no longer. There, as elsewhere, the nineteenth century will do its utmost work before it departs, and the people will assert their will and pleasure in a form neither to be suppressed nor ignored.

Since the days of which Mr. Emerson wrote, more-over, the precedence which he gives to English education, authorship, and scholarship is no longer to be conceded. American education is found to develop the faculties more fully than does the drill of Oxford or Cambridge. The extremely limited horizon of English life produces a national short-sightedness which is unhappily reproduced among us by select youths whose parents view everything through the craze of a false social ambition, and send them abroad, ostensibly to make gentlemen of them, but really to train honest republican natures to the fashion of a pseudo-aristocracy.

Of the English aristocracy of forty years ago Mr. Emerson certainly saw all the good points. He credits them with manners whose charm and value take the place of the thought of which they show small traces. " 'T is wonderful," he says, " how much talent runs into manners : nowhere and never so much as in England." He saw those fine people where they appear best, — at home. Their contempt for other nations leads them to be less regardful of the claims of others on other soil than their own. As I have met them, on the Eastern Continent and on the Western, I should call politeness the exception, rather than the rule, among them.

It is not perhaps as difficult to be polite in cere-monious company, which imposes its own rules, as in the freedom and isolation of country life. How Mr. Emerson excelled as a country host and as a country neighbor is well known in this place. Too sorrowful is the thought of the bread that will be broken with him no more. I will not dwell upon it. But of his home-content he has left us glimpses which have in them a great charm : —

> " Because I was content with these poor fields,
> Low, open meads, slender and sluggish streams,
> And found a home in haunts which others scorned,
> The partial wood-gods overpaid my love,
> And granted me the freedom of their state.
>
> .   .   .   .
>
> And, chiefest prize, found I true liberty
> In the glad home plain-dealing Nature gave.
> The polite found me impolite ; the great
> Would mortify me, but in vain ; for still
> I am a willow of the wilderness,
> Loving the wind that bent me.   All my hurts
> My garden spade can heal."

I quote these lines, as you will all know, from a poem in Mr. Emerson's first volume of verse. Few books, it seems to me, so fully as this reveal the character and habitual thought of the writer. The finest of the poems may aptly be termed " Meditations in Verse." They are pictures, each of a distinct cycle of thought, in which Courage asks the question which Faith and Imagination beautifully answer. Such are, among many others, " The Sphinx," " Each and All," and, above all, " The Problem," sentences of which have now become a part of English speech. These poems have not the flat subjectivity of one who, in every scene, sees himself first, and other things long after, if at all. They pour

forth no unhappy nor unholy passion. They reveal
the fair soul to us without v   'ating its reserves, rapt
as it is in the contemplation f life's sublime mysteries. A charm of unconsciousness is in them. The
poet sings to us with thoughts beyond his song. The
spell of rhythm soothes the Cerberus of his vigilant
caution. What view of sin was ever more polite
than this ? —

> " The fiend that man harries
>   Is love of the Best ;
> Yawns the pit of the Dragon
>   Lit by rays from the Blest.
>
> .   .   .   .   .   .
>
> " Pride ruined the angels,
>   Their shame them restores ;
> And the joy that is sweetest
>   Lurks in stings of remorse."

Polite, too, is Mr. Emerson in his extreme agony, of
which the well-known " Threnody " is the utterance.
Nothing that has been said of this poem seems to me
to express fully its unique merit. It calls up the joys
and beauties which have proved evanescent, sparing
not one dear domestic recollection, — not one of the
beautiful traits of his dead child. But it shows the
mortal fixed in immortality, and the deep serene
persuasion which smiles beyond tears, and which
carries him

> " Past the blasphemy of grief,"

and shows him that

> " Death, with solving rite,
>   Pours finite into infinite."

Death, or the power that lies behind it, has changed his wondrous flower into a wondrous gem, his rose into a ruby, with the rose's perfume. And he bids himself

> " Revere the Maker ; fetch thine eye
> Up to his style, and manners of the sky."

The indignation which Mr. Emerson felt at the great wrongs which have disgraced our social and political history was expressed in a calm and concentrated form, with touches of deep philosophic suggestion, which still speak to us like oracles. We find a striking instance of this in the ode inscribed to William Henry Channing, and written in the days of the Mexican War : —

> " Who is he that prates
> Of the culture of mankind,
> Of better arts and life ?
> Go, blindworm, go,
> Behold the famous States
> Harrying Mexico
> With rifle and with knife ! "

How is this for satire ? —

> " The God who made New Hampshire
> Taunted the lofty land
> With little men ; —
> Small bat and wren
> House in the oak : —
> If earth-fire cleave
> The upheaved land, and bury the folk,
> The Southern crocodile would grieve ! "

And the lesson of all this, what is it ? —

" Let man serve law for man ;
    Live for friendship, live for love,
    For truth's and harmony's behoof ;
    The State may follow how it can,
    As Olympus follows Jove."

But this indignation reached its highest expression in the poems called " Voluntaries," written either during the war of the Southern Confederacy, or just before, and in the " Boston Hymn," whose brave music so fitly accompanied Abraham Lincoln's mandate of emancipation to the colored race in America.

The poem on " Tact," in the first volume, illustrates Mr. Emerson's appreciation of the importance of that quality in all relations and in all successes. But he himself had a finer tact than that which these verses recognize. His was not that ready address which takes advantage of every favoring circumstance in order to carry personal aims, but that fine feeling which weighs and ponders, and is right.

In what I am trying to say, I may not hit precisely the mark set up for me in my present task, which is to speak of Mr. Emerson in his relation to society. With all respect to this philosophic assemblage, I think that some among you may expect to hear something concerning our great friend's appearance at balls and parties, and his success in the light skirmishing which occupies the border between literary and commonplace society. And here, if nowhere else, the example of Mr. Matthew Arnold may help

me. He began his well-known lecture by the assertion that Mr. Emerson was neither a great writer nor
a great poet. I may as aptly say that he was neither
a leader of the German, nor a tailor's model, nor yet
the pet lion of any social *ménagerie.* I must also
confess that in the haunts of high fashion I never, to
my knowledge, met either with him or with his like.
I have seen him at dinners, — have entertained him
myself after that manner. No one here will question
the perfect urbanity of his manners, — fit expression
of the elegance of his nature. As I remember, he
was not a free talker, but was an attentive listener.
He was often very patient of extreme loquacity in
others, but stood ready to redeem the conversation
by some apt word, — a helper in it, not a leader. I
think that he dreaded and disliked over-emphasis,
even in affirming the most important truths; and
am sure that he would have justified Talleyrand's
pregnant saying, — *Point de zèle.*

Most of us easily run into panegyric when speaking of a man so eminent and so faultless as Mr.
Emerson. I confess that for my part I fear more
my own insufficiency in praising than in criticising
him; that is, I fear more to miss the deeper merit
of his work than to overlook the surface traits in it
which may admit of question, and the liberty universally conceded in the saying, — *De gustibus non
disputandum est.*

I have sometimes differed from Mr. Emerson on
points both of feeling and opinion. I think that the

glamour of Eastern thought sometimes overcame his wiser judgment, and that his belief in the absolute logic of organization occasionally led him to utter sayings that savored of fatalism. This, I think, was but a play of his mind, from which his sternly Puritan conscience quickly recalled him. Yet I have felt this vein in him as one which I could not follow. I did not agree with him, either, in wishing that the meetings of the Boston Radical Club should not be reported in the papers. While gladly conceding that a more intimate liberty of communion might have been enjoyed with no such result in view, I thought, and still think, that the earnest encounter of thoughtful oppositions, which gave so much interest to the meetings of the Club, was too instructive and useful to be withheld from the general public.

Yet we must give Mr. Emerson the praise which belongs to a man of faultless intention, without defect of temper or of passion. He was, through some dispensation of grace, exempt from some of the darkest agonies of human nature. He had no brutal impulses to conquer, no raging appetite to contend with. He knew, from the first, the victory of good over evil ; and when he told me, to my childish amazement, that the angel must always be stronger than the demon, he gave utterance to a thought most familiar to him, though at the time new to me.

Mysterious is this inequality of life, by which one thus enters the field armed with the talisman of victory, while the contending ranks around him struggle and bleed to achieve it. When all philosophies, all religions, have done their best, this "why" still remains without its "wherefore."

I suppose that Dean Swift had in his mind the contrast between the great man and the average one when he wrote his humorous tale of Liliput. This contrast was probably greater in his time and region than in the New England of Mr. Emerson's earlier life. And still, when one thinks of him in his study at Concord, and of the *soi-disant* society of that time, one does not wonder that the little creatures so poorly understood the great man. Fortunate for them was it that he had a higher office than to satirize them, or by any lofty gymnastic to illustrate the difference between his proportions and theirs. From that great soul of his the multitude were to be fed and nourished. And well may it be written that "he gave them bread from heaven." For in a certain divine field of culture he gathered and winnowed the choicest grain. The spirit of antiquity was in it, and the life of the present and future. These do, indeed, literally meet in the seed which we sow in the furrows. But this bread with which Mr. Emerson fed the generations of his time had in it such values as only the highest powers of thought could perceive, realize, and transmit. The old historic rivers spoke to him, — Nilus, Strymon, Xanthus, Kephisus, Padus, and Tiber. Poets and philosophers said sooth to him. He saw the unity in their multiplicity, the harmony of their difference, and knew that the secret of the heroic and beautiful is always the same, and always unutterable.

From these rich studies he spoke to us. He gave us the refined quintessence of their elements. Yet he gave us not Homer, nor Plato, nor Hermes, nor Kant, but a woven web in which their imperishable beauties were brought together, sealed by a beauty all his own.

The word " clubable " is, I believe, of English origin. Would one have supposed it likely to apply to Mr. Emerson? It did, I think. He was clubable; that is, capable of enjoying a mixed company gathered with a fixed object. From some of his writings one might have formed a different opinion of him. It might have appeared as if isolation had been an essential condition of his appearing; as if one who had so distinct a doctrine to teach might have found his office incompatible with the encounters of common intercourse. I could name, though I will not, certain clubs which would not have been at all to his taste, — centres of vapid pretension and of fashionable gossip. To imagine him in such surroundings is profane; but where two or three or more were gathered together in the name of any high object, he was likely to be among them and at home with them. All of us remember him in the sittings of the Radical Club. He has often visited the New England Women's Club, and has given his voice as

well as his presence to make its occasions worthy.
A kindred gathering of young damosels, the Saturday Morning Club, has more than once been honored
by his ministration. The club of worthies who for
many years have dined together on the last Saturday
of every month was, I think, a favorite institution of
his. Never having been at one of those dinners, I
cannot tell you what part he took in the accompanying conversation; but I can in my mind picture
him as seated between Agassiz and Longfellow, with
other illustrious people who are now present with
us only in recollection.

Mr. Emerson's treatment of "the comic" in his
work entitled "Letters and Social Aims" shows that
he was fully aware of its importance in human
affairs. I remember very rarely to have seen him
moved to laughter; and when some touch of his fine
humor thrilled his audience, and brought a pleasant
ripple to the surface, I cannot remember that his
countenance underwent any change. The broad grin
which is nowadays so much in fashion would, I
think, have appeared to him a pitiable symptom.
The nearest approach to absolute fun that I can
recall in connection with him was his reading of a
piece called "The Old Cove," which some of you may
remember. He read it in his own parlor, at the
request of one of his daughters, and did not neglect
one of its humorous points.

You are all familiar with the anecdote which represents him as having gone with Margaret Fuller to

20

see Fanny Elsler dance. " Margaret, this is morality." " Waldo, this is religion." I should be glad to
know whether there is any foundation for the story.
A much-esteemed English friend once told me that
the subject of such an anecdote should not spoil it
by denying its truth. He quoted a well-known anecdote about Sydney Smith, and said : Landseer told
me that when they met, after it had been put in cir-
culation, Sydney Smith said to Landseer, "The story
is good ; we had better not spoil it."

With all that we owe in various ways to Mr.
Emerson, I feel most to thank him for his concern
in the common life of humanity. With a refinement
of taste which bordered upon the hypercritical, how
loyal was he to the rights and dignities of the million. Horace said : *Odi profanum vulgus et arceo.*
But Mr. Emerson, as I remember him, was concerned
for the least of those vulgar facts called common
men and women. No claim did he make to a life
apart from his fellows. His interpretation of life —
his and theirs — was heroic, but also sound and
simple. He spoke to ordinary lecture audiences, as
well as to special ones of his own ; to both with the
same grace and with the same patience. I think
he loved homely illustrations, and the smell of earth
and labor. I remember a lecture in which he spoke
of the recent purchase of Neander's library by a Western college, made upon the principle, he said, " that
the longest pole takes the persimmon." The democratic soul which utters itself here and there through-

out his prose and his poetry reached its culmination
in such lines as these : —

> " Who is the master ?   The slave is master,
>   And always was.   Pay him."

I have several times been Mr. Emerson's guest.
The first time was on the occasion of an Antislavery
tea-party which was given in Concord somewhere in
the fifties.   Mr. Garrison and Wendell Phillips were
the principal speakers at this meeting, and were invited, as I was, to stay at the Emerson house.   The
next day some hours intervened between our breakfast and the time of leaving for Boston, and I remember that we passed these hours with Mr. Emerson in
his library, and that the conversation was most easy
and delightful.   I once asked Mr. Emerson's permission to bring a European friend of mine to his house.
This permission was graciously given, and very gladly
improved.   Our host knew how to grant a favor as if
he had been receiving one.

Years after this time I had occasion to attend a
Woman Suffrage Convention held in Concord, and
was fortunately appointed to visit the same hospitable house, which had been burned and rebuilt since
I had last seen it.   The evening was inclement, and
in a comfortless and dripping state I arrived at
the Emerson mansion.   Mr. Emerson immediately
brought me a glass of wine ; and when Mrs. Emerson,
coming in a little later, said, " I am going to give
Mrs. Howe something to eat," her husband replied,

" That 's a good girl, Queenie, that 's a good girl!"
with a heartiness not easily to be forgotten.

I have spoken of Mr. Emerson as a critic and
teacher of society. I would also speak of him as an
exemplar. In an age in which dead statutes ruled
the land, he lifted a courageous voice proclaiming the
holy laws whose spirit underlies the dead letter of
prescription. When Justice was inelegant and un-
acceptable the whole world over, he pointed to her
ermine, and said, " It is ermine still." When wild
crowds shrieked, raged, and hooted against the oppo-
nents of human slavery, he answered the rude symphony with the laughter of the gods. In a time full
of personal pretension, his poise of modest dignity
rebuked the fantastic and shamed the grovelling.
Nobility was in his walk, his word, his every gesture.
What an assurance did we feel in company of which
he made a part! Nothing unworthy would dare to
show itself in his presence. Vulgarity of rustic or of
millionnaire would retire to the background before
him. The wonderful eye, the wonderful smile, not
only rebuked them, but cast them out.

The feminine follies which are so intangible yet
so powerful, at least as withes and nets are powerful,
to entangle and detain, — how well he understood
them! How delicately he unravelled them, knowing
the true womanhood as few know it, despite the
pseudo-feminine caricatures in which fools of both
sexes delight! He spoke for Woman Suffrage more
than once with sober weight and earnestness. The

character and intelligence of the women who ask for it impressed him with the belief that the time for it had come. Mr. Parkman and a good many with him find a number of women to be despicable in character and intelligence because they believe in their right to the franchise. Mr. Emerson considered these women as of a rank to commend any views concerning their own sex which they might adopt, and this one among the number.

And now let me ask one question. What ought I to be able to tell you about Mr. Emerson, you here in Concord, who so long enjoyed his inspiriting and delightful presence ? The only thing that I can supply is the more distant view of what was so near as well as so dear to you. You may say to me: "We know him in his home, and in his home village, where the grass could not grow without him. How did he look outside these familiar bounds ? How did our star shine among the world's great constellations ?" And I can reply, "He shone always with his own peculiar lustre, calm and radiant." Need I say that he still so shines ? So much of his thought and life was cast in forms of immortal beauty, that it endures and will endure, for generations that never heard his voice nor saw his smile, — a joy and an inheritance forever.

XI.

EMERSON'S VIEW OF NATIONALITY.

By GEORGE WILLIS COOKE.

EMERSON was at the same time an American and a cosmopolitan; he believed equally in humanity and in his own country. An American by inheritance, love, and genius, he belongs to the whole world by the breadth of his sympathies, his faith in the great thoughts of all times and men, and his confidence in the individual soul. To him, race, color, and climate had but an external importance; they were but sign-marks to indicate the inferior phases of existence. Where a man is born does not matter, but what is born into him. "If you have man," he says, "black or white is an insignificance. The intellect, that is miraculous. Who has it has the talisman. His skin and bones, though they were of the color of night, are transparent, and the everlasting stars shine through with attractive beams."

He looked upon the nations into which mankind is divided as parts "in the great anthem we call history, a piece of many parts and vast compass;" and he felt that the mighty song of human destiny cannot be well sung out, unless all the races and peoples give utterance to what is in them. "We have no sympathy," he said, "with that boyish egotism, hoarse with cheering for our side, for our State, for our town; the right patriotism consists in the delight which springs from contributing our peculiar and legitimate advantages to the benefit of humanity. Every foot of soil has its proper quality; the grape on the two sides of the same fence has new flavors; and so every acre on the globe, every family of men, every point of climate, has its distinguishing virtues." His view of nationality is, that the special quality of each nation gives it a merit and opportunity enjoyed by no other, and that its genius is to be made a contribution to the universal advancement of humanity.

His faith in the soul was such that he was willing to omit no one from the higher promise of humanity. To him no individual was ever so low as to have lost his capacity for manhood, or to have lost the opportunity of becoming a receptacle of descending truth. His faith in individuality made him regard every one as an agent of the highest, and capable of being, doing, and saying that which is impossible to any other person. In each nation, however, there appear great men who give a tendency to life and thought, adding their personal peculiarity to that of climate and race, to make the national type. Each nation representing some special phase of social and moral development, giving utterance to some great thought and purpose no other nation represents so clearly, it is desirable that reciprocity should exist between nations, for the sake of the common good.

Nothing was dearer to Emerson than the advancement of his own country ; and to this subject he often returned.   In that remarkable paper on " The American Scholar," written at the opening of his career as a public teacher, he said that we must follow the way marked out for us by our own capacities and opportunities.   " Let us be Americans, take new guides and explore the present." The same thought is in his latest appeal to his countrymen on " The Fortune of the Republic," wherein he once more asserted his conviction that we are not to look backward, but trust the ever-fruitful now.   Zealous as he was that America should be American, and not European or Asiatic, he was none the less zealous that we should not be partisans for our own country.   Even when he was urging us to be faithful to this marvellous opportunity put into our keeping, and to take new patterns to ourselves for the making of our national life, he could also urge upon our attention the higher ideal.   " We want men of original perception and original action," he said in 1878, " who can open their eyes wider than to a nationality, — namely, to considerations of benefit to the human race, — can act in the interest of civilization ; men of elastic, men of moral mind, who can live in the moment and take a step forward."   " The civility of no race can be perfect," he said in 1844, " whilst another race is degraded. It is a doctrine alike of the oldest and of the newest philosophy, that man is one, and that you cannot injure any member without a sympathetic injury to all the members."

To be true Americans we must be faithful to humanity ; for the genuinely democratic spirit leads us to consider the rights of all, even those not of our own race. If we can respect the rights of other individuals, we should respect the rights of other nations none the less ; and the demanding of rights for ourselves makes it imperative that, if we would secure them, we demand the rights of others at the same time. A nation may become a guide and inspirer along the way of that brotherhood of the race of which all the prophets have dreamed. Emerson would have America become the inspired teacher of this higher social and national life. " I wish to see America," he says with ringing emphasis, " not like the old powers of the earth, grasping, exclusive, and narrow, but a benefactor such as no country ever was, hospitable to all nations, legislating for all nationalities. Nations were made to help each other as much as families were ; and all advancement is by ideas, and not by brute force or mechanic force."

Such being Emerson's view of nationality, it can be best illustrated, and its truthfulness inquired into, by turning to that field of activity to which he was most strongly attracted. It is as the literary interpreter of America that he can be most clearly understood in relation to his humanitarian and political convictions.

In the doctrine of individuality is the explanation of all his other theories. That doctrine he early declared: "Help must come from the bosom alone." In another statement he makes the meaning clearer: "The world is nothing, the man is all; in yourself is the law of all nature; . . . in yourself slumbers the whole of reason; it is for you to know all, it is for you to dare all." It is a bold doctrine he thus presents, not acceptable to the present time. We are now enamoured with the outward, believing that all truth comes through the senses. To the agnostic nothing can be so repugnant as Emerson's doctrine of the soul. It often happens, however, that the man of intuition and the man of science, when faithful in the search for truth without dogmatic aims, starting from opposite sides come together unexpectedly. It is the same truth they seek, and the same world they seek it in; and so it comes about that outer and inner prove themselves to be one.

The dispute about methods is of little avail; there must be some other test. There can be no better test than that which is suggested by Emerson's career as a man of letters. What is it which has the greatest influence in developing the literary activities of a nation, creating the truest poetry and the most perfect art? Finding the answer to this question, we have found the answer to the question of method in so far as it most deeply concerned Emerson's thought. At the same time we shall find Emerson's point of view as an American, and how it was that in desiring the advancement of humanity he looked for it along the lines of national development.

There are two theories of the sources of literary creation. One of them Emerson has presented with that conciseness and force which mark his best words: "I ask not for the great, the remote, the romantic; what is doing in Italy or Arabia; what is Greek art or Provençal minstrelsy; I embrace the common, I explore and sit at the feet of the familiar, the low. Give me insight into to-day, and you may have the antique and future worlds." To round out this thought of his to its fulness there must be added these words: "Wherever a man comes, there comes revolution. The old is for slaves. When a man comes, all books are legible, all things transparent, all religions are forms."

Matthew Arnold can best present to us the other theory of literary creation, though it must be in words which are as diffuse as Emerson's are concise : —

"What the young writer wants is a hand to guide him through the confusion of the present times, a voice to prescribe to him the aim which he should keep in view, and to explain to him that the value of the literary works which offer themselves to his attention is relative to their power of helping him forward on his road towards this aim. Such a guide the English writer at the present day will nowhere find. Failing this, all that can be looked for, all indeed that can be desired, is that his attention should be fixed on excellent models ; that he may reproduce, at any rate, something of their excellence, by penetrating himself with their works and by catching their spirit, if he cannot be taught to produce what is excellent independently. . . . As he penetrates into the spirit of the great classical works, as he becomes gradually aware of their intense significance, their noble simplicity, and their calm pathos, he will be convinced that it is this effect, — unity and profoundness of moral impression, — at which the ancients aimed; that it is this which constitutes the grandeur of their works, and which makes them immortal. He will desire to direct his own efforts towards producing the same effect. Above all, he will deliver himself from the jargon of modern criticism, and escape the danger of producing poetical works conceived in the spirit of the passing time, and which partake of its transitoriness."

The history of American literature is a sufficient test of the worthiness of these two theories, proving one to be invigorating and creative, while the other has a tendency in it towards what is depressing and destructive. While the Americans, during the first period of our literature, were mere imitators of the English, seeking alike there for great models and for their materials, nothing was accomplished. The literature of that time is forgotten, except as some historian brings to our knowledge remnants of a buried past. When Cooper began to write of American Indians and forest scenery, and Bryant of the hills and rivers and birds about his own home, an American literature began to appear. It was not noble art-models which were wanted, but a living man to see and describe what was about him. Art can never take the place of life ; great models do not go before enthusiasm for the beauty which is all around.

Others had set the example of going to Nature and being independent; but the influence of Emerson in this direction cannot be overestimated. Until he began to exert an influence on our literature, it was possible to say that our writers were mere imitators of the English. It was, indeed, almost impossible for the American writers at the beginning of the century, situated as they were, to keep from being over-powered by a great and noble literature, full of art and genius, presented to them in their own language by the authors of another nation. That literature embodied other ideas than their own, brought before them traditions and memories alien to their own spirit as a people, and describing nature under such forms as were not familiar to them. The traditional influence was upon them as it was upon the English, and they went on imitating the old models.

It was not long after we became politically independent that the desire began to be felt for literary freedom. As early as 1809 Buckminster expressed the hope that our literature would take a bolder flight and form itself on better models. Two years earlier Noah Webster appealed to his countrymen to think and speak for themselves, saying, " It is desirable that inquiries should be free and opinions unshackled." It was one of the fondest dreams of Webster's life, that we should cast off the Old-World models and develop a literature based on our own life and national characteristics. When Bryant wrote his essay on American poetry, in 1818, he treated it as mostly rubbish, and made a demand, according to his biographer, "for a spirit of greater independence, for less imitation of form, for a more hearty reliance upon native instinct and inspiration ; in a word, for greater freedom, greater simplicity, and greater truth." Such was the desire of nearly all the writers who came to have any influence during the first three decades of the century.

It was easier to dream of literary independence, however, than to give an inspiring impulse in the creation of a new form of writing. When Cooper was writing his first novel, in 1820, he long delayed its completion because he distrusted "the disposition of the country to read a book that treated of its own familiar interests." A taste had to be created for what was fresh, native, and original. Though "native Americanism" was developed in politics, in finance, and in social custom, the number of persons who had an interest in literature was so small, and the material interests were so paramount and ever-pressing, there was little hope for an encouragement of what was distinctive in literary art. It was the novelty and freshness of the writings of Cooper, Irving, and Bryant which gave them recognition in England ; and it was the interest awakened by these authors abroad which first really made them popular at home. They had to develop a taste for the work they did, create an audience and train it to a love of what is truly American.

Much as these men did, however, they were never fully emancipated from their reverence for the old models, which influenced even their best work. It was left for a later generation to create an American literature in a more distinctive sense. It was not enough to describe American character and scenery while the old models and ideals were retained. The flavor of the soil must go into the writing before it could be really American. It was that literary movement which began in this country about the year 1835, and with which the name of Emerson is indissolubly connected, which has given to our literature a native flavor not to be mistaken. In America we have breadth, range, and endless promise. Here is every form of scenery, a clear sky, a pure atmosphere, and a horizon stretching boundlessly away. Here are no cramped physical conditions; a continent opens before us, crowded with variety and promise of life. Conventionalisms are no longer oppressive; the nightmare weight of centuries is not upon us; we may go forth in the pure morning air, fresh, natural, joyous, to see with our own eyes and to act with a free spirit. Here is mixing of races, crossing of blood, new combinations of faculty and talent, an untainted race of men, and opportunities as untrammelled as the daylight.

The promise of this new world of Nature and man Emerson was quite awake to, and no hope of his ran higher than that we should have a literature worthy of these physical conditions, and the freedom amidst which it may develop. His expectation did not rest alone on Nature, but on the free opportunity given for the soul's expansion. And it is worthy of notice, that the development of our literature into new forms and ideals came with the awakening of a fresh conception of man's place in Nature, and as a moral and spiritual being. The philosophy of Emerson was creative, it set men to look about them more keenly, and it made them care more for what is real than for what is formal and artistic. He gave an impulse to thought, he made men look directly at the world, he made them say straight out of the heart the things which were in it. He gave them faith in themselves and in their own thoughts, he roused in them a desire to say simply and sincerely how the world and life seemed to them. Here were the elements out of which to create a fresh, vigorous, and national literature. "Look in thy heart and write," was heard by the generation to which Emerson belonged; and as they heeded that eternal word, casting models and formalities aside, they created an American literature. "It is but a few years," says a critic of rare taste and a charming style, "since we have dared to be American in even the details and accessories of our literary work; to make our allusions to natural objects real, not conventional; to ignore the nightingale and skylark, and look for the classic and romantic on our own soil. This change began mainly with Emerson.

Some of us can recall the bewilderment with which his verses on the humble-bee, for instance, were received, when the choice of subject caused as much wonder as the treatment." When we turn to his earlier addresses, and consider what he says in behalf of listening to the voice within and to the voice of Nature, and when we look at his influence on Hawthorne, Thoreau, and Margaret Fuller, we cannot think these words claim too much for Emerson. Though a new generation is now with us, his influence on our literature has not passed away. There are new ideals appealing to us; but his voice is heard above that of every other, and the impulse of his life yet remains a fresh and inspiring creative influence.

Henry James the novelist, in his life of Hawthorne, has attempted to show how that great master was crippled as a literary creator by the absence of the picturesque and romantic in America. He forgets that the highest of all literary motives come from sympathy with man in the daily struggles of his own inward nature, and that literature has other purposes than artistic form and beauty. The best answer which can be made to such literary theorizing is to be found in the words of George Eliot, to whom plain men and women were vastly more interesting than picturesque knights and troubadours, and who turned away from the romantic past to portray the homely present. " Depend upon it," she said in one of the noblest of her novels, " you would gain

21

unspeakably if you would learn with me to see some of the poetry and pathos, the tragedy and the comedy, lying in the experience of a human soul that looks out through dull gray eyes, and that speaks in a voice of quite ordinary tones."

The search for the merely romantic and the artistic casts a blight over some of the best literature of the present hour. It is beautiful without, but there is no life within; it describes the surface of life in glowing colors, but it does not penetrate to the heart. It gives us a magnificent form, a glowing outline, and melody of movement, but there is no living soul to animate the figure. It has no passion, no ardor, nothing heroic, nothing sternly pure, nothing of great manhood. The writers who have accepted the literary theory based on imitation of the past are tame, fashionable, and polished in their style and thought; they are mere describers; not poets, not creators. They look not towards the dawn, they look not about to see how humanity in its possibilities can be portrayed in the light of opening day, when all is fresh and pure. The joy, pain, and tragedy which life everywhere presents they pass by. They do not care for anything so real; they do not see the literary promise there is in these mighty facts of daily existence. There must be as much that is genuinely human and heroic in the life of the toiling millions of America as in the rudeness and savagery of a more picturesque age. Better the rugged verse of Whitman, with its intense appreciation of the struggling and urgent life of America, than the polished prose of James, with its keen-thrusting analysis of that pseudo-Americanism which imitates what is shallow and pretentious in European society.

If we take much of the highest literature of the present hour in England and America, and examine it closely, we find it beautiful without, but full of doubt and weariness within. The English writers since 1865 show too little of the joy, hope, and conviction which marked those of the preceding age. When we turn to their books we find much to admire in the way of artistic perfection and a wonderful development of poetic melody. When we look to the inner motive of their poetry we find it to be retrospective or sceptical. They believe in the past, but not in the present. They are full of praise of the faiths of the dead past, clothing them with beauty and grace ; but toward the faiths of the living now they adopt the philosophy of ignorance. They seem always to be weary and doubtful, to suffer from perpetual ennui. How different the poetry of Wordsworth, Tennyson, and Emerson, with their delight in the near and familiar, their eyes turned towards the present and the future with the expectancy of faith.

Literature demands the thrill of life, deep energy of purpose, tragedy of the inward nature in its searching for a solution of life's meaning, passion, enthusiasm, boundless aims, and a faith pure and sublime. The heart quivering with human sympathy and pity, the heart on fire with high ideal enterprise, the soul aflame with mighty thoughts, the soul aglow with spiritual conviction, — out of these will books grow that have immortality in them. It is said by Wordsworth that poetry is emotion recalled in hours of tranquillity; but there must be emotion, if there is to be poetry, and even deep and surging emotion, worked sternly out into forms of beauty in the hours of calm and pure thought. Only the hero in possibility, however, can write a heroic book, — one who feels the heroic throb of the heart when the brave deed has been done, and the longing to act in the midst of great concerns. He may not have done the hero's deed, but he must be capable of imagining and feeling it, — and of doing it, too, — and then his words will breathe, his pages will have in them the tramp of hosts and the joy of battles won.

That literature is great which is the product of great living. When men are weak and paltry and sensual they have nothing great and wise to say, and their books are worthless. It is the age which is moved by earnest motives which produces a literature of moral power and beauty. A frivolous time may give us finely rounded periods and ornate sentences, but at the heart of them they will be hollow and dead. When mighty thoughts pulsate through a nation's being, uniting the hearts of a people in one common purpose, making them love justice and truth far more than life and its beauty, then will books be written that shall live forever. The times of mental wakening, clash of thought with thought and culture with culture, have been the times of the greatest literary activity. Not all outward influences taken together, however, and fused into one concentrated white heat of environing impulse, could produce the weakest of the world's literary masters ; but they help to bring out what is in men, they give occasion for the outburst and full flush of a capable soul. Only a rose-bush can produce roses, whatever the soil, nurture, and climate. No outward conditions can bring forth mighty thoughts, thoughts which rouse or gladden the world, from the brains of ordinary men. The poet is born ; he comes as a new light into the midst of the world's darkness, to say and to create what has not been said and created before. His appearance is a miracle ; no study of physical or social conditions can account for him. He is a burst of light out of those regions where light always is ; he brings revelations of a world richer and more beautiful than that in which we daily live. The poet does not wait on circumstances ; he creates circumstances, and a world of the romantic and picturesque, out of the flaming sentiments of his own heart. The poet is not the product of an environing past ; he environs himself rather with those ideals which answer to all that is within his own being, as rose-tint answers to rose-tint to make a thing of perfect beauty.

The times when the faces of men have been turned wholly towards the past have not been those of literary fruitfulness. It is the seeing eye without and the burning heart within which are the truest models of literary art. What they do not teach cannot be made up to us by any perfection in words or any richness in music. Thought is the creator of form, and not form the inventor of thought. The true music is to be found in the harmonious soul, and not in the rhythmic concurrence of words. The springs of literary power and beauty are within; the Homers and Shakspeares have sat at the feet of no other masters than their own souls.

No one could more clearly recognize than Emerson has done, that literature must be the outgrowth of life, that it must proceed from thought, sympathy, and experience. What we have not seen, heard, and felt, how can we describe? If we take a scene from the past for our story, for the sake of a picturesque setting, we must infuse into it the life which has been our own, or it will not glow with passion and thrill with energy. It is because our life is like the life of the past, because the heart of man is the same in all ages, touched by the same emotions and played upon by the same experiences, that we are enabled to represent bygone times with reality and justice. Whatever the time or scene, it is our own heart which throbs in its beauty and our own mind which informs it with truth. Emerson has recognized in his characteristic manner that our experience is our test of other men and times. " I am tasting the self-same life," he says, — " its sweetness, its greatness, its pain, which I so much admire in other men. Do not foolishly ask of the inscrutable, obliterated past, what it cannot tell, — the details of that nature, of that day, called Byron or Burke ; — but ask it of the enveloping now. The more quaintly you inspect its evanescent beauties, its wonderful details, its astounding whole, — so much the more you master the biography of this hero, and that, and every hero."

As extravagant as this may seem, a great and pregnant truth lies under it, and the force of it must be recognized wherever literature is to have a living power and charm. To write great books we must be capable of feeling and thinking great things.

He never ceased to criticise us for the spirit of imitation. He did not see in America that original life which he so much desired should be developed amongst us. Men did not sufficiently assert themselves, living and thinking as it seems to them best, to satisfy him. " America is provincial," he said in one of his last addresses. " See the secondariness and aping of foreign and English life, that runs through this country, in building, in dress, in eating, in books. . . . The tendency of this is to make all men alike ; to extinguish individualism and choke up all the channels of inspiration from God to man." From first to last this was his criticism ; and it was needed. Perhaps it was too self-conscious a criticism to have produced the desired effect. It is not when men know their weaknesses that they accomplish the largest results. A life of impulse and energy is the one which develops a literature of enduring quality, and not one that can see its own defects as in a mirror. With the creative skill of a Homer or a Dante, Emerson would have accomplished that in which he has now only partially succeeded.

Urgent as was his demand that we should be American and individual, foregoing the past and trusting to present inspiration, he was himself a diligent student of literature. He loved books, and he knew how to use them, for his essays everywhere show the indications of his literary tastes. Not an omnivorous reader, he contrived to secure what is best, by some process of mental selection which was extraordinary. What is of the highest import he did not hesitate to appropriate to his own page, fitting the quotation into the living structure of his essay, as if it grew there. He knew how to get quickening of thought and inspiration from books, how to assimilate the thoughts of other men into his own life-blood. Nor did he altogether scorn the past, for he took many a lesson from it. He was essentially a cosmopolitan, admiring what is excellent wherever it is to be found.

These seemingly antagonistic tendencies in Emerson were in reality quite in harmony with each other. He scorned imitation for the same reason that he loved original thought. His delight in the great books grew from the same root as his faith in the now and here. He went to the literary masters, not for models, but for quickening of heart and mind. They were to him like the mountain height, the ocean roused by the stormy winds of heaven, or the smile that plays tenderly over the face of a babe, — elementary forces, to be studied as one with flower and star. As he would assimilate the mountain scene, so would he take Homer into his own nature. As God speaks to me, he might have said, so has he spoken to other men and times; the word to others is also good for me to hear.

Emerson felt what all the literary initiators have felt, — the need of liberating the human spirit from the bondage of oppressive forms. He wished to do for America what Lessing did for Germany, — throw off the influence of ideals not in accordance with the genius of his own country. This was also the purpose which animated the great literary pathfinders of the Renaissance; they wished to develop a national literature by writing in the language of the people; and, by setting the example, they did an immense service in the awakening of the modern spirit. So was it when men grew tired of the classic doctrine of the unities, and other such antiquated methods; the old was thrown aside because a new life and power had appeared. The same struggle has gone on in every creative period, and in every nation which has come to a literary expression of its genius, — a struggle for independence of old forms and ideals, and for liberty of uttering the human soul in the words and in the spirit of the present time and place. Until a nation arrives at such measure of genius that it is capable of standing up in its own might and glory to assert its freedom and its manhood, there is little hope for its literature.

When we turn to the great creative age of English literature, that of the time of Elizabeth, one of its characteristics to which our attention is soonest called is the avidity with which its men of letters absorbed what was best, or most to their purpose, in the literature of other lands and times. They borrowed a good plot wherever they could find it; and those who could, sought the inspiration of Italy, then the centre of the world's intellectual activity. But the men of the dawn and full morning glory of English literature, eager as they were to gather the riches of every clime, wrote English books for English people. It was a time when men were awake, when the whole world seemed to be opening to them, when many forces were clashing together. The wealth of the classic ages was being opened before them, the New World was just discovered, and the spirit of commercial adventure being developed; and on every hand influences were at work to rouse and to liberate the human spirit. Feudalism died, and the modern world was born.

Every great literary period has come when men were thus roused by the stirring of new and antagonistic forces. It is not the conflict of civilization with civilization which begets literary power; but when forces long developed apart come in contact with each other, in the movements of peoples or in the progress of discovery, men are thrown out of their old habits, their minds are set free, and they come to act from what is within, not merely by the force of what is without. They find themselves no longer the victims of circumstance and custom, they rejoice in all their powers, and pour out their souls with a joy pure and fresh. For the first time then they live as men, take delight in all their faculties, and pour forth their thoughts, feelings, and ideals with the grace and delight of a child playing in the summer sun. When Greece came in contact with the East, had its imagination roused by the marvels of that fruitful region, and had been stirred to new political activity in defence of its own existence, it produced Plato, Æschylus, and Herodotus. So was it that the energies of Europe, brought into contact with new and widening influences, urging men to fresh exertions for political development and liberty, and appealing to them through loftier ideals, gave to Italy her Dante, Petrarch, and Raphael.

These movements of national genius Emerson recognized; but it is to be said, that he did not see what is the true influence of the past on the present. He did not clearly realize that the past may serve to the individual the same office which the world-movements do to nations and ages. The mind comes in contact with what men have been and done; is quickened and inspired by the riches of that mighty world which lies behind us. The breadth and the wealth of it, liberating them from the material thraldom of the present, sets them free to create new forms and ideals which shall represent what is best out of every human endeavor. This capacity of the past Emerson did not see; it was not open to him to realize it in its fulness of power. He did see, what is even more important, that genuine literary productiveness must be the growth of the impulses of the present. The past may give us materials, it may stimulate and broaden the mind; but the present must give the thrill of life and the beating heart.

Emerson's faith in America is justified, whether we trust in the capacities of the individual soul, or whether our expectation grows from the promises of a new civilization. America brings together the races of the world as no nation or time ever did before; and it centres in itself the freshest impulses of an age full of activity and daring. Its freedom from traditions of its own, after the pattern of which it would need to live and walk, gives it the opportunity to acquire the traditions of all the lands from which it takes its great population. Greece had the traditions of its own past, those of Egypt and of a little corner of Asia; Rome had the traditions of Greece and Egypt and a part of the East in addition to its own; Italy fed on the inherited life of the Christian and classic ages; England turns its eyes to the past of Europe; but America takes to itself the traditions of the whole world. America no castles and feudal romances! What is such trumpery as this compared to those long successions of human effort after the ideal, which have been caught up into the forms of mythology, history, poetry, romance, and art, and which now await the new people who can transform them into its own inheritance, and give them back to the world no longer national traditions, but the poetry of mankind ? We are to have all mythology, all history, all literature, for our possession. As a free people we are to look upon the life of the race, its heroisms and achievements, and, suffusing it with the new spirit, turn it into song and story for the free peoples to come. We shall sing not only of the taking of Troy and of Paradise Lost, but of the triumphs of man as a free soul. A new light will gleam along the pages of the old traditions, and we shall find in them a meaning and a beauty not there before. This is whereto the literature of the present time is feeling, blindly and feebly, amid crudities and weariness, but in hope and promise. It recognizes the wealth of material with which it has to work, but it has not caught that living spirit of faith which must be at the heart of its creative impulse. It awaits a new land for its achievements ; and Emerson's hope for America may yet be justified by a literature in harmony with the new time.

If the anticipations of Emerson were in any degree correct, the literature representing America will have in it the spirit of freedom and equal rights, recognition of man wherever and however found, trust in the powers of Nature and of the mind, and an abiding conviction that the life of the world is that of Spiritual Intelligence. Such forces as these, working in a virgin soil, should produce epics, and dramas, and histories not less great, but truer, than any the past has given us. Genius will fitly sing the new earth and the new peoples.

A nation that would be great must not trust to what other men have done and believed. It may have sympathies so wide as to look with joy on the achievements and traditions of other peoples ; but it must have memories of its own and cherish them, before it can rise to the loftiest attitude of national conviction and self-consciousness. It must have an idea of its own destiny; it must have an ideal capable of uniting its citizens in a common purpose ; it must have the realization of its own individuality as a people. It is not like other nations ; it has a past, a physical environment, and an inner consciousness, quite its own. In being distinctly national it can best serve the universal human interests ; for we do not become cosmopolitan in renouncing the ties which bind us to our own people. We may roam through all lands, but only one place can have given us birth. It is not the negation of individuality which gives a person a wide range of sympathy with his fellows.

America has two ideas which stand out distinctly, — individuality and freedom. Personal and exclusive as they may seem capable, at first glance, of making us, their real effect is to widen our sympathies, and to make us the most cosmopolitan people the world has ever known. Intensely national, our hopes embrace all lands and peoples. Zealously

American, nothing that is human is indifferent to us. Sitting apart, we watch with sympathetic interest the movements of humanity.

These national qualities are in the mind and the writings of Emerson. Concerned as we are rather for the individual than the nation, preferring that persons shall have their rights recognized rather than that the nation shall be powerful, he has become the embodiment of this idea, given it a philosophical, moral, and religious interpretation. It is the thought which finds constant expression in his poems, addresses, and essays; it kindles his most eloquent ideas about the future of mankind. National and yet cosmopolitan is the America he believed in so earnestly. It is a higher type of national being he cherished, that finds its noblest memories and its truest heroisms in the direction of the advancement of humanity. Peace, brotherhood, and universal advancement may give traditions and ideal hopes. Great memories may cluster about the interests of peace and freedom as about the interests of war and heroism. It is these more peaceful, more human, more nobly sympathetic interests to which we give ourselves as Americans; and the ideals of the future are to be formed after this type. The national ideal will cease to be selfish and exclusive and become humane and attractive. It will take form around the thought of our common humanity, giving to freedom and justice the heritage of our best hopes.

When this new national spirit, based on the idea

of individuality, freedom, and a common humanity, has been fully developed, it will take up the past of mankind and interpret it in harmony with its own ideals. It will create a new literary, artistic, and social tendency, which will embody itself in forms suited to its own aspirations. The influence of the past will still be upon us, and we shall be capable of profiting by its lessons; but we shall interpret it in the light of larger experiences. None the less will it feed and stimulate the ideal life, but we shall be less under bondage to it. Around the central thoughts animating the new national life literature will weave its garments of beauty.

A view of nationality which recognizes the distinctive American type as essential, and which is as cosmopolitan as the race, is that to be found in the writings of Emerson. It is not cosmopolitan in the manner of some of his predecessors, who teach that the nation is nothing; but he makes the idea of a universal humanity the very centre of his conception of nationality. Attachment to our country becomes the motive for a recognition of all mankind. Individuals cohere into families in order that they may become true individuals, families into communities, communities into nations, while the family of nations is to include the whole race. The nation remains distinct and individual that it may render a more perfect service to humanity.

The broad and human view is that which appeared most conspicuously in Emerson's Americanism. He was an American in no narrow and sectional spirit ; it was no special spot of earth for which he contended. He was an idealistic American, — an American of the soul, caring for freedom, and morality, and the seeing mind, more than for Concord River or Wachusett Mountain. An American literature of local description and provincial dialect would not have satisfied his desire ; but that rather which grows out of the spirit of high enterprise, loyalty of man to man, and the consciousness of soul-freedom. Faithful as he was to what is local, loyal as he was to the individual, he would have these put in their true relations to the human and universal. Concord had beauties of its own; but Concord was a part of the universe. It was worthy of study because representative of the whole ; it was the whole for which he sought, the universal for which he yearned. This spot of earth is a true indication of the universe. The secrets of the whole universe are to be learned here. This hour of time is a true type of eternity ; the loftiest revelations of eternity may vision themselves before us now. " You may run back," Emerson would say, " through the ages and countries we have travelled from, but what you seek is on this spot and in this time."

Having by the aid of this conception made himself sure of the sacredness of the soul and of the divine life in Nature, he ceased to feel any exclusive interest in time and place. Convinced that man is a living soul, and in contact with the eternal truth here in

22

Concord and America, he turned to Africa and China with the same promise for them. Concord was no Mecca to him; he saw no special sacredness in its flowers, rivers, and ponds. America is not represented by its many kinds of climate and its great variety of scenery, but by its common intelligence and its rights for all. Its ideal is not that of wide-stretching power, but that of a common humanity co-working for the highest ends of intelligent moral beings. The true America is in the soul that is free, intelligent, and aspiring. The country of man is the genuine America. It does not lie here or there, but towards the way of hope and promise, where men rise up to liberty and justice, where they live in the light of the ideal. When the serf is taught to be his own master, when the slave is made to know that he is an intelligent being, when justice speaks in clear-toned voice the rights of all, when the ignorant are educated and the vicious reclaimed, — then America comes to whatever people to whom this light has been given. It lies fresh and fair to the open day wherever it may be; there is a youthful glow and enterprise within it, and its citizens make war no more, but join their hands in the good deeds of peace.

XII.

EMERSON'S PHILOSOPHY OF NATURE.

By WILLIAM T. HARRIS.

THE eminent physicist, Tyndall, has told us that he considers Emerson a profoundly religious influence. Emerson accepted all new discoveries in science without dismay, and without loss of reverence or of faith in the supremacy of the divine in the world. This certainly is a trait that belongs to a religious nature.

There is another aspect of science, that of its relation to poetry or poetic art, that interests us when we take up Emerson's poetry. It has been supposed by some that the age of poetry is now past, and no longer possible, because of the advent of modern natural science and the invention of labor-saving machines. " The Muses have fled and Nature is forever disenchanted." If this were true, the spiritual uses of Nature would have become obsolete. Nature could not be used as a symbol of mind and a means of expression of spiritual nature. An iron age of empty show and pretence would indeed be upon us; for no poetic tropes or metaphors could be found with which we could express invisible nature by visible images. If such were used, they must needs be feigned, — a sham performance imitating consciously the Greek view of Nature, which was a genuine one. An age of hollowness and insincerity, profoundly sceptical of the very existence of spiritual things, is bound to appear when men lose their insight into the correspondence between the material and spiritual, and cease to regard nature as the type whose archetype is mind. Accordingly in this epoch of prose science and machinery an unusual interest attaches to the work of its poets. The original poet of this time is the one that makes incursions into the realm of nature, with the aid of the newest scientific theories, and is able to discover spiritual correspondences in prose realities, whether they be cosmic laws or mere machines.

It is in this important field that Emerson may be regarded as the poet of the future. He sees in their poetic aspect the generalizations of astronomy, geology, and biology, — the theories of nebular consolidation and the evolution of life. The essential characteristic of poetry is to be found in metaphor and personification rather than in the forms of rhythm and rhyme. Hebrew poetry, for example, although the most sublime species of poetry, has no rhythm and rhyme, but only parallelism and correspondence, for its external dress. Much of the so-called poetry lacks metaphor and personification, although it possesses the jingle of rhyme and its metres are perfect.

Such writing lacks the poetic vision that sees the invisible and spiritual in the visible and material. Hence the attempt to use modern discoveries in natural science for poetic matter has for the most part failed, by reason of the lack of a deeper insight which discerned their spiritual significance.

Emerson's poetry abounds in metaphors taken from the modern theories of nature. His spiritual vision pierces through the prose hull to the vital kernel.

The freshness and wildness of nature as depicted by Shakspeare in his lyrics, such, for example, as "Under the greenwood tree," and "When icicles hang by the wall," may be found in Emerson's poems of nature, — especially the "Woodnotes," "May-Day," "The Rhodora," "Hamatreya," "My Garden," "The Titmouse," and "Sea-Shore."

The beauty of nature demands a certain neglect of regularity and symmetry, in order to reach freedom and gracefulness by suggesting boundless resources of form, and emancipation from mechanical conformity to laws and types. There is in this a sort of justification for Emerson's apparent carelessness in respect to metre. In the nature-poems especially there is a suggestion of the transcendency over all mechanism which we always see when we look at the world in masses and put by our analytical spectacles of species and genera and laws. How restful and refreshing are the glimpses of genuine untamed nature offered us in Shakspeare's poem just now alluded to !

> " Under the greenwood tree
>   Who loves to lie with me,
>   And turn his merry note
>   Unto the sweet bird's throat, —
> Come hither, come hither, come hither :
>   Here shall he see
>   No enemy
> But winter and rough weather ! "

Here is abrupt transition of rhythm that suggests freedom from conventionality. The resources of poetry are many and adequate. One may not expect to find all moods and all subjects fittingly expressed in one species of poetry. While one range of subjects demands strict sequence of rhyme and perfect measure of rhythm, another range, involving sudden flashes of insight and vast metamorphoses of objects, may require altogether different treatment. In art, the deepest law is the unity of subject and form.

Merlin's idea of the kind of poetry for the wizard bard was this, according to Emerson, —

> " Great is the art,
>   Great be the manners, of the bard.
>   He shall not his brain encumber
>   With the coil of rhythm and number ;
>   But, leaving rule and pale forethought,
>   He shall aye climb
>   For his rhyme.
>   ' Pass in, pass in,' the angels say,
>   ' In to the upper doors,
>   Nor count compartments of the floors,
>   But mount to paradise
>   By the stairway of surprise.' "

"Machine poetry" is over-careful of its metre and rhyme. Those who "write poetry fit to put round frosted cake," — among whom Emerson places the poets of the epoch of Queen Anne, — seldom take any flights into the realm of the inspired bard. They do not conquer any new realm of nature, and reduce it by trope or personification to the symbol of spiritual nature. They use only the old conventional metaphors. But the realm of true poetry, like "the potent plane of Dæmons, spreads"

> "Close, close to men,
> Like undulating layer of air,
> Right above their heads."

The brave poet may surely ascend into it if he is always true to his aspiration.

In his poem "Woodnotes" Emerson sings the song of the pine-tree; not a song of the idle fancies of the poet on beholding it, but the song of the thoughtful naturalist, who is above all a poet. He sees in the pine-tree the pioneer of vegetation, conquering the drifting sand-heaps, binding together the soil by its roots and covering it with a layer of leaves and branches, by and by to become vegetable mould, in which all plants may flourish. After the pine come other trees, and then animals, and then all is ready for man.

> "Whether is better the gift or the donor?
> 'Come to me,'
> Quoth the pine-tree,
> 'I am the giver of honor.

> My garden is the cloven rock,
> And my manure the snow;
> And drifting sand-heaps feed my stock,
> In summer's scorching glow.' "

He proceeds to interpret like another Merlin the low murmur with which the pine sings when the wind swells, —

> " And the countless leaves of the pine are strings
> Tuned to the lay the wood-god sings."

Here is the prose doctrine of development turned into poetry : —

> "To the open air it sings
> Sweet the genesis of things,
> Of tendency through endless ages."

This is the tendency of which he speaks when he says, in another place, —

> " And, striving to be man, the worm
> Mounts through all the spires of form."

The oracle of the pine continues, and names the great epochs in the " genesis of things," and that endless " tendency "

> " Of star-dust, and star-pilgrimages,
> Of rounded worlds, of space and time.
> Of the old flood's subsiding slime,
> Of chemic matter, force, and form,
> Of poles and powers, cold, wet, and warm :
> The rushing metamorphosis
> Dissolving all that fixture is,
> Melts things that be to things that seem,
> And solid nature to a dream."

In " My Garden " (around Walden Pond) he describes how the deluge ploughed and laid the terraces one by one; how it flowed away at a later period, leaving them to bleach and dry in the sun; how the wind and birds sowed Walden beach. In " Sea-Shore " he makes the chiding sea describe its deeds. It pounds with its hammer the rocky coast, smiting Andes into dust, strewing its bed, and in another age rebuilding a continent of better men.

> " Then I unbar the doors : my paths lead out
> The exodus of nations : I disperse
> Men to all shores that front the hoary main."

In " Merlin " he has laid down his doctrine of poetry in verse. In his prose essay on " Poetry and Imagination " he says that the " Poet discovers that what men value as substances have a higher value as symbols; that nature is the immense shadow of man." So " Poetry is the perpetual endeavor to express the spirit of the thing; to pass the brute body and search the life and reason which cause it to exist." " Nature itself is a vast trope, and all particular natures are tropes."

In Emerson's first published work we find an attempt to make an inventory of the various aspects of the world in time and space. His most important principle reached is this : —

" It is a sufficient account of that appearance we call the world, that God will teach a human mind, and so makes it the receiver of a certain number of congruent sensations, which we call the sun and moon, man and woman, house and trade."

Considering the universe as composed of nature and soul, he defines the former: " Strictly speaking, all that is separate from us, all which philosophy distinguishes as the NOT ME, that is, both nature and art, all other men and my own body, must be ranked under this name, NATURE." Four uses include the purposes served by objects of nature. These are commodity, beauty, language, discipline.

Under commodity we find what is useful for food, clothing, and shelter, — the body's wants. Besides this there is the co-operation of one's fellow-men. " The private poor man hath cities, ships, canals, bridges, built for him. He goes to the post-office, and the human race run on his errands ; to the book-shop, and the human race read and write all that happens, for him." But commodity is not a final end : " This mercenary benefit is one which has respect to a farther good. A man is fed, not that he may be fed, but that he may work."

Nature serves a nobler want than food, clothing, and shelter; namely, the love of beauty. The aspects of beauty he distributes under three heads : (1) delight; (2) as " the mark God sets on virtue ;" (3) as tributary to self-knowledge. " A work of art is an abstract, or epitome, of the world ; it is the result or expression of Nature in miniature. The production of a work of art throws a light upon the mystery of humanity."

That nature serves man in a still more indispensable way, for self-knowledge, not through beauty but directly through language, is obvious. "Nature is the vehicle of thought, and in a simple, double, and threefold degree : (1) words in their literal sense ; (2) in their figurative sense; (3) Nature as a whole being the symbol of spirit.

" Every natural fact is a symbol of some spiritual fact." Here is the key to the poetic use of Nature. " Man is conscious of a universal soul within or behind his individual life, wherein, as in a firmament, the natures of justice, truth, love, freedom, arise and shine." " These are not the dreams of a few poets here and there; but man is an analogist, and studies relations in all objects. He is placed in the centre of being, and a ray of relation passes from every other being to him." In speaking of the relation of language to people whose life is mere use and wont, and to secondary lights in literature, he very strikingly remarks : —

" Hundreds of writers may be found in every long-civilized nation who for a short time believe, and make others believe, that they see and utter truths, who do not of themselves clothe one thought in its natural garment, but who feed unconsciously on the language created by the primary writers of the country, — those, namely, who hold primarily on nature."

Thirdly, Nature as a whole is the symbol of the soul. "The visible creation is the terminus or the circumference of the invisible world." "There seems to be a necessity in spirit to manifest itself in material forms; and day and night, river and storm, beast and bird, acid and alkali, pre-exist in necessary ideas in the mind of God, and are what they are by virtue of preceding affections in the world of spirit."

Coming to the fourth use of Nature, discipline, he finds this to include all the others. "Nature is a discipline of the understanding in intellectual truths." It trains his common-sense year after year by a continual reproduction of annoyances, inconveniences, dilemmas. Debt and credit perform the same good office. Nature disciplines the will. "It offers all its kingdoms to man as the raw material which he may mould into what is useful." "One after another his victorious thought comes up with and reduces all things until the world becomes at last only a realized will, — the double of man."

Moreover, everything has a moral aspect. "All things with which we deal preach to us. . . . The chaff and the wheat, weeds and plants, blight, rain, insects, sun, — it is a sacred emblem from the first furrow of spring to the last stack which the snow of winter overtakes in the fields."

From this idea of discipline in morals Emerson finds a transition to idealism through the thought of the "unity of nature, — the unity in variety which meets us everywhere." In fact, we find everywhere in this remarkable essay what may be called a dialectic, whereby one part joins to the next by a sort of natural growth. Thus commodity becomes beauty through the idea of all society existing for the well-being of each member of it, — the whole existing in the part manifests beauty. So, too, beauty becomes language in its phase of presenting self-knowledge. Language in its highest form, wherein Nature as a whole reflects spirit as a whole, reveals the end of Nature as a discipline, and we reach an ultimate unity.

"So intimate is this unity that it is easily seen; it lies under the undermost garment of nature, and betrays its source in universal spirit."

He finds manifestations of this central unity (*a*) in the fact that every universal truth implies or supposes every other truth; (*b*) "an action is the perfection and publication of thought, and a right action seems to fill the eye and to be related to all Nature;" (*c*) every object in Nature suggests some other.

But "words and actions are not attributes of brute nature. They introduce us to the human form of which all other organizations appear to be degradations." From this he would conclude as to the form of the "central unity" of nature. The basis of all must be truth and virtue. Human forms "are incomparably the richest informations of the power and order that lie at the heart of things." Notwithstanding the defects of humanity, men and women "all rest like fountain-pipes on the unfathomed sea of thought and virtue, whereto they alone of all organizations are the entrances." Thus he believes man to hold a unique place in the world, he alone having the form of the highest principle of nature, and alone having access to that principle.

In the sixth chapter of "Nature" Emerson comes to consider idealism as the view of the world resulting from the foregoing contemplations. All parts of nature conspire to this one end of discipline, and so suggest a doubt whether this object be not the sole purpose of the world. Are not things painted on the firmament of the soul rather than spread out there in space ? It is impossible for us to test the authenticity of the report of our senses.

"Whilst we acquiesce entirely in the permanence of natural laws, the question of the absolute existence of Nature still remains open. It is the uniform effect of culture on the human mind not to shake our faith in the stability of particular phenomena, as of heat, water, azote ; but to lead us to regard nature as phenomenon, not a substance ; to esteem nature as an accident and an effect."

He gives an account of the rise of this idealistic point of view in psychology. (1) The senses have a sort of instinctive belief in the absolute existence of Nature ; (2) so too has the understanding; (3) but reason sees through outlines and surfaces into causes and spirits beneath. "The best moments of life are these delicious awakenings of the higher powers, and the reverential withdrawing of Nature before its God."

He proceeds to make a sort of inventory of the facts that conspire to make the reason an idealist.

(1) A change of view changes the object, and by this most common mechanical means Nature suggests the difference between the observer and the spectacle, — between man and Nature. This may be called the idealistic lesson of spatial perspective. But the perspective of time, too, has its idealistic lesson.

(2) The poet in a higher manner communicates this lesson. He transfigures all material objects, and uses matter as the symbol of his heroic passion. " He unfixes the land and the sea, makes them revolve around the axis of his primary thought, and disposes them anew. He invests dust and stones with humanity, and makes them the words of reason." He gives an extended application of this view of the poet to Shakspeare, quoting especially from the Sonnets.

(3) " The philosopher, not less than the poet, postpones the apparent order and relations of things to the empire of thought."

" It is, both with the poet and the philosopher, a spiritual life imparted to nature ; that the solid seeming block of matter has been pervaded and dissolved by a thought ; that this feeble human being has penetrated the vast masses of nature with an informing soul, and recognized itself in their harmony, — that is, seized their law. In physics, when this is attained, the memory disburthens itself of its cumbrous catalogues of particulars, and carries centuries of observation in a single formula."

(4) If the presuppositions of science are idealistic, so, too, are its results. " It fastens the attention upon immortal necessary uncreated natures, — that is,

upon ideas; and in their presence we feel that the outward circumstance is a dream and a shade. Whilst we wait in this Olympus of gods we think of nature as an appendix to the soul. We ascend into their region, and know that these are the thoughts of the Supreme Being."

Although this region of divine ideas is accessible to few men as a matter of science or philosophy, yet, says Emerson, "all men are capable of being raised by piety, or by passion, into their region." In the company of such ideas the mind sees its immortality as a necessary fact.

(5) Finally, the ground of the doctrine of idealism is to be found in religion and ethics. He defines and distinguishes the two provinces; both agree in that their function is " the practice of ideas, or the introduction of ideas into life." " Ethics and religion differ herein: that ethics is the system of human duties commencing from man; religion, from God. Religion includes the personality of God; ethics does not." Here, in this earliest essay of Emerson, how completely is expressed the doctrine of the personality of God and the moral and intellectual character of his Being!

Religion is for the uneducated mind what philosophy is for the cultured. " It does that for the unschooled which philosophy does for Berkeley and Vyasa. The first and last lesson of religion is, ' The things that are seen are temporal; the things that are unseen are eternal.' "

While he loves nature, therefore, with a love amounting to a passion, Emerson announces idealism as indicating the "true position of nature in regard to man, wherein to establish man all right education tends, as the ground which to attain is the object of human life, — that is, of man's connection with nature."

With this theory of Nature the soul "sees the world in God and beholds the whole circle of persons and things, of actions and events, of country and religion, not as painfully accumulated, atom after atom, act after act, in an aged, creeping past, but as one vast picture which God paints on the instant eternity, for the contemplation of the soul."

Hence the soul "sees something more in Christianity than the scandals of ecclesiastical history or the niceties of criticism. . . . It accepts from God the phenomenon as it finds it, — as the pure and awful form of religion in the world."

In the six chapters that are devoted to this discussion we have progressed by a natural growth of the subject — by what would be called a dialectical evolution of the idea of nature — to the doctrine of the first principle of the world as a personal being. In the seventh chapter, to which we have arrived, this result is made a special theme. It is the doctrine of Spirit as the absolute. "Idealism is a hypothesis to account for nature by other principles than those of carpentry and chemistry." But as merely negative it is a defective view. "If it only deny the existence of matter, it does not satisfy the demands of the spirit. It leaves God out of me. It leaves me in the splendid labyrinth of my perceptions, to wander without end."

Idealism, then, is only a useful introduction to the positive doctrine of spirit. In answering the questions, Whence is matter, and whereto? we reach this positive doctrine. "The world proceeds from the same spirit as the body of man. It is a remoter and inferior incarnation of God, — a projection of God in the unconscious."

Up to this point the doctrine of nature has been what we may call that of evolution, or at least in harmony with the modern doctrine of that name. Indeed, there is prefixed to the essay one of those oracular pieces of verse that Emerson often used to sum up his prose essays. The key-note which expresses the theme sounds forth : —

> " A subtle chain of countless rings
> The next unto the farthest brings ;
> The eye reads omens where it goes,
> And speaks all languages the rose ;
> And, striving to be man, the worm
> Mounts through all the spires of form."

Here is the doctrine of evolution substantially set forth. It does not say that the lower produces the higher. Nor does the doctrine of evolution, when rightly understood. In saying "there is a survival of the fittest," it says that mind is the goal of nature. The farther from mind, the farther from survival. The chaotic and inorganic is an unstable equilibrium which is continually changing and attempting some new form. But individuality begins when nature ascends to mind, and the power of self-preservation increases with the increase of mind. Does not this point clearly towards the supremacy of mind, if nature moves always to attain the form of intelligence? That which comprehends itself and the world, and is able to act with directive intelligence, is able to conquer all other beings and make all serve him. Evolution of the fittest, therefore, points to man or spiritual being as the final cause of nature. All beings are on their way thither. In the result of the process of nature one may read the character of the supreme first principle revealed in it. If nature is so constituted that left to its own laws it does evolve and can evolve only rational creatures as the fittest, evidently the absolute Being must be rational. Here is the view of nature that Emerson had reached and announced in his own doctrine of evolution before 1836. While it is substantially the doctrine of evolution, it is spiritual evolution ; being an insight into the fact that nature reveals spirit as its final cause, and into the fact that the universe is not alien to man, but throughout the projection of a being like man, or divine-human.

Turning from the contemplation of evolution to the final chapter of this treatise on "Nature," we come to the question of "Prospects." In the eighth chapter we rise to take a survey of the whole. "Prospects" shall mean both history and prophecy.

He unfolds in this chapter an altogether new and surprising theory of the world, — a theory that one would pronounce incompatible with the evolutional theory developed thus far. It is no less than the theory of "Lapse," or Descent of the Soul, somewhat like that found in the fourth Ennead of Plotinus.

There are, indeed, a few notes in the preceding chapter on "Spirit," at the close, which form the transition to this remote doctrine of Lapse. The inadequacy or imperfection of the individual is the connecting link. "As we degenerate, the contrast between us and our house is more evident. We are as much strangers in nature as we are aliens from God. We do not understand the notes of birds. The fox and the deer run away from us; the bear and the tiger rend us. We do not know the uses of more than a few plants, as corn and the apple, the potato and the vine."

How do we reconcile this inadequacy with the positive doctrine of spirit? This had been stated thus:

"We learn that the highest is present to the soul of man; that the dread universal essence, which is not wisdom, or love, or beauty, or power, but all in one and each entirely, is that for which all things exist, and that by which they are; that spirit creates; that behind nature, throughout nature, spirit is present; one and not compound, it does not act upon us from without, — that is, in space and time, — but spiritually, or through ourselves; therefore that spirit — that is, the Supreme Being — does not build up nature around us, but puts it forth through us as the life of the tree puts forth new branches and leaves through the pores of the old. . . . Man has access to the entire mind of the Creator, and is himself the creator of the finite."

If man is the creator of the finite, then all imperfect beings have arisen through his agency. From this the doctrine of Lapse is easily deduced. But the doctrine of Evolution does not account for the existence of lower orders of being by supposing a lapse, or degeneration, of higher beings. It supposes that an All-Good Highest Being desires to share his blessedness with creatures, and therefore creates them by an eternal process, giving them the possibility of developing by freedom into all knowledge and goodness. All lower and lowest creatures belong to the process necessary in the Divine Wisdom for creating beings with free individuality. Such free individuality must be reached by the exercise of will power. Natural selection involves this exercise of such rudiments of will and intellect as belong to lowest organisms. Arrived at man, individuality is reached that can know universal truth, and will universal good; and thus the final type is attained.

As the view of evolution here described makes nature a process of creating new spirits, and thus of increasing the number of blessed beings, it is thoroughly optimistic in its character. The other view, that explains nature by the fall of spirits from an Eden of blessedness or by a lapse from holiness, is, on the contrary, pessimistic.

With these suggestions we turn to the most important part of the final chapter, which he introduces with the following words : —

" I shall therefore conclude this essay with some traditions of man and Nature which a certain poet sang to me ; and which, as they have always been in the world, and perhaps reappear to every bard, may be both in history and prophecy."

Either because he wishes to indicate that the theory is one delivered to him by tradition, and one which he has not fully verified in his own intuitions, or because he has a feeling of the discrepance between this theory and that of evolution already approved, he calls it " some traditions," and intimates that he received it from " a certain poet," whom he quotes or feigns to quote.   Note especially the difference in style between the foregoing essay and these " traditions."   There is a sort of poetic rhythm in the latter, and a sonorous balance of sentences quite in contrast to the epigrammatic style of the remainder of the treatise : —

" The foundations of man are not in matter, but in spirit ; but the element of spirit is eternity.   To it, therefore, the longest series of events, the oldest chronologies, are young and recent.   In the cycle of the universal man, from whom the known individuals proceed, centuries are points, and all history is but the epoch of one degradation.

" We distrust and deny inwardly our sympathy with

nature. We own and disown our relation to it, by turns. We are, like Nebuchadnezzar, dethroned, bereft of reason, and eating grass like an ox. But who can set limits to the remedial force of spirit?

"A man is a god in ruins. When men are innocent, life shall be longer, and shall pass into the immortal as gently as we awake from dreams. Now, the world would be insane and rabid if these disorganizations should last for hundreds of years. It is kept in check by death and infancy. Infancy is the perpetual Messiah, which comes into the arms of fallen men, and pleads with them to return to paradise.

"Man is the dwarf of himself. Once he was permeated and dissolved by spirit. He filled nature with his overflowing currents. Out from him sprang the sun and moon, — from man the sun, from woman the moon. The laws of his mind, the periods of his actions, externized themselves into day and night, into the year and the seasons. But having made for himself this huge shell, his waters retired ; he no longer fills the veins and veinlets ; he is shrunk to a drop. He sees that the structure still fits him, but fits him colossally. Say, rather, once it fitted him, now it corresponds to him from far and on high. He adores timidly his own work. Now is man the follower of the sun, and woman the follower of the moon. Yet sometimes he starts in his slumber, and wonders at himself and his house, and muses strangely at the resemblance betwixt him and it. He perceives that if his law is still paramount, if still he have elemental power, if his word is sterling yet in nature, it is not conscious power, it is not inferior but superior to his will. It is Instinct. Thus my Orphic poet sang."

He comments on these oracles in his former sober vein: "At present man applies to nature but half his force. He works on the world with his understanding alone." Apparently commenting on the passage beginning, "Yet sometimes he starts in his slumber," he continues: "Meantime, in the thick darkness there are not wanting gleams of a better light, — occasional examples of the action of man upon nature with his entire force, — with reason as well as understanding." Ancient miracles, the history of Christ, prayer, eloquence, and the like, occur to him. Far more profound, and in harmony with his optimism and evolution, is the following : —

"The ruin or the blank that we see when we look at nature is in our own eye. The axis of vision is not coincident with the axis of things, and so they appear not transparent but opaque. The reason why the world lacks unity, and lies in broken heaps, is because man is disunited with himself. . . . When a faithful thinker, resolute to detach every object from personal relations and see it in the light of thought, shall, at the same time, kindle science with the fire of the holiest affections, then will God go forth anew into the creation."

He returns to the "Orphic" poet, and closes his book with the following quotation : —

"Nature is not fixed, but fluid. Spirit alters, moulds, makes it. The immobility or bruteness of nature is the absence of spirit ; to pure spirit it is fluid, it is volatile, it is obedient. Every spirit builds itself a house ; and beyond its house a world ; and beyond its world a heaven.

" Know, then, that the world exists for you. For you is the phenomenon perfect. What we are that only can we see. All that Adam had, all that Cæsar could, you have and can do. Adam called his house heaven and earth, Cæsar called his house Rome ; you perhaps call yours a cobbler's trade, a hundred acres of ploughed land, or a scholar's garret. Yet, line for line and point for point, your dominion is as great as theirs, though without fine names. Build, therefore, your own world. As fast as you conform your life to the pure idea in your mind, that will unfold its great proportions. A correspondent revolution in things will attend the influx of the spirit. So fast will disagreeable appearances, swine, spiders, snakes, pests, madhouses, prisons, enemies, vanish ; they are temporary, and shall be seen no more. The sordor and filths of nature the sun shall dry up and the wind exhale. As when the summer comes from the south, the snow-banks melt, and the face of the earth becomes green before it, so shall the advancing spirit create its ornaments along its path, and carry with it the beauty it visits, and the song which enchants it ; it shall draw beautiful faces, warm hearts, wise discourse, and heroic acts, around its way, until evil is no more seen. The kingdom of man over nature, which cometh not with observation, — a dominion such as now is beyond his dream of God, — he shall enter without more wonder than the blind man feels who is gradually restored to perfect sight."

This form of the Lapse differs from the Oriental tradition of it, found in Neoplatonism and Gnosticism, in having two forms of paradise, — a past and a future. Since the soul lapsed from a past perfection, how can it be assured against a future lapse if it recovers its state once more ?   More especially, how can it recover at all ?

The inconsistency of Asiatic philosophy ever reappears in the mysticism of the Occident.   But this special form of it, — one is piqued to ask : Does it belong to some earlier studies of Emerson which marked his first insights into Plato's Phædrus, or the Enneads of Plotinus, or Jacob Boehme ?   And did he feign to quote it in order (like a favorite device of Carlyle) to avoid the necessity of making a steep transition to such an Orphic style ?   Or, are the quotation-marks no mask, after all, and did he quote the substance of his friend Alcott's Orphic rhapsodizings ? Perhaps, however, these words were written before the acquaintance with Alcott began ; perhaps, too, before Alcott himself adopted the theory of the Lapse. But it is certain that nowhere else (not even in the " Tablets ") could one find such a complete statement of the Lapse theory, held by Alcott ever since the Orphic sayings were written for " The Dial " in 1842.

I cannot think that Emerson ever held the doctrine of the Lapse, or believed it seriously to be the true view of the world.   He makes occasionally a poetic allusion to it, and sometimes seems to be attracted by its intimation of a former union with God which the soul may attain again ; but for his own genuine theory of the world one must look to his statement of evolution — an *ascent* rather than a lapse.

I quote in conclusion, as one of the completest of his statements, this poem on "Wealth," — illustrating how science can be turned into spiritual metaphor:

" Who shall tell what did befall
Far away in time when once
Over the lifeless ball
Hung idle stars and suns ?
What god the element obeyed ?
Wings of what wind the lichen bore,
Wafting the puny seeds of power,
Which, lodged in rock, the rock abrade ?
And well the primal pioneer
Knew the strong task to it assigned,
Patient through Heaven's enormous year
To build in matter home for mind.
From air the creeping centuries drew
The matted thicket low and wide,
This must the leaves of ages strew
The granite slab to.clothe and hide,
Ere wheat can wave its golden pride.
What smiths, and in what furnace, rolled
(In dizzy æons dim and mute
The reeling brain can ill compute)
Copper and iron, lead and gold ?
What oldest star the fame can save
Of races perishing to pave
The planet with a floor of lime ?
Dust is their pyramid and mole.
Who saw what ferns and palms were pressed
Under the tumbling mountain's breast
In the safe herbal of the coal ?
But when the quarried means were piled
All is waste and worthless, till
Arrives the wise selecting will,
And out of slime and chaos, Wit
Draws the threads of fair and fit.

Then temples rose, and towns and marts,
The shop of toil, the hall of arts ;
Then flew the sail across the seas
To feed the North from tropic trees ;
The storm-wind wove, the torrent span,
Where they were bid, the rivers ran ;
New slaves fulfilled the poet's dream,
Galvanic wire, strong-shouldered steam.
Then docks were built and crops were stored
And ingots added to the hoard.
But, though light-headed man forget,
Remembering Matter pays her debt ;
Still, through her motes and masses, draw
Electric thrills and ties of Law,
Which bind the strengths of Nature wild
To the conscience of a child."

XIII.

EMERSON AS SEEN FROM INDIA.

By PROTAP CHUNDER MOZOOMDAR.

To speak frankly, the meditative Hindoo feels that much of all this Anglo-Saxon muscularity might be spared. India is networked with iron roads, warped and woofed with electric wires, measured, triangulated, dock-yarded, garrisoned, planted with 90-pounder guns, inundated with mum and whiskey. We ask in innocent wonder where all this will end. The English newspapers, when they do not fight against the " natives," fight against each other, or speak of wars and amnesties in other lands, or deal with trade statistics, parliamentary triumphs, ball-room dresses, and marriages in high life. They bring us in ship-loads of literature from England about romantic attachments and refined flirtations and aristocratic rascalities. They write books to prove that men have as little soul as oysters, that animals show their passions and intelligence by affections of the same nerves as human beings, and that some handsome women when angry display their canine teeth. Europe has conquered us, and now she is trying to materialize us. We cannot cope with her tremendous muscularities.

> "The brooding East with awe beheld
>   Her impious younger world, —
> The Roman tempest swelled and swelled,
>   And on her head was hurled.
> The East bowed low before the blast,
>   In patient, deep disdain ;
> She let the legions thunder past,
>   And plunged in thought again."

While wandering last year under the classic shadows of your great trees at Concord, my dear friend Dr. Putnam often talked to me of the rapt, thought-plunged figure of Emerson so often seen in those Arcadian walks. My reverence for him was great. Every scene of beauty seemed to be haunted by his spirit. The fragrance of his presence, removed but so lately, still hovered over all that I saw. And now you want me to say what we think of him in India. Where the blue Narbudda, so still, so deep and pure, flows through the high, milk-white walls of the marble hills near Jubbulpoor, in the natural alcoves of the virgin rocks there are devotional inscriptions in Sanscrit. I wish Emerson had composed his essays on Nature there. The azure dome above, the azure floor beneath, the pure white hills around, without a blade of grass, the mysterious calmness and coolness, the hum of the wild bees, the cooing of the wild doves, remind one of the spirit, depth, sweetness, pureness, and stillness of Emerson's genius.

Amidst this ceaseless, sleepless din and clash of Western materialism, this heat of restless energy, the character of Emerson shines upon India serene as the evening star. He seems to some of us to have been a geographical mistake. He ought to have been born in India. Perhaps Hindoos were closer kinsmen to him than his own nation, because every typical Hindoo is a child of Nature. All our ancient religion is the utterance of the Infinite through Nature's symbolism. The sky, the luminous atmosphere, the sun, the sea, and the swift night-winds, twilight and the dawn, — daughters of the heavens, — called out the Hindoo sage into the bosom of the unspeakable *Dyaus Pitar* (*Diespater*, Jupiter), the Heavenly Father. Emerson speaks of his sense of childhood in the green mansions of Nature; his rapt communion with the spirit of "the august Mother;" his starlight wanderings; the upward gazing into the infinite depths; his sense of homogeneity with the woods and wilderness. The tranquil landscape and the distant line of the horizon gave him that perception of occult relationship between man and all things which is the key to the sublime culture known as *Yoga* in the history of Hindoo philosophy. "I become a transparent eyeball," says he; "I am nothing; I see all; the currents of universal being circulate through me. I am part or parcel of God. . . . I am the lover of uncontained, immortal beauty."

Keshub Chunder Sen in his last work on *Yoga* says: "The face-wall of Nature's cathedral is opaque to the ordinary eye, but to the spiritual eye of *Yoga* it is transparent. Hence the *Rishi* (devotee) saw through the diversified forms of gross matter the presence of a resplendent person." Such God-vision is possible only to the favored eye of the *Yogi*. Western intellect has disenchanted, hardened, vulgarized Nature ; driven all soul, all poetry, all religion and supersensible meaning out of it. Emerson has rehabilitated the deepest revelations in this outward frame of the universe. He has re-established the priestly functions of man in the mysterious temples of Nature. You will have to admit now that the great fathers of our people in going to discover the secrets of all things in the animated symbols of this vast creation, read Truth at its very source. Emerson read from that same mysterious volume, and scattered beauty, wisdom, and spiritual plenty over all his land.

The evolution of Hindoo spirituality shows in its second stage the wonderful development of insight. The *Vedas* are the religious interpretation of Nature, the *Upanishads* or *Vedantas* are the concentrated religion of the soul. All the varied powers of Nature, all names, and all forms resolve into *Atman*, or self. The Vedic poet asks : " Who saw him [the soul] when he was first born ; when he who has no bones bore him who has ? Where was the breath, the blood, the self of the world ? Who went to ask this from any that knew it ? Though solitary, still he [the soul] walks far ; though lying down, he goes everywhere.

Who save myself is able to know that God who rejoices and rejoices not ? " All at once, in this stage
of Vedic theology, the solid universe vanishes as an
illusion, and religion soars sublime in the azure infinitude of soul. Who but Emerson, in the West,
represents this illumined, spiritual introspection ?
True, his intercourse with Nature was part of his
daily food; but it did not shut out, it unsealed his
insight into, that grander heaven and earth within
himself. Nature was but the outer halo of the deep,
inner fire ; the soul overshadowed everything ; the
universe became pale before its grandeur. " Go out
of the house," says he, " to see the moon, and it is
mere tinsel." Who discovered so well as he that
Nature teaches us nothing but what we ourselves
contribute to it ? The spirit is the centre and archetype of all things, and beauty, beneficence, law, and
wisdom only lead us to ourselves. Emerson laid the
foundation of the true philosophy of man by tracing
phenomena to their real source in reflective humanity.
He laid the foundations of the true philosophy of the
world by viewing matter, not as a soulless succession
of appearances, nor yet a creation of the brain of
man, but as a mysterious, marvellous putting forth
in outward form of beauty that which he inwardly
realizes in the spirit. His writings, too, often recall to
mind the utterances of Hindoo philosophy, — that all
the universe is a divine dream, passing away ; but in
passing it reminds us of the meaning, glory, presence, and life, which it reveals and conceals at the

24

same time.   Creation rests on the bosom of man, and man rests on the bosom of the Infinite.   "No mortal," says the *Vedanta,* " lives by the breath that goes up or by the breath that goes down.   We live in another, in whom both repose."

Amidst all this soul-absorbing philosophy of things, it is a true happiness to find that Emerson so deeply felt the reality and earnestness of life, — the reality of the inner and outer world as well.   There are two orders of devotees in India, — those who renounce their homes and retire into the forests, and those who live in their houses, but, with everything that pertains to them, devote themselves to the culture and the perfection of virtue.   *Shiva* himself, the prince of *Yogis,* belongs to the latter order.   " All the fetters of the heart here on earth are broken, all that binds us to this life is undone ; the mortal becomes immortal."   This is the lofty idea of emancipated humanity which *Krishna* inculcates in the *Bhagavat Gita.*   And to Emerson surely belonged that beatified humanity.   I do not know why, but as often as I study his features in the imperfect photograph which I possess, the idea of *Nirvana* as taught by the great *Sakya Muni* suffuses my soul.   There is that hushed, ineffable, self-contained calmness over his countenance so familiar to us who have studied the expression of Gotama's image in every posture.   In Japan, China, Burmah, Ceylon, Nepaul, Thibet, — Buddha has the same mysterious calmness.   The Egyptians prefigure it in the awful face of the Sphinx.   It is

Nirvana made flesh and visible. It is the "peace past understanding" which lights up the face of every true child of God. Emerson had it in a wonderful measure. It did me good to hear of his broad, warm, many-sided humanity. Did he not welcome work, spirituality, aspiration, obscure excellence, from every quarter of the globe into his house ? Did he not identify himself with every good movement, however unpopular, which had for its object the amelioration of his race ?

Long, long had we heard of his name and reputation. We wondered what manner of man he was. When at last I landed on your continent, how glad I should have been to sit at his feet and unfold before him the tale of our woe and degradation ! But he had gone to his rest; and instead of touching his warm hand, which had blessed so many pilgrims, I could but kiss the cold dust of his nameless grave at the Concord cemetery.

Yes, Emerson had all the wisdom and spirituality of the Brahmans. Brahmanism is an acquirement, a state of being rather than a creed. In whomsoever the eternal Brahma breathed his unquenchable fire, he was the Brahman. And in that sense Emerson was the best of Brahmans.

PEACE COTTAGE, CALCUTTA, July, 1884.

XIV.

EMERSON'S ORIENTALISM.

By W. T. HARRIS.

In his " Representative Men " Emerson describes Plato as visiting Asia and Egypt, and imbibing " the idea of one Deity in which all things are absorbed." Asia, according to him, is " the country of unity, of immovable institutions ; the seat of a philosophy delighting in abstractions, of men faithful in doctrine and in practice to the idea of a deaf, unimplorable fate, which it realizes in the social institution of caste." Europe, on the other hand, is active and creative in its genius ; " it resists caste by culture ; its philosophy was a discipline ; it is a land of arts, inventions, trade, freedom. If the East loved infinity, the West delighted in boundaries." Plato, according to him, is the balanced soul who sees the two elements and does justice to each. What Emerson says of Plato we may easily and properly apply to himself. But he goes farther than Plato towards the Orient, and his pendulum swings farther West into the Occident. He delights in the all-absorbing unity of the Brahman, in the all-renouncing ethics of the Chinese and Persian, in the measureless images of the Arabian and Hindoo poets. But he is as practical as the extremest of his countrymen. His practical is married to his abstract tendency. It is the problem of evil that continually haunts him, and leads him to search its solution in the Oriental unity which is above all dualism of good and evil. It is his love of freedom that leads him to seek in the same source an elevation of thought above the trammels of finitude and complications. Finally, it is his love of beauty, which is the vision of freedom manifested in matter, that leads him to Oriental poetry, which sports with the finite elements of the world as though they were unsubstantial dreams.

Perhaps nowhere in our literature may one find so complete a characterization of the East Indian philosophy as is contained in the short poem called "Brahma," which appeared in the first number of the "Atlantic Monthly" in 1857. There is no subject farther from the thought of the average common-sense of the modern European or American than the all-absorbing unity which the East Indian conceived under the name *Brahma*. Hence the mirth excited at first by the strange conceits of the poem in question. To the reader of the *Bhagavat Gita*, "Brahma" seemed a wholly admirable epitome, or condensed statement, of that wonderful book. One may illustrate each stanza by parallel passages from the Indian episode.

> " If the red slayer think he slays,
>   Or if the slain think he is slain,
> They know not well the subtle ways
>   I keep, and pass, and turn again."

Brahma is pure Being, the same in all things that exist, the same under all changes. In the second chapter of the *Bhagavat Gita* (J. Cockburn Thomson's translation), the following passage occurs : —

" He who believes that this spirit[1] can kill, and he who thinks that it can be killed, both of these are wrong in judgment. It neither kills, nor is killed. It is not born, nor dies at any time. It has no origin, nor will it ever have an origin. Unborn, changeless, eternal, both as to future and past time, it is not slain when the body is killed."

In the same chapter the "subtle ways" of Being are described thus: " All things which exist are invisible in their first state, visible in their intermediate state, and again invisible in their final state." The visible state is the passing state, and the invisible state is that which Being returns to and keeps.

> " Far or forgot to me is near ;
>   Shadow and sunlight are the same ;
> The vanished gods to me appear ;
>   And one to me are shame and fame."

To pure being there is no distinction. Even one so important as separation in space and time is nothing, and all is " near." Light and darkness, too, the most wonderful of material distinctions, are the

---

[1] The word translated "spirit" here, signifies pure being rather than consciousness, as it does with us ; for the spirit is something above mind (*buddhi*) and heart (*manas*), which are its external instruments. The "red slayer" is a member of the warrior caste, the Kshatriyas.

same to pure being. Even the invisible ("vanished") gods are pervaded by Being, and invisibility has no validity. But a far deeper distinction to humanity is that between good and evil, shame and fame. Even this, however, does not enter the divine essence of Brahma; to him one is the same as the other. This moral indifference is Indian, but not Persian. To the Persian, good and evil are absolute, and irreducible to a common ground. At first, light and darkness — shadow and sunlight — were the ultimate elements of the absolute dualism. Then came Zoroaster, who elevated the thought to good and evil, as being more ultimate natures than light and darkness. Ahura Mazda and Ahriman are in eternal conflict. A primeval unity for the two — *Zerruane Akerene* — is a comparatively modern thought, resulting from an attempt to reduce the Persian doctrine to a monism, like Brahmanism. In the ninth chapter of the *Bhagavat Gita* Krishna says : —

"I am the same to all beings. I have neither foe nor friend. But those who worship me with devotion dwell in me and I also in them. Even if one who has led a very bad life worship me, devoted to no other object, he must be considered as a good man ; for he has judged aright. He soon becomes religiously disposed, and enters eternal rest ; he who worships me never perishes. For even those who are born in sin — even women, Vaishyas, and Shúdras — take the highest path if they have recourse to me. How much more, then, sacred Brahmans and pious Rajarshis."

In the thirteenth chapter we recognize the indifference of space and time in this : " It [spirit, or pure being] cannot be recognized, on account of its subtility, and it exists both far and near."

The network of distinctions in the world forms a divine illusion (*Maya*), by which those men are deluded who do not take refuge in Brahma. This is described in the seventh chapter of the *Bhagavat Gita.* Here, too, occurs the mention of the *Over-Soul,* or *Adhyatma,* an expression which Emerson used as a title for one of the greatest of his essays. In the eighth chapter we read : " The supreme universal spirit is the One simple and indivisible ; and my own nature is called Adhyatma " (*Adhi,* meaning *above,* superior to, or presiding over ; and *atma,* the soul, — not the soul that presides over all, but that which is above the soul itself).

> "They reckon ill who leave me out ;
>   When me they fly, I am the wings ;
> I am the doubter and the doubt,
>   And I the hymn the Brahmin sings."

The last line recalls the passage in the tenth chapter of the *Bhagavat Gita,* where we are told which one is *the* hymn : " Of the Vedas, I am the Sáma-Veda. I am the Vrihatsaman among the hymns (of the Sáma-Veda) ; the Gaytri among rhymes."

> "The strong gods pine for my abode,
>   And pine in vain the sacred Seven ;
> But thou, meek lover of the good !
>   Find me, and turn thy back on heaven."

The "strong gods" are : Indra, the god of the sky, the wielder of the thunder-bolt; Agni, the god of fire; and Yama, the god of death and judgment. These and all the inferior gods are absorbed into Brahma at the close of the Kalpa, or day of Brahma (four thousand three hundred and twenty millions of our years) ; and after the night of Brahma are again created at the beginning of the next day. The "sacred seven" are the seven Maharshis (*Maha*, great, and *rishi*, saint), or highest saints. In the tenth chapter we are told : " The seven Maharshis . . . were born of my mind, and from them these inhabitants of the world are sprung." They preside over each *manwantara* (one of the fourteen divisions of the Kalpa).

Brahma exhorts man to come to him through attaining a state of mental indifference to all distinctions. He may even neglect the holy Vedas, if he will turn his back on Indra's heaven and seek to know " the single imperishable principle of existence in all things ;" and when he is in a condition where "he neither rejects nor hopes," then "he enters me without any intermediate condition." In the eighteenth chapter is this injunction : —

"Place thy affections on me, worship me, sacrifice to me, and reverence me. Thus thou wilt come to me. I declare the truth to thee. Abandoning all religious duties, seek me as thy refuge. I will deliver thee from all sin. Be not anxious."

Thus it happens that, as we learn in chapter eighteenth, " He whose disposition is not egotistical, and whose mind is not polluted, does not kill, even though he slay yonder people."

This *Bhagavat Gita,* an episode in the *Mahabharata,* represents a field of battle; and Arjuna, commanding the younger branch of the Kuru tribe, is seized with irresolution at the sight of his relatives in the opposing army. Krishna the god, disguised as his charioteer, delivers the doctrines of the book as an argument to induce him to fight, and succeeds. " A treatise of metaphysics before a battle, in eighteen lectures, under the form of a dialogue between Arjuna and his companion Krishna, — such is the *Bhagavat Gita,*" says Cousin in his " History of Modern Philosophy" (vol. ii. ch. vi.). He well characterizes (in the same chapter) the nature of Brahma as conceived by the Indian consciousness : —

" In fact, what is the sole exercise of the sage ? Contemplation ; the contemplation of God. And what is this God ? We have seen what ; the abstraction of being. But the abstraction of being, without fixed attribute, is realized quite as well in a dog as in a man ; for there is being in everything, as Leibnitz has said ; there is being in a clod of earth as well as in the soul of the last of the Brutuses. The indifference of the Yogin is, therefore, consistent ; he searches only for God, but he finds him equally in everything."

In his article on Plato, in the " Representative Men " (first edition, page 53), Emerson has fully described this idea in the form that he held it, and as he understood the East Indians to hold it, thus : —

" The Same, the Same : friend and foe are of one stuff;
the ploughman, the plough, and the furrow are of one
stuff; and the stuff is such, and so much, that the variations of form are unimportant. 'You are fit,' says the
supreme Krishna to a sage, 'to apprehend that you are
not distinct from me. That which I. am, thou art, and
that also is this world, with its gods, and heroes, and
mankind. Men contemplate distinctions, because they are
stupefied with ignorance. . . . The words I and Mine constitute ignorance. What is the great end of all, you shall
now learn from me. It is soul, — one in all bodies, per-
vading, uniform, perfect, pre-eminent over Nature, exempt
from birth, growth, and decay, omnipresent, made up of
true knowledge, independent, unconnected with unreali-
ties, with name species, and the rest, in time past, present,
and to come. The knowledge that this spirit, which is
essentially one, is in one's own, and in all other bodies, is
the wisdom of one who knows the unity of things. As
one diffusive air, passing through the perforations of a
flute, is distinguished as the notes of a scale, so the nature
of the Great Spirit is single, though its forms be manifold, arising from the consequences of acts. When the
difference of the investing form, as that of god, or the
rest, is destroyed, there is no distinction. . . . The whole
world is but a manifestation of Vishnu, who is identical
with all things, and is to be regarded by the wise, as not
differing from, but as the same as themselves. I neither
am going nor coming; nor is my dwelling in any one place;
nor art thou, thou ; nor are others, others; nor am I, I.'
As if he had said, 'All is for the soul, and the soul is
Vishnu ; and animals and stars are transient paintings, and
light is whitewash, and durations are deceptive, and form

is imprisonment, and heaven itself a decoy.' That which the soul seeks is resolution into being, above form, out of Tartarus, and out of heaven, — liberation from nature."

It is remarkable that while Emerson has given us this wonderful summary of the spirit of the Indian mind, Alcott should have made a somewhat similar statement of the Egyptian mind. In his "Tablets" (page 167) he develops his theory of man as the author of Nature : —

"Man is a soul, informed by divine ideas, and bodying forth their image. His mind is the unit and measure of things visible and invisible. In him stir the creatures potentially, and through his personal volitions are conceived and brought forth in matter whatsoever he sees, touches, and treads under foot, — the planet he spins."

He then proceeds with this remarkable epitome of the Egyptian mind as the Neoplatonists interpreted it : —

> "He omnipresent is,
> All round himself he lies,
> Osiris spread abroad,
> Upstaring in all eyes ;
> Nature his globèd thought,
> Without him she were not,
> Cosmos from Chaos were not spoken,
> And God bereft of visible token."

This is spoken of man, as though the Egyptian Sphinx had brooded over the riddle of human life, its universal significance in the world, as the final object of all creation.

The problem of evil and finitude receives a solution in Emerson's "Uriel." In this poem the substantiality of evil is denied and the supremacy of good asserted. Not merely this doctrine but a much concreter form is set forth; namely, that all deeds return upon their doer, and that all influences return to their source in such a manner that all pain or evil is but good in the process of making. The return of injury upon the doer does not annihilate him, but punishes him into goodness, heals and blesses him. The form of this poem is a suggestion of Persian or Arabic poetry. It refers to Seyd (sultan), suggesting a favorite Persian poet, and hints at the seven archangels, of whom Uriel was one, by the term Pleiads (the famous seven). Uriel was the archangel of the Sun, endowed with the fulness of divine light. Milton speaks of him as the interpreter of God's will : —

> " Uriel, for thou of those seven spirits that stand
> In sight of God's high throne, gloriously bright,
> The first art wont his great authentic will
> Interpreter through highest heaven to bring."

Uriel would be the spirit most fitting to see the deepest solution of the problem of life. In the profound discussion with the other archangels on the question of "what subsisteth and what seems," he gives "sentiment divine" against the subsistence of evil. Nothing in the universe exists except self-relation, — all will return to itself, — all is circular.

Evil returned on itself will neutralize itself so that its subsistence or continuance can only be in the form of the good.

> " Line in nature is not found ;
> Unit and universe are round ;
> In vain produced, all rays return ;
> Evil will bless, and ice will burn."

This oracle causes a shudder in heaven : —

> " Seemed to the holy festival
> The rash word boded ill to all ;
> The balance-beam of Fate was bent ;
> The bounds of good and ill were rent;
> Strong Hades could not keep his own,
> But all slid to confusion."

If good and evil are only two roads, both leading to the same goal, where, then, is the distinction between heaven and hell ? Strong Hades cannot keep its devils ; who entering heaven, among the angels, all will slide into confusion. Here is the same issue that is found in the second stanza of " Brahma" : —

> " Shadow and sunlight are the same ;
> . . . . .
> And one to me are shame and fame."

Taken directly, without the mediation provided for in the self-return, it paralyzes the will and denies morality and religion. Of what use is it to choose the right and renounce the wrong, if all comes to the same in the end? But consider the mediation: If you do evil, it will come back to pain you, and you must be purified by its fire. Uriel sees that evil changes on its return into a purifying fire, — a purgatory. The universe does not suffer, but the individual writhes in pain, although he is purified by it.

The universe is not made for happiness, but for the development of free individuality. To free individuality happiness, or rather blessedness, is incidental. But pain is the means by which it is enabled to grow into freedom, — the pain of struggle and exertion, the pain of returning evil deeds, by which it comes to self-knowledge and learns its identity with the universe : —

> " With damning conceit and self-assertion
>   To say *Thou* in addressing the rest of existence,
>   Nor hear the answer, in agony echoed : —
>   ' I, the prime All, am within as without thee ;
>   Who worketh woe, to himself doth work it.' " [1]

Such knowledge of the conversion of evil into good tends to quietism. Uriel retires from the holy festival into his cloud after this sad self-knowledge, although it is doubtful whether he lapsed into the sea of generation, or whether he grew too bright to be seen; at all events, he withdrew from sight : —

> " A sad self-knowledge, withering, fell
>   On the beauty of Uriel ;
>   In heaven once eminent, the god
>   Withdrew, that hour, into his cloud ;
>   Whether doomed to long gyration
>   In the sea of generation,
>   Or by knowledge grown too bright
>   To hit the nerve of feebler sight.

[1] Jordan's " Sigfridsage," Mr. Davidson's translation.

> Straightway, a forgetting wind
> Stole over the celestial kind,
> And their lips the secret kept, —
> If in ashes the fire-seed slept.
> But now and then, truth-speaking things
> Shamed the angels' veiling wings ;
> And, shrilling from the solar course,
> Or from fruit of chemic force,
> Procession of a soul in matter,
> Or the speeding change of water,
> Or out of the good of evil born,
> Came Uriel's voice of cherub scorn,
> And a blush tinged the upper sky,
> And the gods shook, they knew not why."

Another most remarkable poetic statement of the law of return, which Emerson saw to be the foundation of the universe, is the oracle prefixed to the essay on "Spiritual Laws" : —

> " The living Heaven thy prayers respect,
> House at once and architect,
> Quarrying man's rejected hours,
> Builds therewith eternal towers ;
> Sole and self-commanded works,
> Fears not undermining days,
> Grows by decays,
> And, by the famous might that lurks
> In reaction and recoil,
> Makes flame to freeze and ice to boil ;
> Forging, through swart arms of Offence,
> The silver seat of Innocence."

The universe is here spoken of as the living Heaven, which contains and upholds, and at the same time is active builder or architect ; using the hours that man has not moulded by his feeble will, it erects eternal towers. It is sole and self-commanded, not co-ordinate with any one, but supreme. It does not fear overthrow of its divine good through the evil works of wicked men who have not learned to will the good for its own sake. By the famous might of this law of return, the deepest of Heaven's laws, flame will freeze and ice will boil; evil will bless, by curing the perverse will through the pain of its recoil. Through the dark ministration of offending deeds the silver seat of Innocence will be forged. The universe is so made that as a whole it always brings out good from evil, and " better thence again." The individual is prevented from subsisting contentedly in evil through the ministration of pain. "He makes the wrath of man to praise Him."

XV.

EMERSON'S RELATION TO GOETHE AND CARLYLE.

By WILLIAM T. HARRIS.

In our study of the great man and his environment we must consider, before all, his contemporaries. By common consent Emerson is joined with Carlyle as co-author of the stream of influence which has acted so powerfully on the thinking and literary expression of the nineteenth century.

Other sources of the same stream of influence are Coleridge and Wordsworth. The latter, — Wordsworth, — indeed, stands for the great English poet of the century with a large and increasing number of highly cultured people. We have already, in discussing the relation of Emerson to Nature, spoken of the characteristics of poetry. Poetry performs the office of imposing a spiritual view of some sort upon the world as it exists for us. The poet passes it through his mind, and forthwith his version of nature, of men and things, is accepted by his readers and becomes their view of the world. There goes with poetry music of rhythm and rhyme; but that is less essential than the trope and personification by which the poet makes over the things of the world into means of spiritual expression. They were prose facts, mere opaque things; now they become transparent, and a sort of spiritual light shines through them. They express facts of human experience, — facts that were unutterable before. The deep spiritual truths which could not be communicated nor even conceived clearly, now by the poet's aid become expressible in trope and metaphor and through the personification of natural things. The invisible is now visible.

This function of poetry in revealing spiritual experience and the structure of our moral and intellectual selves by metaphor and personification goes on from age to age. There are poets of various degrees of universality. Homer's revelation underlies all our literature, all the literature of European civilization. He taught man to recognize in nature the presence of human spirit. Every object is an expression of some spiritual being: the fountains, groves, mountains, streams, clouds, winds, waves, plants, animals, — all express in their motions, sounds, appearances, some passion, some desire or meaning of invisible conscious beings. Nurtured in this view of the world, it is not strange that the European man has learned to know himself in the course of three thousand years by seeing his reflection in an ideal world created for him by the Muse.

In the line of Homer have followed other poets, great and small. The great poets since Homer have taken new themes, new experiences of the inner world of man, and found their expression in terms of correspondence with external nature. Dante has revealed thus the inner world of Christianity. Shakspeare has made visible the genesis of human institutions from the individual man; he has shown man as a social animal creating the social forms and evolving social unities, — the colossal institutions in which he lives. We may study the individual, and see how these greater selves come to manifest themselves in his thinking and feeling. Each individual shows fragments of his larger self; he indicates his place in some institution which supplements his deficiencies. If Shakspeare is the revealer of the essential character of human institutions, teaching us in what sense they are the substance of individual men, Goethe is the revealer of a new phase of human experience, of still deeper and subtler spiritual laws. Goethe shows the individual not so much the source, as the result, of institutions. All returns to the individual. The institution which man generates and places over himself as a supreme self to nurture and preserve him, educates him; all that he gives to it returns to him. By sufficient intelligence he shall be able to turn all manner of fortune into blessing. The attitude of the individual towards the world is therefore all-important. The Christian religion had taught from the beginning the germ of this doctrine. It is the attitude of the soul towards the world that determines its state of weal or woe. The soul, in the Inferno of Dante, seeks directly the gratification of its finite wants and desires, careless of the welfare of its fellows. This produces collision. The individual against society — the one against the many — fights, to lose the battle. Pain is the only result. The individual has neglected his higher self, the social whole, and has assumed that man possesses completeness as a mere individual, without institutions; but he learns by the suffering of the Inferno that he is, after all, a mere fragment, and that by selfish isolation he maims and wounds himself.

In the Inferno, the soul pursues this hopeless struggle of selfishness against altruism, growing more deeply imbittered against his fellow-men and the universe. This attitude changes in the Purgatory. The individual sees the nature of his sin, and repents. He strives to reunite himself to his higher self by conforming to institutions, family, civil society, Nation, Church. He gradually eliminates from himself the habits and tendencies of antagonism and selfishness. He attains at last the Paradise. This is the state of soul wherein the individual lives in conscious harmony with institutions, — the state wherein he enjoys the complete fruition of his higher self. He sees and feels his unity with all, and he enjoys the life of all. All returns to him. He has found that by giving all he receives all. Selfishness has given place to love.

The natural consequence of the Christian revelation unfolds by and by this idea of culture of the individual, not as a different revelation, but as its own result.

Goethe is the world-poet of this movement. He shows in the Faust that if the individual would find a permanent state of blessedness, and be able to say to the happy moment, "Stay, for thou art fair," he must energize not against the institutions of the world, as he does in the first part of the drama, nor attempt to find his supreme object in any subordinate institution, as in the second part of the drama. He must find the paradise in altruism. Only the reflection of the well-being of others can fill his soul with gladness that does not weary or turn to sorrow. Accordingly Goethe, in the last scene of the second part of Faust, paints the four phases of Christian history in the three typical holy fathers and the Doctor Marianus.

The perfection of the soul by asceticism in Pater Ecstaticus — repelling the social world for the sake of personal salvation — is an imperfect Christianity, because it preserves the form of selfishness although it practises supreme renunciation. The recognition of divine reason in nature by Pater Profundus is still partial, because only a theoretical attitude towards the world. Pater Seraphicus is higher, because he actively engages in the work of lifting up others towards perfection, using his knowledge to illuminate the imperfectly developed. Doctor Marianus announces the view of the world on which all this is based, — the doctrine of grace. It is what Goethe calls in his great prose romance the "worship of sorrow." Wilhelm Meister hears this discussed in the Pedagogical Province:[1]—

[1] Carlyle's Translation.

" No religion that grounds itself on fear," said the Three,
" is regarded among us. With the reverence, to which a
man should give dominion in his mind, he can, in paying
honor, keep his own honor ; he is not disunited with himself, as in the former case. The religion which depends
on reverence for what is above us we denominate the
Ethnic ; it is the religion of the nations, and the first
happy deliverance from a degrading fear. All Heathen
religions, as we call them, are of this sort, whatsoever
names they bear. The second religion, which founds itself
on reverence for what is around us, we denominate the
Philosophical ; for the philosopher stations himself in the
middle, and must draw down to him all that is higher,
and up to him all that is lower, and only in this medium
condition does he merit the title of Wise. Here, as he
surveys with clear sight his relations to his equals, and
therefore to the whole human race, his relation likewise
to all other earthly circumstances and arrangements necessary or accidental, he alone, in a cosmic sense, lives in
Truth. But now we have to speak of the third religion,
grounded on reverence for what is beneath us ; this we
name the Christian, as in the Christian religion such a
temper is with most distinctness manifested : it is a last
step to which mankind were fitted and destined to attain.
But what a task was it, not only to be patient with the
Earth, and let it lie beneath us, we appealing to a higher
birthplace ; but also to recognize humility and poverty,
mockery and despite, disgrace and wretchedness, suffering
and death, to recognize these things as divine ; nay, even
on sin and crime to look not as hindrances, but to honor
and love them as furtherances of what is holy ! Of this,
indeed, we find some traces in all ages ; but the trace is

not the goal ; and this being now attained, the human species cannot retrograde ; and we may say, that the Christian religion, having once appeared, cannot again vanish ; having once assumed its divine shape, can be subject to no dissolution."

To a remark of his, the Three reply to Meister:

" Our confession has been adopted, though unconsciously, by the greater part of the world." And "Where?" he asks. " In the Creed !" exclaimed they ; " for the first Article is Ethnic, and belongs to all nations ; the second, Christian, for those struggling with affliction and glorified in afflic- tion ; the third, in fine, teaches an inspired Communion of Saints, — that is, of men in the highest degree good and wise."

In another connection the eldest of the Three, after discussing the other aspects of Christ's life, says : —

" Now, omitting all that results from this consideration, do but look at the touching scene of the Last Supper. Here the Wise Man, as it ever is, leaves those that are his own utterly orphaned behind him ; and while he is careful for the Good, he feeds along with them a traitor by whom he and the Better are to be destroyed."

He continues, describing the rules and methods of the Pedagogic Province : —

" All that is external, worldly, universal, we communi- cate to each from youth upwards ; what is more particularly spiritual and conversant with the heart, to those only who grow up with some thoughtfulness of temper ; and the rest, which is opened only once a year, cannot be imparted save to those whom we are sending forth as finished. That last religion which arises from the reverence of what is beneath us ; that veneration of the contradictory, the hated, the avoided, we give each of our pupils in small portions, by way of outfit, along with him into the world, merely that he may know where more is to be had, should such a want spring up within him. I invite you to return hither at the end of a year, to visit our general festival, and see how far your son is advanced : then shall you be admitted into the Sanctuary of Sorrow."

In this idea of the worship of sorrow Goethe rises to his highest and purest thought, and joins his own epoch to the preceding epoch. History is made continuous. Without this insight the modern world breaks off from the old world with the idea of individual culture, and reverts to a sort of barbarism. Refined selfishness, enlightened self-interest, cold, calculating understanding, supreme individualism, is the dry-rot of character ; and it is the special form in which the diabolic makes its appearance in an age of science. This is the meaning of Mephistopheles, whose spiritual import is so well expressed by Emerson in his "Representative Men," in a passage that shows the significance of Goethe's work in literature : —

" Take the most remarkable example that could occur of this tendency to verify every term in popular use. The devil had played an important part in mythology in all times. Goethe would have no word that does not cover a thing.   The same measure will still serve : ' I have never heard of any crime which I might not have committed.' So he flies at the throat of this imp.   He shall be real ; he shall be modern ; he shall be European ; he shall dress like a gentleman, and accept the manners, and walk in the streets, and be well initiated in the life of Vienna, and of Heidelberg, in 1820, — or he shall not exist.   Accordingly, he stripped him of mythologic gear, of horns, cloven foot, harpoon tail, brimstone, and blue-fire, and, instead of looking in books and pictures, looked for him in his own mind, in every shade of coldness, selfishness, and unbelief that, in crowds or in solitude, darkens over the human thought, — and found that the portrait gained reality and terror by everything he added and by everything he took away.   He found that the essence of this hobgoblin, which had hovered in shadow about the habitations of men ever since there were men, was pure intellect, applied — as always there is a tendency — to the service of the senses ; and he flung into literature, in his Mephistopheles, the first organic figure that has been added for some ages, and which will remain as long as the Prometheus."

Mephistopheles is the devil that tempts men of culture.   Not merely nor chiefly in sensuous things, but rather in sceptical coldness towards one's fellowmen.   The preference of one's higher self it may be, — the higher self of culture, — of refined taste, insight, purity that keeps aloof and is pharisaic — is Mephistophelian.

This element, — the element of Goethe's devil, — strange to say, is the element that is generally recognized as Goethe's ideal.   Olympian serenity and self-seeking in the midst of all the sorrow and evil that prevails in the world is supposed to be Goethe's conception of the divine.

Even Emerson, although possessed of the piercing vision of a seer, discovers only so much in him. He does justice to this ideal by accrediting it with a comparatively lofty aim. He says of Goethe : —

"The old Eternal genius who built the world has confided himself more to this man than to any other. I dare not say that Goethe ascended to the highest grounds from which genius has spoken. He has not worshipped the highest unity ; he is incapable of a self-surrender to the moral sentiment. There are nobler strains in poetry than any he has sounded. There are writers poorer in talent, whose tone is purer and more touches the heart. Goethe can never be dear to men. His is not even the devotion to pure truth ; but to truth for the sake of culture. He has no aims less large than the conquest of universal nature, of universal truth, to be his portion ; a man not to be bribed, nor deceived, nor overawed ; of a stoical self-command and self-denial, and having one test for all men, — What can you teach me? All possessions are valued by him for that only ; rank, privileges, health, time, being itself."

"From him nothing was hid, nothing withholden. The lurking dæmons sat to him, and the saint who saw the dæmons ; and the metaphysical elements took form. 'Piety itself is no aim, but only a means, whereby through inward peace we may attain the highest culture.'"

"Enmities he has none. Enemy of him you may be, — if so you shall teach him aught which your good-will cannot, — were it only what experience will accrue from your ruin. Enemy and welcome, but enemy on high terms. He cannot hate anybody ; his time is worth too much."

" In this aim of culture, which is the genius of his works, is their power. The idea of absolute eternal truth without reference to my own enlargement by it, is higher. The surrender to the torrent of poetic inspiration is higher ; but compared with any motives on which books are written in England and America, this is very truth, and has power to inspire which belongs to truth. Thus has he brought back to a book some of its ancient might and dignity."

This view of Goethe is illustrated still further, and its limitation indicated in what Emerson tells us of " Wilhelm Meister " : —

" ' Wilhelm Meister ' is a novel in every sense, the first of its kind, called by its admirers the only delineation of modern society, — as if other novels, those of Scott, for example, dealt with costume and condition, this with the spirit of life. It is a book over which some veil is still drawn. It is read by very intelligent persons with wonder and delight. It is preferred by some such to Hamlet, as a work of genius. I suppose no book of this century can compare with it in its delicious sweetness, so new, so provoking to the mind, gratifying it with so many and so solid thoughts, just insights into life, and manners, and characters ; so many good hints for the conduct of life, so many unexpected glimpses into a higher sphere, and never a trace of rhetoric or dulness. A very provoking book to the curiosity of young men of genius, but a very unsatisfactory one. Lovers of light reading, those who look in it for the entertainment they find in a romance, are disappointed. On the other hand, those who begin it with the higher hope to read in it a worthy history of genius, and the just award of the laurel to its toils and denials, have also reason to complain. We had an English romance here, not long ago, professing to embody the hope of a new age, and to unfold the political hope of the party called 'Young England,' in which the only reward of virtue is a seat in Parliament, and a peerage. Goethe's romance has a conclusion as lame and immoral. George Sand, in 'Consuelo' and its continuation, has sketched a truer and more dignified picture. In the progress of the story the characters of the hero and heroine expand at a rate that shivers the porcelain chess-table of aristocratic convention : they quit the society and habits of their rank; they lose their wealth ; they become the servants of great ideas, and of the most general social ends ; until, at last, the hero, who is the centre and fountain of an association for the rendering of the noblest benefits to the human race, no longer answers to his own titled name: it sounds foreign and remote in his ear. ' I am only man,' he says ; ' I breathe and work for man,' and this in poverty and extreme sacrifices. Goethe's hero, on the contrary, has so many weaknesses and impurities, and keeps such bad company, that the sober English public, when the book was translated, were disgusted. And yet it is so crammed with wisdom, with knowledge of the world, and with knowledge of laws ; the persons so truly and subtly drawn, and with such few strokes, and not a word too much, the book remains ever so new and unexhausted, that we must even let it go its way, and be willing to get what good from it we can, assured that it has only begun its office, and has millions of readers yet to serve.

" The argument is the passage of a democrat to the

aristocracy, using both words in their best sense. And this passage is not made in any mean or creeping way, but through the hall door. Nature and character assist, and the rank is made real by sense and probity in the nobles. No generous youth can escape this charm of reality in the book, so that it is highly stimulating to intellect and courage."

Were it true, as Emerson supposes, that Goethe's view of the world places self-culture supreme, and without subordinating it to altruism, there would be the most serious grounds for denying to Goethe his rank as one of the four great world-poets, — a rank, as we shall see, that is actually assigned to him by Emerson himself. Emerson sees clearly enough the place of Goethe in literature, but without being able thoroughly to account for it.

Dante, too, he ranks with Homer and Shakspeare; not because he sees the validity of Dante's message to mankind, but for his obvious historic importance in literature.

One of the most wonderful and instructive of Emerson's poems is the " Test and Solution," giving us his supreme critical insight, and his canon of highest honor in literature.

The Muse speaks : —

> "I hung my verses in the wind,
>   Time and tide their faults may find.
>   All were winnowed through and through,
>   Five lines lasted sound and true;
>   Five were smelted in a pot
>   Than the South more fierce and hot;

> These the siroc could not melt,
> Fire their fiercer flaming felt,
> And the meaning was more white
> Than July's meridian light.
> Sunshine cannot bleach the snow,
> Nor time unmake what poets know.
> Have you eyes to find the five
> Which five hundred did survive?"

The Muse makes her own answer to the riddle; the same Muse that "sung alway by Jove," even "at the dawn of the first day." This Muse sat alone, crowned with stars, and for long ages strove to mix the stagnant earth with thought. Her song prevailed on the spawning slime; the fierce elements were tamed; wolves shed their fangs; and the earth smiled in flowers when man was born. The shepherd races of Asia with their tents, the civilization of Egypt with its granite architecture, came first; and then stepped forth the perfect Greek:—

> "That wit and joy might find a tongue,
> And earth grow civil, Homer sung."

Homer then wrote the first of the five lines that survived the five hundred. But who is the second of the five gifts of the Muse?

The Muse proceeds to tell how, having flown from Greece to Italy, she brooded long and held her peace, being accustomed to sing when not expected. Sometimes she unlocks doors of new delight, singing wit and joy to men in evil times; on other occasions she appalls men with a bitter horoscope, and fills them with spasms of terror:—

> " So I folded me in fears,
> And Dante searched the triple spheres,
> Moulding nature at his will,
> So shaped, so colored, swift or still,
> And, sculptor-like, his large design
> Etched on Alp and Apennine."

Dante, then, is the second of the great world-poets. The characterization of his genius is by no means so happy as that of the next following : —

> " Seethed in mists of Penmanmaur,
> Taught by Plinlimmon's Druid power,
> England's genius filled all measure
> Of heart and soul, of strength and pleasure,
> Gave to the mind its emperor,
> And life was larger than before:
> Nor sequent centuries could hit
> Orbit and sum of Shakspeare's wit.
> The men who lived with him became
> Poets, for the air was fame."

The first three favorites of the Muse do not surprise us; they have long been chosen by the world at large. But the fourth has not yet been found by the common consent of mankind. He is regarded as a religious genius, but not as a poet : —

> " Far in the North, where polar night
> Holds in check the frolic light,
> In trance upborne past mortal goal
> The Swede Emanuel leads the soul.
> Through snows above, mines underground,
> The inks of Erebus he found;
> Rehearsed to men the damnèd wails
> On which the seraph music sails.
> In spirit-worlds he trod alone,
> But walked the earth unmarked, unknown.

> The near by-stander caught no sound, —
> Yet they who listened far aloof
> Heard rendings of the skyey roof,
> And felt, beneath, the quaking ground;
> And his air-sown, unheeded words,
> In the next age, are flaming swords."

Recalling to mind our definition of the poetic, and laying stress on the function of seeing the spiritual meaning of the natural, we may perhaps feel the force of the same reasons that led Emerson to place Swedenborg in the rank of the great poets. We certainly gain a hint of the powerful personal influence which he exercised on Emerson. In the "Representative Men" one may find the account of Swedenborg much more definite and satisfactory than that of any other personage honored with mention there. His inventory of the Swede's ideas and achievements is of a character to justify the high place he assigns to him. The central doctrine of correspondence comes near to a scientific statement of the contents of the poet's vision, and we may well believe that it was this especially which attracted Emerson's admiration and study. However that may be, certainly literature, philosophy, and religion have " caught no sound,' and his ' air-sown words " are yet unheeded; although it is still possible that the prophecy may come true, and those unheeded words

> " In the next age be flaming swords."

The four great names in literature are usually made to include Homer, Dante, Shakspeare, and

26

Goethe. If Swedenborg is added as a fifth, one would expect that Plato would also form the sixth, or even take precedence of the Swede. Goethe's claims for a place among the five immortals are set forth by the Muse in these lines : —

> " In newer days of war and trade,
>   Romance forgot, and faith decayed,
>   When Science armed and guided war,
>   And clerks the Janus-gates unbar,
>   When France, where poet never grew,
>   Halved and dealt the globe anew,
>   Goethe, raised o'er joy and strife,
>   Drew the firm lines of Fate and Life,
>   And brought Olympian wisdom down
>   To court and mart, to gown and town;
>   Stooping, his finger wrote in clay
>   The open secret of to-day."

And with these the Muse concludes : —

> " So bloom the unfading petals five,
>   And verses that all verse outlive."

In discussing Emerson's appreciation of the import of Goethe to the world, we come upon the relation of both these men to Carlyle. For it is undoubtedly to Carlyle that Emerson's diligence in the study of Goethe is due. Most profitable, too, it is to consider the differences of attitude in these men towards Goethe.

" Close thy Byron, open thy Goethe," says Carlyle to the gloomy individual plunged in the lake of the " everlasting no."

"Well did the wisest of our time write: 'It is only

with renunciation that life, properly speaking, can be said to begin.'"

The "worship of sorrow" finds in Carlyle a readier votary than in Emerson. Here is his most eloquent apostrophe to it, from the "Sartor Resartus" (book ii. chap. 9) : —

"Poor, wandering, wayward man ! Art thou not tried, and beaten with many stripes, even as I am ? Ever, whether thou bear the royal mantle or the beggar's gabardine, art thou not so weary, so heavy-laden ; and thy Bed of Rest is but a grave. O my Brother, my Brother, why cannot I shelter thee in my bosom, and wipe away all tears from thy eyes ! Truly, the din of many-voiced Life, which in this solitude, with the mind's organ, I could hear, was no longer a maddening discord, but a melting one : like inarticulate cries, and sobbings of a dumb creature, which in the ear of Heaven are prayers. The poor Earth, with her poor joys, was now my needy Mother, not my cruel step-dame ; Man, with his so mad Wants and so mean Endeavors, had become the dearer to me ; and even for his sufferings and his sins, I now first naméd him brother. Thus was I standing in the porch of that 'Sanctuary of Sorrow ;' by strange, steep ways, had I too been guided thither ; and ere long its sacred gates would open, and the 'Divine Depth of Sorrow' lie disclosed to me. . . .

"Small is it that thou canst trample the Earth with its injuries under thy feet, as old Greek Zeno trained thee : thou canst love the Earth while it injures thee ; for this, a Greater than Zeno was needed, and he too was sent. Knowest thou that 'Worship of Sorrow'? The Temple hereof, founded some eighteen centuries ago, now lies in ruins, overgrown with jungle, the habitation of doleful creatures : nevertheless, venture forward ; in a low crypt, arched out of falling fragments, thou findest the Altar still there, and its sacred Lamp perennially burning."

In that most wonderful of all recent books, the "Correspondence of Carlyle and Emerson,"[1] the highest interest attaches to this interpretation of Goethe and to the practical lessons drawn by each of the friends from it. Nov. 20, 1834, Emerson writes : —

" Truth is ever born in a manger, but is compensated by living till it has all fools for its kingdom. Far, far better seems to me the unpopularity of this Philosophical Poem (shall I call it ?), 'Sartor Resartus,' than the adulation that followed your eminent friend Goethe. With him I am becoming better acquainted, but mine must be qualified admiration. It is a singular piece of good nature in you to apotheosize him. I cannot but regard it as his misfortune, with conspicuous bad influence on his genius, — that velvet life he led. . . . Then, the Puritan in me accepts no apology for bad morals in such as he. We can tolerate vice in a splendid nature whilst that nature is battling with the brute majority in defence of some human principle. The sympathy his manhood and his misfortunes call out adopts even his faults ; but genius pampered, acknowledged, crowned, can only retain our sympathy by turning the same force once expended against outward enemies now against inward, and carrying forward and planting the standard of Oromasdes so many leagues farther on into the envious Dark."

[1] Boston : James R. Osgood & Co., 1883.

Carlyle replies : —

" Your objections to Goethe are very natural, and even bring you nearer me : nevertheless, I am by no means sure that it were not your wisdom, at this moment, to set about learning the German Language, with a view towards studying *him* mainly ! I do not assert this ; but the truth of it would not surprise me. Believe me, it is impossible you can be more a Puritan than I ; nay, I often feel as if I were far too much so : but John Knox himself, could he have seen the peaceable impregnable fidelity of that man's mind, and how to him also Duty was Infinite, — Knox would have passed on, wondering, not reproaching. But I will tell you in a word why I like Goethe : his is the only healthy mind, of any extent, that I have discovered in Europe for long generations ; it was he that first convincingly proclaimed to me (convincingly, for I saw it done) : Behold, even in this scandalous Sceptico-Epicurean generation, when all is gone but hunger and cant, it is still possible that Man be a man ! For which last Evangel, the confirmation and rehabilitation of all other Evangels whatsoever, how can I be too grateful ? On the whole, I suspect you yet know only Goethe the Heathen (Ethnic) ; but you will know Goethe the Christian by and by, and like that one far better."

In another letter (Dec. 9, 1840) : —

" Even what you say of Goethe gratifies me ; it is one of the few things yet spoken of him from personal insight, the sole kind of things that should be spoken ! You call him *actual*, not *ideal ;* there is truth in that too ; and yet at bottom is not the whole truth rather this : The actual well seen *is* the ideal? The *actual*, what really is and exists: the past, the present, the future no less, do all lie there! Ah yes! one day you will find that this sunny-looking, courtly Goethe held veiled in him a Prophetic sorrow deep as Dante's, — all the nobler to me and to you, that he could so hold it. I believe this; no man can see as he sees, that has not suffered and striven as man seldom did."

In a certain obvious sense Goethe and Carlyle and Emerson preach the same doctrine, — the doctrine of our age. The age of science is the age of ascent out of conventionalities, out of mere prescription and ignorant following of law and custom into individual insight into the rational necessity of the law.

But which of the three has seen and stated the problem of the time in its entirety? Which has found the solution? Goethe, it must be confessed, and Goethe alone. Goethe has understood human history as a growth, and has seen the inevitable approach of democracy as something to be prepared for by all nations. Goethe has studied the spirit and appliances of the Middle Ages, and seen that the rise of the scientific tendency is the rise of scepticism against what is prescribed. Faust has studied "Philosophie, Juristerei, und Medicin . . . auch Theologie," and finds himself wise but unhappy because he doubts the possibility of knowing the Divine, or of ascending into the image of the First Principle of the Universe. Not only is he unequal to the comprehension of Nature, but even to that of human nature. He cannot approach the Erd-Geist, the Microcosm, or have a comprehension of the mind of the race except through loss of individuality. The lesson that through social union the individual is divinely reinforced and comes to equal the Absolute, he has not yet learned. This lesson, however, it shall be the mission of the entire drama of Faust to teach.

Carlyle fulminates during his entire literary career against the doctrine of individualism in its form of revolutionary protest, and in favor of individualism as manifested by men in power or supported by institutions. This is an implicit contradiction, and utterly misses the point of Goethe's solution. Carlyle sees the divinity of institutions, but not the mediation of the individual by them.

Emerson, on the other hand, sets forth personal morals as the solution of individualism. He confirms Goethe's belief in individual perfection as the result of the entire human process on the planet. All the world is for man, and all human institutions are for the perfection of the individual. But Emerson does not lay great stress on the cardinal institutions of man. The Church and the State are not exhaustively studied by him as developments of essential humanity. Even civil society and the family are not specially prized as something divine, above the accidents of the individual. The Transcendental reformers attacked in one way or another all of these institutions. It is true that Emerson did not partake in the merely negative excursions of the Transcendentalists, but always saw the affirmative aspect of things that had got into existence. In his lecture on " The Reformer and the Transcendentalist," in 1841, he said : If the institution of property seems to deprive the individual of his birthright to a piece of land to live on, yet it has preserved for him the rational achievements of the race, " libraries, museums and galleries, colleges, palaces, hospitals, observatories, cities, — Rome and Memphis, Constantinople and Vienna, and Paris and London, and New York." But what socialist could state better the negative side ? " There is a cunning juggle in riches. I observe that they take somewhat for everything they give. I look bigger, but am less ; I have more clothes but am not so warm, more armor but less courage, more books but less wit."

Goethe, who lived through all the phases of the French Revolution, saw the truth in the conservative instinct that supports institutions even when they have become worn out, as well as the truth of the radicalism that wishes to reform what it does not understand. Goethe was a prophet in discerning the fruits of the era of labor-saving machinery in forms of government and creeds and social caste. Especially in the novelettes that are found in Meister's *Wanderjahre* one may find our social problem of the readjustment of vocations stated, as well as the solution by means of a systematic migration and a general education. How to manage in order to meet an age of revolutions in the State and in civil society is indicated by the particulars of an organization formed by the leading spirits as described in that novel for the purchase and improvement of property in various parts of the world.

Carlyle shows in the " Sartor Resartus " how deeply he had pondered the problems of sociology ; but in all the latter years of his life he seems to have treated such problems from the stand-point of the nation, and to have made the State of the most importanoe. His " French Revolution " is an epic poem, and the " Frederick the Great" must altogether precede every history yet written as a complete study of the genesis and mature development of one of the greatest powers of the world. It is the history of Europe in essential particulars for its most important century. But the problems in sociology and the meaning of the movements in natural science and labor-saving machinery, the printing-press and the daily newspaper and local self-government, humanitarianism, — all these things which were so significant in Goethe's eyes are not seen in their true light by Carlyle. Perhaps we may say, too, that Emerson undervalues them in comparison with the ethical culture of the individual. With ethics, it is true, man is complete in all ages. But the Orientals are precocious in their ethics only for the reason of the meagre development of the State with them. Crude States without written constitutions, pure despotisms, require the best ethical education of their rulers to make them tolerable. Where all government is conducted by an irresponsible ruler, the happiness of the people depends entirely upon the wisdom and moderation of the despot. Where the superior in rank or in age holds despotic power over the inferior or the younger, ethics alone can ameliorate the lot of the people; for each citizen has his despot above him, even though he may be despot in his turn to those below him. The invention of constitutional forms protects the governed from those who govern; and Europe and America care very little whether their rulers are personally amiable or otherwise. Hence the ethical message is not itself of so weighty a character as the one based on institutions, — on the realization in the world, of man's higher self in social forms, — the " Grand Man," as called by Swedenborgians.

Froude tells us [1] in a very pointed manner that he regards Carlyle's message as negative to the tendencies of the nineteenth century. If modern civilization is on the right road, then Carlyle was all wrong : —

" An adequate estimate of Carlyle's work in this world is not at present possible. He was a teacher and a prophet in the Jewish sense of the word. The prophecies of Isaiah and Jeremiah have become a part of the permanent spiritual inheritance of mankind, because events proved that they had interpreted correctly the signs of their own times, and their prophecies were fulfilled. Carlyle, like them, believed that he had a special message to deliver to the present age. Whether he was correct in that belief, and whether his message was a true message, remains to be seen. He has told us that our

[1] Thomas Carlyle : A History of the first Forty Years of his Life ; Preface.

most cherished ideas of political liberty, with their kindred corollaries, are mere illusions, and that the progress
which has seemed to go along with them is a progress
towards anarchy and social dissolution. If he was wrong,
he has misused his powers. The principles of his teaching are false. He has offered himself as a guide upon a
road of which he had no knowledge ; and his own desire
for himself would be the speediest oblivion both of his
person and his works. If, on the other hand, he has been
right ; if, like his great predecessors, he has read truly
the tendencies of this modern age of ours, and his teaching is authenticated by facts, then Carlyle, too, will take
his place among the inspired seers, and he will shine on,
another fixed star in the intellectual sky. Time only can
show how this will be."

To Americans who have faith in their form of
government as the coming State-form for all civilized
nations, this method of putting Carlyle's claims
seems cruel and unjust. If local self-government
shall triumph in history, then Thomas Carlyle shall
have been only a false prophet ! One hopes there is
a different alternative.

Emerson's praise of the "History of Frederick"
shows how an optimist and a thorough democrat could
find in Carlyle's latest work the most discerning book
ever written : [1] —

" Meantime here has come into the country three months
ago a book of Carlyle, 'History of Frederick,' infinitely

[1] From Emerson's Diary ; see "Correspondence of Carlyle and
Emerson," vol. ii. p. 272.

the wittiest book that ever was written, a book that one
would think the English people would rise up in mass
to thank him for, by cordial acclamation, and congratulate themselves that such a head existed among them,
and much-sympathizing and on-its-own-account-reading
America would make a new treaty extraordinary of joyful, grateful delight with England, in acknowledgment of
such a donation, — a book with so many memorable and
heroic facts. . . . And withal a book that is a Judgment
Day, for its moral verdict on the men and nations and
manners of modern times; with its wonderful new system of mnemonics, whereby great and insignificant men
are ineffaceably ticketed and marked in the memory by
what they were, had, and did."

With this transcendent esteem for the "Frederick,"
Emerson could write the following to Carlyle in
1864, severely rebuking the latter's disparagement of
America : —

"I have in these last years lamented that you had not
made the visit to America which in earlier years you projected or favored. It would have made it impossible that
your name should be cited for one moment on the side
of the enemies of mankind. Ten days' residence in this
country would have made you the organ of the sanity of
England and of Europe to us and to them, and have shown
you the necessities and aspirations which struggle up in
our Free States, which, as yet, have no organ to others,
and are ill and unsteadily articulated here. . . . Are
English of this day incapable of a great sentiment? Can
they not leave cavilling at petty failures, and bad manners,

and at the dunce part (always the largest part in human affairs), and leap to the suggestions and finger-pointings of the gods, which, above the understanding, feed the hopes and guide the wills of men?"[1]

Directly after the close of the war (Jan. 7, 1866) Emerson wrote on the same theme: —

"I am very sorry that Jonathan looks so unamiable seen from your island. Yet I have too much respect for the writing profession to complain of it. It is a necessity of rhetoric that there should be shades, and, I suppose, geography and government always determine, eyen for the greatest wits, where they shall lay their shadows. But I have always the belief a trip across the sea would have abated your despair of us. The world is laid out here in large lots, and the swing of natural laws is shared by the population, as it is not — or not as much — in your feudal Europe. My countrymen do not content me, but they are susceptible of inspirations. In the war it was humanity that showed itself to advantage, — the leaders were prompted and corrected by the intuitions of the people, they still demanding the more generous and decisive measure, and giving their sons and their estates as we had no example before. In this heat they had sharper perceptions of policy, of the ways and means and the life of nations, and on every side we read or heard fate-words, in private letters, in railway cars, or in the journals. We were proud of the people, and believed they would not go down from this height. But peace came, and every one ran back into his shop again."

[1] Correspondence of Carlyle and Emerson, vol. ii. pp. 285, 286.

And again (Jan. 5, 1872) : —

" Meantime, I know well all your perversities, and give them a wide berth. They seriously annoy a great many worthy readers, nations of readers sometimes, — but I heap them all as style, and read them as I read Rabelais' gigantic humors, which astonish in order to force attention, and by and by are seen to be the rhetoric of a highly virtuous gentleman who *swears.*"

In this connection here are a few passages from Carlyle showing the value he set on Emerson's writings, and also the limitations he set on his admiration of the themes selected : —

" And so now by a direct transition I am got to the Oration. My friend ! you know not what you have done for me there. It was long decades of years that I had heard nothing but the infinite jangling and jabbering, and inarticulate twittering and screeching, and my soul had sunk down sorrowful, and said there is no articulate speaking then any more, and thou art solitary among stranger-creatures ! and lo, out of the West comes a clear utterance, clearly recognizable as a man's voice, and I have a kinsman and brother ; God be thanked for it ! I could have wept to read that speech ; the clear high melody of it went tingling through my heart ; I said to my wife, ' There, woman ! ' She read ; and returned, and charges me to return for answer, ' that there had been nothing met with like it since Schiller went silent.' My brave Emerson ! And all this has been lying silent, quite tranquil in him, these seven years, and the ' vociferous platitude ' dinning his ears on all sides, and he quietly answering no word ; and a whole world of Thought has silently built itself in these calm depths, and, the day being come, says quite softly, as if it were a common thing, ' Yes, I am here too.' " (Dec. 8, 1837.)

" I love your ' Dial,' and yet it is with a kind of shudder. You seem to me in danger of dividing yourselves from the Fact of this present Universe, in which alone, ugly as it is, can I find any anchorage, and soaring away after Ideas, Beliefs, Revelations, and such like, — into perilous altitudes, as I think ; beyond the curve of perpetual frost, for one thing ! . . . Surely I could wish you returned into your own poor nineteenth century, its follies and maladies, its blind or half-blind, but gigantic toilings, its laughter and its tears, and trying to evolve in some measure the hidden Godlike that lies in it ; — that means to me the kind of feat for literary men. Alas, it is so easy to screw one's self up into high and ever higher altitudes of Transcendentalism, and see nothing under one but the everlasting snows of Himmalayah, the Earth shrinking to a Planet, and the indigo firmament sowing itself with daylight stars ; easy for you, for me : but whither does it lead ? I dread always, To inanity and mere injuring of lungs ! . . . Well I do believe, for one thing, a man has no right to say to his own generation, turning quite away from it, ' Be damned ! ' It is the whole Past and the whole Future, this same cotton-spinning, dollar-hunting, canting and shrieking, very wretched generation of ours. Come back into it, I tell you ! " (Aug. 29, 1842.)

And this passage is the most severe reassertion of his stand-point as against that of Emerson : —

" You are bountiful abundantly in your reception of those ' Latter-Day Pamphlets ; ' and right in all you say of them ; — and yet withal you are not right, my Friend, but I am! Truly it does behoove a man to know the inmost resources of this universe, and, for the sake both of his peace and of his dignity, to possess his soul in patience, and look nothing doubting (nothing wincing even, if that be his humor) upon all things. For it is most indubitable there is good in all ; — and if you even see an Oliver Cromwell assassinated, it is certain you may get a cart-load of turnips from his carcass. Ah me, and I suppose we had too much forgotten all this, or there had not been a man like you sent to show it us so emphatically! Let us well remember it ; and yet remember too that it is not good always, or ever, to be 'at ease in Zion;' good often to be in fierce rage in Zion ; and that the vile Pythons of this Mud-World do verily require to have sun-arrows shot into them, and red-hot pokers struck through them, according to occasion : woe to the man that carries either of these weapons, and does not use it in their presence ! " (Nov. 14, 1850.)

" We read, at first, Tennyson's Idyls, with profound recognition of the finely elaborated execution, and also of the inward perfection of vacancy, — and, to say truth, with considerable impatience at being treated so very like infants, though the lollipops were so superlative. We gladly changed for one Emerson's 'English Traits,' and read that with increasing and ever-increasing satisfaction every evening; blessing Heaven that there were still Books for grown-up people too ! That truly is a Book all full of thoughts like winged arrows ! " (Jan. 27, 1867.)

Two paragraphs relative to the United States, written, the one nearly forty years after the other, are pleasant reading to Americans, by reason of vivid memories of words of a different tenor from the same source : —

"And so here, looking over the Water, let me repeat once more what I believe is already dimly the sentiment of all Englishmen, Cisoceanic and Transoceanic, that we and you are not two countries, and cannot for the life of us be ; but only two parishes of one country, with such wholesome parish hospitalities, and dirty temporary parish feuds, as we see ; both of which brave parishes Vivant ! vivant ! And among the glories of both be Yankee-doodle-doo, and the Felling of the Western Forest, proudly remembered ; and for the rest, by way of parish constable, let each cheerfully take such George Washington or George Guelph as it can get, and bless Heaven ! I am weary of hearing it said, ' We love the Americans,' 'We wish well,' etc., etc. What in God's name should we do else ? " (Aug. 12, 1834.)

"And indeed I may confess to you that the doings in that region are not only of a big character, but of a great ; — and that in my occasional explosions against ' Anarchy,' and my inextinguishable hatred of it, I privately whisper to myself, ' Could any Friedrich Wilhelm, now, or Friedrich, or most perfect Governor you could hope to realize, guide forward what is America's essential task at present faster or more completely than " anarchic America " herself is now doing ? ' Such ' Anarchy ' has a great deal to say for itself (would to Heaven ours of England had as much !), and points towards grand Anti-Anarchies in the future ; in fact, I can already discern in it huge quantities of Anti-Anarchy in the 'impalpable-powder' condition ; and hope, with the aid of centuries, immense things from it, in my private mind ! " (June 4, 1871.)

27

There is an interesting passage in "The Represen-tative Men," in which Emerson criticises the literary form of Goethe's works. It is suggested by the criti-cism that Carlyle makes on Emerson's style : —

"This law-giver [Goethe] of art is not an artist. Was it that he knew too much, that his sight was microscopic, and interfered with the just perspective, the seeing of the whole ? He is fragmentary ; a writer of occasional poems, and of an encyclopædia of sentences. When he sits down to write a drama or a tale, he collects and sorts his obser-vations from a hundred sides, and combines them into a body as fitly as he can. A great deal refuses to incor-porate. This he adds loosely, as letters of the parties, leaves from their journals, or the like. A great deal is left that will not find any place. This the book-binder alone can give any cohesion to ; and hence, notwithstand-ing the looseness of many of his works, we have volumes of detached paragraphs, aphorisms, xenien, etc."

I have on another occasion discussed the mooted question of the artistic unity of Emerson's prose essays, endeavoring to show that the unity is of a high order, and deserving to be called "dialectic," or even "or-ganic" unity.[1] This topic is not of special interest on this occasion.

In conclusion, I will refer to the "Song of Nature," in which Emerson has given us the counterpart of Goethe's speech of the Erd-Geist, — an altogether

[1] See "Atlantic Monthly" for August, 1882, and "Journal of Speculative Philosophy" for April, 1884.

noteworthy performance, by reason of its hopeful look towards the future of man. There is commentary in it, too, for the poems called "The Test" and the "Solution," which we have already considered. I quote the closing stanzas : —

> "Twice I have moulded an image,
> And thrice outstretched my hand,
> Made one of day, and one of night,
> And one of the salt sea-sand.

> "One in a Judæan manger,
> And one by Avon stream,
> One over against the mouths of Nile,
> And one in the Academe.

> "I moulded kings and saviours,
> And bards o'er kings to rule; —
> But fell the starry influence short,
> The cup was never full.

> "Yet whirl the glowing wheels once more,
> And mix the bowl again;
> Seethe, Fate! the ancient elements,
> Heat, cold, wet, dry, and peace, and pain.

> "Let war and trade and creeds and song
> Blend, ripen race on race,
> The sunburnt world a man shall breed
> Of all the zones, and countless days.

> "No ray is dimmed, no atom worn,
> My oldest force is good as new,
> And the fresh rose on yonder thorn
> Gives back the bending heavens in dew."

XVI.

ION: A MONODY.

By A. BRONSON ALCOTT.

I.

Why, oh, ye willows, and ye pastures bare,
Why will ye thus your blooms so late delay,
Wrap in chill weeds the sere and sullen day,
And cheerless greet me wandering in despair?
Tell me, ah, tell me! ye of old could tell —
Whither my vanished Ion now doth fare —
Say, have ye seen him lately pass this way,
Ye who his wonted haunts did know full well?
Heard ye his voice forth from the thicket swell,
Where midst the drooping ferns he loved to stray?
Caught ye no glimpses of my truant there?
Tell me, oh, tell me, whither he hath flown —
Belovèd Ion flown, and left ye sad and lone,
Whilst I through wood and field his loss bemoan.

II.

Early through field and wood each Spring we sped,
Young Ion leading o'er the reedy pass;

How fleet his footsteps and how sure his tread!
His converse deep and weighty; — where, alas!
Like force of thought with subtlest beauty wed?
The bee and bird and flower, the pile of grass,
The lore of stars, the azure sky o'erhead,
The eye's warm glance, the Fates of love and dread, —
All mirrored were in his prismatic glass;
For endless Being's myriad-minded race
Had in his thought their registry and place, —
Bright with intelligence, or drugged with sleep,
Hid in dark cave, aloft on mountain steep,
In seas immersed, ensouled in starry keep.

III.

Now Echo answers lone from cliff and brake,
Where we in springtime sauntering loved to go,
Or to the mossy bank beyond the lake, —
On its green plushes oft ourselves did throw, —
There from the sparkling wave, our thirst to slake,
Dipped in the spring that bubbled up below
Our hands for cups, and did with glee partake.
Next to the Hermit's cell our way we make,
Where sprightly talk doth hold the morning late.
Departed now — ah, Hylas, too, is gone!
Hylas, dear Ion's friend and mine, — I all alone,
Alone am left by unrelenting fate, —
Vanished my loved ones all, — the good, the great, —
Why am I spared? why left disconsolate?

IV.

Slow winds our Indian stream through meadows green,
By bending willows, tangled fen and brake,
Smooth field and farmstead doth its flow forsake :
'T was in far woodpaths Ion, too, was seen,
But oftenest found at Walden's emerald lake
(The murmuring pines inverted in its sheen) ;
There in his skiff he rippling rhymes did make,
Its answering shore echoing the verse between.
Full-voiced the meaning of the wizard song,
For wood and wave and shore with kindred will,
Strophe, antistrophe, in turn prolong : —
Now wave and shore and wood are mute and still,
Ion, melodious bard, hath dropt his quill,
His harp is silent and his voice is still.

V.

Blameless was Ion, beautiful to see,
With native genius, with rich gifts endowed,
He might of his descent be nobly proud,
Yet meekly tempered was, spake modestly,
Nor sought the plaudits of the noisy crowd,
When duty called him in the thick to be.
His life flowed calmly clear, not hoarse nor loud ;
He wearied not of immortality,
Nor like Tithonus begged a time-spun shroud,
But life-long drank at fountains of pure truth,
The seer unsated of eternal youth.

'T is not for Ion's sake these tears I shed,
'T is for the Age he nursed, his genius fed —
Ion immortal is; he is not dead.

VI.

Did e'en the Ionian bard, Mæonides
(Blind minstrel, wandering out of Asia's night,
The Iliad of Troy's loves and rivalries
In strains forever tuneful to recite),
His raptured listeners the more delight?
Nor dropt learned Plato 'neath his olive-trees,
More star-bright wisdom in the world's full sight,
Well garnered in familiar colloquies,
Than did our harvester in fields of light;
Nor spoke more charmingly young Charmides
Than our glad rhapsodist in his far flight
Across the continents, both new and old;
His tale to studious thousands thus he told
In summer's solstice and midwinter's cold.

VII.

Shall from the shades another Orpheus rise
Sweeping with venturous hand the vocal string;
Kindle glad raptures, visions of surprise,
And wake to ecstasy each slumberous thing;
Flash life and thought anew in wondering eyes,
As when our seer transcendent, sweet, and wise,
World-wide his native melodies did sing,
Flushed with fair hopes and ancient memories?
Ah, no! his matchless lyre must silent lie.

None hath the vanished minstrel's wondrous skill
To touch that instrument with art and will.
With him winged Poesy doth droop and die,
While our dull age, left voiceless, with sad eye
Follows his flight to groves of song on high.

VIII.

Come, then, Mnemosyne, and on me wait,
As if for Ion's harp thou gav'st thine own !
Recall the memories of Man's ancient state,
Ere to this low orb had his form dropt down,
Clothed in the cerements of his chosen fate ;
Oblivious here of heavenly glories flown,
Lapsed from the high, the fair, the blest estate,
Unknowing these, and by himself unknown : —
Lo ! Ion, unfallen from his lordly prime,
Paused in his passing flight, and, giving ear
To heedless sojourners in weary time,
Sang his full song of hope and lofty ·cheer ;
Aroused them from dull sleep, from grisly fear,
And toward the stars their faces did uprear.

IX.

Why didst thou haste away, ere yet the green
Enamelled meadow, the sequestered dell,
The blossoming orchard, leafy grove, were seen
In the sweet season thou hadst sung so well ?
Why cast this shadow o'er the vernal scene ?
No more its rustic charms of thee may tell,

And so content us with their simple mien : —
Was it that memory's unrelinquished spell
(Ere men had stumbled here amid the tombs)
Revived for thee that Spring's perennial blooms,
Those cloud-capped alcoves where we once did dwell?
Translated wast thou in some rapturous dream ?
Our once familiar faces strange must seem
Whilst from thine own celestial smiles did stream !

X.

I tread the marble leading to his door
(Allowed the freedom of a chosen friend),
He greets me not as was his wont before,
The Fates within frown on me as of yore ;
Could ye not once your offices suspend ?
Had Atropos her severing shears forbore,
Or Clotho stooped the sundered thread to mend !
Yet why dear Ion's destiny deplore ?
What more had envious Time himself to give ?
His fame had reached the ocean's farthest shore.
Why prisoned here should Ion longer live ?
The questioning Sphinx declared him void of blame,
For wiser answer none could ever frame ;
Beyond all time survives his mighty name.

XI.

Now pillowed near loved Hylas' lowly bed,
Beneath our aged oaks and sighing pines,
Pale Ion rests awhile his laurelled head ;
(How sweet his slumber as he there reclines !)

Why weep for Ion here ?   He is not dead,
Nought of him Personal that mound confines;
The hues ethereal of the morning red
This clod embraces never, nor enshrines.
Away the mourning multitude hath sped,
And round us closes fast the gathering night;
As from the drowsy dell the sun declines,
Ion hath vanished from our clouded sight.
But on the morrow, with the budding May,
A-field goes Ion, at first flush of day,
Across the pastures on his dewy way.

CONCORD, May, 1882.

INDEX.

INDEX.

[For many subjects, referred to only therein, see *Emerson's Books, Essays, Poems, Poetic and Prose Quotations*.]

ABBOTT, JACOB, publications, 42. Abraham, incomparable, 142. (See *Bible*.)

Adam: inward voice, 140 ; possessions, 351. (See *Bible*.)

Adams, Samuel: public schools, 6 ; Tea Party, 21.

Addison, Joseph, poetry, 180.

Advertiser, Boston, on Alcott's book, 49.

Æolian Harp, illustration, 20.

Æschylus: allusion, 182 ; an ideal, 331. (See *Greek*.)

Africa, human interest, 338.

Agassiz, Louis : on materialism, 119 ; on evolution, 135 ; companionship, 305.

Agnosticism, 134, 162, 314. (See *Ethics, Religion*.)

Albee, John, allusion, 211.

Alcott, A. Bronson : a guest, 20 ; club, 22 ; relation to Emerson, 36-67 ; Diaries, 37-39, 41-67 ; American Institute, studies, 40 ; Boston record, 42 ; conception of life, 42, 43 ; order of spiritual precedence, 44 ; trip to Concord, 44, 45 ; mob, 46 ; religion, 47 ; conversations on the Gospels, 48-50 ; on Nature, 51, 52 ; estimate of Emerson, 53-58 ; English experiences with reformers, 58-65 ; Fruitlands, 59, 65 ; Wayside, 65 ; on Carlyle's Cromwell, 66, 67 ; advice from Emerson, 143 ; Orphic rhapsodizings, 332 ; Tablets, 362, 380 ; poem of Ion, 420-426.

Allston, Washington : pupil, 31 ; an evening, 37 ; in Diary, 42, 44.

America : town-meetings, 8, 9 ; original style, 56 ; peculiar origin, 69 ; Puritan colonies, 70 ; two Americas, 73 ; fewer limitations, 78 ; parasites, 79 ; Independence, 80 ; majorities, 81 ; quadrupedal age, John and Jonathan, 84 ; not causeless, 85 ; hill voices, 87 ; the Land, 89 ; literature, 138 ; righteousness, 143 ; rational religion, 235 ; description of Christ, 243 ; a new religion, 250 ; jubilees, 268 ; literary interpreter, 313 ; faith in, 332 ; part of universe, 337, 338 ; rulers, 410, 411. (See *New England, United States*.)

American Institute of Instruction, 40.

Americans : Emerson one, 68-91, 106, 107 ; born in other countries, 71 ; early families, 72 ; typical, 88 ; Emerson's nationality, 310 ; point of view, 314, 315 ; literature, 316, 320 ; writers, 317 ; literary independence, 318 ; character and scenery, 319 ; future literature, 333 ; two distinct ideas, 334-336.

Anarchy, 417.

Andrew, John Albion, anecdote, 17, 18.

Anne, Queen, epoch, 343.

Anselm, on belief and knowledge, 274.

Antislavery : Emerson's position, 25-28 ; excitement in Boston, 45, 46 ; slavery inward, 80 ; pride, 106 ; Concord tea-party, 307 ; a stand, 308.

Apollo : word, 167 ; how described, 243.

Appleton, Nathan, dinner, 288.

Arabia : Mahomet, 139 ; and America, 315 ; poets, 373, 381.

Architecture, different modes, 165.

Aristophanes, allusion, 182. (See *Greek*.)

Aristotle : Alcott's study, 47 ; on love, 200 ; poetic test, 201-203 ; on Homer, 210 ; on freedom, 268.

Arnold, Matthew: criticism, 52; a French answer, 95; quotation, 112, 113; poetry criticised, 118; on Emerson's style, 130; answered, 180; comparisons, 181–184; hints, 185; definition of poetry, 201–204; on Gray, 204–210; Mrs. Howe's reply, 301; literary creation, 315.

Art and Life, 317.

Artists, painting their own portraits, 109.

Asia: travellers, 140; righteousness, 143; America not Asiatic, 312; a corner, 332; philosophic inconsistency, 362; Plato in, 372; shepherd races, 399. (See *India, Oriental.*)

Atheism: lecturer, 137; lamented, 284. (See *God, Religion,* etc.)

Athens, Greece: fondness of Socrates for, 2; Pericles, 12; panorama, 151.

Atlantic Monthly: papers, 22; international, 63, 64; Brahma, 373; essays, 418.

Australia, gold, 142.

Azores, illustration, 112.

BAAL, allusion, 153.
Babel, confusion, 167. (See *Bible.*)

Bacon, Francis: Alcott's study, 47; French quotation on poetry, 94; on verse, 179.

Balzac, Honoré de, his Breton gentleman, 126.

Bancroft, Mrs. George, 40.

Baptists, their Tritheism, 153.

Barham, an English reformer, 63.

Bartol, Cyrus Augustus, Emerson's religion, 109–145.

Bees, metaphor, 103, 104, 261.

Beethoven, Ludwig von: to be surpassed, 125; gold, 142.

Behmen (Boehme), Jacob Christian: symbol, 238; insights, 362.

Belleisle, René de Poyen: Essay, 92–108; poem, 107, 108; town, 206.

Bellows, Henry Whitney, congratulations, 110.

Berkeley, Bishop, philosophy, 352.

Berlin, centre of Germany, 10. (See *Germany.*)

Bermudas, illustration, 112.

Bhagavat Gita: translation, 179, 374; teaching, 370; episode, 378. (See *Hindoo, India, Vedas.*)

Biber, George E., apostasy, 62.

Bible: in school, 6; Balaam's ass, 18; Saul prophesies, 23; Alcott's study, 40; "voice of one," etc., 50; nations born of flesh and spirit, 69; inspiration, 111; David and Paul, Joseph's coat, 112; "Yea, yea!" 114; Hebrew, 115; "an ear to hear," 116; Paul and Moses in retirement, 117; David's prayer, Adam, 118; Exodus, not Genesis, 119; amanuenses, 130; gall and vinegar, 133; star differing from star, 135; "the way called heresy," 136; "Thus saith the Lord," 146; letter and spirit, 148; collision, 239; with covers, 245; wrath of man, 385. (See *Jews, Religion, St. John,* etc.)

Bismarck, Baron von: quoted, 129; rugged, 134.

Blackberries, anecdote, 137.

Blarney Groves, verses, 180, 181.

Bockshirmer, Alcott's study of, 42.

Boëthius, Alcott's reading, 42.

Books, not finalities, 242. (See *Literature, Poetry, Shakspeare,* etc.)

Borgias, the, manuring the Reformation, 284.

Boston, Mass.: Emerson's birthplace, 1, 2; old landmarks, 4; prosperity, 5; public schools, 6; embargo, 7; party spirit, Noddle's Island, 8; a centre, 9; alliance with Cambridge, 11; Second Church, 12, 151; pulpit, 13, 152; North End places, 14; lectures, 15, 16; Bethel, 17; War meeting, 18; circle of souls, 19; social gatherings, 20; Emancipation celebration, 21; Town and Country Club, 22; individuality, 23; Lyceum, 24; Boston Parish, Athenæum, 25; deeper heart, 26–28; the Hub, 29; witchcraft, 30; six lectures, 31; in poetry, 32–35; Channing's pulpit, 37; Masonic Temple, 38, 39; Institute of Instruction, 40; spirit of life, 42; Garrison mob, 45, 46; twelve lectures, 57; Bay, 70; Washington St., 71; dozen great men, 79; Beacon Hill, 87;

nearness, 122; First Church, 148; Federal St. home, 150; Everett's lectures, 151; Chardon St. home, 151, 158; allusions, 154; Philistines, 157; Milton lecture, 175; turning from, 287; Radical Club, 302; Woman's Club, 304.

Bradford, George P., ride with Alcott, 44.

Brahmans, spirituality, 371, 372. (See *Emerson's Poems, Hindoos, India, Vedas.*)

Bread, brown, illustration, 123.

Brown, John: sympathy with, 21; cross, 134, 135. (See *Antislavery, Southern Rebellion.*)

Browne, Sir Thomas, his English, 55.

Browning, Robert, his Bishop Blougram, 127.

Brownson, Orestes A.: reasonings, 58; urgency, 163.

Bryant, William Cullen: allusion, 316; on American poetry, 318.

Buckminster, Joseph Stevens: preaching, 13; a hope, 317.

Buddhism: mysterious calmness, 370; spirit, 374. (See *India, Religion,* etc.)

Bulkeley, Peter: Emerson's ancestor, 147; sermons, 148.

Burke, Edmund: quoted, 141; nature, 327.

Burmah. (See *Buddhism, India,* etc.)

Burns, Robert, on the Daisy, 29.

Burroughs, John, in The Century, 105.

Byron, Lord: verdict, 210; nature, 327; and Goethe, 402.

CABOT, ELIOT, literary care, 154. Cæsar, allusion, 361. (See *Julius Cæsar.*)

Calderon, genius, 183.

California: students, 27; Golden Gate, 70; the Forty-niners, 79; Homeric, 88; Shasta, 89; Yosemite, 140; gold, 142. (See *America.*)

Calvinism: a little, 115; decline, 248; a disease, 266. (See *Religion,* etc.)

Cambridge, Eng., scholarship, 185.

Cambridge, Mass.: doubtful about Emerson, 288; drill, 296. (See *Harvard University.*)

Canaan, conquest, 148. (See *Bible, Jews,* etc.)

Canada, students, 27.

Carlyle, Thomas: letters to, 3, 9, 10; product of London, 9; merit, 23, 24; not appreciated, 25, 27; Alcott's study, 40, 41; undertaking a magazine, 41; Sartor Resartus, 42; ideal of Emerson, 45; on Emerson's first Essays, 50; interest in reforms, 63; Alcott's antagonism, 64; letter, 65; Cromwell, 66; hero-worship, 68; thought and act, 120; irony, 127; rugged, 134; absorption in, 151; religious essence, 246, 247; spiritual asphyxia, 277; feigned quotations, 362; stream of influence, 386; relation to Emerson, 386–418; Wilhelm Meister, 390–393; relation to Goethe, 402; worship of sorrow, 403; Correspondence, 404–406; same doctrine, 406; fulminations, 407; labor-saving machinery, 408; sociology, epic poem, 409; negative message, History of his Life, 410; among the seers, 411; disparagement of America, 412, 413; value of Emerson, 414–416; pleasanter words on American affairs, 417.

Cathedral, face-wall illustration, 367. (See *Architecture.*)

Century, The, on Emerson, 105.

Cerberus, soothed, 298.

Ceylon, religion, 370. (See *Asia, India,* etc.)

Channing, Edward, professorship, 11.

Channing, William Ellery, the divine: eloquence, 11; discourses, 13; pulpit, 37; interviews, 38; anxiety about a new magazine, 41, 42; spiritual rank, 44; ethics, 58; parallel in England, 62; the breast a church, 114; a gift of Unitarianism, 133; Miss Peabody's interest, 152; influence declining, 248; pulpit, 293. (See *Religion, Unitarianism,* etc.)

Channing, William Ellery, the poet: Ode to Emerson, 216–222; to Emerson's son, 223, 224.

Channing, William Henry, Ode to, 299.

Character: always current, 143; building, 246; nature's highest form, 254, 255. (See *Ethics, Religion,* etc.)

Chaucer, Geoffrey : quotation, 54; criticised, 203.

Chelsea, Eng. : Carlyle's residence, 64 ; letter, 65.

Cheney, Mrs. Ednah D., Emerson and Boston, 1-35, 171.

Child, D. L., and wife, 39.

Child, Mrs. Lydia Maria: Emerson's eyes, 16 ; in Diary, 42.

China : emigration, 71; human hopes, 338; religion, 370 ; ethics, 372. (See *Asia, Buddhism,* etc.)

Choate, Rufus, anecdote, 129.

Christian Examiner, in Diary, 42.

Christianity : an Eastern monarchy, 159 ; the word dropped, 161 ; revelations, 176 ; different Christianities, 238 ; doctrine, 239 ; aim, 246; essence, 247 ; inner world, 388 ; four phases painted, 390 ; third religion, 391. (See *Calvinism, Ethics, Religion,* etc.)

Church : support of reforms, 62 ; freedom, 66 ; a seceder from, 114 ; councils, 115 ; not a finality, 116 ; fandango, 122, 123 ; corrupt, 126 ; artificial, 129 ; supposed treason, 136 ; leadership, 152 ; attendance, 172 ; Emerson's attitude, 237-248 ; founded on science, 245, 246 ; decadence, 285 ; Dante, 389 ; studied, 407. (See *Ethics, Religion, Worship,* etc.)

Cicero, poetry, 180.

Cities : man-made, 1-4 ; aid from library, 5 ; cockneyism, 9 ; not prisons, 10, 11 ; advantages, 408. (See *Berlin, Boston, New York,* etc.)

Civilization : dependent on morality, 261, 276.

Clairvoyance, in art, 183. (See *Symonds.*)

Clarke, James Freeman, in Diary, 42, 44.

Clarke, Sarah, letter, 31-33.

Clubs, 304. (See *Boston.*)

Coins, illustration, 132.

Coleridge, Samuel [Taylor : republication, 42; Alcott's study, 47; definition of poetry, 178; stream of influence, 386.

Columbus, Christopher, discovery, 70, 85. (See *America.*)

Common-sense, basis of prose, 178. (See *Milton, Poetry,* etc.)

Concord, Mass. : Emerson stock, 1 ; pines, 2 ; town-meeting, 9 ; stars shining, 11 ; Emerson's residence begun, 15 ; club, 21 ; war-meeting, 28 ; Emerson day, 31; Ode in 1859, 32, 33 ; circle, 40 ; Alcott's first trip, 44-48 ; other visits, 48, 53, 54, 56 ; abiding greatness, 64 ; Wayside, 65 ; Mystic of, 66 ; monument, 86 ; Walden, 89 ; reputation made, 90 ; nearness, 122 ; discourse, 136 ; old families, 148 ; drives, 156 ; in poetry, 227 ; School of Philosophy, 233 ; studious home, 293 ; study, 303 ; tea-party, 307 ; part of the universe, 337, 338 ; classic trees, 366.

Congregationalism, Tritheism, 153.

Conscience : inner light, 247 ; voice of God, 269-272. (See *Ethics,* etc.)

Conservatism, stands on man's limitations, 83. (See *Religion,* etc.)

Constantinople, its appliances, 408. (See *Asia, Oriental,* etc.)

Conventionalism, 319. (See *Church, Worship,* etc.)

Conway, Moncure D., apotheosis, 150.

Cooke, George Willis : French quotation, 97 ; Emerson's View of Nationality, 310-338. (See *America.*)

Cooper, James Fenimore, first books, 316, 318.

Cord, untwisted, 137.

Corneille, Pierre, genius, 183.

Cousin, Victor, Modern Philosophy, 373.

Cromwell, Oliver : Carlyle's Life, 66, 67; war, 259 ; assassinated, 416.

Cupid, in poetry, 191, 196. (See *Emerson's Poems,* — Three Loves.)

DANA, RICHARD HENRY : in Diary, 44 ; on Emerson, 288.

Dante: love of Florence, 2 ; hell, 126 ; verse and insight, 174 ; new verse, 185 ; on love, 200 ; poetry defined, 201 ; criticism of life, 203 ; creative skill, 328 ; an ideal, 331 ; revelation, 388 ; great poem, 389 ; rank, 398, 400, 401 ; prophetic sorrow, 406. (See *Poetry, Swedenborg,* etc.)

Darwin, Charles, theories, 262–264. (See *Evolution.*)

Davidson, Professor Thomas: on Aristotle, 202 ; Jordan's Sigfridsage, 383.

Decalogue : original, 248 ; echoed, 256. (See *Bible, Laws, Religion*, etc.)

Demons, theory, 194–196. (See *Emerson's Poems*, — Dæmonic Love.)

Dervishes, illustration, 124. (See *Emerson's Poems*, — Days.)

Devil, "dear old," 122. (See *Goethe, Mephistopheles*, etc.)

Dial, The : begun, 42 ; on Reformers, 59–61 ; discussed, 62 ; Orphic Sayings, 362 ; Carlyle's opinion, 415.

Dickens, Charles, his Little Marchioness, 288.

Diodati, Charles, Milton's friend, 176.

Dorcas, incomparable, 142. (See *Bible*.)

Dryden, John, not a classic, 204.

EAST LEXINGTON : pulpit, 154, 156 ; Emerson understood, 157.

Eden, the Fall, 357. (See *Bible, Man*, etc.)

Edinburgh, Scotland, a prayer, 25.

Edwards, Jonathan, menaces, 126. (See *Calvinism, Puritanism*, etc.)

Egypt : vote of a prophet, 81 ; architecture, 165 ; traditions, 332 ; Sphinx, 370 ; Plato in, 372 ; mind, 380 ; civilization, 399. (See *Emerson's Poems*, — The Sphinx, — *Oriental*, etc.)

Elias, inspiration, 242. (See *Bible*.)

Elijah, whirlwind, 156. (See *Bible*.)

Eliot, George, quoted, 321, 322.

Elizabeth, Queen, her era, 182–184, 248, 330.

Elliotson, John, meeting Alcott, 61.

Elsler, Fanny, anecdote, 306. (See *Fuller*.)

Emerson Family, settlement, 148. (See *Bulkeley, Concord, Haskins*, etc.)

Emerson, Charles Chauncy : Ralph Waldo's brother, 39 : talk with Alcott, 45 ; law, 149 ; death, 169, 170.

Emerson, Edward Bliss, brother of Ralph Waldo, 149.

Emerson, Edward Waldo, son of Ralph Waldo, 175.

Emerson, Ellen Louisa (Tucker), Ralph

Waldo's first wife : marriage, 22 ; death, 151.

Emerson, George B., cousin of Ralph Waldo, 150.

Emerson, Lydia Jackson, second wife of Ralph Waldo : chat, 158, 159 ; eminently Christian, 172 ; hospitality, 307, 308.

Emerson, Mary Moody, aunt of Ralph Waldo : paper on, 22 ; a guest, 40 ; reading a paper, 151 ; expression, 152.

Emerson, Ralph Waldo : Boston relations, 1–35 ; birth, 1 ; fondness for cities, 2 ; on New York, 3 ; childhood, 4, 5 ; schools, 6, 7 ; orphaned youth, 8 ; cockney spirit, 9 ; hailing from Boston, 10 ; college, 11 ; preaching, 12 ; settlement and sacrament, 13 ; sermon notes, 14 ; European trip, 15 ; old admirers, portrait, 16 ; punctuality, 17 ; friendship for Father Taylor, 17, 18 ; patriotic indignation, 18 ; flippantly misunderstood, 19, 20 ; friendly influences not to be spared, — "The Common or Emerson," 20 ; Music Hall occasions, localities, Freedom's utterances, 21 ; clubs, marriage, 22 ; pride in Boston, 23 ; the Lyceum power, 24 ; theological tempest, 24, 25 ; reading Carlyle, 25 ; looking below the surface, 26 ; perennial youth, 27 ; side of freedom, 28 ; homely traits, 30 ; Greek and Puritan blended, 30 ; note of authority, 31 ; growth in favor, 32 ; intellect and sentiment, 32–35 ; relations to Alcott, 36–67 ; loyalty in friendship, 36, 37 ; Alcott's record, 37, 38 ; on Angelo, 38 ; Luther, 39 ; gatherings, 39, 40 ; educational lecture, 40 ; advanced thought, 41 ; spiritual rank, 44 ; new idea of life, 45 ; antislavery, 46 ; topics discussed, 47, 48 ; defence of Alcott, 49 ; comments, 50 ; as a lecturer, 51, 52 ; advice, 52, 53 ; characteristics, 53, 54 ; on conscience, 54 ; style, 55 ; qualities, 56 ; on politics, 57 ; present failure, 58 ; encouragement about the foreign trip, 59 ; review of it, 60, 61 ; two friends antipathetic, 64 ; Wayside, 65 ; Americanism, 68–91 ;

no hero-worshipper, 68; catholic acceptance of truth, 69; ancestry clerical, Puritan, and American, 74; adipose tissue, 75; absence of system and consistency, 76; nothing solved, coherence, 77; cosmopolitan, 78; comfortable words towards England, 79; broad sympathies, 80; a questioner, 81, 82; Providence, 83; the fundamentals illuminated, 84; foremost in patriotism, 85, 86; nature's voices, 87–89; a champion, 89; making Concord's reputation, 90; an experimenter, 91; French view, 92–108; as a poet, 93, 94; not a philosopher, 95; a thinker, sage, and prophet, 96; attitude towards God, 97, 98; symbolism of nature, 99; lyriques, 100; first laws, 101; self-confidence, 102; served by all materials, 103, 104; conception and treatment, 105; a reformer, 106; honor to the country, 107; Belleisle's tribute, 107, 108; religion, 109–145; a volcano, own portrait, 109; Christianity queried, 110; optimist and critic, 111; an immigrant and interrogator, 112; New Bedford installation, 113; the Church, 114; Puritanism and parties, 115; a bidden guest, churchgoing, 116; next door to truth, 117; a cheerful Adam before the Fall, 118; mind from matter, morality not the whole of religion, 119; *chant* and *cant*, 120; indecency repellent, 121; old couplet translated, 122; humorous picture of the Church, 123; his own forerunner, 124; severity towards class and person, 125; majorities, a mountain mind, 126; beat and mission, 127; shielded from coarseness and vanity, 128; atomic style, 129; clarion oracle, 130; literary style, 131; philanthropy and trickery, early sermons, 132; war against injustice, expectance of God, 133; gownless minister, ruggedness, 134; admiration of onslaught, 135; ecclesiastical prejudice overcome, 136; "fair creature," etc., 137; faith in immortality, enduring books, 138; in the air, 139; his own company, 140; night-

flower of faith, reply when ill, 141; in heaven, 142; understating, 143; swallow flights, mystic sense, no one great book, 144; a perceiver, 145; as a preacher, 146–172; out of the pulpit, 146; ancestry, 147; relations to Concord explained, 148; brothers, 149; a fair pupil, 150; first trip to Europe, wife's death, leaving the Second Church, 151; studying under Channing, 152; sermon on Mr. Sampson, 153; East Lexington preaching, 154; two Divinity addresses, 155; Concord home, 156; simple people's appreciation, 157; transcendentalism, denial of Christ, life-purpose, 158; consulting the ladies, 159; Ware misunderstanding, unselfish courtesy, 160; silence about Christ, 161; humility hopeful, agnosticism, 162; intuition of God, 163; reserve and utterance, 164; poetic parables, 165, 166; tongue of fire, 167; deepest secret, 168; bereavements, 169, 170; apocalyptic chants, 171; church-going resumed, 172; among the poets, 173–214; feeling the impulse, 173; a poet without verse, 174; parallel, 175; description applied to self, 175–177; perfect expression denied, 178; true standard, 179, 180; resemblances, 181; concentrating, 182; clairvoyance, environment, 183; best poems, 185; every line valuable, 186; homage to love, 187; friendship, 188–190; a poem analyzed, 191–197; mysticism, 197; ethical lesson, 198; extraordinary language, 199; commentaries on love, 200, 201; wild rule, 202; sustained virtue, 204; comparison with Gray, 205; epitaphs, 206–210; delight in his own poetic expression, 211; magic power, 212; poetic tributes, 215–232; ethics, 233–285; biography, 233; harmonizing idealism, 234; morality the law of the universe, 235; first and last religious utterances, depth, 236; impatient of church doctrines, 237, 238; present deity, 238–245; future religion, 245–251; morality and philosophy, 252; thinking stones, 253; fundamental law, 255;

subjective idealism, 257; will-conformity, 258; superiority to Kant, 259; idea of *right*, 260; utilitarianism, 261, 262; evolution, 262-266; freedom and fate, 267, 268; obedience, 269, 270; conscience, 271; worker with God, 272; disaster of wrong, 277; highest inspirations, 280; laws alive, 281; talk with a missionary, 282; immoral year, 284; relation to society, 286-309; threescore, 287; eccentric disturbers of peace, 288; eloquent on foot, 289; seraph's armor, Phi Beta Kappa oration, 290; coral reefs, 291; politeness, 292; unwillingness to enter the pulpit, 293; critical appreciation of England's aristocracy, 293-296; country host, 296; first volume of verse, 297; child's death, 298; indignation, 299, 300; a tailor's model, 301; Radical Club, 302; in his study, 303; *clubbable*, 304; on the comic, reading The Old Cove, 305; stage-dancing, anecdotes, vulgar facts, 306; entertaining Mrs. Howe, 307; nobility, 308; woman question, inspiriting presence, 309; view of nationality, 310-338; inheritance, 310; faith in the soul, 311; advancement of his country, 312; literary field, 313; repugnant to agnosticism, literary career, 314; two theories of literary creation, 315, 316; going to Nature direct, 317; promise of a new world, 319, 320; pioneer, 321; outgrowth of life, 326; imitation criticised, 327; diligent student, cosmopolitan, antagonistic tendencies, 328; a liberator, 329; morning-glory, 330; world - movements recognized, 331; faith in America, 332; hopes, 333; national qualities in his mind, 335; garments of beauty woven, 336; broad and human, 337; localism, 338; philosophy of nature, 339-364; acceptance of discoveries, 339; poet of the future, 340; metaphors from modern theories, 341; rhythmic transitions, 342; machine and frosted-cake poetry, 343; evolution in poetry, 344; inventory of nature, 345; nobler wants, 346, 347; transition to idealism, 348; central unity, 349; psychology, 350; ground of idealism, 352-354; evolution, 354, 357; individuality, 355; surprising world theory, 356; traditions, 358; comments on Oracles, 360; doctrine of the Lapse, 361, 362; seen from India, 365-371; Arcadian walks, 366; sense of childhood, 367; priestly functions, 368; introspection in the West, 369; earnestness of life, 370; manner of the man, 371; Orientalism, 372-385; words about Plato applied to self, 372; haunted by the problem of evil, 373; analysis of Brahma, 373-378, 382; summary of the spirit of Indian mind, 379, 380; Neoplatonism, 380; problem solved, 381; foundation of the universe, law of return, 384, 385; relation to Goethe and Emerson, 386-419; stream of influence, 386; understanding Mephistopheles, 393-396; self-culture, 398; influenced by Swedenborg, 401, 402; sorrow-worship, 403; interpretation of Goethe, 404; Puritanism, 405; doctrine of the age, 406; solution of individualism, 407; the Civil War, 412-416; valued by Carlyle, 414; English Traits preferred to Tennyson, 416; style criticised, 418; Alcott's Monody, 420.

EMERSON'S BOOKS: —
English Traits: allusions, 78-80; shunning the shame, 121; critical appreciation, 293; value, 416.
Essays, first volume, 50.
First Philosophy in Boston, projected, 23.
Nature: allusions, 10, 78; Alcott's insight, 51, 52; French allusions, 99, 106; first publication, 158, 236; opening lines, 239; all things moral, 256; evolution, 262-265; quoted and analyzed, 345-362; written in India, 366.
Representative Men, 68, 372, 378, 393, 394, 401, 418.

EMERSON'S ESSAYS, LECTURES, SERMONS, SPEECHES, etc. : —
American Scholar, The, 312.

EMERSON'S ESSAYS, LECTURES, SERMONS, SPEECHES, etc. : —

Aunt Mary Moody Emerson, 22.
Beauty, 99, 346, 347, 349. (See *Emerson's Poems*.)
Commodity, 99, 346, 349.
Discipline, 99, 256, 348, 349.
Divinity School Address, 106, 155, 156, 158, 235, 236, 244, 245.
Ethics, 54–56.
Eulogy on Parker, 247–250.
Fate, 266, 267.
Fortune of the Republic, 312.
Free Religious Association, address, 236.
Friendship, 37. (See *Emerson's Poems*.)
Historical Discourse, Concord, 136.
Idealism, 256, 257, 350–354.
Judgment Seat of Christ, 154.
Language, 99, 349.
Lapse, or Descent of the Soul, 356–362.
Luther, 39.
Means of Inspiring a Taste for English Literature, 40.
Memory, 19.
Method of Nature, 158.
Methods and Philosophy of History, 57, 58.
Michael Angelo, 33.
Milton, 39, 175–178.
Over-Soul, The, 73; among Brahmans, 376.
Plato, 251.
Poetry and Imagination, 345.
Preacher, The, 155, 156, 236, 245, 246, 251.
Progress of Culture, 106.
Prospects, 355.
Reformer, The, and Transcendentalist, 408.
Sermon on Mr. Sampson, 153.
Soul, 347, 348.
Spirit, 353–356.
Sumner Outrage, 28.
Traditions, 358.
Unity, 349.
Wealth, 5. (See *Emerson's Poems*.)
Worship, 245, 251 (See *Emerson's Poems*.)

EMERSON'S POEMS : —

Boston Hymn, 21, 32–35, 300, 307.
Brahma, 167; compared, 373–378, 382.
Concord Monument, Hymn, 32, 86.
Days, 186 ; (Day's Ration) 124.
Dirge, The, 149, 186, 205.
Discontented Poet, The, 210.
Each and All, 171, 297.
Earth Song, The, 86.
Emancipation Hymn, 32.
Epode, The, 208. (Voluntaries.)
Forerunners, The, 185.
Fourth-of-July Ode, 32. (Concord Hymn.)
Friendship, 37, 188–190. (See *Emerson's Essays*.)
Hamatreya, 86, 171, 341.
Hermione, 36, 37, 185, 187, 188.
Humble Bee, The, 120, 321, 366.
Initial, Dæmonic, and Celestial Love, 191–201. (Three Loves.)
In Memoriam, 205, 206.
Lines to J. W., 171.
May-Day, 341.
Merlin, 185, 202, 211, 212, 342, 345. (Merlin's Song.)
Monadnoc, 126.
Mountain and the Squirrel, 171.
My Garden, 341, 345.
Ode to Bacchus, 165–167, 212–214.
Ode to Beauty, 165, 185. (See *Emerson's Essays*.)
Ode to Channing, 299.
Ode, The, 206, 207, 230. (Voluntaries.)
Problem, The, 2, 111, 113, 165, 271, 297.
Rhea, 171, 186, 190.
Rhodora, The, 104, 171, 341.
Saadi, 126, 139, 186, 270.
Sea-shore, 341, 345.
Solution, 396, 399, 400–402, 419.
Song of Nature, 418, 419.
Sphinx, The, 168, 185, 297.
Spiritual Laws, 384.
Tact, 300.
Terminus, 186.
Test, The, 143, 398, 399, 419.
Three Loves, The, 185. (Initial, Dæmonic, and Celestial.)
Threnody, 169–171, 186, 205, 298, 299.

EMERSON'S POEMS : —

Titmouse, The, 186, 341.

Uriel, 165, 167, 185, 381–383.

Wealth, 363, 364. (See *Emerson's Essays.*)

Wood Notes, 166, 167, 185, 341, 343, 344.

Worship, 169. (See *Emerson's Essays.*)

Voluntaries : When Duty whispers, 30, 206, 300. (Ode and Epode.)

EMERSON'S POETRY : —

(Brief quotations not referred to in the previous section.) Politics, 3; "The inevitable morning," 3, 4; "We love the venerable house," 13, 14; "The being that I am," 28; patriotic, 85, 86; "A subtle chain," 100, 354; French translations, 101–104; ears of stone, 105; eyes and light, 109; vest, 110; good from all, 111; an owl, 112; time coined, 113; star-axis, conscious law, 114, 281; harvest, 116; beneath the pines, 117; neighbor's creed, 121; joy in remorse, 122; nine lives, 123; mountain-measure, 129; science and hurt, grief and balsam, 134; knowing as known, 138; biding at home, 140; clothed eternity, old Niles, 142; loudest requiem, 164; unsightly root and bright flower, 184, 185; love, 189, 190; feeding men, 262; rivers of God, 270; "The fiend that man harries," 272, 298; cheerfulness, 278; permanence of excellence, 281; "Good-by, proud world," 287, 288; home content, 297; omnipresence, 380; line in nature, 382.

EMERSON'S PROSE : —

(Quotations on different subjects.) Cities, 4; wealth, 5; town-meetings, 9; Boston, 10; Everett, 12; a Thinker let loose, 13; the Lyceum, 24; young men, 26, 27; no demand, 27; Abolitionism, 28; quiet manners, 29; bulletin-boards, 30, 31; The Transcendentalist, 41;

EMERSON'S PROSE : —

defence of Alcott, 49; advice to him, 52, 53; his English trip, 59–61; one Reason, 75; dozen great men, 79; angry bigot and Abolitionism, 81; sturdy New Hampshire lad, 88; the Land a sanative influence, 89; gentle liberators, 90, 91; experimenters, 91; divine personality, 97; externization of soul, 98; definition of poetry, imagination, 99; fire from Etna, 100; self-trust, 101; working with God, 101, 102; fate, 102; promise of the future, 106; converse aside, 110, 111; original relation to nature, 112; poppy and corn, 115, 116; forsaking tasks, 116; censure tempered by acquaintance, 125; blackberries, 137; egotism, 139; wrangle and wonder, 144; moral sentiment, 156; friend of man, 158; silence about Christ, 161; in the midst of truth, 163; God's sensibility, 169; death an absurdity, 170; parish of young men, 172; on Milton, 175–178; poetry defined, 180; loquacity, 182; new verse valuable, 185; nature a hieroglyphic, 186; Shakspeare's Phœnix, 200; Byron *mot*, 210; new teacher looked for, 235; foundation of belief, law of gravitation, 236, 252; mind not divided, 237; creeds outgrown, Swedenborg's failure, and Behmen's, 238; foregoing generations seeing nature face to face, 239; miracles, 239, 240; connection of Church and New Testament, 241; traditions, false theology, 242; Oriental pictures of Jesus, 243; his character, 244; a new Church, 245; founded on science and ethical laws, 246; essence of Christianity, 247, 248; pure ethics, 249; a new religion, 250; laws alive, divine essence, mere morality, 251; power, law in sentiment, 252; living stones, choral life-song, live universe, 253; fate, loaded dice, morals generated, the side of right, nature's highest form, 254; character, moral force of grav-

EMERSON'S PROSE: —
ity, 255.; all things moral, noble doubt, 256 ; centre of nature, 257 ; virtuous man, *moral* defined, 258 ; moral discipline, impregnable principle, wagon and star, world's open secret, 259 ; bee and hive, moral institutions, 261 ; greatest good of greatest number, low prudence, 262 ; source and tap, injustice, snake-skin, eternal moral force, 263 ; melioration, a tropical swamp, 264 ; evil serving good, 265 ; human culture unfinished, 265, 266 ; organization behind, liberty before, 266, 267 ; huckabuck woven, 266 ; razors and suicides, 267 ; obedience, will-education, 268, 269 ; first experiences, 269 ; the moral sentiment, 269, 270 ; soul of God in men, 270 ; genius and conscience, 271, 272 ; identity of law, one Reason, 273 ; love, perception, intellect, morals, 273, 274 ; poetry and wickedness, 275 ; crime and punishment on one stem, 276 ; health in every department, 277, 278 ; evil and good unequal, 278 ; secret belief in law, Providence, 279 ; man near to Nature, 280 ; God everywhere, 281 ; immortality, 281, 282 ; other-world questions, 282, 283 ; moral interregnums, regenerated conscience, 284 ; divine presence, 286 ; English hero, 294 ; talent and manners, 296 ; Fanny Elsler anecdote, 306 ; manhood all-important, anthem of history, 310 ; new guides for America, 312 ; higher national life, 313 ; help from within, 314 ; man and revolution, 315 ; writing from the heart, 320 ; tasting the same life, 326 ; provincialism, 327 ; running backward in vain, 337 ; nature a vast trope, 345 ; aspects of the world, 345, 346 ; mercenary benefits, 346 ; threefold vehicle of thought, symbolism, poet-dreams, shallow writers, 347 ; Nature's kingdoms, moral aspects, 348 ; ultimate unity, 349 ; absolute existence of **nature, 350** ; philosophy of nature,

EMERSON'S PROSE: —
.351 ; presuppositions of science, 351, 352 ; unity of religion with ethics, personality of God, 352 ; true position of nature, 353 ; idealism, 353, 354 ; same spirit in earth and man, 354 ; degeneracy, understanding nature, 356, 357 ; traditions quoted, 358 ; miracles, ruin in nature, nature fluid, 360 ; the world for *us*, 361 ; Hindoo thought, 367 ; the moon, 369 ; Plato, the East, 372 ; Krishna, doctrine of appearances, 379, 380 ; Faust and his devil, 393, 394 ; Goethe criticised, 395, 396 ; Wilhelm Meister, 396, 398 ; Goethe's velvet life, Truth born in a manger, 404 ; accumulated property, 408 ; praise of Carlyle's Frederick, 411, 412 ; rebuking Carlyle on the American War question, 412, 413 ; unamiable Jonathan, 413, 414 ; perversities of style, 414 ; Goethe's literary form, 418.

Emerson, William, father of Ralph Waldo, settlement in Boston, 1, 148, 149.

Emerson, William, brother of Ralph Waldo : education, 149 ; school, 150.

Enchanted Princess, 295.

Endicott Family, in Massachusetts, 72. (See *New England*, etc.)

England : characteristics, 9 ; critics, 27 ; traits, 29 ; Alcott's visit, 58–67 ; "doleful daughters," 64 ; local limitations, 69 ; full of Americans, 71 ; literature, 138 ; poetry, 182, 184 ; dramatists, 204 ; lectures, 293 ; society, 295 ; scholarship, manners, 296 ; literary models, 317 ; present literature full of doubt, 323 : traditions, 332 ; exportations to India, Young, 397 ; one with America, 417. (See *Alcott, America, Emerson, R. W., Emerson's Books, — English Traits, — Europe*, etc.)

Episcopacy, Tritheism, 153. (See *Unitarianism*.)

Epistles, in the original, 248. (See *Bible, St. Paul*, etc.)

Ethics: Essay, 233-285; different from religion, 352; precocious, 409. (See *Conscience, Religion*, etc.)

Europe: origin of nations, 69; full of American ideas, 70; and people, 71; precedents, 72; travellers, 140; Everett's return, 151; Emerson's, 153; description of Christ, 243; America not European, 312; pretentious society, 323; traditions, 332; genius, 372; civilization, 387; history in Carlyle's books, 409; rulers, 410; feudal, 413. (See *America, England*, etc.)

Everett, Alexander H., notice, 23.

Everett, Edward: his professorship, 11; genius, 12; oratory, 150, 151.

Evolution: deals with structure, 119; greeted, 135; rational ground, 234; sympathy, 262-264; in poetry, 344; philosophy, 354, 355; natural selection, 357; Hindoo, 368. (See *Darwin, Emerson's Prose Quotations*, etc.)

Experience, a disciple of, 47.

FAITH: lost in the city, 3; groundwork, 257. (See *God, Religion, Worship*, etc.)

Family, freedom in, 66.

Fancy, in literature, 178.

Fate: loaded dice, 254; amelioration, 263. (See *Emerson's Essays*.)

Felton, Cornelius Conway, notice of Emerson, 288.

Fénelon, Bishop, influence, 248.

Feudalism: dead, 330; none in America, 332. (See *England, Europe*, etc.)

Fichte, Johann Gottlieb: tribute to Christ, 242; thought, 251; on faith, 257.

Fields, James T., quoted, 123.

Firdûsî, his poetry, 179.

Fisher, James, hospitality, 20.

Fiske, James, career, 86.

Florence, Italy: Dante's fondness for, 2; local prejudices yielded, 10. (See *Cities, Italy*, etc.)

Follen, Charles: wife, 42; in Diary, 42, 44.

Forces, and powers, 292.

Fox, W. J.: dinner, 61; wife, 64.

France: character, 9; view of Emerson, 92-108; brilliant age, 184; heroes, 294; Revolution, 408, 409.

Francis, Convers, in Diary, 42.

Franklin, Benjamin, Poor Richard, 5, 262.

Frederick the Great, 10. (See *Carlyle*.)

Freedom: in all departments, 66; of man, 253; two great ideas, 334.

Free Religion: switching off, 114; party in error, 159. (See *Ethics, Religion*, etc.)

Free Religious Association, address, 236.

Friendship: genius for, 36; love without wings, 189. (See *Emerson's Poems*.)

Froebel, Friedrich, understood, 155.

Frothingham, Nathaniel L., in Diary, 44.

Froude, James Anthony: on morality, 261; on Carlyle, 410.

Fruitlands, Alcott's scheme, 59, 65.

Fuller, Margaret: allusion, 11; art-clairvoyance, 183; in society, 289; anecdote, 305, 306; influenced by Emerson, 321.

Furness, William Henry: educational paper, 40; spiritual rank, 44.

Furies, converted, 266.

GARRISON, WILLIAM LLOYD: mobbed, 45, 46; reforms, 58; speaking, 62; church within, 114; divergence, 134; Concord speech, 307. (See *Antislavery, John Brown*, etc.)

George III., "George Guelph," 417.

German: words, 257; heroes, 294; the dance, 301; language, 405.

Germany: central city, 9, 10; personified, 129; study inducing Radicalism, 149; tribute to Christ, 242; Lessing's influence, 329. (See *Goethe, Carlyle*, etc.)

Gibraltar, illustration, 260.

Gnosticism, the Lapse, 361.

God: heroes his instruments, 68; first-hand, 112; eating veal, 128; river, 131; out of hiding, 133; not to be analyzed, 145; eternal relations, 152; face to face, 153; incarnate, 160;

name translated, 163; beauty, 165; love demanded, 196; seeing deity, 245; pitiable, 251; thoughts, 272; speaking to men, 329; personality, 352; Hindoo view, 367-371; Plato's *one*, 372; serene genius, 280. (See *Bible, Brahma, Buddhism, Ethics, Religion*, etc)

Goethe: quoted, 117; man's business, 120; Faust disagreeable, 121; reverence, 133; introspection, 137; on individuality, 143; absorption in, 151; unity, 174; on poetry, 275; relations to Emerson, 386-419; a revealer, 388; world-poet, 390; Wilhelm Meister, 390-393; Mephistopheles, 393-395; analysis, 395, 396; Meister analyzed, 396-398; view of the world, 398; Byron, 402; adulation, 404; objections, 405; present age, 406; solution, 407; French Revolution, 408, 409; lawgiver, 418. (See *Carlyle, Germany*, etc.)

Goodwin, H. B., Concord minister, 48.

Gordian Knot, of slavery, 134. (See *Antislavery, John Brown*, etc.)

Gospels, in the original, 248. (See *Bible*.)

Gould, Jay, typical, 86. (See *America*.)

Graham, Sylvester, dietetics, 58. (See *Reformers*, etc.)

Grand Man, of Swedenborg, 410. (See *Man*, etc.)

Gray, Thomas, rank, quotations, 204-210.

Greaves, Mr., his principles, 59, 62. (See *Reformers*, etc.)

Greece: climate, etc., 258; contact with the East, 331; traditions, 332; the Muse, 399. (See *Pindar*, etc.)

Greek: perceptions, 29, 30; apogee, 88; study, 150; architecture, 165; gods, 167; poetry, 179, 182; clairvoyance, 183; anthology, 186; chorus, 196; dramatists, 201; description of Christ, 243; professorship, 288; heroes, 294; art, 315.

Greenough, Horatio, anecdote, 135.

HAFIZ: poetry, 179; new verse, 185. (See *Persia*, etc.)

Happiness, not the aim of the universe, 383. (See *Ethics, Religion*, etc.)

Harris, William T.: on evolution, 262; Emerson's Philosophy of Nature, 339-364; Orientalism, 373-385; Emerson's Relations to Goethe and Carlyle, 386-419.

Harte, Bret, reporter of California, 86. (See *Homer*.)

Harvard University: in 1817, 11, 12; Divinity School, 19; Address, 24, 25, 113, 235, 236, 244; benefaction, 27; prayer, 113; Observatory, 131; lobbying, 132; overseer, 134; last word, 136, 137; Emerson's graduation, 150; two theological Addresses, 155, 156; Greek professorship, 288. (See *Cambridge, Emerson's Lectures*, etc.)

Harvard, Mass.: residence, 1; community, 59.

Harwood, English reformer, 61.

Haskins Family, Emerson's mother, 149.

Hastings, battle of, 294.

Hawthorne, Julian, Essay, 68-91.

Hawthorne, Nathaniel: fellowship, 183; influenced by Emerson, 321.

Heaven, not to be analyzed, 145. (See *Happiness, Religion*, etc.)

Hebrew: oracle, 130; poetry, 179, 340. (See *Bible*, etc.)

Hedge, Frederic Henry: editorship, 41, 42; sermon, 44; conversation, 48.

Hegel, Georg Wilhelm Friedrich, a definition, 163.

Heidelberg, the Devil in, 394. (See *Mephistopheles*.)

Heraud, John A.: Alcott's interviews, 59; apostasy, 62; evening, 63. (See *Reformers*.)

Hermes, quintessence, 304.

Herodotus, an ideal, 331.

Hesiod: Alcott's study, 42; poetry, 123. (See *Greek. Homer*, etc.)

Higginson, Thomas Wentworth, quoted, 106.

Hillard, George Stillman, not understanding Emerson, 19.

Himmalayah, snows, 415.

Hindoos: hushed devotion, 163; meditation, 365; geography, 366; kinship, 367; Vedas, 368; philosophy, 369; deities, 370; Brahmans, 371; poets, 373; gods, 377, 378.

History, defined, 202.

Hoar, Elizabeth, a guest, 40.

Holmes, Oliver Wendell, the *hub*, 29.

Holy Ghost: Montanist opinion, 114; conflict with world-spirit, 131; not exhausted, 242. (See *God, Jesus, Religion*, etc.)

Holy Land, of the soul, 140.

Homer: comparison, 24; excluded, 123; hell, 125; genius, 143, 144; quoted, 173; verse, 174; allusions, 181; criticism of life, 203; words, 210; *one*, 243; environment, 258; quintessence, 304; springs of power, 326; creative skill, 328; assimilated, 329; Troy taken, 333; revelation, 387; rank, 398, 401. (See *Greek, Poetry*, etc)

Horace, quoted, 306.

Howe, Julia Ward, Emerson and Society, 286-309.

Hugo, Victor: motto quoted, 92; God bankrupt, 118, 119; unity, 174.

Humanity, Seer of, 2. (See *Great Man, Immortality, Jesus*, etc.)

Hume, Joseph, heard, 62.

Huntington, Frederick D., on character, 246.

IMAGINATION: makes the universe one vast metaphor, 99; basis of poetry, 178.

Immortality: Alcott's study, 43; in poetry, 118; Emerson's assurance, 138; Whence? 234; questions, 283; in poem, 426. (See *God, Heaven, Jesus, Religion*, etc.)

Independents: extremists, 137; Emerson's ancestry, 147, 148.

India: Emerson as seen from, 365-371; Brahma, 373; moral indifference, 375-378; two orders of devotees, 370. (See *Emerson's Poems, Hindoos, Vedas*, etc.)

Indians, church among, 147, 148.

Individualism, doctrine of, 407.

Individuality: two great ideas, 334-336; begins, 355.

Innocence, silver seat, 384, 385.

Inspiration: larger, 242; channels, 327. (See *Bible, Holy Ghost*, etc.)

Instinct, spiritual, 359.

Ion, Alcott's poem, 420-426.

Ireland, emigration, 72.

Irving, Washington, freshness, 318.

Isaiah, prophecies, 410. (See *Bible*, etc.)

Italy: its centre, 10; local limitations, 69; poetry, 179; art-clairvoyance, 183; heroes, 294; query, 315; inspiration, 330; ideal men, 331; traditions, 332; the Muse, 399. (See *Florence, Michael Angelo*, etc.)

JACKSON, ANDREW, anecdote, 135.

James, Henry, quoted, 134.

James, Henry, Jr. : Life of Hawthorne, 321; polish, 323.

James I., age, 183.

Japan, religion, 370. (See *Buddhism, Orient*, etc.)

Jehovah, name sacred, 163. (See *Brahma, God*, etc.)

Jena, Fichte at, 251.

Jeremiah, prophecies, 410. (See *Bible*.)

Jerusalem, robbed, 142. (See *Bible*.)

Jesus: retirement and love of cities, 2; Alcott's study, 42, 46-48; person, 111; pre-existence, 113; not a finality, 116; wilderness, 117, 139; hell, 125; prayer through, 128; Gethsemane, 134, 135; incomparable, 142; judgment-seat, 154; realizing divinity, 155, 156; denial, enemy of man, 158; *puppy* criticism, 159; preached by silence, 161; bloodless victory, 163; parables, 164; eclipsed, 167; secret, 168; why better, 240; Church doctrine, 242; excellence, 243, 244; a prophet, 244, 245; environment, 258; grace and truth, 260; answers to queries, 283; history, 360; aspects, 392. (See *Christianity, Ethics, God, Religion*, etc.)

Jews: their cultus, 238; teachers, 410. (See *Bible, Hebrew, Worship*, etc.)

Johnson, Samuel, on rascality, 278.

Jonathan, fictitious personage, 413. (See *America, New England*, etc.)

Jonson, Ben, poetry, 180.

Jordan's Sigfridsage, quoted, 383.

Journal of Speculative Philosophy, essays, 418.

Jubbulpoor, hills, 366. (See *India*, etc.)

Julius Cæsar, genius, 144. (See *Cæsar.*)

Jupiter, Dyaus Pitar, 367. (See *God, Jehovah,* etc.)

Justice: comparison, 295; inelegant, 308.

KANSAS, raids, 124.

Kant, Immanuel: constructive genius, 95; ethics, 234; his Kritik, 258; inferiority, 259; theory, 260; on freedom, 268; quintessence, 304.

Kearney, Denis, and the Chinese, 71. (See *California.*)

Kennebec River, sojourn, 150.

Keshub Chunder Sen, last work, 367, 368. (See *India,* etc.)

Khayam, Omar, quoted, 117. (See *Persia*)

Kinney, Mrs. E. C., Sonnets on Emerson, 231, 232.

Kirkland, John Thornton, presidency, 11.

Knox, John, Carlyle's allusion, 405. (See *Calvinism, Puritanism,* etc.)

Kossuth, Louis, shut out, 26.

Krishna, deity, 370, 378, 379. (See *Hindoos, Jehovah,* etc.)

LALOR, MR., Alcott's interview, 61. Landseer, Thomas, anecdote, 306.

Lane, Charles, socialism, 59, 62.

Latin Poetry, 179. (See *Greek,* etc.)

Laud, Archbishop, a persecutor, 147. (See *Emerson Family.*)

Laws, alive, 251, 281. (See *Ethics,* etc.)

Lazarus, Emma, sonnet, 215.

Leibnitz, Gottfried Wilhelm, quoted, 378.

Lens, illustration, 137.

Lessing, Gotthold Ephraim, influence, 329.

Liberty, before us, 264, 267.

Life, theory of, 38, 39.

Lincoln, Abraham: proclamation, 21; lily, 133. (See *America,* etc.)

Literature, methods of creation in America, 315–333 *passim.* (See *Milton,* etc.)

London, Eng.: effect, 4; everywhere known, 9; advantages, 408.

Longfellow, Henry Wadsworth, companionship, 305.

Lord's Supper: refusal to administer, 13, 110; table and sideboard, 127; Parker's view, 128; sermon, 152; attitude, 172; scene, 392.

Louis XIV., era, 184.

Love, compared with friendship, 189. (See *Emerson's Poems.*)

Lovelace, sympathy with, 80

Lowell Family, in the War, 26, 27.

Lowell, James Russell, pathos, 27.

Lucretius: higher meaning, 193; poetry defined, 201.

Luther, Martin: principles, 66; prayer, 118; private judgment, 147.

Lyceum: Emerson's place, 24; pulpit, 157.

Lyman, Theodore, gift to Harvard, 151.

MAB, QUEEN, in poetry, 192.

Macdonald, George, Maurice's apostle, 162.

Madonna, shrine, 247. (See *Roman Catholicism.*)

Mahomet, in the desert, 139.

Man: as a study, 43; the universal, 45; eternal relations, 152. (See *Ethics, Immortality, Great Man,* etc.)

Marcus Antoninus, ethical sculpture, 274.

Marcus Aurelius: comparison, 181; on morals, 258.

Marietta, Ohio, letter, 31–33.

Marlowe, Christopher, genius, 184.

Marston, a reformer, 62, 63. (See *Alcott.*)

Mason, Jeremiah, understanding Emerson, 19.

Massachusetts, literary soil, 184. (See *New England.*)

Materialism: science, 134; Western, 367.

Maurice, Frederick Dennison, on Christianity, 161, 162.

May, Samuel Joseph: allusion, 39; in Diary, 42.

Mead, Edwin D., Emerson's Ethics, 233–285.

Mecca, Concord not one, 338.

Medicis Family, 284. (See *Italy.*)

Memory, in composition, 178.

Memphis, appliances, 408. (See *Egypt.*)

Mephistopheles, meaning, 393-395. (See *Goethe*, etc.)

Mercutio, allusions, 191-193, 200. (See *Emerson's Poems*, — Three Loves.)

Mermaid, illustrative fable, 71, 72.

Messiah, infancy a perpetual, 155, 359. (See *Jesus*, etc.)

Methodism, its gift, 133.

Michael Angelo : allusion, 144 ; inspired, 271. (See *Emerson's Lectures*.)

Microcosm, approached, 406.

Middle Ages : architecture in the, 165 ; Goethe's study, 406.

Milan, and Rome, 10.

Mill, John Stuart, essay, 260.

Milton, John : Satan routed, 125 ; magnificent fable, 163 ; verse and insight, 173-178 ; ploughman, 185 ; poetic test, 201 ; Paradise Lost, 333 ; Uriel, 381.

Miracles : disbelieved, 239-241 ; ancient, 360. (See *Ethics, Nature, Religion*, etc.)

Miriam, incomparable, 142. (See *Bible*.)

Mnemosyne, invoked, 424.

Molière, Jean Baptiste Poquelin, literary rank, 93.

Moloch, fire, 148.

Montaigne, Michel Eyquem : quoted, 103, 104 ; allusion, 115 ; on style, 201, 202.

Montanists, on the Holy Spirit, 114.

Montanus, Roman, 115.

Morality : 233-285 *passim* ; defined, 235. (See *Ethics, Religion*, etc.)

Morgan, J. M., design, 62.

Morley, on Nature, 52.

Moses : incomparable, 142 ; inspiration, 242 ; law, 260. (See *Bible*.)

Mozoomdar, Protap Chunder, Emerson seen from India, 365-371.

Muses, the : converted, 266 ; fled, 339 ; answer, 399 ; favorites, 400. (See *Emerson's Poems*, — Test and Solution.)

NAPLES, Italy, yields to Rome, 10. Napoleon Bonaparte, genius, 144.

Narbudda River, 366. (See *India*.)

Nationality, Emerson's view, 310-338. (See *America*, etc.)

Nature : a touch in old age, 1 ; poet of outward, 2 ; town under the care of, 3 ; in Boston, 4 ; French allusions, 92-108 *passim* ; nurse, 138 ; hermitage, 140 ; eternal relations, 152 ; a hieroglyphic, 186 ; ally of religion, 256-259 ; independence, 317 ; new world of, 319 ; man's place, 320 ; trust in, 333 ; Emerson's philosophy, 339-364 ; disenchanted, 339 ; Greek view, 340 ; temples, 368 ; Emerson's relation to, 386 ; cathedral, 367. (See *Emerson's Books*.)

Neander, Johann August Wilhelm, library, 306.

Nebuchadnezzar : allusion, 181 ; dethroned, 359. (See *Bible*.)

Neoplatonism : the Lapse, 361 ; in verse, 380.

Nepaul, Buddhism, 370. (See *India*, etc.)

Neptune, statue, 180. (See *Blarney*.)

New Bedford, Mass. : pulpit, 12 ; installation, 113.

New England : its centre, 10 ; Everett a classic, 12 ; youth, 25 ; best voice, 28 ; Van Buren's presidency, 58 ; social reform, 61 ; Puritans, 70 ; influence in Europe, 71 ; Mayflower, 72 ; farmers, 86 ; lads, 88 ; literature, 184. (See *America*, etc.)

New England Woman's Club, formed, 22.

New Testament, praise, 241. (See *Bible*.)

New World, discovered, 330.

New York : letter about, 3, 4 ; Castle Garden, 70 ; Broadway, 71 ; dozen great men, 79 ; Fifth Ave., 89 ; lectures, 288 ; advantages, 408.

Newman, Cardinal, running hand, 129, 130.

Newspapers, not appreciative, 16.

Newton, Sir Isaac, his laws, 266

Nicodemus, 180. (See *Blarney*.)

Nirvana, Hindoo, 370, 371.

Noah, his sons' reverence, 121. (See *Bible*.)

North American Review : on Milton, 39, 175 ; in Diary, 42.

North Pole, travellers, 140, 145.

Norton, Andrews, hearing a sermon, 123, 124.

OBSERVER, THE, in Diary, 42.
Occident: mysticism, 362; swinging towards, 372. (See *Orient.*)
O'Connell, Daniel, heard, 62.
Oldham, his apostasy, 63. (See *Alcott.*)
Old Manse, The, window, 148. (See *Concord.*)
Olmsted, Frederick Law, religion, 116.
Olympus, waiting in, 352.
Orient: spirit in Emerson, 197; peculiar religion, 238; Christ, 243; thought, 302; Lapse, 361, 362; swinging towards the, 372; Emerson's Orientalism, 372–385; precocious ethics, 409. (See *Brahma, India, Occident,* etc.)
Orpheus, in poem, 423.
Orphic Poet: quoted, 359, 360; style, 362.
Osgood, J. R., & Co., 404.
Osiris, how described, 243.
Ovid, advice, 189.
Owen, Robert: denied, 62; Alcott's interview, 63; surgical smile, 135.
Oxford, Eng.: a prayer, 25; crushing a flower, 185; drill, 296. (See *Cambridge.*)

PAGANISM: oracle, 130; philosophy, 243.
Paris, advantages, 408. (See *France.*)
Parker, Theodore: thanks, congregation, 21; Lord's Supper, 128; friends in college, 132; sword, 134; on conscience, 269; hammer, 291; pulpit, 293.
Parkman, Francis, woman's suffrage, 309.
Parliaments of the Times, 22.
Partitions, illustration, 141.
Pascal, Blaise: a new, 248; piety, 274.
Peabody, Elizabeth Palmer: enthusiasm, 11; reminiscences, 14; hospitality, 20; on a lecture, 38; in Diary, 42; on Emerson's preaching, 146–172; on Bacchus, 212.
Peabody, Ephraim: in Diary, 42, 44; sermon, 123, 124.
Peabody, Mary (Mrs. Mann), 40.
Peel, Sir Robert, letter, 63.
Pentateuch, translation, 163. (See *Bible, Moses,* etc.)
Pentecostal Muse, 167. (See *Holy Ghost.*)

Pericles, eloquence, 12.
Persian: Muse, 167; poetry, 179, 182; ethics, 372, 375; moral indifference, 375; Seyd, 381. (See *Orient.*)
Pestalozzi: a Connecticut, 37; a disciple, 59.
Petrarch, love-advice, 189; ideal, 331.
Phi Beta Kappa oration, 290. (See *Harvard University.*)
Philistines, in Boston, 157.
Phillips, Wendell: speaking, 62; divergence, 134; artillery, 291; tea-party, 307.
Phocion, environment, 258.
Pindar: allusion, 182; new verse, 185; definition of poetry, 201; environment, 258.
Pine-tree, oracle, 343, 344.
Plato: Alcott's study, 40, 42, 47; constructive ability, 95; pre-existence, 113; picture-book, 117; exercise of intellect, 121, 122; Republic, 123; the ideal, 125; childhood, 133; hitting the apple, 145; understood, 153; allusions, 182; in Emerson, 197; Platonic poet, 200; definition of poetry, 201; on freedom, 268; piety, 274; quintessence, 304; how produced, 331; Phædrus, 362; in Asia, 372; contemplation in religion, 378; poetic rank, 402; allusion in poem, 423.
Plotinus, Fourth Ennead, 356, 362.
Plutarch: statue, 180; comparison, 131, 132.
Poe, Edgar Allan, melodies, 198.
Poetry: French view, 92–105; basis, 178; defined, 201–204; rhythm, 342, 343; characteristics, 386, 387.
Poets, Emerson among the, 173–214. (See *Emerson's Poems, Shakspeare,* etc.)
Politics: universal theme, 8; degraded, 25; parties in 1884, 71.
Pons, Capdueil, couplet, 275.
Pope, Alexander, criticised, 204.
Power, unity, 252.
Prayer: approved at Harvard, 134; allusion, 360.
Preaching, Essay on Emerson's, 146–172.
Princeton Review, on evolution, 262.
Prometheus, enduring, 394.
Prophets: Jesus one, 244, 245; dream

of brotherhood, 313. (See *Bible, Inspiration*, etc.)

Prose, basis, 178. (See *Emerson's Prose*.)

Protestantism : in 1846, 66 ; service a reminder, 128.

Provençal ministry, 315.

Psychology, idealistic view, 350.

Purgatory : in the Orient, 383 ; Dante's, 389.

Puritanism : blending, 30 ; in New England, 70 ; ancestry, 74, 115, 175, 404 ; not to be confounded with Independence, 147, 148 ; Milton amidst, 176 ; conscience, 302 ; Carlyle's, 405. (See *Calvinism*, etc.)

Putnam, Dr., conversation, 366.

Pyramids, wheat-grains, 116.

QUAKERISM : its gift, 133 ; Lord's Supper, 172.

Quincy, Josiah : on town-meetings, 8 ; classmate, 11.

RABBI, title, 152.

Radical Club, 302, 304. (See *Free Religion*, etc.)

Raleigh, Sir Walter, genius, 184.

Raphael : Marriage of the Virgin, 132 ; ideal, 331.

Reason, basis of poetry, 178.

Reformation, the manure of the, 284.

Reformers : in England, 59–65 ; Emerson as one, 106.

Reforms : long lists, 60–62 ; relying on infinitude, 83. (See *Alcott*, etc.)

Religion : in old age, 1 ; Alcott's Diary, 43 ; French view, 94, 95 ; one that degrades not, 122 ; architecture, 127 ; Emerson's, 109–145 ; ethical side, 233–285 ; defined, 255 ; ally of nature, 256 ; different from ethics, 352 ; heathen, 391. (See *God, Jesus*, etc.)

Renaissance : art-clairvoyance, 183 ; pathfinders, 329.

Revolutionary War, chaplaincy, 148.

Richter, Jean Paul Friedrich, on faith, 141.

Ripley, George, in Diary, 42, 43.

Rivers, historic, 303.

Roman Catholicism, mass a reminder, 128.

Rome : architecture, 165 ; traditions, 332 ; achievements, 408.

Rubinstein, Anton : secret of worship, 109 ; advice, 124, 125 ; piano recital, 143 ; quoted, 145.

Russia, her exiles, 71.

SAADI : a line, 139 ; poetry, 179. (See *Emerson's Poems*.)

Sabbath, observance compulsory, 147.

Sadduceeism, desolating, 128.

Saint Augustine, triumphs, 115.

Sainte-Beuve, Charles Augustin, quoted, 105.

Saint John : gospel, 151 ; reporting Jesus, 161. (See *Bible*.)

Saint Paul : his Arabia, 139 ; incomparable, 142 ; inspiration, 242.

Salem witchcraft, 30.

Salter, his philosophy, 250.

Sampson, the ideal merchant, 153, 154.

Sanborn, Frank B. : Essays, 36–67, 173–214 ; quoted, 118 ; invitation to Miss Peabody, 146 ; Ode of 1882, 224–231.

Sand, George, her Consuelo, 397.

Sanscrit poetry, 179. (See *India, Vedas*, etc.)

Saturday Club, 22. (See *Boston*.)

Saturday Morning Club, 305.

Saturn, devouring, 134.

Saxon, in Emerson's diction, 55.

Scepticism, of this age, 340.

Schiller : on religion, 116 ; silence, 414.

School-ship, boys, 16, 17.

Science, an idol, 117.

Scientists, weary, 119.

Scott, David, portrait of Emerson, 16.

Scribes, authority, 186.

Septuagint, translation, 163. (See *Bible*.)

Seyd, Sultan, poet, 381.

Shakspeare : " green fields," 1 ; boldness, 51 ; his English, 55 ; his name everywhere, 93 ; Sonnets, 99, 185, 200, 351 ; Seven Ages, 124 ; genius, 144 ; verse and insight, 174, 175, 178 ; knowledge, 182 ; imperishable genius, 183, 184 ; love-advice, 189 ; Romeo, love, Phœnix and Turtle, 200 ; test of poetry, 201 ; criticism of life, 203 ; era, 204 ; *one*, 243 ; springs of power,

326; lyrics of nature, 341; quoted, 342; human institutions, 388; Hamlet, 396; wit, rank, 400.

Shaw, Colonel, Ode to, 206.

Sidney, Sir Philip: his English, 55; blossoming, 184.

Sigfridsage, 383.

Silence, anecdote, 160–162.

Sinai, the Kantian, 260.

Smith, Sydney: heard, 62; anecdote, 306.

Society, Emerson's relations, 286–309.

Society for the Diffusion of Useful Knowledge, 38.

Society for Ethical Culture, 250.

Socrates: love of Athens, 2; comparison, 22, 24; a new, 248; surroundings, 258.

Solitude, benefits, 30, 31.

Sophocles, creations, 183.

Soul, origin and destiny, 234. (See *Ethics, Religion*, etc.)

Southern Rebellion: Emerson indignant, 18–20, 26–28, 73, 74; Harper's Ferry, 134; Carlyle letters, 412, 413. (See *Antislavery, Emerson's Poetry*, etc.)

Sparks, Jared, historic mission, 59.

Spencer, Herbert: ethics, 234; theory, 260; Data of Ethics, 263.

Spenser, Edmund, blossoming, 184.

Sphinx: its calmness, 370; riddle, 380; in poem, 425. (See *Emerson's Poems*.)

Spinoza, constructive ability, 95.

Spiritual Intelligence, life of the world, 333. (See *God, Religion*, etc.)

Stoics, pain no evil, 118.

Storm, privacy of, 140.

Sturge, Joseph, once heard, 62. (See *Alcott*.)

Sumner, Charles, outrage, 28. (See *Antislavery, Southern Rebellion*, etc.)

Sun, Emerson his own, 139.

Swedenborg, Emanuel: keenness, 144; Christian symbol, 238; waning influence, 248; on piety, 274; poetic rank, 400–402; sect, 410.

Swift, Jonathan: suggests Sartor Resartus, 127; poetry, 180; comparison, 181; Liliput, 303.

Symonds, an English critic, 182–184. (See *Clairvoyance*.)

Syria, ancient, 148.

System, lacking in Emerson, 75–77.

TALLEYRAND, his *mot*, 301.
Taylor, Edward: Bethel, 14; poetic insight, 17; *bon mot*, 18; in Diary, 42; tacking, 111; a gift from Methodism, 133; estimate of Emerson, 136.

Teleology, 263, 264.

Tennyson, Alfred: poetry, 323; Idyls, 416.

Thayer, James B., quoted, 156.

Thibet. (See *Buddhism*.)

Thompson, George: antislavery eloquence, 45, 46; Alcott's interview, 62.

Thomson, J. Cockburn, translation, 374.

Thoreau, Henry D.: definition of a philosopher, 96; making a pencil, 137; a wise word, 282; influenced by Emerson, 321.

Tiberius, a gymnasium, 284.

Ticknor, George, professorship, 11.

Titus, Emperor, stolen candlestick, 142.

Traditions, not authoritative, 242.

Tramps, illustration, 139.

Transcendentalism: disciples, 46; spring time, 49; main track, 115; its gift, 133; hell for its disciples, 157; in Boston, 158; age, 184; reformers, 407; altitudes, 415.

Transcendentalist, The, new, 41. (See *Alcott*.)

Truth: in the midst of, 163, 164; infinite, 165; at its source, 368.

Turin, Italy, precedence of Rome, 10.

Tyndall, John, on Emerson, 339.

UNITARIANISM: ministry, 14; American Association, 62; pale negations, 115; great gift, 133; protest, 149; leaders, 153; physical, 266. (See *Puritanism, Religion*, etc.)

United States, Carlyle correspondence, 416, 417. (See *America*.)

Upham, T. C., Alcott's reading, 42.

Utilitarianism, discussed, 261, 262.

VAN BUREN, MARTIN, presidency, 58. (See *New England*.)
Van Helmont, on piety, 274.
Vaughan, Henry, bird metaphor, 118.
Vedas. Hindoo, 368, 370, 376, 377. (See *Bhagavat Gita, India*, etc.)
Venus, in poetry, 191, 192. (See *Emerson's Poems*.)
Vienna, Austria: life in, 394; advantages, 408.
Villon, French scamp-poet, 204.
Violin, illustration, 124.
Vishnu, deity, 379. (See *Hindoos*, etc.)
Voltaire: poetry, 180; comparison, 181.
Vyasa, philosophy, 352.

WAAGEN, GUSTAV FRIEDRICH, art-mission, 59.
Wachusett Mountain, 337.
Walden Pond, 422. (See *Concord, and Thoreau*.)
Walker, James: in Diary, 42, 44; dull sermon, 123.
Ward's English Poets, introduction, 203.
Ware, Henry, Jr.: colleague, 12; in Diary, 42; sermon controversy, 160.
War of 1812, disastrous effect, 7.
Washington, George: prayers, 109; rank, 133; allusion, 417.
Watches, illustration, 131.
Waterston, Robert Cassie, in Diary, 42
Watt, James, illustration of politics, 81.
Wayside, Concord, Alcott's residence, 65.
Webster, Daniel: blood, 111; logic, 135.
Webster, Noah, appeal, 317.
Wesley, John, waning influence, 248. (See *Methodism*.)

White Hills, travellers, 140.
Whitman, Walt: estimate of him, 121, 135; rugged verse, 322.
Whittier, John Greenleaf, the gift of Quakerism, 133.
Williams, Sir William, epitaph, 206. (See *Gray*.)
William the Conqueror, followers, 294. (See *Emerson's Books*, — English Traits.)
Winthrop Family, in New England, 72.
Wit, in authorship, 178.
Woman: clubs, 22; suffrage convention, 307, 309.
Woman's Club, 304.
Words, woven, 130. (See *Emerson's Essays*, — Language.)
Wordsworth, William: French view, 93; insight into nature, 104; light, 110; prayer, 118; blessings, 122; insight and verse, 174; poetry, 323, 324; stream of influence, 386.
Worship: Bartol's paper, 109–145 *passim*; Miss Peabody's essay, 146–172 *passim*; Mead's essay, 238–250 *passim*; of sorrow, 393, 403. (See *Church, Religion*, etc.)
Wright, Henry C.: association with Alcott, 59–64.

YOGA, Hindoo religion, 367, 368.
Yogin, in India, 378.

ZENO: a new, 248; allusion, 403.
Zion, Scriptural allusions, 416.
Zoölogy, the Fourth-of-July of, 140.
Zoroaster: on poetry, 179, elevation, 375.